MUSIC
SOUND AND SENSE

MUSIC
SOUND AND SENSE

Ronald L. Byrnside

Agnes Scott College, Decatur, Georgia

wcb
Wm. C. Brown Publishers
Dubuque, Iowa

wcb group

Wm. C. Brown
Chairman of the Board
Mark C. Falb
President and Chief Executive Officer

MT
6
.B998
M9
1985

wcb

Wm. C. Brown Publishers, College Division

Lawrence E. Cremer
President
James L. Romig
Vice-President, Product Development
David A. Corona
Vice-President, Production and Design
E. F. Jogerst
Vice-President, Cost Analyst
Marcia H. Stout
Marketing Manager
Marilyn A. Phelps
Manager of Design
William A. Moss
Production Editorial Manager

Book Team

Karen Speerstra
Editor
Fred Westphal
Consulting Editor
Sharon R. Mueller
Editorial Assistant
Mark Elliot Christianson
Designer
Moira Urich
Production Editor
Mary Jean Gregory
Production Editor
Mary M. Heller
Visual Research Editor
Vicki Krug
Permissions Editor

Cover image by Mark Elliot Christianson.

To my friends
Ellen and Marvin Perry

CONTENTS

SECTION *ONE*   11

TERMS AND CONCEPTS

1 TIME AND MUSIC   12

2 SOUND AND MUSIC   24

3 FORM AND MUSIC   50

SOUND AND SENSE LISTENING GUIDES

COLORPLATES

PREFACE

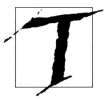The purpose of *Music: Sound and Sense* is to guide students in their search for an understanding and genuine pleasure of many kinds of music. Further, the book suggests ways to think about any kind of music as a part—a very important part—of the cultural context from which it develops. Virtually no one needs to be taught how to "appreciate" music of some kind, but everyone, including the students for whom this book is intended, is enriched by an expansion of personal musical boundaries and tastes. *Music: Sound and Sense* encourages students to engage in such expansions and offers specific guidelines for doing so.

ORGANIZATION AND SCOPE

There are fifteen chapters that divide into three subsections, covering the range from basic terms and concepts (chapters 1–4), to the various periods of Western art music (chapters 5–11), to American popular music, rock, jazz, and an introduction to three non-Western musical cultures (chapters 12–15).

For the historical periods (chapters 5–11) I have elected to proceed from the baroque era through the twentieth century and then treat the music of the Middle Ages (chapter 10) and the Renaissance (chapter 11). My feeling is that students new to the subject matter are more likely to be drawn to and involved in the more familiar-sounding music of the baroque than to earlier music, and it is important to actively involve students from the start.

Professors who prefer a historical approach may wish to start with the earlier music and proceed in chronological fashion. The book is designed to facilitate that approach also. It is simply a matter of the instructor's choice.

All of us who have taught courses of this kind are keenly and, I might add, painfully aware of the limitations of class time; it seems there is never enough time to cover all of the material and rarely is there sufficient time for students to reflect upon what has been presented. The instructor must make some choices concerning the use of class time. It would be a luxury if we could begin classes of this kind assured of student exposure to the basic terms and concepts, but experience has proven that this assumption cannot be made. I believe that some attention and time must be given to basic terms and concepts. After covering the fundamentals, the instructor can proceed to give time and attention to the various chapters as he or she prefers. Ideally, all of the materials should be explored.

SPECIAL FEATURES

The art work featured has been carefully selected and positioned to offer students insights into the cultural context of the music they are learning. "Sound and Sense" listening exercises are found throughout the text. These elements are designed to draw students into active listening. Most instructors doubtless have a collection of works which they regularly use to illustrate various styles and genres of music. Such works can easily be used as supplements to, or in some cases substitutes for, the pieces discussed and analyzed in the text.

Each chapter begins with a "Sounds of the Chapter" element featuring all the musical pieces that will be encountered in the chapter. Within the text special names, terms, and concepts appear in boldface, and margin notes highlight important information.

Each chapter concludes with a comprehensive summary and a list of the key terms. A section called "Thinking About It" poses leading questions that invite creative responses.

Appendix A is a list of the recordings included in the record set, with instructions for the best use of each piece. Appendix B offers a brief list of major composers and their works. The Glossary offers definitions of the key terms and concepts introduced in the text. (The sources I used for dates and for editorial treatment of composition titles are: *The International Cyclopedia of Music and Musicians* and *Webster's Biographical Dictionary*.) Finally, a cultural time chart integrating the chronological development of the arts is offered at the end of the book.

The Instructor's Manual to accompany this text contains many diverse components. I suggest alternative course organization formats, goals and means for each chapter, along with outlines, summaries, and a test item file. Further listenings are offered and insights into the "Sound and Sense" listening exercises are provided.

THE RECORD SET

The text is accompanied with a set of five long-playing records on which are contained all or part of many of the works discussed and/or analyzed. A list of the works contained on these recordings appears in Appendix A, in the record set itself, and in the Instructor's Manual. ♪
This symbol will be used throughout the text to indicate musical pieces that appear on the record set.

Ultimately, the success of courses of this kind is closely tied to the expertise and concern of the instructor, whose role in the learning process cannot be altered by any textbook. I believe, however, that *Music: Sound and Sense* can be a useful tool for the instructor and an informative and challenging book for students.

ACKNOWLEDGMENTS

"I wish I had thought of that"—a phrase often expressed by one stimulated or touched by an idea or perspective that comes from someone else. No one can possibly recall the sources of all these ideas. In my case, now, only a few of the most obvious come to mind. To the countless others I extend my honest thanks.

My particular thanks go to four people who were mentors, colleagues, and who are my friends: Charles Hamm, Ben Johnston, Bruno Nettl, and Alex Ringer. I also want to thank their students and mine at the University of Illinois in years past.

I acknowledge with gratitude the tireless help of my friend Lillian Newman, librarian at Agnes Scott College, and the encouragement of my special friends at Agnes Scott: Linda Woods, "Betts" Zenn, and Jay Fuller.

Whatever merit this book may have is due, in large measure, to the expertise of several people who reviewed the manuscript with rigor and compassion:

Robert B. Van Voorhis
University of North Dakota

David Nyman
Southern Utah State College

Lu Elrod
California State University, Los Angeles

Jack Boyd
Abilene Christian University

Wayne C. Smith
Spokane Falls Community College

Finally, my thanks go to the fine staff people at Wm. C. Brown who worked on this project, especially my editor, Karen Speerstra, whose intelligence, wit, and patience made my work a joy.

MUSIC

SOUND AND SENSE

INTRODUCTION

There is no evidence that people have any physiological need for music, yet throughout history and in all parts of the world, people have everywhere and always had music. It must be concluded, then, that music is very important to humankind. Music is, in fact, one of our self-created treasures.

Throughout the centuries it has been made evident that music occupies a special place in our existence. Music has provided a means for expressing something deep inside; it has been a joy, a comfort, and an adjunct to religion. It has been a call to battle, a mnemonic device, and a didactic tool. Mystical, evil, even healing powers have been attributed to music. A given ritual may be invalidated for failure to perform the specified musical accompaniment in some cultures, and in more than one culture a song is viewed as personal property, to be sung only by its possessor. The powers of music have been recognized and jealously guarded by people from many cultures and eras.

In Plato's *Republic,* he suggests some things about music that may at first astonish us. He says, in part

> "What, then, are the dirge-like harmonies? Tell me, for you are a musician."
>
> "The Mixolydian," he said, "and the intense Lydian, and others similar to them."
>
> "These, then," said I, "we must do away with. For they are useless. . . . But again, drunkenness is a thing most unbefitting guardians, and so is softness and sloth."
>
> "Yes."
>
> "What, then, are the soft and convivial harmonies?"
>
> "There are certain Ionian and also Lydian ones that are called relaxed."

"Will you make any use of them for warriors?"

"None at all."

"And gracelessness and evil rhythm and disharmony are akin to evil speaking and the evil temper, but the opposites are the symbols and the kin of the opposites, the sober and good disposition."

Can so fertile a mind as Plato's actually have believed that music is capable of good or evil? He definitely inferred that some music is wicked and dangerous to the existence of the state.

Writing in the fourteenth century, Jacob of Liège also made some startling claims about music.

Would that it pleased the modern singers that the ancient music and the ancient manner of singing were again brought into use! For, if I may say so, the old art seems more perfect, more rational, more seemly, freer, simpler, and plainer. Music was originally discreet, seemly, simple, masculine, and of good morals; have not the moderns rendered it lascivious beyond measure?

Did he really believe that music can be imbued with good morals? Can sounds and rhythms be moral or immoral?

A mythical Eastern prince, concerned that his subjects were not attending to the affairs of state because they were spending too much time making music, proclaimed that music should die before the dawn of a specified day. On the evening before that day, a group of musicians performed a mournful dirge under the prince's balcony. They said to him, "You have decreed that music must die; we have come to bury it." The prince responded, "Bury it deep."

Music, then, not only offers entertainment, but also reveals characteristics of the culture to which it belongs.

Music does not submit to a singular definition. How music is defined depends upon whom we ask, and also when we ask. For instance, if we were to ask a Tibetan monk, "What is music?" he would produce sounds that many of us in the Western world would be unwilling to call music. At least, it would not be music as we perceive it. But the gravelly, subterranean vocal sounds and the honking of the elongated trumpet are an integral part of the Tibetan monk's spiritual existence. This music is equally important to him as our music is to us.

Tibetan monks with trumpets

If we ask a young composer from the 1980s to define music, he or she may respond with a series of electronically generated sounds. Some may say, "No, those are squeaks and pops, not music." Still, for the composer and the audience, this is music.

When we listen to "Scarborough Fair" we may say, "Now that's music." This is so because our conditioning, our heritage, tells us that this particular piece contains the properties of music and behaves as music should. It is one of tens of thousands of works that we could offer in response to the question, "What is music?" It could serve as our definition of music. But it would be a mistake to assume that our definition is any more valid than the definition offered by the Tibetan monk or the composer of electronic music or a performer from the Kabuki theater or a Pygmie from the Ituri forest or an anonymous ninth century peasant from northern Europe. Ultimately, there is no singular definition of music. There are many, and each depends on whom we ask and when.

The mention of "Scarborough Fair" suggests another question, namely, "Whose music is it?"

An anonymous seventeenth century ballad begins,

Are you going to Scarborough Fair? Savory, sage, rosemary and thyme.

Simon and Garfunkel

Surely the author of this two hundred-year-old verse would have reason to claim ownership of this song. But we know that Paul Simon and Art Garfunkel, two young men from the twentieth century, composed and recorded "Scarborough Fair." The old song had so moved them that they borrowed it and added to it a canticle of their own. However, it could be argued that "Scarborough Fair" is our music. We listen to it and sing it in the shower; we have made it part of us. So despite the great diversity of music and the many possible definitions of it, it is possible for people from different eras and cultures to derive mutual satisfaction from the same music.

As we approach the study of Western classical music or art music, the question "Whose music is this?" may emerge again. Those who are cautious may fear that art music is simply too foreign to them. But remember that before you became a computer science major or a French major, those languages were probably foreign to you and seemingly beyond your grasp. Or before you became a math major, differential equations were hopelessly foreign to you. And before you decided to pursue premedical studies, even the simplest organism seemed an unfathomable mystery. But the desire to know and the willingness to work at learning helped you to override these obstacles. Now the understanding of many concepts in your field are simple and automatic to you. Too often we forget that such mastery is acquired cumulatively, step-by-step over a period of time. The same condition prevails in the study of music, though the mode of study may be new to you.

In the study of most disciplines the brain, eyes, hands, and ears are employed. The hearing apparatus is, however, merely a conduit for the information sought. That which we seek is not what we hear; rather, what we seek is the meaning behind what we hear. The ear provides a convenient means of getting to the data, the concept, or the interpretation. It serves only as a means to an end. But in music, what we hear is what we are after. It is the end, not a means to an end. Thus, our study is conducted by the ear in cooperation with the brain. Sometimes, students new to this subject believe this isn't enough—that the eyes and hands ought to be doing something as well. The old adage "seeing is believing" connotes that if the subject matter is visible, our grasp of it is more secure. The first step in our study is to rid ourselves of this notion and to allow the ear to work for us.

Broadly speaking, we can identify three categories of music in the Western world: (1) art music, or classical music; (2) folk music, and (3) popular music. Western art music is a cultivated tradition as its composers are normally equipped with certain technical/learned skills, and its audience has acquired the capacity to assimilate lengthy and often complex musical structures and ideas. The music (or most of it) is fixed through notation so that it remains approximately the same each time it is recreated or performed.

Popular music tends to be simpler and technically less complex than classical music. The demands on the audience are less rigorous, and the audience is more diverse and vast. Popular music is generally aimed at commercial success, and its primary goal is entertainment rather than edification.

Folk music in its purest form is generated neither by commercial nor artistic considerations. It is often functional within the culture, created to accompany or to commemorate certain events important in the lives of its folk: work songs, lullabies, and accounts of cataclysmic events. The music lives in oral tradition. It is not notated; instead, it is passed on from generation to generation through live performances. A folk song tends to change from time to time, due to the whim and fancy or to the faulty memory of some purveyor of the song in the chain of its life.

Folk musicians

We must also take into account the distinction between sacred and secular music. The difference is evident not so much in purely musical terms, for the two types use or can use essentially the same materials. Rather, the distinction derives from the different functions of the two. In the Middle Ages, the Church fostered and nourished the production of music, some of which exists today in manuscript form. Clearly, this music was designed for sacred purposes. Today, however, we view it not only as the sacred music of the Middle Ages, but also as the art music from that period.

The history of Western art music can be divided into the following stylistic periods:

A.D. 1 through the first millennium	The early Middle Ages. The era of Gregorian chant. All of the music from this era that we will study is sacred music from the early Christian church.
1150–1300	The Gothic period. The emergence of polyphony. Thirteenth century motet.
1300–1450	The Ars Nova period, the late Middle Ages. Sacred music: Mass, motet. Secular music: songs of the trouvères.

1450–1600	The Renaissance. Sacred music: Mass, motet, chorale. Secular music: Italian madrigal, English madrigal.
1600–1750	The baroque. Opera, oratorio, concerto grosso, trio sonata, cantata, keyboard music.
1720–1760	The Rococo or preclassic era. The early symphony and string quartet, keyboard music, concerto, opera.
1760–1800	Classical era. Symphony, string quartet, sonata, concerto, opera, oratorio.
1800–1900	The nineteenth century or romantic era. Symphony, string quartet, sonata, concerto, opera, Lied (art song), tone poem, ballet, music for piano.
1900—	The Modern or contemporary era. Symphony, string quartet and other chamber music, sonata, concerto, opera, the emergence of electronic music.

The indicated years of each of these style periods are not definite. The romantic period, for instance, did not begin at 12:01 A.M. on January 1, 1800. An old style fades away only gradually and a new one emerges as slowly. Still, however general these dates are, the history of Western art music is a history of periodic stylistic changes and the dates serve as a reminder of these periods.

There are discernible differences between the music of the baroque and the music of the classical periods, and there are reasons for these differences. In part, this study focuses on the characteristics of several styles of music, the differences between those styles and some reasons for the style and taste changes in music. American popular music, rock, jazz, and music of some non-Western cultures are dealt with in section III.

To facilitate this study, it is necessary to deal with some preliminaries. These will develop a fund of information, terminology, and precepts, both technical and aesthetic, that are common to all music.

The question may arise, "What do I have to do to succeed in knowing these materials?" Regardless of the scope of your musical background in art music, you should approach this study as a student of music. More than anything else, this will involve listening to music—not simply hearing it, but listening to it—in recorded form and, as often as possible, in live performances. The understanding and love of music are not dependent upon the ability to read musical notation (though of course there is great value in having that ability). Consequently, few examples of musical notation appear in this text. It will, however, be useful to develop some skill in reading rhythmic notation. Particular attention should be given to the discussion of note values and meters in chapter 1.

All of the musical examples mentioned and discussed in the text should be readily available to you in recorded form, and it is important to listen to these recordings. You should have little trouble locating recorded anthologies and song collections of American popular music, rock, and jazz.

TERMS AND CONCEPTS

1

TIME
AND
MUSIC

Fur Traders Descending the Missouri, George Caleb
Bingham

The Metropolitan Museum of Art, Morris K. Jessup Fund, 1933

SOUNDS OF THE CHAPTER

J. S. Bach
Brandenburg Concerto no. 2 ♪

Chopin
Waltz, op. 34, no. 2 ♪
Waltz, op. 69, no. 1

Handel
"Halleluia" Chorus, *Messiah* ♪

Haydn
Symphony no. 101 ♪

Scott Joplin
"The Entertainer" ♪

Fig. 1.1
St. Louis Arch

TIME CREATES MOVEMENT AND CHANGE

Buildings, statues, paintings, and even photographs do not stand still. In our memories they may be stationary, immobile objects, but when we actually confront them, we perceive movement. When, for example, we view the magnificent St. Louis Arch, created by Eero Saarinen, we don't see something frozen whole and intact. (See fig. 1.1.) Rather, our eyes and brain perceive a structure that begins someplace, moves upward and across, then moves on to a landing point elsewhere.

A certain amount of time is required to complete this perception—perhaps only microseconds. Nevertheless, the eyes and brain traverse this span and perceive this structure through a flow of time. Time is the mode of transportation for movement. Movement creates change; thus, time is responsible for both movement and change.

Notice the psychological and emotional changes that occur when time is arrested and movement is thwarted, as in figures 1.2a and b.

Fig. 1.2

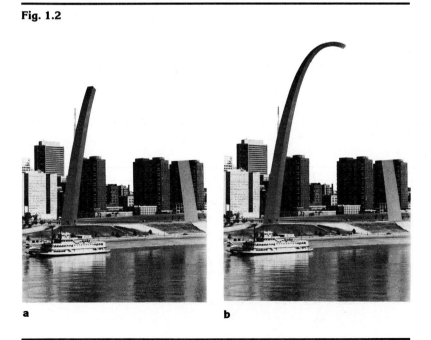

a   b

RHYTHM ORGANIZES TIME

Time is a fundamental reality of our existence. The minutes and hours of the clock; the seasons and tides; our every heartbeat, breath, and step; our infancy, childhood, youth, and old age; and all of the countless movements and changes that attend these phenomena, happen in and are distributed through time. Time is as real to the archaeologist as it is to the hourly employee, and as important to the astronomer as it is to the dispatcher.

None of us can ignore, destroy, or will time out of existence. Indeed, we are inclined to make time useful and pleasurable by organizing it in one way or another. When time is organized, it is endowed with **rhythm.**

Notice that the fence in figure 1.3 has a temporal organization, or a rhythm, consisting of a series of regularly spaced posts of equal size. The series of posts is but one dimension. Notice in figure 1.4 how the personality of the fence changes as we impose another dimension of rhythm upon it: every third post is accented with color.

Rather than being a flat, single-dimensional phenomenon, rhythm has many layers or dimensions. The rhythm of the fence now has two layers: (1) the original series of regularly spaced posts, and (2) the recurring pattern of brown, white, white. Each brown post marks the beginning of a group of three posts, so it could be called a three-post pattern.

In figure 1.5 the fence has yet another rhythmic pattern: each brown post marks the beginning of a group of four posts—a four-post pattern.

Organized time displays rhythm.

Layers of rhythm produce patterns.

Fig. 1.3

Fig. 1.4

Fig. 1.5

Beats

The succession of regularly spaced posts of equal size that we see is analogous to a succession of **beats** that we cannot see, but which we hear and feel. Graphically illustrated they appear as:

We often respond to these beats in music by tapping our toe or snapping our fingers along with them.

A succession of beats can be organized into patterns by systematically **accenting** or stressing some beats more than others: the accented beats, which receive more emphasis or force than the other beats, are analogous to the black posts. A three-beat pattern is created by accenting or stressing every third beat:

An accented note often has the sign $>$ above or below it.

By accenting every fourth beat, a four-beat pattern is created:

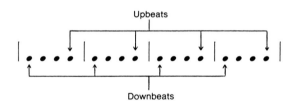

Meter

In music, patterns such as we have just described are called **meters.** Each repetition of the pattern is marked off into a **bar,** or **measure,** and in notating music, a **bar line** is drawn at the end of each repetition.

Thus we say that the preceding example displays four bars (or measures) of a three-beat meter. The first beat of each bar is usually the **downbeat** (the accented beat), and the last beat of each bar, the **upbeat.**

The preceding example shows four bars of a four-beat meter.

This, though, is not always the case. Many kinds of music—classical, popular, folk, jazz, old, and new—make some use of a rhythmic device called **syncopation.** Syncopation puts the accent on a beat other than the downbeat of a measure or on some portion of a beat other than its beginning. This creates a kind of metrical jerk. Notice how these examples of syncopation put the emPHAsis on the wrong sylLAbles.

Example:

A meter is a pattern of beats.

Use bar lines to separate each repetition of a metrical pattern.

Add odd accents and interest through syncopation.

Generally, syncopation seems to work best when it is not overdone; still, the piano rag makes extensive and satisfying use of syncopation in the right-hand part, while the left-hand part steadily plays "on the beat."

The presence of beats and meter in music is almost immediately evident in the first movement of Johann Sebastian Bach's *Brandenburg Concerto no. 2.*

The total rhythmic personality of this piece of music consists of many layers, since time is organized in different ways. The orderly succession of beats of equal duration is merely the simplest and most obvious layer of the music's rhythm. The meter pattern is another layer.

Tempo

In listening to the opening portion of the second movement of the *Brandenburg* Concerto no. 2, a succession of beats and a metrical pattern occurs once more. There is, however, an important and notable difference between the beats of the two movements: the beats of the first movement have a fast pace, while the beats of the second movement have a slow pace. The pace or speed at which music moves is called **tempo.** Tempo is another layer of rhythm. A wide variety of tempos is available in all gradations from very fast to very slow. Here is an abbreviated list of tempo indications commonly used in music.

The tempo of the music is the speed at which it moves.

Term	Translation	Speed or Pace
largo	broad	very slow
lento	slow	slow
adagio	slowly	slow
andante	walking pace	moderately slow
andantino	diminutive of andante	a little faster than andante
moderato	moderately	moderate
allegro	lively	fast
presto	very quick	very fast

In some kinds of music it seems somehow "right" to maintain a steady, unflagging tempo from start to finish, perhaps slowing down only at the very end. In other types of music it seems equally appropriate and satisfying to alter the steady tempo by accelerating **(accelerando)** at some points, and by slowing down or retarding **(ritardando)** at other points. This kind of music requires the periodic, purposeful "breaking" of the tempo; the accelerandos and ritardandos seem to add a sense of drama.

Tempo changes within a piece often add drama.

The *Brandenburg* no. 2, first movement, is an example of a kind of music that seems to thrive on and gain its rhythmic vitality from a steady tempo. In contrast, Chopin's *Waltz,* op. 69, no. 1, seems to gain its rhythmic and dramatic punch through the occasional breaking away from a steady tempo. Notice how the tempo speeds up at some points and applies brakes at others. The term applied to a tempo that makes extensive use of accelerando and ritardando is **rubato.** The Chopin *Waltz* is a clear example of the use of rubato.

A tempo can be temporarily broken with a **fermata** ⌢ , a note held for longer than its notated duration. Usually a fermata is used for some dramatic purpose, as in "O'er the land of the FREEEEEEEEEEEE, and the home of the brave."

Note Value

A piece of music that had only three layers of rhythm—beat, meter, and tempo—would be hopelessly dull and monotonous. To be compelling and satisfying, music requires at least one other layer of rhythm where activity occurs between the beats. In this fourth layer of rhythm, some durations are longer than the basic beat, and some are shorter. The duration of every sound in music, whether it lasts for a beat, for more than a beat, or for less than a beat, has what is called a **note value.** That is, some notes are held through the durational value of two beats, three beats, or more, and some notes last for only a fraction of a beat—one-half of a beat (or toe tap), one-fourth of a beat, one-third of a beat, and so on.

> Notes indicate duration of sound.

Organization is achieved on this fourth layer of rhythm with notes. There are several kinds of notes, each having a durational value relative to the others. For example, a figure that looks like a beat with a stem attached to its side— ♩ —is called a quarter note. A half note— ♩ — has the durational value of two quarter notes. In other words, a ♩ lasts exactly twice as long as a ♩ lasts. An eighth note— ♪ —lasts exactly half as long as a ♩ lasts. Thus, it takes two eighth notes, which can be notated as ♪ ♪ or as ♫ , to equal the value of one quarter note. Allowing for minor changes and refinements, this has been the standard notational system in the Western world since about the late seventeenth century.

Using the quarter note as the standard note value, it is evident from the following chart that all other note values are either multiples or fractions of it.

> All notes are either multiples or fractions of quarter notes.

Note values

Quarter notes

Half notes

Whole note

Quarter notes

Eighth notes

Sixteenth notes

Eighth note triplets

(Here an ♪ = 1/3 the value of a ♩)

Silences between notes are designated by rests.

Every note value has an equivalent value in silence. In music these silences are called **rests**.

	Note value		Equivalent rest	
Quarter note	♩		𝄽	Quarter rest
Half note	𝅗𝅥		▬	Half rest
Whole note	𝅝		▬	Whole rest
Quarter note	♩		𝄽	Quarter rest
Eighth note	♪		𝄾	Eighth rest
Sixteenth note	♬		𝄿	Sixteenth rest
Eighth note triplets	♫₃		𝄾 𝄾 𝄾 ₃	Triplet rests

There are two ways to increase the duration of a note or rest. One method is to place a dot (•) after the note or rest, thereby increasing its duration by fifty percent. For example, a half note has the value of two quarter notes, but a dotted half note has the value of three quarter notes.

A dot next to a note or a rest increases its duration.

Half note

Dotted half

The other way to prolong the duration of a note is to join it to another note by means of a **tie**— ‿ . Thus:

= 3 eighth notes

= 3 quarter notes

A **meter signature** has two factors—an upper and a lower number. The upper number indicates how many beats are in the metrical pattern; the lower number indicates which note value is the basic beat for the piece of music. Thus, 4/4 indicates a four-beat meter in which the quarter note is the basic beat. A three-beat pattern, in which the eighth note is the basic beat, is indicated by 3/8.

What does the meter signature 3/8 mean?

The rhythmic notations of the opening few bars of several different pieces of music are illustrated here. They demonstrate a variety of meters, tempos, and note values, the layers of rhythm.

1. 4/4 Allegro: Handel's "Halleluia" from *Messiah*

2. 3/4 Lento: Chopin's *Waltz,* op. 34, no. 2

3. 6/8 Presto: Haydn's Symphony no. 101, first movement
   (following the slow introduction)

Begins on an upbeat

4. 2/4 Moderate: Scott Joplin's "The Entertainer"

SUMMARY

In chapter 1 you have encountered some of the most basic elements in music—elements that will help you to understand and enjoy the music to come.

Rhythm is the term applied to the organization of time in music, and rhythm is discovered layer by layer. Basic to rhythm are beats. Beats are then organized into patterns called meters. To provide variety in rhythm, the meters are arranged in various patterns. Another layer of rhythm determines the speed at which these patterns progress. This is termed tempo.

Still organizing time, various types of notes and their durations were presented as either fractions or multiples of the quarter note. If longer duration is necessary, dots and ties can be used. Finally, the method of accenting off of the beat was described and termed syncopation.

Armed with these basics, let's move on.

KEY TERMS

rhythm	syncopation	presto
beat	tempo	accelerando
meter	largo	ritardando
bar	lento	rubato
measure	adagio	fermata
bar line	andante	note value
downbeat	andantino	rest
upbeat	moderato	tie
accent	allegro	meter signature

THINKING ABOUT IT

Using some of the terms you have encountered in this chapter, describe some of the rhythmic differences between Handel's "Halleluia" Chorus (example 1) and the Chopin *Waltz* (example 2).

The Guitar Player by Vermeer

The Iveagh Bequest

SOUNDS OF THE CHAPTER

J. S. Bach
Well-Tempered Clavier ♪

Barber
Adagio for String Orchestra ♪

Bartók
Music for Strings, percussion and celesta

Beethoven
Symphony no. 5
Symphony no. 6 ♪

Berlioz
Harold in Italy

Borodin
In the Steppes of Central Asia ♪

Brahms
Clarinet Quintet in B Minor

Britten
Young Person's Guide to the Orchestra

Debussy
Danse sacrée and *Danse profane*
La Mer
Prélude à l'Après-midi d' un faune
    (Prelude to the Afternoon of a Faun)
Sonata for Flute, Viola, and Harp

Dvorak
Concerto for Cello and Orchestra
Symphony no. 9, *From the New World*

Benny Goodman
"Avalon"

Griffes
The White Peacock ♪

Handel
"Halleluia," *Messiah* ♪

Haydn
String Quartet, op. 33, no. 2

Mendelssohn
Violin Concerto in E Minor

Mozart
Queen of the Night aria, *The Magic Flute*
Horn Concertos

Mussorgsky/Ravel
Pictures at an Exhibition ♪

Palestrina
"Agnus Dei," Mass: *Veni sponsa Christi*

Purcell
Variations on a New Ground Bass

Saint-Saëns
"Elephants," *Carnival of Animals*

Stravinsky
*Le Sacre du Printemps (The Rite of
    Spring)*

Tchaikovsky
"Dance of the Sugar Plum Fairy," *The
    Nutcracker*

Varese
Ionisation ♪

Wagner
Overture from *Tannhäuser*

Wonder
"Isn't She Lovely"

"Amazing Grace"
"Farmer in the Dell"
"Laudate pueri"
"Laus Deo Patri"
"Scarborough Fair"

Music must have both time and sound.

Music, however defined, has a temporal aspect and a sonorous aspect. Without time and sound, music cannot exist. In chapter 1, some of the ways in which time relates to music were examined. In this chapter something of the nature and uses of sound in music are explored.

When a flexible body such as a taut string, a strip of wood or metal, or a column of air is set into motion, it vibrates until its energy is spent. As it vibrates it displaces the air molecules that rested on its formerly dormant surface. This sets off a chain reaction in which wave after wave of molecules is displaced. If you are situated close enough to such an activity, and if the motion is begun with enough force, your eardrums will pick up the motion and will begin to vibrate. At this moment you experience the sensation of hearing.

Sound is created by vibration.

Unless you have a hearing impediment, your ears pick up sounds more or less constantly: sounds produced by nature, traffic, other mechanical devices and, of course, music. Fortunately we have the capacity to block out some unwanted sounds while we focus on other sounds that are more interesting and pleasurable at the time. If such were not the case, it would be very difficult for us to listen attentively to music.

Experience tells us that there is a great variety and differentiation of sounds: thunder does not sound like a canary, a snare drum does not sound like a guitar, nor does applause sound like an airplane.

Most *musical* sounds, however, have the following attributes in common:

The frequency of the vibration determines the pitch.

1. Definite pitch. A given sound is perceived as relatively high or low because of **pitch.** For example, the keys on the far left-hand side of the piano keyboard produce very low pitches; those on the far right-hand side produce high pitches. Every definite pitch vibrates with a specific **frequency**—it vibrates a certain number of times per second. The higher the frequency, the higher the pitch.

The same pitch sounds different on different instruments because of timbre.

2. Timbre, or tone color. **Timbre** is the quality characteristic of and peculiar to a given instrument. A flute playing a given pitch sounds distinctly different from a trumpet playing the same pitch, and the trumpet sounds different from a piano, a banjo, or a bagpipe playing the same pitch.

It is often necessary to note how loudly or softly music is to be played.

3. Volume, or amplitude. **Volume** or **amplitude** is the degree of loudness or softness. In music, volume is notated with these symbols:

p	(soft)	*mp*	(moderately soft)	*pp*	(very soft)	*ppp*	(softer still)
f	(loud)	*mf*	(moderately loud)	*ff*	(very loud)	*fff*	(louder still)

These are referred to as **dynamics.**

PITCHES AND INTERVALS

Pitches are the basic units of which musical sounds are created. Every pitch is assigned a letter name, or a letter name plus one of these symbols: ♯ (called a **sharp**), or ♭ (called a **flat**). Both sharps and flats are termed **accidentals.** A ♯ raises the pitch of a letter name; thus C♯ is higher in pitch than C, but lower than D. A ♭ lowers the pitch of a letter name; thus B♭ is lower in pitch than B, but not as low as A.

The distance that separates one pitch from another (either higher or lower) is called an **interval.** A brief survey of the piano keyboard will help us to identify the names of pitches, and to understand the nature of various intervals used in making music.

> An interval is the distance between two pitches, and an octave is the purest interval.

The Octave System

Refer to figure 2.1, which illustrates a portion of a piano keyboard. Notice that the white keys have been assigned the letter pattern c-d-e-f-g-a-b, followed by the same sequence, C-D-E-F-G-A-B. C is the octave of c, D is the octave of d, and so on. The **octave** is the simplest, purest interval in our tuning system. C sounds almost exactly like c except that its pitch is higher. Similarly, D sounds like d, E like e, and so forth. This is acceptable without knowing its mathematical-acoustic foundations because it is sensed quite naturally. D does not sound like the octave of c, nor do any of the other letter names; only C sounds like the octave of c.

The black keys, arranged in groups of twos and threes on the keyboard, also have letter names. As seen in figure 2.1, each black key has two letter names such as c♯ and d♭, and d♯ and e♭. This is simply a notational convenience. In some musical contexts it is appropriate to call a given black key c♯; in other contexts it is appropriate to call the same black key d♭ instead of c♯. The important point to remember is that a black key (like a white key) produces only one pitch that sounds the same regardless of whether it is called c♯ or d♭.

> Each piano key produces one pitch.

Notice, too, that the octave system also applies to the black keys: C♯ is the octave of c♯, B♭ is the octave of b♭.

Fig. 2.1

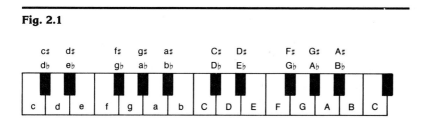

If you play any two adjacent keys, you've produced a minor, and if you skip one key in between you've produced a major second.

Majors and Minors

The smallest interval commonly used in Western music is called a **minor second** (or a half step, or semitone). A minor second can be produced by playing successively or simultaneously any two adjacent keys on the keyboard: for example, c to c♯, or e to f, or g to g♯, or b to c. The next largest interval is called a **major second** (or a whole step, or whole tone). This interval can be produced by playing any two keys that are separated from each other by one intervening black or white key. For example, c to d is a major second, as are e to f♯, g to a, and b to c♯.

Another way of determining the size of a major second is to note that it encompasses the distance of two minor seconds. Thus, the major second, c to d, contains within it the minor seconds c to c♯ and c♯ to d. An octave encompasses the distance of twelve minor seconds: c to c♯, c♯ to d, d to d♯, d♯ to e, e to f, f to f♯, f♯ to g, g to g♯, g♯ to a, a to a♯, a♯ to b, b to C.

This is a convenient way of judging other intervals such as minor third, major third, perfect fourth, augmented fourth, perfect fifth, minor sixth, major sixth, minor seventh, major seventh, as well as those intervals larger than an octave, such as minor ninth, major ninth, minor tenth, and major tenth. Figure 2.2 illustrates various intervals in music notation.

Fig. 2.2

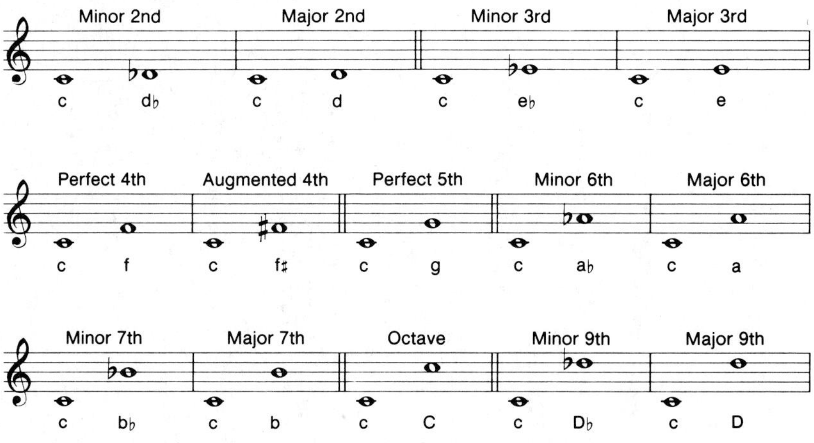

Plate 1
Music, the universal language.

The Old Musician; Edouard Manet; National Gallery of Art, Washington, D.C., Chester Dale
Collection 1962.

Plate 2

Motion, time, and rhythm are discussed in chapter 1. Despite this painting's seemingly placid surface, these three elements are apparent in the water, bridge, clouds, and oarsmen.

Max Schmitt in a Single Scull; Thomas Eakins; The Metropolitan Museum of Art, New York. Alfred N. Punnett Fund and Gift of George D. Pratt 1934.

Plate 3

Rhythmic patterns and meters are discussed in chapter 1. Notice the many patterns and repetitions in this visual image.

Mahantango Valley Farm; Unknown artist; National Gallery of Art, Washington, D.C.; Gift of Edgar William and Bernice Chrysler Garbish 1953.

Plate 4

Time, rhythm, and memory have been universal sources of inspiration in all of the arts. Musical time is different from so-called real time: a fascinating piece of music may seem to be all too brief, while a dull piece may seem annoyingly long and drawn out.

Persistence of Memory; Dali; Collection, The Museum of Modern Art, New York.

Plate 5

The nature and quality of musical sounds are discussed in chapter 2. Notice how the player listens with great care.

The Guitar Player; Vermeer; The Greater London Council as Trustees of the Iveagh Bequest, Kenwood.

Plate 6

Consonance and dissonance are discussed in chapter 2. Notice how the letter O creates dissonance.

Love; Robert Indiana; Collection of Whitney Museum of American Art; Gift of the Howard and Jean Lipman Foundation, Inc.

Plate 7

Form, as discussed in chapter 3, makes a given work perceptible and memorable.

Stonehenge; photograph by Jill Cannefax/EKM-Nepenthe.

Plate 8
. . . daffodils,
That come before the swallow dares, and take
The winds of March with beauty . . .
(See meaning as discussed in chapter 4.)

Daffodils; photograph by John Maher/EKM-Nepenthe.

Plate 9

As mentioned in chapter 4, Cezanne said that this painting is not about apples—it is about appleness.

Basket of Apples; Paul Cezanne; The Art Institute of Chicago, H. B. Bartlett Memorial Collection.

Plate 10

The long, lonesome stretches of land, the sky, with its mixture of heaviness and lightness, dark, cool trees, and the solitary traveller combine to create a mood. How would you describe that mood? How do motion and texture contribute to the mood? (For a discussion of meaning and mood, see chapter 4.)

Wheatfields; Ruisdael; The Metropolitan Museum of Art, New York, Bequest of Benjamin Altman 1913.

Plate 11

Color, shape, and texture combine to create the mood of this painting. (See chapter 4.)

Norham Castle, Sunrise; JWN Turner; The Tate Gallery, London.

Plate 12

Can you detect the motion, meter, rhythm, tempo, texture, form, and mood in this painting?

Winter (Return of the Hunters); Pieter Brueghel the Elder; Art Resource.

As we have just mentioned, an octave contains twelve half steps; for example, the octave c–C contains:

c	c♯	d	d♯	e	f	f♯	g	g♯	a	a♯	b	C
1	2	3	4	5	6	7	8	9	10	11	12	

This succession is one kind of musical scale—the chromatic scale—which includes all of the pitches from c to its octave C.

Another very important kind of scale, called the diatonic scale, contains fewer pitches and has a different internal intervallic structure from the chromatic scale. There are, in fact, two kinds of diatonic scales: major and minor. Each has seven pitches plus the octave, for a total of eight pitches; 1 indicates a whole step, and ½ indicates a half step.

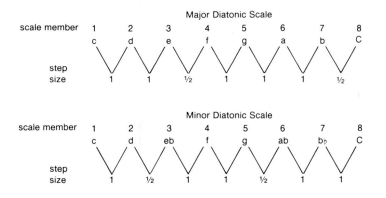

Notice the different placement of whole steps and half steps in the major and minor diatonic scales.

Melody

When a series of pitches and its attendant intervals is wedded to a set of note values a **melody** results. A melody has no fixed shape; it may be very active and employ many different pitches and intervals, or it can be fairly static, restricting itself to only a few pitches and intervals. Whatever the case, nearly all melodies have some upward and downward motion, some variety of pitches and intervals. A melody stuck on one pitch invites boredom. Prove this to yourself by singing any song you know, using the correct rhythm, but singing it in its entirety on only one pitch.

The **range** of a melody is the distance between the lowest and highest notes. Without even being able to read the specific pitches notated in figure 2.3, it should be evident that melody A covers a wide range, while melody B has a narrow, restricted range.

We combine a series of pitches and a set of note values to produce a melody.

Melodies exhibit both wide and narrow ranges.

Fig. 2.3

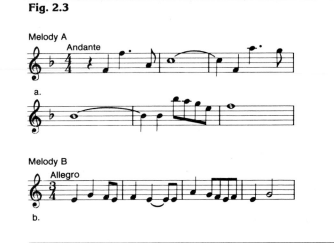

Melody A

a.

Melody B

b.

There is also no standard or ideal length for a melody. Moving at a moderate tempo in 3/4 meter, "Amazing Grace" takes sixteen bars to unfold (fig. 2.4), while "Farmer in the Dell," moving at a quicker tempo and in 2/4 meter, is complete in only eight bars (fig. 2.5).

Melodies are made up of phrases.

Generally speaking, melodies contain shorter bursts of activity called **phrases.** The end of a phrase is a temporary resting place—a place to catch a breath, similar to a comma in a sentence. The melody "Amazing Grace" contains four phrases: the first phrase ends in bar four on the word *sound;* the second phrase ends in bar eight on the word *me;* the third phrase ends in bar twelve on the word *found;* and the concluding phrase of the melody ends in bar sixteen on the word *see.*

Very short melodies are termed motives.

An even shorter piece of melodic material is referred to as a **motive.** The opening seconds of Beethoven's Symphony no. 5 present what may well be the best-known motive in the history of Western art music. Like most motives, this one consists of only a few notes, is very brief, and yet is memorable.

In large-scale instrumental works the word **theme** is often used in place of melody. For now, it is wise to accept this as a convention without worrying about the technical differences that exist between a melody and a theme.

Fig. 2.4

Amazing Grace

Amazing grace how sweet the sound that saved a wretch like me;
I once was lost but now am found, was blind but now I see.

Fig. 2.5

The Farmer in the Dell

Contour of a horizon—analogous to the up and down motion of a melody.

CHORDS AND HARMONY

Thus far, we have been talking about pitches and intervals that are emitted successively; one after another, one at a time. In conjunction with rhythm, these successions create melodies, motives, or themes. These are linear, similar to the line that defines the horizons observed in nature.

But we know from experience that sounds in music can be emitted more than one at a time. Different pitches can be sounded simultaneously. When two or more differing pitches are sounded together, they

Fig. 2.6

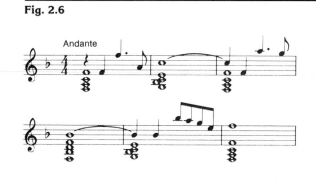

Often, two or more pitches are sounded together, creating a chord.

Harmony is created by a group or succession of chords.

create a **chord.** A group or succession of chords creates **harmony,** which usually accompanies the melody of a given song. Without reading the actual pitches in figure 2.6, notice the diverse natures of melody and harmony. The pitches of the melody are emitted successively while the pitches of each chord sound simultaneously as the melody unfolds.

The melody constitutes one **line** or part of this conglomeration; each of the individual members of the chords constitute additional lines or parts. Thus, in this example, both the melodic line and the accompanying chordal lines are present.

Harmony Reflects Change

While it is presumed that the earliest music in the Western world was strictly melodic, there is proof that musicians were aware of harmony by at least the early Middle Ages. The history of harmony reveals a series of periodic changes in attitudes and preferences where sonorities, or chords, are concerned. The chords and the harmony preferred by the medieval world differed in some ways from the chords and harmony favored in the Renaissance. Still another set of chordal and harmonic preferences was evident in the baroque, and tastes and preferences have continued to change up to the present.

The nature of harmony has changed over the ages.

The notion of what is satisfying and beautiful harmony, then, has not remained constant. Twentieth century audiences may perceive medieval harmony as crude and filled with displeasing sounds, yet, were it somehow possible for a person from the eleventh century to hear the harmony of "Scarborough Fair," it is safe to assume that the modern rendition would sound chaotic to that person.

Fig. 2.7

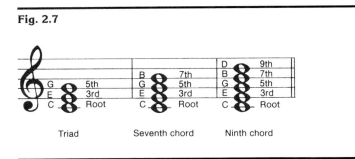

Triad   Seventh chord   Ninth chord

Chords Create Harmony

A chord may contain many different pitches. If you gently place your forearm on the keyboard of a piano and depress as many keys as is possible, a chord with many pitches is produced. The sound of the chord may be unpleasant and would not likely be used to accompany any part of the melody "Amazing Grace." The chord wouldn't sound appropriate. If the same operation were performed on only the black keys of the keyboard, the resultant chord might seem less abrasive, but it probably wouldn't sound like the correct accompaniment for "Amazing Grace" either. Only certain carefully selected chords, arranged in a particular order, seem to harmonize the hymn's melody in a satisfactory way.

The System of Functional Harmony

Of the many possible combinations of pitches, relatively few form the basis of the harmonic system that has prevailed and dominated musical practice in the Western world for the past 250 years. This system is known as **functional harmony,** or **tonality.** This is a system of organizing chords to produce the sense of being in a key. Music written in accordance with the principles of this system produces a central chord around which all other chords revolve. The chords in this system are built of stacks of major and minor thirds, forming **triads** (consisting of root, third, and fifth), **seventh chords** (consisting of root, third, fifth, and seventh), **ninth chords** (consisting of root, third, fifth, seventh, and ninth) and so forth, as shown in figure 2.7.

Properly arranged, these chords produce harmony. A central chord to which all other chords progress—rather like a gravitational system—emerges from this harmony.

In music this phenomenon is referred to as "keyness," or being in a **key.** Every key has seven pitches, which are family members. They belong to the key and can be used melodically and as members of chords.

Functional harmony is presently the dominant harmonic system in the Western world.

Each key has seven diatonic pitches, while all other pitches are chromatic pitches in that key.

These seven pitches are called **diatonic.** For example, the key of C has the following diatonic pitches:
C D E F G A B (C)
1 2 3 4 5 6 7 (8—octave)

All other pitches—C♯, E♭, F♯, B♭, etc.—are nonfamily members of the key of C and are called **chromatic** pitches. The central or key chord is called the **tonic** (or I). The way in which the chords are arranged in the system of functional harmony gives the tonic a sense of repose and finality. No other chord has this distinct quality, and indeed, a primary function of the tonic chord is to end a piece of music. The piece would not sound as if it were truly ended if it terminated on any chord other than the tonic.

A function of the tonic chord is to end the piece of music.

The dominant seventh functions to create harmonic tension and to progress to the tonic.

The **dominant seventh** (or V_7) chord has two primary functions: to create harmonic tension by sometimes resisting the gravitational pull of the tonic; and to progress ultimately to the tonic. Thus V_7 resolves into I. The function of the **subdominant** (or IV) chord is to lead to the dominant. Essentially then, the system of functional harmony operates in a cyclical fashion: I leads to IV, which leads to V_7, which leads to I. In practice this simple formula is overlaid and interlaced with a rich diversity of other chords and chord progressions, both diatonic and chromatic, that interrupt, forestall, and greatly enhance this inexorable cyclic flow. The chord vocabulary of functional harmony is thus greatly expanded.

Modulation allows changes in key within a piece of music.

The horizons of functional harmony are also expanded by use of a process known as **modulation.** This process makes it possible to shift temporarily in the course of a piece of music from the original, central, overriding key to another key. This allows a piece of music that begins in one key to modulate to one or more other keys and then return to the starting key. The process is different from, but related to, a visual experience called an optical illusion. But a critical difference between a modulation and an optical illusion is that once established, an optical illusion remains unstable, whereas a modulation in music is a temporary move and the return to the original key is both inevitable and stabilizing.

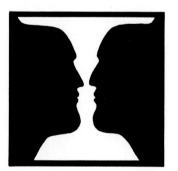

The system of functional harmony is further enriched by two related but differing **modes:** the major and minor mode. A piece can be in the key of C major (major mode) or in the key of C minor (minor mode). In either case, the chord built on the pitch C will be the tonic. If the tonic triad is minor, the key and the mode are minor. If the tonic triad is major, the key and the mode are major. Usually, the minor mode sounds "darker" than the major mode.

Love, by Robert Indiana, illustrates the dissonance of the letter "O."

Whitney Museum of American Art, Gift of the Howard and Jean Lipman Foundation, Inc.

Nearly all harmonic systems, including functional harmony, have the conflicting forces of **consonance** and **dissonance** built into them. Consonance, or a consonant chord, is analogous to a state of repose or relaxation, as in sinking into a comfortable chair after running a mile. Dissonance, created by chromatic pitches and chords, is, on the other hand, similar to a state of restlessness and tension, as in the actual heart-pounding, foot-thumping running of the mile. For reasons of health and sanity, this action must eventually wind up in an easy chair. The tension (dissonance) must, sooner or later, resolve into relaxation (consonance). In music, too, both dissonance and consonance are required. Endless running would result in heart failure; endless sitting would result in atrophy. Similarly, the mixture of consonance and dissonance in music is, and always has been, necessary. We must remember, however, that dissonance and consonance are relative terms, and that what was dissonant to the ears of one era or culture might be consonant, or relatively so, to another era or culture.

Consonant chords convey relaxation, while dissonant chords convey tension. Music demands a combination of the two.

TEXTURE

Texture refers to the number of lines or voices in a piece of music, and to the quality and activity of those lines. A few technical terms are useful in the description and comprehension of the texture of music. Other descriptive, nontechnical adjectives will also help account for the number and quality of voices, as well as the activity of those voices as they create a musical texture.

Monophonic Texture

A melody with no complementary harmony has monophonic texture.

A texture consisting of only one musical line or voice is called **monophonic.** Singing, whistling, or humming without any accompaniment creates a monophonic texture. It is important to remember, however, that monophony does not necessarily imply a single or solo voice; several people singing the same melodic line without adding any harmony creates a texture that is monophonic.

If you sing a song alone at a volume level of *p, mp,* or *mf,* the monophonic texture created might be further described as thin or light. If the song is sung at the top of your lungs, the texture will still be monophonic, but a different descriptive adjective, such as full or heavy, would be more appropriate. If ten of your friends sing the song in unison with you, the texture would still be monophonic, but is more accurately described as dense.

Polyphonic Texture

A polyphonic texture has a melody and harmony.

Two branches of polyphonic music are (1) homophonic, where the melody dominates the harmony, and (2) contrapuntal, where two or more lines are equally prominent.

When two or more different lines are performed simultaneously, as in harmony, the texture is defined as **polyphonic.** The two major branches of polyphonic music are (1) **homophonic** and (2) **contrapuntal.**

In a homophonic texture, one line, the melody, predominates any of the accompanying or harmonizing lines. A church hymn in four-part harmony and a solo song with chordal accompaniment are examples of homophonic texture.

In **counterpoint,** or in a contrapuntal texture, two or more different lines are equally prominent and compelling. Thus, attention is divided between two or more independent melodies rather than focused on one. This kind of texture is also known as **nonimitative counterpoint** because the voices do not repeat, or imitate, one another. In some contrapuntal textures, however, a given melody or subject may be stated in one voice and then restated or imitated in another voice or voices of the texture. This special kind of contrapuntal texture is imbued with **imitative counterpoint.** The lead voice performs the subject first and then proceeds to other material while, in succession, a variable number of voices follow and echo the subject. Graphically illustrated, imitative counterpoint looks like this:

In imitative counterpoint, the theme in the lead voice is restated or imitated in another voice or voices of the texture.

```
voice 1  XXXXX (the subject)_____(other material)_____
voice 2            XXXXX_____
voice 3               XXXXX_____
voice 4                  XXXXX_____
```

A **fugue** is a type of composition based on imitative counterpoint.

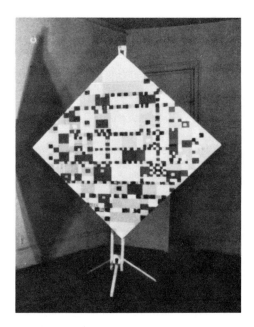

Broadway Boogie-Woogie by Mondrian—non-imitative counterpoint.

Some contrapuntal works employ a subsidiary melody or subject which is combined with and, in fact, competes with the main subject. A subsidiary subject or melody of this kind is called a **countermelody.**

The following examples illustrate the various kinds of harmonic language and textures.

1. Antiphon—"Laus Deo Patri," Psalm 113, "Laudate pueri." (Found in the recorded anthology *Masterpieces of Music Before 1750,* no. 1.) This is an example of monophonic music. The rhythm is nonmetrical.
2. Parallel Organum. (Found in the previously mentioned anthology, no. 6.) This is the earliest known type of polyphony in the Western world. It dates from about the ninth century AD. Notice the hollow, mysterious quality of the harmony.
3. "Agnus Dei" from the Mass *Veni sponsa Christi* by Palestrina. (Found in the same anthology, no. 24.) This is a polyphonic texture with imitative counterpoint. We are still not in the realm of functional harmony, but the harmony here has a lovely, almost ethereal quality. This kind of harmonic language and texture was favored in the late Renaissance.

4. Henry Purcell: *Variations on a New Ground Bass* (seventeenth century). (Found in the same anthology, no. 38.) Notice the repetitive nature of the lowest line in the texture, the bass line. This repetitive bass line, called a **ground bass,** is one kind of **ostinato.** An ostinato is a figure, line, or rhythm, usually fairly short, that is repeated doggedly throughout the course of a piece or an extended section of it.

5. J. S. Bach: any fugue from the *Well-Tempered Clavier* (eighteenth century). The baroque fugue is considered the soul of imitative counterpoint. By Bach's time, functional harmony definitely had been established as *the* harmonic system of the Western world.

6. Handel: "Halleluia" from *Messiah* (1741). The harmony in this piece is definitely functional. Some sections of the piece are homophonic, as at the beginning, while some sections are contrapuntal, as for example, "And He shall reign forever and ever."

7. Dvorak: Symphony no. 9, *From the New World,* second movement (1893). The majestic introduction and the solo that follows are both homophonic. Notice that the harmonic language is more lush, more melancholy, and somewhat more dissonant than the previous examples.

8. Griffes: *The White Peacock* (1915–16). The texture is essentially homophonic. The harmonic language is lusher still, almost to the point of being exotic.

MUSICAL INSTRUMENTS

Considering the diversity and geographical distribution of the many, many cultures throughout recorded history, and remembering that these cultures have always created music, it should not be a surprise that hundreds, if not thousands, of different musical instruments have been invented. However, only a fraction of these are in consistent use in the Western world today. The modern major symphony orchestra is composed of about one hundred members; still it normally employs only a few types of string, woodwind, brass, keyboard, and percussion instruments. A typical rock group usually employs only one or two kinds of guitar, keyboard, and percussion.

Musical instruments are manifold, and whatever their age, provenance, or type, they have at least one thing in common: they are all man-made, with the exception of the oldest and most universal of all, the human voice.

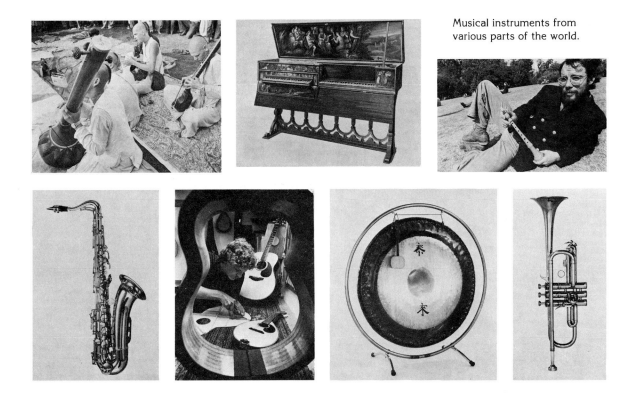

Musical instruments from various parts of the world.

Voices

This instrument is listed in the plural since there are so many different kinds of voices, all of which produce a nearly infinite variety of timbres and nuances. Consider, for example, the differences between the singing voices of children and those of adults, and the differences between male and female, high and low adult voices.

Adult voices are categorized as follows:

Male		Female	
tenor	high	coloratura	very high
baritone	medium	soprano	high
bass	low	mezzo soprano	medium
		contralto (or alto)	low

Different styles of music require different vocal qualities and techniques. The quality of the rock singer's voice is different from that of the church choir singer, the country/western singer, the folk singer, the jazz singer, or the opera singer. Even within the framework of rock music, voice qualities vary considerably from performer to performer—

Consider your voice as an instrument. Which category is it in?

from Elvis Presley, to Little Richard, to Frankie Avalon, to the Beach Boys, to the Beatles, to Boz Skaggs, to Billy Joel, to Kim Carnes, and so forth.

Human voices are very satisfying as solo instruments, as accompanied soloists, in small and large groups, in groups of men or women, and in mixed groups. The remarkable human voice also blends well with many kinds of man-made instruments.

A spectacular display of the prowess of one human voice is evident in a rendition of the Queen of the Night's aria for a coloratura soprano from Mozart's opera, *The Magic Flute.* Equally compelling and electric, in its own way, is Stevie Wonder's rendition of his song, "Isn't She Lovely."

The Orchestra Family

The concept of the orchestra dates back to the baroque era. At that time the orchestra was considerably smaller than it is today. It employed some instruments that have since dropped from use, and did not include some others that have been incorporated gradually since the baroque.

The seating arrangement of the symphony orchestra, diagramed in figure 2.8, shows the various instruments arranged in groups or families: stringed instruments, woodwinds, brass, percussion, plus the piano and harp. Every family has several members, each with particular capabilities. Some members of a family are designed to play the high part

Fig. 2.8
Seating arrangement for orchestra

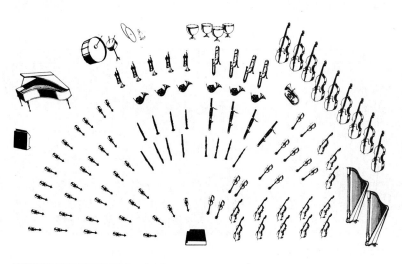

of the texture, some a little lower, some in the middle range, and some at the bottom of the texture. This corresponds roughly to the distribution of human voices: soprano, alto, tenor, and bass.

Strings   Generally speaking, the string family has been the backbone of the orchestra since its inception. This family consists of 1st violins, 2nd violins, violas, violincello (or cello), and double basses.

   The two basic ways of producing sounds from these instruments are: **bowing**—pulling the bow across the strings to produce a smooth or **legato** sound; and **pizzicato**—plucking the strings with the end of the finger. A small wooden device called a mute can be placed over the strings to produce a veiled or muffled sound.

   The violin, viola, cello, and string bass have proven to be re-markably versatile, and a considerable repertoire of solo, chamber, and

The string family is made up of first violins, second violins, violas, violincellos, and double basses.

String instruments can be played in two ways: by bowing and by plucking (pizzicato).

Stringed instruments

The cello lesson

Viola   Violin

Guitar, bass, violin, banjo

Double bass   Cello

String duet

Harp

orchestral music has been written for them. Listen, for example, to the solo violin in Mendelssohn's Violin Concerto in E Minor; to the solo viola in Berlioz's *Harold in Italy;* to the solo cello in Dvorak's *Concerto for Cello and Orchestra;* and to the string bass in Saint-Saëns' "Elephants" from *Carnival of Animals.* The wonderful way in which the voices of violins, violas, and cellos blend has inspired many composers to write string quartets. Haydn's String Quartet, op. 33, no. 2, is but one glorious example. Samuel Barber's *Adagio for String Orchestra* reveals the warmth and beauty of an entire string section.

The modern chromatic harp, with all its heavenly connotations, has many ancient ancestors who are found virtually all over the world. The harp in today's orchestra was developed in the late eighteenth century, but came into real prominence only about a century later with works such as Debussy's *Danse sacrée* and *Danse profane,* and his *Sonata for Flute, Viola, and Harp.* Several of Debussy's orchestral scores also feature important and prominent parts for harp, *Prélude à l'Après-midi d'un faune (Prelude to the Afternoon of a Faun),* and *La Mer,* among them.

Woodwind instruments are: flutes, oboes, English horns, clarinets, saxophones, bassoons, and French horns.

Many woodwinds have long histories.

Woodwinds   The woodwind family is composed of the flute, oboe, English horn, clarinet, various saxophones, bassoon, and French horn, many of which have historical prototypes. The flute, in one form or another, is an ancient instrument. Around the time of Joseph Haydn in the mid-eighteenth century, the flute entered the orchestra as a permanent member.

The oboe, too, has ancient ancestors, but its modern form was developed mainly by the French in the late seventeenth century. The English horn, whose tonal quality resembles that of the oboe, entered the orchestra in the early nineteenth century. The bassoon and its deeper-voiced brother, the contrabassoon, were known in the sixteenth century and were part of the orchestra in the baroque. The oboe, English horn, and bassoon are double-reed instruments. They produce a woody and somewhat nasal sound.

The saxophone is not an official member of the orchestra.

The clarinet and saxophone are single-reed instruments that produce a more mellow sound, particularly in their middle ranges. Although some composers, beginning in the late nineteenth century, wrote parts for the saxophone, they never became official, permanent members of the symphony orchestra. However, they found a home in jazz and in some forms of popular music. The clarinet, on the other hand, became a permanent member of the orchestra beginning in the very late eighteenth century.

Woodwind instruments

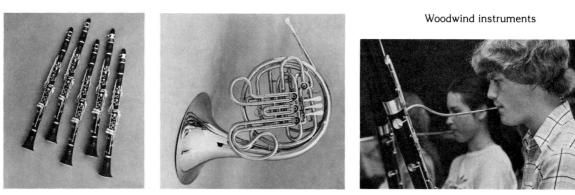

Clarinet   French horn   Two bassoonists

A flute duet   Tenor sax   Jazz on baritone sax

    Though the French horn is made of brass instead of wood, it is grouped with the woodwind family. What was once the strictly utilitarian hunting horn was transformed into an artistic instrument sometime in the seventeenth century. By the end of the eighteenth century the modern French horn with valves supplanted its older relatives.

    To get acquainted with the timbres of the woodwinds, listen to the following works in which they are prominently featured.

Flute—

    Debussy: *Prélude à l'Après-midi d'un faune (Prelude to the Afternoon of a Faun).*
    J. S. Bach: Any of the sonatas for flute and harpsichord.

Oboe—
> Beethoven: Symphony no. 6, third movement, allegro. After an opening passage, mainly for strings, the oboe has a playful solo. The oboe is then joined by a solo bassoon, a solo clarinet, and a solo French horn. This passage is repeated a little later in the movement.

English horn—
> Borodin: *In the Steppes of Central Asia.*
> Dvorak: Symphony no. 5, *From the New World,* second movement, largo.

Clarinet—
> Brahms: Clarinet Quintet in B Minor
> Benny Goodman: "Avalon" (this should be available on many recorded anthologies of the big dance band era).

Bassoon—
> Stravinsky: *Le Sacre du Printemps (The Rite of Spring),* beginning.

French horn—
> Mozart: Any of the four *Horn Concertos.*

A woodwind quintet is made up of a flute, oboe, clarinet, bassoon, and French horn.

The woodwind quintet, consisting of flute, oboe, clarinet, bassoon, and French horn, is an integral part of chamber music, especially in more recent times. Woodwind quintets by Anton Reicha, Jacques Ibert, and Walter Piston are available in recorded form.

The members of the brass family are the trumpet, the trombone, and the tuba.

Brass The brass family of the orchestra includes the trumpet, trombone, and tuba. In one form or another the trumpet and trombone were known in the late middle ages, while the tuba is a more recent invention. By the early nineteenth century these instruments were members of the symphony orchestra, and the trumpet and trombone have become standard instruments in jazz as well. Various mutes can be inserted into the bell end of brass instruments to dramatically alter their tone colors.

Mutes can be used to change the tone color of brass instruments.

The following examples will help acquaint you with the sounds of the brass instruments.

Trumpet—
> Mussorgsky/Ravel: *Pictures at an Exhibition,* beginning.

Trombone—
> Wagner: Overture from *Tannhäuser*

Tuba—
> Britten: *Young Person's Guide to the Orchestra*

Tuba   The high school concert band   Brass instruments

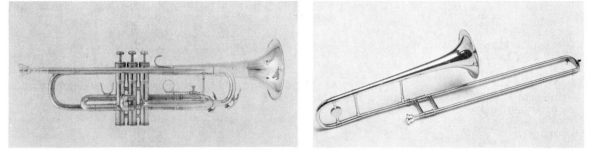

Trumpet   Trombone

Percussion Some percussion instruments are among the oldest musical instruments known, and yet in the Western world, at least, the percussion family has only recently received the special attention that other instrumental families have enjoyed for some time. In this respect many African and Asian musical cultures are far ahead of the Western world, and have been for a very long time. Fortunately, in our century some composers have begun to tap the rich, manifold vein of percussion instruments.

      Of the percussion instruments most commonly employed in the modern symphony orchestra, some have definite pitch and some do not. Those with definite pitch include the timpani (tunable "kettle" drums), glockenspiel, chimes, xylophone, and vibraphone (having either wooden or metal bars or tubes that are struck with mallets). The snare drum, bass drum, cymbals, gongs, triangle, tambourine, wood blocks, castanets, gourds, and maracas have indefinite pitches. These latter are essentially rhythm instruments and are rarely played alone or for solos.

Percussion instruments include the timpani, glockenspiel, chimes, xylophone, vibraphone, snare drum, bass drum, cymbals, gongs, triangle, tambourine, wood blocks, castanets, gourds, and maracas.

Percussion

Gettin' into it

Trap set with bass drum, snare drum, side drums,
two tom-toms, ride cymbal, high hat cymbals.

Cymbals of various sizes

Edgard Varese's *Ionisation* (1931) is an excellent introduction to
the special qualities and capabilities of percussion instruments. The piece
requires thirteen players and thirty-seven percussion instruments. Bartok's Music for strings, percussion and celesta provide other excellent
examples. Technically, the celesta is a member of the percussion family
even though it is a keyboard instrument, and in practice is usually played
by the pianist in the orchestra. The most celebrated celesta solo is Tchaikovsky's "Dance of the Sugar Plum Fairy" from *The Nutcracker*.

SUMMARY

This chapter is essentially about two things: musical sounds and the instruments that produce these sounds.

Pitches are the basic sound material of music. Every pitch has certain characteristics including frequency (highness or lowness), volume (loudness or softness), and timbre or tone color (determined by the instrument playing the pitch). In cooperation with rhythm, pitches can be combined in several different ways to create melody, harmony, and texture.

A melody, motive, or theme consists of a rhythmized succession of pitches and intervals (or distances). The texture of an unaccompanied melody is called monophonic.

When two or more pitches are sounded together, they create a chord. A succession of chords produces harmony. Most of the music with which we are most familiar adheres to the principles of a system called functional harmony. In that system certain kinds of chords and chord progressions are used to produce the sense of being in a key. The tonic, dominant seventh, and subdominant chords are central to this "keyness," and all chords, consonant and dissonant, must ultimately resolve to the tonic.

A contrapuntal texture is a special type of polyphonic texture in which two or more musical lines are equally compelling. Imitative counterpoint consists of a lead voice or line and one or more following voices. The following voices, each in turn, imitates or echos the subject first presented by the lead voice.

In addition to the various ranges of the human singing voice, every instrument has its special tone quality or timbre. The instruments of the modern symphony orchestra are divided into the following groups or choirs: strings, woodwinds, brass, and percussion.

KEY TERMS

pitch

frequency

timbre

volume (amplitude)

dynamics

sharp

flat

accidental

interval

octave

minor second (half
    step, semitone)

major second (whole
    step, whole tone)

melody

range

motive

theme

phrase

chord

harmony

functional harmony

triads

seventh chords

ninth chords

key

diatonic

chromatic

tonic

dominant seventh

subdominant chord

modulation

modes

consonance

dissonance

texture

monophonic

polyphonic

homophonic

contrapuntal

counterpoint

imitative counterpoint

fugue

countermelody

ground bass

ostinato

bowing

legato

pizzicato

THINKING ABOUT IT

In terms of texture, what is the difference between the Bach fugue (example 5 on page 38) and *The White Peacock* (example 8 on page 38)?

Example 4 on page 38 features an ostinato. How would you describe an ostinato? Can you think of a rock song or songs that contain an ostinato?

3

FORM AND MUSIC

Ste. Sernin, Toulouse—an intricate, multifaceted formal design

SOUNDS OF THE CHAPTER

J. S. Bach
St. Matthew Passion
French Suite no. 1 in D Minor

Beethoven
Piano Sonata in F Minor, op. 2, no. 1
Piano Sonata no. 8 in C Minor, op. 13 ♪
Piano Sonata, op. 13
Piano Sonata, op. 26 ♪
Symphony no. 3, *Eroica*

Brownie and Sonny
"I'm a Stranger Here" ♪

Ray Charles
"Someday"

Chopin
Mazurka, op. 63, no. 3 ♪
Mazurka, op. 67, no. 3 ♪

Debussy
"Beau Soir"
"La Flute de Pan" ♪

Handel
Alcina
Messiah

Haydn
Minuet, Symphony no. 92
Piano Sonata no. 50 in D Major ♪
Piano Sonata in E Minor
String Quartet, op. 76, no. 3

Joel
"Just the Way You Are"

Little Richard
"Tutti Frutti"

Glen Miller
"In the Mood"

Mozart
G Minor Symphony
Piano Sonata in B♭ Major
Symphony no. 40 ♪

Elvis Presley
"Hound Dog"

Ravel
Boléro
Pavane pour une Infante défunte

Jimmy Reed
"I Was So Wrong"

Scarlatti
Sonata in C Minor, K. 158

Schubert
Die Erlkönig
"Gute Nacht," *Die Winterreise*
"Who is Sylvia?"

Pinetop Smith
"Pinetop's Boogie Woogie"

Sondheim
"Send in the Clowns"

Otus Spann
"Good Morning Mr. Blues"

Tchaikovsky
"March," *The Nutcracker*
"Overture Miniature," *The Nutcracker*

"A Froggie Would A-Courtin' Go"
"Amazing Grace"
"Battle Hymn of the Republic"
"Down in the Valley"
"Maple Leaf Rag" ♪
"My Country 'Tis of Thee"
"The Entertainer" ♪
"The Star Spangled Banner"
"Wonderous Things of Thee Are Spoken"

MUSIC: THE EVOLVING MESSAGE

It has been said that "Time ensures that everything doesn't happen all at once." This quote is applicable to the experience of listening to pieces of music, as well as to life in general.

If a piece of music were really a "piece" in the ordinary sense of the word, then it should be tangible and observable as a whole. Clearly, "piece of" is not the intended meaning where musical compositions are concerned, for a piece of music is neither tangible nor something that happens all at once. Music unfolds over a span of time; it does not appear as an entity that is visible as a whole. It becomes meaningful to us as we absorb the content of each passing phase of the span and relate each phase to the others. The more fully we grasp the contents and sense the interrelationships of a given piece of music, the more intimately we know it. In essence, then, knowledge of the form or structure of a given work rests on the perception and understanding of its various parts and how they relate to one another.

The composer's work involves piecing together the various separate musical ideas he or she invents to form a larger musical whole that has continuity. We as listeners do not have the burden of inventing these ideas, but our grasp of a piece is dependent upon our ability to perceive its continuity. Musical chaos would result without this ability. Where the true appreciation of music is concerned, it would be difficult to overrate the importance of being able to hear form.

To grasp a piece of music, we must be able to perceive its continuity.

It is important to analyze form on more than one level. If a landscape were observed from 10,000 feet in the air, its structure is perceived in one light. From an altitude of 500 feet, the perception of the structure begins to change in some ways: the general outlines observed from 10,000 feet are out of sight (but not out of memory), but new and significant information is gained. For example, the shaded areas are now revealed as patches of trees, and the snakelike line comes into focus as a river. A walking tour of the landscape presents an infinite variety of detail and the interrelationships of the many parts, large and small, are visible.

Similarly, the structure of musical compositions can be examined. This examination can proceed from the general to the particular or vice versa. Either the whole piece or merely individual movements of a multimovement work can be examined, as can the sections that make up the piece or movement, the subsections, the phrases, or even the motives.

MUSICAL BOOKKEEPING

To assist these analyses, a kind of musical-structural bookkeeping method is employed. Capital letters designate sections of a piece, and lower case letters designate subsections. If a section or subsection is repeated exactly or nearly exactly during a piece, its letter is repeated in the analysis. For example, the diagram *ABA* indicates that there are three sections in the piece, the last of which is a repetition of the first. When a nonliteral repetition occurs, the analysis reads: *ABA'*. The *A'* indicates that the repetition is nonliteral but nevertheless recognizable as the content of *A*.

There is no fixed length for a section of music; in a large-scale work, such as a symphonic movement, a section may be lengthy. In a small work, such as a song or a short piece for the piano, a section of music may be brief. Whatever the scale, a section can be loosely defined as a musical unit that has internal cohesion and reaches a conclusion. A section can terminate with a momentary pause or it can run directly into the next section. In either case, the beginning of a new and contrasting section is usually marked by some notable change in content. Many popular songs such as "Send in the Clowns" (Stephen Sondheim) and "Just the Way You Are" (Billy Joel) have the form *AABA* on the level of the section.

Lower case letters are used to mark the constituents of sections. Again, the length and duration of a subsection is variable. In some works a subsection can be a short phrase; in others it can consist of several phrases. A diagram of the formal structure of "Send in the Clowns" looks like this:

level of the section ----	A	A	B	A
level of subsections ----	abc	abc	def	abc

Some forms have been used consistently through long periods of music history: the ternary, binary, rondo, twelve-bar blues, and sonata-allegro forms.

Ternary: *ABA* or *AABA*

The simple **ternary** form *ABA* is found in many kinds of music throughout a long chronological span. It has proven to be not only aesthetically pleasing, but also psychologically rewarding. The reiteration of *A* creates a pleasing sense of symmetry. Moreover, the restatement of *A*, given its particular location within the form, has another value: it reintroduces the familiar. When confronted with a series of events, each of which is new and unpredictable, we tend to become uneasy or bored. But the recurrence of one or more of the events has a reassuring effect.

Capital letters designate sections of a piece, and lower case letters designate subsections.

What does ABA indicate?

A' indicates a nonliteral repetition of A.

Length and duration of sections and subsections can vary.

A section is a musical unit that has internal cohesion and reaches a conclusion.

It is true that in a fine piece of music each component has a purpose, but it does not necessarily follow that every element is as important as others. In most ternary forms, the content of *A* is the most important material. In a sense it is ultimately what the piece is all about, and so lingers in our memory of the piece. In an *ABA* form, *A* is clearly in a position of prominence: the *A* section is stated twice; it is the first thing we hear, as well as the last.

However, *B,* too, is important in the ternary form. It must be present to ensure the success of the form. If *B* were not included, nothing would remain but a succession of *A* statements. No musical material, however compelling and gripping, can stand alone for very long. The constant, uninterrupted repetition of *A* would almost certainly lead to listener boredom. The presence of *B* prevents such an undesirable situation; it interrupts *A* and focuses our attention on something new before we begin to get "too much of a good thing." The *B* section is designed to be diversionary, but not reactionary. It contains enough interest and contrast to attract our attention, yet it does not overpower *A*. The return to *A* is all the more satisfying precisely because of the diversionary activity of *B*.

Listeners find the ternary form *ABA* especially pleasing.

Composers have made frequent use of the *ABA* form, and audiences from different cultures and eras have long found it satisfying. The ternary form, for example, is found in the literature of nineteenth century piano music. The form of Mazurka, op. 67, no. 3, by Frederic Chopin (1810–49), is diagramed and discussed in the following "Sound and Sense." (The term **opus** [or op.] means work or composition. Many composers, including Chopin, used opus numbers in ordering their compositions chronologically.)

♪ SOUND AND SENSE: ABA *Form*

Title: *Mazurka,* op. 67, no. 3
Composer: Chopin
A Closer Look:

A	B	A
aa' aa'	bb'	aa'

This is a brief example in which *A* is dominated by a single idea, and the short *B* section consists of a single, contrasting idea.

Notice that the material in B of this piece contrasts with that in *A* in terms of harmony, melody, rhythm, and, to some extent, range, although its range is more restricted than the range in *A*.

Coda means tail—and acts as a musical stop sign.

Mazurka, op. 67, no. 3, concludes with a section called a **coda** (Italian for "tail"). A coda is simply an ending formula or a musical stop sign. (A more extensive examination of the nature of the coda at various stages of history appears in a later chapter.)

Chopin's Mazurka, op. 63, no. 3, is a longer and somewhat more complex example of ternary form.

♪ SOUND AND SENSE: *Complex* ABA *Form*

Title: Mazurka, op. 63, no. 3
Composer: Chopin
A Closer Look:

A	B	C
aa' bb'	cc' (or d)	aa''

The two subsections of *B* resemble each other, yet the second of them seems to grow organically and develop a unique structure from the first. Hence we have the option of calling it either *c'* (if we feel strong about its relationship to *c*) or *d* (if we feel it is more autonomous).

The return to the *A* section includes a subsection that is a nonliteral repetition of neither *a* nor *a'*. Still it is clearly derived from the content of *a*, so it is designated *a''*.

Large compositions—symphonies or concertos—consist of a number of individual entities called **movements.** For example, a classical symphony normally consists of four movements.

A large-scale ternary form was used as the third movement of most eighteenth and nineteenth century symphonies. Beethoven and other romantics used a dance in 3/4 time called the **scherzo** for this purpose. Classical composers, Haydn and Mozart among them, preferred another triple-meter dance called a **minuet.** The minuet has the form minuet-trio-minuet *(ABA)*. The third movement, "Minuet," from Symphony no. 92 by Joseph Haydn (1732–1809), is diagramed here.

The minuet has an *ABA* form.

SOUND AND SENSE: *Minuet*

Title: Symphony no. 92, third movement
Composer: Haydn
A Closer Look:

A (minuet)	B (trio)	A (minuet)
aba'ba'	ccdc'dc'	aba'

As you listen to this example you will notice that the diagram does not list everything that happens. For example, four smaller segments are subsumed under *a*. Notice, too, that the most notable change in content occurs at section *B* with the entrance of the French horns.

The third movement of Symphony no. 40 by Wolfgang Mozart (1756–91) is another minuet-trio-minuet.

♪ **SOUND AND SENSE:** *Minuet-Trio-Minuet*

Title: Symphony no. 40, third movement

Composer: Mozart

A Closer Look:

A (minuet)	*B* (trio)	*A* (minuet)
aa'a''a'''	*bcb*	*a*

This movement is somewhat more compact than the Haydn example, as all of the material of Section *A* is derived from a single idea—*a*—and several nonliteral repetitions of it. Here again, the most notable change in content begins at *B,* a section that is largely dominated by the woodwinds. This contrasts with the two *A* sections that are dominated by the string instruments.

Beethoven's *Eroica* symphony exhibits the *ABA* form in its third movement.

The third movement of Symphony no. 3, the *Eroica* symphony, by Ludwig van Beethoven (1770–1827), is a scherzo-trio-scherzo—*ABA* design. Once more, the most obvious change in content occurs at the trio *(B)* with the entrance of the French horns.

Ternary form is also found in the field of vocal music. A special kind of operatic song called a da capo aria was particularly favored by opera composers in the baroque era. "Tonami a vagheggiar," from the opera *Alcina* by George Frederick Handel (1685–1759), is a da capo aria having the formal structure *ABA.* The same is true of the arias, "He was despised" from Handel's *Messiah,* where the *B* section begins with the words "He gave his back to the smiters," and of "Grief and pain" from J. S. Bach's *St. Matthew Passion,* where the *B* section begins with the words, "May the anguish of my spirit." (Additional examples of ternary form, as well as other forms discussed in this chapter, are listed at the end of this chapter.)

Binary: *AB* or *AABB*

Although it seems logical that a two-part structure would be easier to grasp than a three-part structure, it is generally not true in music. The

Binary form means two-part structure.

impact of **binary** *AB* is very different from that of ternary *ABA.* Binary form lacks the return to *A* and the psychological comfort that accompanies this return. *A* must make its point without the benefit of a restatement. *B* must be equal in force with its partner *A,* otherwise the

In binary form *A* and *B* are of equal importance.

piece would have a lame ending, and would lack justification.

The dance suite from the baroque era contains many examples of binary form. The French Suite no. 1, in D minor, by J. S. Bach, contains six short dance movements: allemande, courante, sarabande, menuet I, menuet II, and gigue. All are cast in the binary form *AABB* (the menuet II does not repeat *B*). In most cases, *A* begins on tonic and ends on dominant, and *B* begins on dominant and ends on tonic.

In these pieces, one of the functions of *B* is to provide contrast to *A*. The degree of contrast, however, presents a problem. If the contrast is violent and overpowering, the piece loses all sense of unity, particularly in view of the fact that *A* is not repeated. *A* and *B* would sound like two different pieces rather than as partners in a single work. It is the composer's difficult task, then, to make *A* and *B* sound like separate entities that are recognizable as related parts of a larger entity.

> **The composer must make the *A* and *B* sections in binary form work as partners in the piece.**

Bach provided an ingenious solution to this problem in the six movements of the French Suite no. 1, in D minor. The *B* section begins with a variation of the opening material of the *A* section in each case. In the allemande, the opening gesture of *A* is inverted (turned upside down) at the beginning of *B*. The same is true of the courante and the gigue. In the sarabande, the opening gesture of *A* is in the highest part; the same gesture at the opening of *B* is found in the lowest part. Once this unifying connection is made, the *B* section is free to proceed to contrasting material.

> **How did Bach handle binary form?**

Rondo: *ABACA, ABACADA,* or *ABACABA*

It is evident from the **rondo** diagram that it keeps "coming 'round to" the *A* section. The recurrences of *A* are separated by sections of contrasting materials. In many rondos, the *A* sections are all in the tonic key and the contrasting sections are in some other key(s). Two movements, one by Haydn and another by Beethoven, both diagramed below, illustrate how the rondo works.

> **The rondo form is characterized by the recurrence of *A*.**

♪ SOUND AND SENSE: *Rondo*

Title: Piano Sonata no. 50 in D Major, last movement

Composer: Haydn

A Closer Look:

A—aabb (tonic key)
B—ccdd (tonic key)
A—aabb (tonic key)
C—eee'e'f (subdominant key)
A—a'b'b' (tonic key)

♪ **SOUND AND SENSE:** *Rondo*

Title: Piano Sonata, op. 13, second movement

Composer: Beethoven

A Closer Look:

A—aa
B—bc
A—a
C—dd′
A—a′a′
Coda

"The Entertainer" has a slightly different rondo form.

Many American rags have a structure that is reminiscent of the rondo. The typical rag, like the rondo, has five or more sections. But unlike a rondo, the sections are often all in the tonic key, and the *A* section is repeated only once instead of two or more times. On the section level, both "The Entertainer" and "Maple Leaf Rag" have the form *ABACD,* compared to a common rondo form *ABACA.*

Twelve-Bar Blues: *AA′B*

All twelve-bar blues have the melodic and poetic structure *AA′B.*

The **twelve-bar blues** probably developed as a poetic form about one hundred years ago. Early in its history, however, singer-musicians and instrumentalists breathed music into it and created an extraordinarily versatile musical form.

Both the melodic and poetic structures follow the same format. The poetic structure consists of an opening line in which a problem or situation is presented, a second line in which, for the sake of emphasis, the problem or situation is repeated, and a third line in which a conclusion or outcome is introduced.

A Well, I'm feelin' so bad all the live long day.
A Well, I'm feelin' so bad all the live long day.
B Think I'll go down to the river and throw my poor self in.

The melodic form, likewise, has the same melodic phrase for both the first and the second *A;* a different melodic phrase is sung to *B.* Examples of this poetic/melodic form are plentiful in the three record anthology, *The Best of the Blues* (Sine Qua Non 103/3), one of several fine recorded anthologies of blues readily available to the public. A few of the twelve-bar blues from this collection are "Good Morning Mr. Blues" (Otis Spann), "I Was So Wrong" (Jimmy Reed), "I'm a Stranger Here" (Brownie and Sonny) and "Someday" (Ray Charles).

Most twelve-bar blues are in 4/4 time—all of the above examples are in 4/4. Return to the examples and determine the length of each of the three sections: How many measures or bars long is *A?* the second *A? B?* When it has been determined that *AAB* equals four bars plus four bars plus four bars, the reason this form is called the twelve-bar blues is obvious. There are also blues patterns of eight bars, sixteen bars, and others, but the twelve-bar blues is employed most often.

The twelve-bar blues also has a basic harmonic formula:

Content	*A*				*A'*				*B*			
bar	1	2	3	4	1	2	3	4	1	2	3	4
chord	I	–	–	–	IV	–	I	–	V_7	–	I	–

With only slight modifications, the twelve-bar blues form and its attendant harmonic scheme are found in a variety of music that succeeded the blues. The scheme is often found in boogie woogie, of which "Pinetop's Boogie Woogie" by Pinetop Smith is a good example. It is also found in the big band repertoire of the swing era, as in Glenn Miller's "In the Mood." Little Richard's "Tutti Frutti," and Elvis Presley's "Hound Dog" are examples of the twelve-bar blues format in early rock and roll music. Contemporary rock music, too, often employs the twleve-bar blues form.

Sonata-Allegro

The word sonata has two meanings in music. It can designate a genre of musical composition, such as a piano sonata, a violin sonata, or in the baroque era, a trio sonata. Or, as it is used in this text, the **sonata-allegro** form (for short, sonata form) can refer to a specific musical structure.

As the twelve-bar blues is to blues, jazz, and some types of popular music, so the sonata-allegro form is to Western art music of the past two hundred years. The form is ubiquitous; it is found in one or more movements of the symphony, the concerto, the string quartet, and the sonata.

The form crystallized in the classic era of the mid-eighteenth century after a period of experimentation. With some modifications, the sonata-allegro form has survived to the present day.

The form has the following elements: exposition-development-recapitulation-coda.

The **exposition** section introduces the dominant thematic materials of the movement. Often, but not always, there are two contrasting themes—*A* and *B,* and a closing theme, *C,* which frequently is reminiscent of the *A* theme. The themes don't follow one another back to back, but are joined by a connective non-thematic section called a **bridge.** The

Twelve-bar blues format is found in boogie woogie, big band, early rock and roll, and today's rock music.

The sonata-allegro form contains: exposition-development-recapitulation-coda.

In the sonata-allegro form, the exposition introduces the dominant themes.

exposition section is normally repeated verbatim. Materials bracketed by these signs,  , are repeated literally. Thus the exposition section of the sonata form is diagramed:

A ————————————————— B   (Bridge)
                                              C (or A')
(Tonic key) (modulatory bridge   (Dominant key or
            section)   relative minor)

This diagram is obvious in the exposition section of the first movement of Mozart's Symphony no. 40. When listening to the piece, note the contrasting characters of A and B. A is rather jagged, whereas B is more lyrical.

    After the repetition of the exposition section, the form proceeds to the development section wherein one or both of the themes introduced in the exposition section are developed. The **development** section has no set length, nor does it have to behave in any prescribed way, but it usually deals with thematic materials from the exposition section. These materials are developed so that new characteristics are revealed.

    A theme can be developed in any or all of the following ways:

In the development section of the sonata-allegro form, new characteristics of the theme are revealed.

Can you describe the four methods of developing a theme?

1. All or part of a theme can be cast in a series of different keys. The development section is usually harmonically restless and is marked by frequent changes of key.
2. A theme can be tossed about the orchestra (in the case of instrumental works), played first by one group of instruments, then by another group.
3. A theme can be combined with a countermelody that vies equally for attention.
4. A theme can be pulled apart or broken into fragments. Notice that in the Mozart example an extended patch of the development plucks the first three notes from the A theme and repeats them several times at different levels. It is as if this fragment of the theme were being put under a microscope.

The development section is filled with tension and struggle; the developing theme seems to fight for its life. This turmoil is resolved with the **recapitulation,** where everything is reordered. This section is very similar to the exposition in terms of content and the order of events. A major difference, however, is that in the recapitulation, both A and B are in the tonic key, so the movement ends in the tonic rather than the dominant.

The turmoil experienced in development is resolved in the recapitulation.

    The sonata-allegro form concludes with a coda. Sometimes the coda is little more than the ending formula mentioned earlier. Often, though, in large-scale movements such as the Mozart example, the coda is extended. In fact, the coda has nearly the proportions and the activity of another development section in the Mozart G Minor Symphony.

Sonata-allegro form ends with a coda.

THEME AND VARIATIONS: A PROCESS

All of the forms discussed thus far are means of organizing musical ideas to make them comprehensible. Theme and variations is not so much a set structure as it is a process, but, like any useful form, it too is a means of organizing musical ideas. In a theme and variations, there is no set length, no prescribed number of sections, and no established policy governing repetition and contrast. The process allows considerable freedom so composers from the Renaissance to the twentieth century have displayed great affection for it.

The purpose of devising form is to organize musical ideas.

Creating Variations

A theme and variations begins with a full statement called, logically, the theme. **Theme** in this case implies not only the melody, but the harmony and the formal structure of the section called the theme. A number of other sections, called **variations,** follow. These variations are created in two basic ways: the melody itself is varied (through ornamentation, change of note values, other added notes, or rhythmic devices); or the melody is retained in its original state, but its environment is changed from one variation to the next.

Variations are created by changing note values, adding notes or rhythmic devices and changing the environment.

The second movement of the Haydn String Quartet, op. 76, no. 3 is an example of the environmental variation. Listen first to the theme section itself—the melody may be familiar as the hymn "Wondrous Things of Thee are Spoken." This section has the form *aa'bcc,* and is retained in each of the four variations that follow the theme section. In each of these four variations, the melody is stated in its original form and is clearly recognizable. However, the environment in which the melody is found changes. In the first variation, the texture is reduced to two instruments, one carrying the melody, the other weaving a countermelody around it. In variation 2 the melody is given to the cello, and two of the other strings carry a new countermelody. All four instruments are active in variation 3: the viola has the melody and there are new countermelodies above and below it in the texture. In the fourth and last variation, the melody is returned to the first violin which quietly carries it to a high singing range. The movement concludes with a brief coda.

Haydn's String Quartet, op. 76, no. 3 and Beethoven's Piano Sonata, op. 26, are two examples of theme and variation.

The first movement of Beethoven's Piano Sonata, op. 26 is an example of a theme and variations in which the melody itself is varied. The theme section has the ternary form *aa'ba'.* Notice as you listen to the five variations that this structure is retained throughout. Each of the variations has a traceable relationship to the melody of the theme section, although some are more clearly discernible than others. For example, in the first variation, the quick notes added in the right-hand part do not obliterate the original melody; in the second variation, the left-hand part is closely related to the melody; but the third variation only faintly echoes the melody.

SONG STRUCTURES

There are two basic types of song structure: strophic and through-composed. These terms apply only to songs, not instrumental or keyboard music.

Strophic

"O'er the land of the free and the home of the brave" are usually the last words heard in "The Star Spangled Banner" although they are not the last words in the song. They are merely the final words in the first stanza of the national anthem. The other four stanzas are rarely sung, but when they are, they are sung to the same music as the first stanza. This structure, where there are multiple stanzas that are all sung to the same strand of music, is called **strophic.** Many hymns, art songs, folk songs, and popular songs are strophic. "Amazing Grace," "Battle Hymn of the Republic," "Down in the Valley," "A Froggie Would A-Courtin' Go," and "My Country 'Tis of Thee" are all strophic, as are the art songs "Who is Sylvia?" by Franz Schubert (1797–1828) and "Beau Soir" by Claude Debussy (1862–1918).

A strophic song has multiple stanzas, all sung to the same strand of music.

Through-Composed

The opposite of strophic is **through-composed,** a type of song in which new music is composed for each stanza of the poem and no section of music is repeated. Through-composed songs are not numerous outside the field of art song, but Schubert's "Erlkönig" and Debussy's "La Flute de Pan" are fine examples of the type.

New music is composed for each stanza of a through-composed song.

Modified Strophic

A third type of song structure—**modified strophic**—combines aspects of both strophic and through-composed. In Schubert's "Gute Nacht" from the song cycle *Die Winterreise,* the first two stanzas are sung to the same music, the third stanza is sung to a slightly different version of the same music, and the fourth and last stanzas employ the same music, changed from the minor mode to the major.

Modified strophic combines the strophic and the through-composed types of song structure.

ADDITIONAL EXAMPLES OF THE FORMAL TYPES DISCUSSED IN THIS CHAPTER

SOUND AND SENSE: *Ternary ABA Form*

Title: Piano Sonata in F Minor, op. 2, no. 1, second movement
Composer: Beethoven

A Closer Look:

A—aa'ba''
B—cc'd
A—aa (both ornamented) ba (both ornamented)
Coda

SOUND AND SENSE: *Ternary* **ABA** *Form*

Title: "March" from *The Nutcracker*

Composer: Tchaikovsky

A Closer Look:

A—a (trumpets) *b* (strings) *aba'* (low brass *abab*)
B—c (flutes) *c*
A—a''b'aba''abab

SOUND AND SENSE: *Binary* **AABB** *Form*

Title: Sonata in C Minor, K. 158, Longo 4

Composer: D. Scarlatti

A Closer Look:

A—abbccd
*A—*repeated
B—efc'c'd'd'
*B—*repeated
Notice that the *B* section uses some of the material from the *A* section, thus ensuring unity.

SOUND AND SENSE: *Binary* **ABAB** *Form*

Title: "Overture Miniature" from *The Nutcracker*

Composer: Tchaikovsky

A Closer Look:

A—aaba
B—cc
A—aaba
B—cc
Coda

SOUND AND SENSE: *Rondo Form*

Title: Piano Sonata no. 8 in C Minor, op. 13, second movement

Composer: Beethoven

A Closer Look:

A—aa
B—b (begins in minor mode)
A—a
C—c (also begins in minor mode, but a different key)
A—aa
Coda

SOUND AND SENSE: *Rondo Form*

Title: *Pavane pour une Infante défunte* (orchestral version)

Composer: Ravel

A Closer Look:

A—a, French horn dominates
B—b, oboe and winds dominate; *b,* strings
A—a, clarinet and flute dominate
C—c, flute; *c',* clarinet; *c* and *c'* repeated
A—a, flute dominates

SOUND AND SENSE: *Sonata-Allegro Form*

Title: Piano Sonata in B♭ Major, K. 333

Composer: Mozart

A Closer Look:

Exposition

A—a   *a'* tonic key
Bridge   modulates to
B—b   *b'* dominant key
Bridge
C—c

(repeat entire exposition verbatim)

Development
The *A* theme is developed and there are several changes of key.

Recapitulation
A—a (tonic key) *a'*
Bridge
B—b (tonic key) *b'*
Bridge
C—c
Coda

SOUND AND SENSE: *Sonata-Allegro Form*

Title: Piano Sonata in E Minor, first movement

Composer: Haydn

A Closer Look:

Exposition
A—a (tonic key) *a'*
Bridge
B—b (new key of relative major), *b'*
(repeat entire exposition verbatim)

Development
The *A* theme is developed and there are several changes of key.

Recapitulation
A—tonic key
Bridge
B—*b* (tonic key), *b'*
A—a fragment of *a* closes the movement

SUMMARY

In this chapter you have been exposed to the various forms composers use to organize their musical ideas. You've learned to identify and record many of the most frequently used forms.

Musical bookkeeping allows us to record the intangible forms of the music we hear. Capital letters designate sections of pieces and lower case letters designate subsections. The ternary form *ABA* indicates a piece of music made up of three sections, with section three repeating section one. This repetition offers reassurance and satisfaction to the listener.

Binary form, *AB* or *AABB*, offers no repetition. In this form the two sections must work hand in hand to create cohesion within the piece.

In rondo form we return to the *A* section repeatedly. Rondos can be composed in a variety of ways, including *ABACA, ABACADA,* and *ABACABA.*

Twelve-bar blues form has the common poetic and melodic structure *AAB,* along with a basic harmonic formula. You've probably heard this form in current rock music.

The sonato-allegro form is recognized by its structure: exposition, development, recapitulation, and coda. Mozart's Symphony no. 40, first movement, is a good example of this form.

Using theme and variations, the composer establishes a theme and then employs numerous devices to vary that theme. The note values or the rhythm or the environment might change from one variation to the next.

Songs usually display one of two basic structures. If a song has several stanzas sung to the same music, the structure is strophic. If each stanza of the song is sung to a different music, and no music line is repeated, the structure is through-composed. A third structure alternative is merely a combination of the two basic forms. Modified strophic shows characteristics of both.

Your newly acquired knowledge of form, and the method for recording this nontangible aspect of music, will help you to improve your listening skills and to appreciate similarities and differences found in various types of music.

KEY TERMS

ternary	twelve-bar blues	theme
coda	sonata-allegro	variations
scherzo	exposition	strophic
minuet	development	through-composed
binary	recapitulation	modified strophic
rondo		

THINKING ABOUT IT

Construct a Sound and Sense listening guide for Simon and Garfunkel's "Scarborough Fair." Include a formal analysis on the level of the section and the subsection, and comment on meter and other rhythmic details, texture, and instrumentation.

Repeat the assignment for Ravel's *Boléro.*

4

Daffodils

SOUNDS OF THE CHAPTER

Bartók
Suite *Out of Doors*

Beethoven
Pastoral Symphony
Symphony no. 7

Berlioz
*Symphonie Fantastique (Fantastic
    Symphony)*

Debussy
"Nuages," *Nocturnes*

Ives
The Unanswered Question ♪

Mendelssohn
Hebrides Overture
Italian Symphony
Violin Concerto

Vivaldi
"Spring," *The Seasons* ♪

von Weber
Der Freischütz ♪

MUSIC TRANSCENDS WORDS AND OBJECTS

Emotions, thoughts, and visions are difficult to express without stumbling over too many words or groping for a single word that escapes consciousness. Yet some individuals are capable of expressing their thoughts with an economy of words and an accuracy that invites others to thrill in the emotion.

William Shakespeare undoubtedly possessed this capability. The following extract exemplifies the superior quality of his work.

> . . . daffodils,
> That come before the swallow dares, and take
> The winds of March with beauty . . .

(Shakespeare: *The Winter's Tale* IV, iv. 118–20)

Is this *only* an assemblage of words? If the answer is yes, then perhaps there is no such thing as poetry. If the answer is no—this is not *only* an assemblage of words—then perhaps it is true that there is something meaningful beyond the words: something inspired by the words, but not limited to them. The meaning transcends the words themselves.

But what is the meaning? Does this pair of lines mean something about daffodils? About swallows? About the winds of March? The lines speak of all three, but ultimately they evoke a condition, a season, an atmosphere, and a mood to which the daffodils, swallows, and winds are only accessories.

In a context other than this poetry, the daffodil has its own phenomenological identity that is observable, knowable, and appreciable. The same is true of the swallow and the wind. But in the context of this poetry, something of the separate identities is lost or forgotten—they are no longer *only* phenomena. The separate identities are surrendered to a larger entity having a meaning of its own.

Perhaps then, the special magic of the poet is that he or she can take well-known phenomena, such as daffodils, swallows, and wind, and blend them together to produce a more profound meaning.

The great French painter, Paul Cezanne, once exhibited a painting entitled *Apples*. A critic chided him, saying, "That doesn't look like apples." Cezanne replied, "It's not apples, it's appleness." Clearly the larger essence was more important than the objects, and the meaning of Cezanne's painting far exceeded the boundaries of the objects.

Basket of Apples, by Paul Cezanne, described by the artist as "appleness."

The Art Institute of Chicago, H. B. Bartlett Memorial Collection

The profundity of Shakespeare's poetry cannot be explained by words beyond a very general level. The impact of the poetry and the meaning it communicates is undeniably real. The fact that we cannot express it in so many words does not deny its existence, but merely demonstrates the occasional poverty of words.

The force of poetry cannot be expressed in words.

It is possible to speak of meaning in generalities. For example, a particular piece of music might evoke tears in most listeners. Obviously, sadness is embedded in the meaning of the piece. But certainly the specific meaning, the reason for the sadness, will vary from listener to listener. Each listener brings a unique set of experiences, memories, associations, and expectations to the piece. The listeners are alike enough to recognize the general quality of sadness, but sufficiently individual to have personal, particular interpretations of it.

The meaning of music varies with each listener.

THE LANGUAGE OF MUSIC

Many of the temporal and sonorous aspects of a piece of music are exposed with careful study—its meter, tempo, melody, harmony, texture, form, and instrumentation. It is also possible to speak confidently about the style, genre, date of composition, and composer of a given piece. The fact that a piece is in 4/4, is essentially homophonic, is in rondo

Structural aspects of music can be identified, but the meaning is individualized by the listener.

form, and is played by a string quartet can be verbalized, but it is impossible to state with certainty what the piece means even when the composer states the meaning. Only individual interpretations or a general consensus are possible.

In an age and a culture so dependent on proof, it seems strange that the inability to identify the specific meaning of a given poem or composition does not matter. In fact, the pleasure and the profound experience of the poem or the composition is not depreciated by this inability. This is perhaps the magic, not of the poet, but of poetry itself—the experience is so real that any attempted explanation would only be an interference. Felix Mendelssohn wrote, "The thoughts which are expressed to me by music that I love are not too indefinite to be put into words, but, on the contrary, too definite."

Not all feeling evoked by music should be confined to words.

Music is a special kind of language, but like any language, it is merely a conduit for communication. Some of these messages are explored here.

Music and Description

Music has the capacity to produce believable **descriptions** or imitations of things beyond itself. These things are found primarily in nature and possess sound and motion, such as babbling brooks, bird calls, thunder, breezes, falling rain, and lightning. The attempt to describe these things in music has intrigued composers for a long time: pieces with bird call imitations were known at least as long ago as the fourteenth century. But music made exclusively of these descriptions is very limited, and tedium develops quickly. The music is impoverished and robbed of its more profound functions. The meaning of the music is evident, but it quickly induces boredom.

Music composed to imitate nature's sounds exclusively becomes tedious.

Used judiciously and sparingly, however, descriptions of this kind can be useful and meaningful in music. Writing in the mid-eighteenth century, the British critic, Joseph Avison, said, "If the composer uses imitation [i.e., description] in a general way, it should succeed in bringing the object before the hearer, rather than in forcing a comparison between the object and the sound."

Judicious use of descriptive music is found in Vivaldi's "Spring."

Vivaldi's "Spring" from *The Seasons* is a delightful piece of music that uses descriptions judiciously. Listen to the first movement of this work in which bird calls, gentle breezes, a rainstorm, and the calm after the storm are described. Another convincing use of descriptive music is found in the Wolf's Glen Scene from act 2 of Carl Maria von Weber's opera, *Der Freischütz*. In the last four minutes of the scene, a series of magic bullets is cast. The casting of each is followed immediately by

Editions Ides et Calendes

Barbizon in the Snow,
Ferdinand Chaigneau. The wind
and the cold are expressed in
this picture.

patches of extraordinary music, describing in succession a flock of night birds, a wild boar, a hurricane, wheels, cracking of whips, trampling of horses, barking of wild dogs, and thunder and lightning. Here the descriptions are ingenious, not so much because they are so strikingly realistic, but because they add so much to the overall atmosphere of the scene.

Music and Interpretive Description

Music has the additional and more subtle capacity to rise above a simple description of nature to an interpretation of, or commentary upon, it. Interpretive description offers not the "musical photograph" of birds, raindrops, or lightning, but rather expresses the density of the forest, the majesty of the mountains, the depth and action of the sea, or the force of the storm. This appears to be Beethoven's intent when he produced his *Pastoral Symphony* (Symphony no. 6). On the back of the title page of the first violin part of this symphony, and in one of his sketchbooks, Beethoven wrote:

> Pastoral symphony, or recollections of country life (expressive of feeling rather than painting). . . . All painting in instrumental music, if pushed too far, is a failure. Anyone who has an idea of country life can make out for himself the intentions of the author without many titles.

Beethoven employs interpretive description in his *Pastoral Symphony.*

Beethoven, adhering to this belief, provided only a brief title for each of the five movements of this symphony: (1) "Cheerful feelings aroused on arrival in the country"; (2) "Scene at the brook"; (3) "Joyful gathering of the peasants"; (4) "Thunderstorm"; and (5) "Glad, thankful feelings after the storm."

Breakers on the Headland at Granville 1853, Paul Huet. The active sea, as at Fingal's Cave.

Courtesy, The Louvre

Ironically, another great composer, Claude Debussy, a lifelong admirer of Beethoven's music, felt that this particular work was less successful than many of Beethoven's others because it was, in his view, too imitational. Debussy wrote:

> How much more profound an interpretation of the beauty of a landscape do we find in other passages in the great Master, because, instead of an exact imitation, there is an emotional interpretation of what is invisible in Nature. Can the mystery of a forest be expressed by measuring the height of the trees? Is it not rather its fathomless depths that stir the imagination?

In 1829, Felix Mendelssohn visited Fingal's Cave, located on one of the Hebrides Islands off the coast of Scotland. In August of that year he wrote to his beloved sister, Fanny:

> . . . in order to make you understand how extraordinarily the Hebrides affected me, the following came into my mind there.

Fig. 4.1
This is what came to Mendelssohn's mind as he viewed Fingal's Cave.

Figure 4.1 shows the opening measures of the *Hebrides* Overture by Mendelssohn.

Three years later he wrote to Fanny concerning the *Hebrides* Overture or, as it is sometimes called, *Fingal's Cave*:

> I cannot bring the *Hebrides* to a hearing here because I do not consider it finished as I originally wrote it. The middle section in D major is very stupid, and the whole so-called development smells more of counterpoint than of whale blubber, gulls, and salted cod.

Mendelssohn was often very critical of himself and his work. Several of his best known and most admired works, including the *Italian Symphony* and the *Violin Concerto,* displeased him. The composer's opinion notwithstanding, the *Hebrides* Overture has thrilled audiences for more than a century and a half. The piece is cast in a sonata-allegro form, as seen in the following Sound and Sense.

Mendelssohn depicted his impression of Fingal's Cave through music.

SOUND AND SENSE: *Sonata-Allegro Form*

Title: *Hebrides* Overture (''Fingal's Cave'')
Composer: Mendelssohn
A Closer Look:

Exposition (not repeated)
A (theme in violas, cellos). In the tonic key of B minor.
Bridge section. Modulating to the key of D major.
B (theme in cellos). In the key of D major.

Development
Begins with several statements of the rhythm:

Frequent modulations, tonally restless, finally leading back to the recapitulation.

Recapitulation
A (theme in violas and cellos). In the tonic key of B minor.
Bridge section.
B (theme in clarinets) B minor/major.
Brief reference to the *A* theme.
Coda, in B minor.

Many musical pieces cleverly combine imitation and interpretive description to bring a scene to life.

The suite *Out of Doors,* an example of Béla Bartók's ''Night Music,'' both describes and reflects upon nature's sounds. Once more, the occasional chirping of insects is not as fascinating as is the overall atmosphere and eeriness of night that the piece evokes.

From an extensive list of works that operate this way, listen to one more: Claude Debussy's ''Nuages'' (''Clouds''), from the *Three Nocturnes for Orchestra.* Debussy said of this piece:

> ''Nuages'' represents the unchanging aspect of the sky, with the slow and melancholy passage of the clouds dissolving in a gray vagueness tinged with white.

Program Music

Program music is based upon a story, painting, poem, character or scene.

Instrumental music that is alleged to be inspired by or connected to a story, painting, poem, character, or scene, is often referred to as **program music.** The program, or extramusical idea behind the piece, may consist of nothing more than a title, or it may consist of a fairly detailed verbal sketch. When a composer provides such a program, he or she is emphasizing that the program is intimately tied to the meaning of the piece. Given foreknowledge of the program, listeners may be persuaded to find a similar meaning in the piece. Without knowledge of the program this may not happen, but the audience may still be moved by and find meaning in the piece.

Some have persistently held that program music is somehow "cheaper" than **absolute music** (music without an indicated program). It is argued that the verbal program is a crutch used to support wobbly music, and that absolute music stands on its own, nobler legs. Our task here is not to defend or to attack program music, but rather to try to understand what it is.

Obviously, the composer intends the program to serve as a means of focusing attention on the general meaning he or she feels is expressed in the music. The good composer knows that no written program can be devised that will add to or detract from the quality of the music. The program may, however, invite a perception of the music and its general meaning that is more closely related to the *composer's* perception.

Hector Berlioz prepared a detailed program for his *Symphonie Fantastique (Fantastic Symphony)*. Although he later shortened the program, it is printed here in its entirety.

Absolute music has no program.

The program may bring our perception of the music closer to that of the composer.

Consider the program Berlioz prepared for his *Symphonie Fantastique*.

Berlioz: *Symphonie Fantastique,* op. 14.

In the score of this work Berlioz published the following scenario (translated by Brett).

"A young musician of unhealthy sensitive nature and endowed with vivid imagination has poisoned himself with opium in a paroxysm of lovesick despair. The narcotic dose he had taken was too weak to cause death, but it has thrown him into a long sleep accompanied by the most extraordinary visions. In this condition his sensations, his feelings, and his memories find utterance in his sick brain in the form of musical imagery. Even the Beloved One takes the form of a melody in his mind, like a fixed idea which is ever returning and which he hears everywhere. [This recurring melody, or **idée fixe,** which typifies the Beloved One, is first heard in the Allegro, in C major.]

"*First Movement: Reveries, Passions* (Largo, C minor, 4/4; Allegro agitato e appassionato assai; C major, 4/4). At first he thinks of the uneasy and nervous condition of his mind, of somber longings, of depression and joyous elation without any recognizable cause, which he experienced before the Beloved One had appeared to him. Then he remembers the ardent love with which she suddenly inspired him; he thinks of his almost insane anxiety of mind, of his raging jealousy, of his reawakening love, of his religious consolation.

"Second Movement: A Ball (Allegro non troppo, A major, 3/8). In a ballroom, amidst the confusion of a brilliant festival, he finds the Beloved One again.

"Third Movement: Scene in the Country (Adagio, F major, 6/8). It is a summer evening. He is in the country, musing when he hears two shepherd lads who play, in alternation, the *ranz des vaches* (the tune used by the Swiss shepherds to call their flocks). This pastoral duet, the quiet scene, the soft whisperings of the trees stirred by the zephyr wind, some prospects of hope recently made known to him, all these sensations unite to impart a long unknown repose to his heart and to lend a smiling color to his imagination. And then She appears once more. His heart stops beating, painful forebodings fill his soul. Should she prove false to him! One of the shepherds resumes the melody, but the other answers him no more . . . Sunset . . . distant rolling of thunder . . . loneliness . . . silence . . .

"Fourth Movement: March to the Gallows (Allegretto non troppo, G minor and B-flat major, 4/4). He dreams that he has murdered his Beloved, that he has been condemned to death and is being led to execution. A march that is alternately somber and wild, brilliant and solemn, accompanies the procession. . . . The tumultuous outbursts are followed without modulation by measured steps. At last the fixed idea returns, for a moment a last thought of love is revived—which is cut short by the death blow.

"Fifth Movement: Dream of the Witches' Sabbath (Larghetto, C major, 4/4; and Allegro, E-flat major, C minor, and C major, 6/8). He dreams that he is present at a witches' revel, surrounded by horrible spirits, amidst sorcerers and monsters in many fearful forms, who have come together for his funeral. Strange sounds, groans, shrill laughter, distant yells, which other cries seem to answer. The Beloved Melody is heard again, but it has lost its shy and noble character; it has become a vulgar, trivial grotesque dance tune. She it is who comes to attend the witches' meeting. Riotous howls and shouts greet her arrival . . . She joins the infernal orgy . . . bells toll for the dead . . . a burlesque parody of the *Dies irae* . . . the Witches' round dance. . . . The dance and the *Dies irae* are heard together."

Philosophical Program Music

Charles Ives, an American composer, expressed his opinion of program music in *Essays Before a Sonata*. Some of his statements from that publication appear here:

> Does the success of program music depend more upon the program than upon the music? If it does, what is the use of the music, if it does not, what is the use of the program? Does not its appeal depend to a great extent on the listener's willingness to accept the theory that music is the language of the emotions and *only* that?

Ives continues, suggesting that descriptive program music that plays only on the sensuousness of raw emotion is shallow. He seeks, rather, meaning and emotions in a deeper sense "which may be a feeling influenced by some experience perhaps of a spiritual nature in the expression of which the intellect has some part." For him the ideal music must bring to bear the cooperation of heart and mind in the production of meaning in this deeper sense. He suggests that our conception of program music should not be limited simply to descriptive pieces. He understands program music in a broader sense, for he says:

> On the other hand is not all music, program-music—is not pure music [absolute music], so called, representative in its essence?

Thus another type of program music in which imitation, interpretation, and description have little or no role is introduced. This is **philosophical program music,** which attempts to relay the essence and power of ideas and attitudes, and is not content merely to describe objects or scenes. Ives himself produced such a work in *The Unanswered Question* (1908). Ives's program appears here:

> The strings play *ppp* throughout, with no change of tempo. They are to represent "The Silences of the Druids" who speak, see, and hear nothing. The trumpet intones "The Perennial Question of Existence" and states it in the same tone of voice each time. But the hunt for the "Invisible Answer" undertaken by the flutes and other human beings becomes gradually more active, faster and louder through an *animando* to a *con fuoco*. The "Fighting Answerers," as time goes on, seem to realize a futility, and begin to mock "The Question"—the strife is over for the moment. After they disappear, "The Question" is asked again for the last time, and the "Silences" are heard beyond in undisturbed solitude. . . .

The American composer Charles Ives questioned the purpose of program music.

Imitation, interpretation and description play little or no role in philosophical program music.

The Unanswered Question **is an example of philosophical program music.**

Your sense of meaning in a piece of music will evolve during repeated listenings.

But can a composer communicate something meaningful to us in instrumental music for which he provides no program, descriptive or otherwise? It is possible, but to paraphrase Mendelssohn, the specific meaning is too definite to put into words. The possible meaning of a given work can be approached, however, in a general way. This vantage at least assists audiences in thinking about the work in an active rather than a passive manner. The first listening of the piece is likely to make an impact. But on repeated listenings, the nature of that impact, indeed, the sense of meaning in the piece, changes and evolves.

Unlike Symphony no. 6, Beethoven provided no program at all for Symphony no. 7, and yet there is something in this music that suggests a program. In the second movement of this symphony, for example, a sense of weakness transformed into great power, and a sense of humility transformed into glorification and great dignity, are created.

The following Sound and Sense illustrates the formal structure of this movement on the level of the section and subsection.

SOUND AND SENSE: *Structure*

Title: Symphony no. 7, second movement

Composer: Beethoven

A Closer Look:

The dominant theme—*a*—whose environment is varied with each repetition, is notated:

A	*B*	*A'*	*B'*	*A''*
aa'a''a'''	*bcc'*	*a''''*-fugue	*b'*	*a*

Notice first of all the rather common or humble nature of this theme that spends so much time on one pitch and traverses only a very limited range. Its plodding rhythm is restricted to two note values— ♩ and ♪ . This would appear to be the commonest, most unpromising musical clay, but Beethoven has a magnificent destiny in mind for it.

The theme is first heard in *a*, where it is placed at the bottom of the texture and played by violas, cellos, and double basses. It enters almost apologetically at a very quiet dynamic level. Notice in *a'* that the theme rises in the texture to the second violins and speaks no longer in a whisper, but in a clearly audible voice. Further, a lovely countermelody is wound around it. In *a*, the theme may seem ridiculous, but something happens to it in *a'* that eliminates this possibility.

In *a''* the theme continues its ascent in the texture, and is sung in a higher, louder voice by the first violins. It is joined by another, equally compelling, countermelody. Metaphorically speaking, it is as if the theme has gotten off its knees, risen, and has begun to walk in a steady, dignified gait.

The full-voiced orchestra takes the theme in *a'''* while the first violins wrap a high, soaring countermelody around it. Moving from its humble, unpretentious beginning, the theme has achieved magnificence.

The *B* section provides the necessary contrast and diversion. Notice, however, that the cellos and double basses retain the rhythm of the *a* theme in the background. Upon its reentry in *A'*, the theme becomes the subject of a fugue. Beethoven has now bestowed upon this theme the ultimate musical dignity.

The movement ends with *A''* almost as quietly as it began, but in the course of the movement the theme has been completely transformed. It bids its noble, though understated, adieu.

SUMMARY

In the first three chapters you learned to analyze the special nature of rhythms, themes, harmonies, textures, instruments, and forms. When these elements are joined together to create music, however, they collectively produce the sense of something beyond themselves. In this chapter, we identified that essence as meaning.

When music merely imitates, its meaning is quite clear. When music begins to describe, the meaning we find is colored by our individual experiences. To bring our perceptions closer to theirs, composers such as Vivaldi, Beethoven, Mendelssohn, Berlioz, Debussy, and Ives provided a set of clues regarding the meaning of their music. These clues are termed programs.

Programs may influence our interpretation of musical pieces. But in each piece of music, whether program or absolute, we are likely to discover meanings both unique to ourselves, and meanings universal.

KEY TERMS

musical description   absolute music
program music   philosophical program music

THINKING ABOUT IT

Grappling with meaning can be difficult since there are no clear-cut answers to questions. Still, it seems to be in our nature to seek meaning in music. Even after you have firmly established in your own mind the meaning of a given piece of music, you may discover that the meaning changes, sometimes dramatically, as you discuss the work with friends who also know the work. As time permits, you should involve yourself in such discussions.

STYLES IN WESTERN ART MUSIC

5

Baroque Grandeur: The Palace of Versailles

SOUNDS OF THE CHAPTER

J. S. Bach
Brandenburg Concerto no. 2
Brandenburg Concerto no. 5
Cantata no. 80
Six English Suites
Six French Suites
Well-Tempered Clavier ♪

Caccini
Le Nuove musiche

Corelli
Trio Sonata in F Minor, op. 3, no. 9

Handel
Alcina
Israel in Egypt
Messiah ♪
Trio Sonata in F Major, op. 2, no. 5 ♪

Haydn
Surprise Symphony

Lully
Alceste

Monteverdi
Orfeo

Mozart
G Minor Symphony

Purcell
Dido and Aeneas
Variations for Harpsicord

Vivaldi
The Seasons ♪

THE BAROQUE: MUSICAL LINK WITH THE PAST

The road leading back through history is expansive but much of the terrain as far back as the seventeenth century is familiar to us. Beyond this time, the road narrows dramatically, and familiar signposts become scarce. The music and the philosophical foundations of the Renaissance and pre-Renaissance eras may intrigue and inspire us, but still seem foreign to us, as if they belong to the history of another world. The music, especially, seems alien. Its rhythm is difficult to appreciate because our appetite for upbeat/downbeat and meter is not satisfied; melodies and themes may not emerge in a clear fashion; the sense of key, and of tonic or dominant is not present, and the formal structure of much of the music does not coincide with our notions about how music is put together.

Baroque music seems modern to us.

The baroque, on the other hand, seems somehow modern. The music from the baroque (ca. 1600–1750), though clearly different from ours in some ways, is nonetheless music with which we can empathize. This is because many of our twentieth century musical practices and genres were born in the baroque, were nurtured through the years, and have survived into our time. Meter and functional harmony, discussed in chapters 1 and 2, became the standard means of organizing musical time and chords in the baroque, and remain the standard today. Opera, chamber music, orchestral music, keyboard music, and the concerto, all of which are staples of Western art music today, were invented in the baroque. Even the concept of the ticket-buying public is traceable to the baroque era.

The Enlightenment includes the middle and late baroque, the preclassic, and classic eras.

The Enlightenment era stressed emperical proof.

It sometimes happens that catch words or phrases from a certain period in history are retained to identify the character or summarize the accomplishments of a given age. Thus, the period comprising the second half of the seventeenth and all of the eighteenth centuries is frequently called the age of the Enlightenment, of which the middle and late baroque, preclassic, and classic eras are elements. This age placed the highest premium on reason, and viewed rationality, rather than experience or tradition, as the true source of knowledge. Because sensory perceptions vary greatly from person to person or from culture to culture, the leaders of the Enlightenment viewed the senses as unreliable sources of knowledge. Rather, the detached and unyielding proofs of mathematics and the wisdom accumulated by empirical investigation were viewed as the unquestionable sources of human knowledge. Consequently, the sciences and mathematics flourished during the Enlightenment.

This spirit of inquiry and the slow but steady drift toward individual liberty were characteristics of the enlightened baroque. Indeed, the Enlightenment represented a fundamental shift in the Western world. Culture was reoriented, from deeply entrenched authority to the establishment of the modern republic that became manifest in the late eighteenth century with the success of both the American and the French revolutions.

For a time, however, the forces of the Enlightenment had to share the stage with a power that was very nearly the antithesis of the Enlightenment. This power was the Absolute Monarch, of whom France's Louis XIV is the most notable example. All power, all authority and, by extension, all knowledge were invested in the person of the monarch. Individual liberties were minimal or nonexistent in such a situation.

The baroque was thus witness to a titanic struggle between these two opposing forces—Absolutism, representing the old order, and the Enlightenment, a new order that eventually won the battle. Oftentimes, the arts of the baroque period reflected this conflict between these major forces and their ideologies.

Because of the change and conflict characteristic of the baroque, the artistic style that emerged was distinctly different from its predecessor, the Renaissance style. Baroque art was first viewed as wild and undisciplined; the term baroque originally meant "anything in bad taste." Flourishes, extravagance, and intricate detail characterized this new art style, and though wild and undisciplined, it soon shed this unfavorable connotation and was legitimized as a stylistic label for music and the other arts of the seventeenth and early eighteenth centuries.

Baroque Art: A Stylistic Comparison

Two paintings, one by Giorgione, the other by Rubens, shown in figures 5.1 and 5.2, illustrate this drastic change in all art forms from the Renaissance to the baroque. The former is a product of the Italian Renaissance; the latter of the early baroque. Even a cursory examination of the two paintings reveals some marked stylistic differences characteristic of the eras during which they were painted.

Perhaps the most striking element of the Renaissance work is the abundant use of geometric shapes: the squares on the floor, the superimposed rectangles of the throne and the circle at the base of the throne, the triangles formed by the banner held by St. George (left front), the one formed by the head and hand positions of St. Francis (right front), and the larger triangle formed by the heads of Mary, St. George, and St. Francis. These are all firm, even self-confident shapes, where everything is fixed in place, giving the painting a stable and static quality.

A spirit of inquiry and a drift toward individual liberty characterized the enlightened baroque.

Baroque arts reflect the struggle between Absolutism and the Enlightenment.

Baroque originally meant "anything in bad taste."

Compare Renaissance and baroque styles in art.

Fig. 5.1
Virgin and Child with Saints by Giorgione—Renaissance serenity and control.

Biblioteca Comunale di Castelfranco Veneto

Fig. 5.2
Rape of the Daughters of Leucippus by Rubens—baroque action and voluptuousness.

The characters are neither overweight nor underweight; they are, in fact, ideally proportioned, healthy, and beautiful. Their countenances reflect no fear, no desperation, nothing trivial. Rather, they are faces that reflect thoughtfulness, serenity, and, once more, self-confidence. Mary's left hand grips the throne with assurance and comfort; there is no suggestion that she is holding on out of fear; no chance that she will fall. She is in control.

Renaissance figures appear ideally proportioned.

Nature is visible, though secondary in importance to the characters in the painting. Notice that nature is contained by the wall behind Mary and the others. Aside from the symbolic content of the painting, it is clear that the characters are the subject of a passive, serene, self-contained world.

The Rubens presents a very different vision. The painting exudes action. Everything—the people, the horses, even the sky—strain with motion and threaten to burst beyond the frame and escape the canvas. The horse at the left arches its head to one side revealing huge, tense muscles. The front legs of the horse at the right are also tense with action. There is a sweeping, spiraling quality running from the lower left-hand corner to the woman's outstretched hand near the top right corner. The generous swatches of cloth echo this motion; the material is heavy and dense.

Baroque figures exude action.

The figures are all muscular and fleshy, their robustness sharply contrasting with the cool, ideally proportioned figures in the Giorgione painting. The faces, particularly the eyes, of these characters are animated rather than coolly passive. The eyes of the central woman peer beyond the bounds of the frame in an entreaty for assistance. The world of this baroque painting is charged with drama, unlike the Italian Renaissance Giorgione.

The human affections were of particular interest to baroque artists. René Descartés (1596–1650), one of the most influential thinkers of the seventeenth century, described the baroque concept of emotion, or "passions," in his treatise *The Passions of the Soul* (1649). The following is a paraphrase of an excerpt.

Descartes wrote on human passion in *The Passions of the Soul* in 1649.

Descartes: Spokesman for the *Doctrine of Affections.*

> The human soul is located in a small gland in the middle of the brain. The body creates one variety of passions, the soul itself creates another variety. When the two varieties work together in a common effort they create a response to some object. The principal effect of the passions is that they incite the soul to desire those things for which they prepare the body. So it is that the feeling of fear incites a desire to fly; the feeling of courage incites a desire to fight. There are six basic passions: wonder, love, hatred, desire, joy, and sadness. All other human passions are related to one or more of these.

Fig. 5.3
Prescriptions for painters, in accordance with the *Doctrine of Affections.*

Attention   Desire   Rapture   Simple Bodily Pain   Laughter

Terror or Fright   Anger   Despair   Sadness   Hatred or Jealousy

Philosophers, artists, and music theorists of the time codified the many works on this topic and compiled them in the *Doctrine of Affections.* The ideas contained in the *Doctrine of Affections* became the aesthetic creed for baroque artists, composers, and others in the arts.

Charles LeBrun (1619–90), an artist and aesthetician, spoke to the artist in terms of the *Doctrine of Affections.* The proper expression of a given passion was, as far as he was concerned, measurable: the precise tilt of the head, the opening of the eyes, and the line of the mouth all had to be properly proportioned in order to incite in the viewer the desired passion (see fig. 5.3).

MUSIC OF THE BAROQUE

The music of the baroque, like the art, reflected the Enlightenment characteristics of ornamentation and extravagance. Furthermore, it was the pleasure of the composer, as well as an obligation, to find the musical means to express various states of the soul so as to involve the emotions of the audience. The composer was not seeking self-expression, but the expression of generalized states to which any rational person could respond. During the baroque, a whole catalog of **musical recipes** was developed; a collection of musical figures, rhythms, and chord progressions, each of which was the means of expressing one or another affection. The intent was to create a one-to-one relationship between a given musical configuration and a specific affection.

The baroque composer expressed various states of the human soul.

It seems likely that the most convenient means of achieving this goal would be with the type of musical description discussed in chapter 4, where, for example, a rippling figure would represent water. But the baroque composer and his audience were interested in something much more profound than mere description, although this, too, abounds in baroque music. Nor were they concerned with the simple imitation of natural phenomena such as bird calls, water, or thunder. They strove to imitate states of the soul such as wonder, love, joy, and sorrow.

Description and imitation were not enough for the baroque composer.

The composer's job was to present these passions in the clearest and most forceful way. In vocal music, the composer sought the dominant affection of a passage of text, combined it with the appropriate musical configuration, and retained that configuration throughout the duration of that portion of the text. There are countless examples of these movements or sections generated by one figure. Handel's oratorio, *Israel in Egypt,* provides some striking examples. Listen first to the air for alto, based on the text "Their land brought forth frogs, yea, even in the king's chambers. He gave their cattle over to the pestilence. Blotches and blains broke forth on man and beast." Notice that the opening figure, the little hopping motive presented by the violins, runs throughout almost the entirety of the air, and is even incorporated into the singer's vocal line. The following chorus, "He spake the word and there came all manner of flies and lice in all their quarters," is similarly dominated by the initial whirling figure presented by the violins, and the chorus subsequent to this, "He gave them hailstones for rain . . ." is built the same way.

The opposite approach to this kind of text setting involves spotlighting every individual word in a text that is rich with word-painting possibilities. This approach is frequently encountered in the sixteenth century Italian madrigal and was one of the principal items against which the emerging baroque composers reacted most strongly.

One (bright) day we all went (up) the hill,
There we heard the sweet (song of the bird.)
(Suddenly) (lightning) flashed and the (rain) came.
We all ran (down) the hill and were (very sad)
that the weather had stopped our (happy time.)

For each of the circled words a musical figure or device could be invented that would sound like the thing represented by the words. The baroque composer would consider such a setting a hopeless mishmash from which no central or dominant affection could arise. Rather, he would determine the general feel of the whole text and invent one musical figure to serve the entire passage.

CHARACTERISTICS OF BAROQUE MUSIC

Functional Harmony

The principles of functional harmony are a product of the baroque period.

In the examination of harmony in chapter 2, the nature of functional harmony was described as a systematic ordering of chords from which the sense of key and also of tonic, dominant, and subdominant emerge. This harmonic system, still in use today, is a product of the baroque. It is not possible to say precisely when the system first came into existence, but from the mid-to-late seventeenth century onward, functional harmony was universally employed. In 1722 the French composer Jean-Philippe Rameau published his *Treatise on Harmony* in which most of the basic principles of functional harmony are explained and codified, and in which the terms tonic, dominant, and subdominant are introduced. Rameau did not invent the system, but his treatise describes harmonic practices that were prevalent before and during his time. Tonality is a unifying factor in nearly all music from the middle and late baroque, despite composers' individual styles.

Basso Continuo

Basso continuo is common to nearly all baroque music.

Another feature common to nearly all baroque music, is the **basso continuo,** or thorough (meaning throughout), bass. The continuo was played on a keyboard instrument, either harpsichord or organ, or on a lute, and was usually joined by a cello, bassoon, or some other instrument capable of playing a bass line. Thus, the continuo employed an instrument that could play chords supported by an instrument that could play the lowest single line in the musical texture. The two instruments served essentially as accompaniment, fleshing out the harmonies and supplying the underlying bass line that supported the solo singers or instrumentalists. As the name continuo implies, the basso continuo played nonstop for the duration of a work. It usually did not call attention to itself, but unobtrusively supplied the necessary harmonic backdrop.

Plate 13
This painting from the Renaissance is discussed in chapter 5.

Madonna with Child and Saints; Giorgione; Biblioteca Comunale di Castelfranco Veneto.

Plate 14
This painting from the baroque is discussed in chapter 5.

Rape of the Daughters of Leucippus; Rubens; Art Resource.

Plate 15
An example of the fanciful, decorative rococo style. (See chapter 6.)

Hofkirche; photo by Jeff Smith.

Plate 16

A rococo scene (see chapter 6)—notice how the muted colors and the slender
figures contrast with those in the baroque painting in plate 14.

A Party in the Open Air; Watteau; Bildarchiv preussischer Kulturbesitz.

Plate 17

The romantic fascination with nature is evident in this nineteenth century landscape painting. (See chapter 8.)

A View Near Volterra; Jean-Baptiste-Camille Corot; National Gallery of Art, Washington, D.C., Chester Dale Collection 1962.

Plate 18
The dual romantic themes of freedom and heroism are expressed in this
nineteenth century painting. (See chapter 8.)

Liberty Leading the People; Delacroix; Art Resource.

Plate 19

Once more, the romantic fascination with nature is evident in this landscape.

Forest at Fountainbleau; Jean-Baptiste-Camille Corot; National Gallery of Art, Washington, D.C., Chester Dale Collection 1962.

Plate 20

A new vision and a reshaping of elements—analogous to new forms and the dissolution of tonality as discussed in chapter 9.

Three Musicians; Picasso; Philadelphia Museum of Art, The A. E. Gallatin Collection.

Plate 21
Notice how the blurred outlines distort photographic reality, analogous to
Debussy's distortion of tonality. (See chapter 9.)

Woman Seated Under the Willows; Claude Monet; The National Gallery of Art, Washington, D.C.,
Chester Dale Collection 1962.

Plate 22
Tiffany Lamp, an example of Art Nouveau style. (See chapter 9.)

Photograph by Robert V. Eckert/EKM-Nepenthe.

Plate 23
The thick texture, dark colors, and haunted eyes are typical of expressionistic paintings. This vision is analogous to the expressionistic music of Schönberg and Berg. (See chapter 9.)

The Holy Face; Roualt; The Museum of Modern Art, Paris.

Plate 24
This is a different sort of expressionistic painting, lighter in texture and color than the Roualt in plate 23. Still, it exemplifies the pent-up raw emotion that we find in the music of Anton Webern. (See chapter 9.)

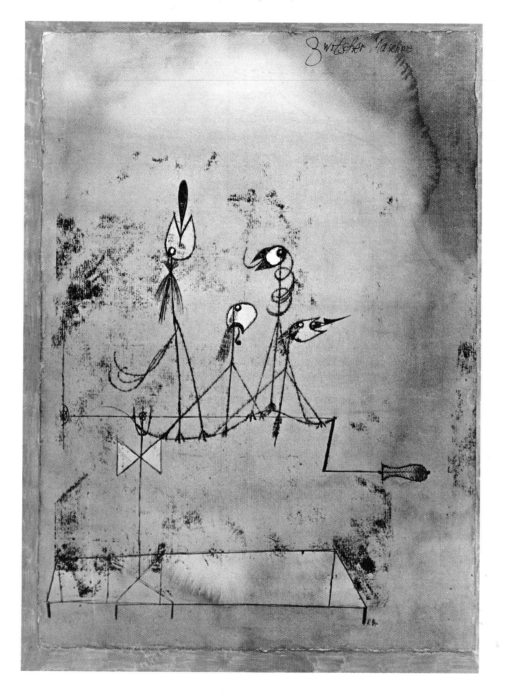

Twittering Machine; Paul Klee; The Museum of Modern Art, New York, Purchase.

Fig. 5.4

Fig. 5.5

Figured Bass

The keyboard player of the continuo was not delegated a textual part, but was expected to play or "realize" a fully fleshed-out part. The instrumentalist had to rely on his ability to read and interpret a baroque musical shorthand called a **figured bass.** This consisted of the bass line of the composition written out in musical notation, above which were written various numbers and symbols telling the performer which chords to play above the bass line. Figure 5.4 shows a figured bass for the opening phrases of the chorale: "Was bist du dock, o Seele." Figure 5.5 shows the realization of the same figured bass.

> **The figured bass noted the bass line of the composition, as well as the chords to be played.**

Some of the adjectives applied to the Rubens painting are also descriptive of baroque music. Most music from the baroque could be described as dramatic, active, ornamental, or virtuosic. Composers at that time were fond of the vivid contrast between loud *(f)* and soft *(p)*, and the contrast in volume that results from playing a small group of instruments against a larger group. Precise tempo indications are not plentiful in baroque manuscripts, but evidence suggests that composers were also fond of dramatic contrasts between fast and slow.

> **Dramatic contrasts typify baroque music.**

A great deal of baroque music is infused with what a jazz musician would call "a beat"—a steady, relentless pulsation. It has been suggested that this music has an atomic rhythm; an ever-present smallest note value, beyond which there is no further significant subdivision. This is evident in J. S. Bach's *Brandenburg* Concerto no. 2. Notice as you listen

> **Can you hear the atomic rhythm in Bach's *Brandenburg* Concerto no. 2?**

to the opening minutes of the first movement that there is a constant tick-a-tick-a-tick-a in the rhythmic background. As the concerto progresses to the slow movement, notice that the atomic unit slows down dramatically, but is still present.

This kind of beat is present in all of the movements of the six *Brandenburg* Concertos. Listen for it also in the first prelude, the first fugue, and throughout Bach's *Well-Tempered Clavier,* book I. Indeed, this sense of action derived from atomic rhythm is found in a great many works by Bach and other composers from the late baroque.

Baroque melodies are expansive.

There is action, too, in prototypical melodies from the baroque. Baroque melodies tend to be long, spiraling and complicated, unlike those from the classical era. The length and expansive quality of baroque melodies can be tested by taking a deep breath as the melody begins and attempting to hold it until the first major stopping place. The opening statement from *Brandenburg* Concerto no. 5, or Bach's well-known melody "Jesu, Joy of Man's Desiring" are excellent pieces with which to experiment.

Compare the classical and baroque melodic types.

Compare, for example, the Bach melodies just mentioned with the opening theme of Mozart's G Minor symphony, and the theme from the second movement of Haydn's *Surprise* symphony. In contrast to the baroque themes, the classical melodies are expended in short bursts of energy—small bits that create a larger whole. Graphically illustrated the two types appear thus:

Baroque melodic type /YYYYYYYYYY)

Classical melodic type

The spiraling character creates natural ornamentation.

Baroque melodies are marked also by a profusion of such ornaments as trills, mordents, and turns. In contrast to some other styles, the ornamentation in baroque music seems to grow organically from the spiraling character of the melody. It does not seem to be an afterthought or something pasted on to the melody; it is, rather, a natural part of the action of the melody.

Many works from the baroque, whether vocal or instrumental, are designed for performance by highly skilled master musicians. Baroque music has a regal quality and the sense of a style somehow "bigger than life." This idea automatically calls for performers with better than average skills. Some sense of the vocal prowess demanded of an opera singer in the baroque era is apparent in the aria "Tonami a vagheggiar" from the opera *Alcina* by Handel.

Baroque music exhibits drama, activity, ornamentation and virtuosity.

Thus, the general stylistic ingredients of baroque music are drama, activity, ornamentation, and virtuosity. These ingredients are evident in most genres and forms of the era.

GENRES OF ORCHESTRAL MUSIC

The Concerto Grosso

The **concerto grosso** was the dominant form of orchestral music in the baroque era. It emerged in the second half of the seventeenth century as a multimovement piece. Usually, it alternated a number of fast, slow, and dance movements, and featured a small group of soloists (usually two or three) called the **concertino.** The concertino was pitted against and played in alternation with a larger group of instruments called the **tutti.** The basso continuo discussed earlier completed the ensemble.

Important composers of early concerto grossi include Alessandro Stradella (1645–82), Arcangelo Corelli (1653–1713), Georg Muffat (1645–1704), and Giuseppe Torelli (1658–1709). The genre underwent some changes in the course of its history, and as it evolved in the hands of Vivaldi, J. S. Bach, and Handel in the late baroque, it normally had three movements: fast-slow-fast. (There are, however, some important exceptions to this general rule.)

In an earlier chapter we discussed the various effects and information that emerge from viewing a landscape from 10,000 feet in the air, from 500 feet in the air, and from ground level. As our perspective changes so does the scene. The *Brandenburg* Concerto no. 2 is a glorious example of the concerto grosso as it existed in the late baroque. It can be examined from these same perspectives.

This metaphorical view from 10,000 feet reveals the fast-slow-fast superstructure of the work and the presence of an atomic rhythm. Return to the first few minutes of the opening movement to pick up the rhythm. We feel more comfortable when we are able to tap our toes, snap our fingers, or in some other way empathize with the rhythm of the music at hand. From 10,000 feet we may be aware that other, more complex things are happening in this movement. As we become at ease with the rhythmic feel of the piece our curiosity will likely begin to wander to some of them. At that point, we will want a closer look at the work.

Keeping the rhythm in mind, descend to 500 feet and listen to the same excerpt again. Now we detect that sometimes the tutti plays, and sometimes one or more members of the concertino play. Our view from this perspective confirms that the concertino consists of four members—violin, oboe, flute, and trumpet—which enter successively, each solo entrance being preceded by a statement from the tutti. A pattern emerges: tutti-concertino-tutti-concertino-tutti-concertino-tutti-concertino.

As we approach ground level and listen to the piece once more, we may be prompted to ask specifically what the tutti plays each time it enters, and what the four members of the concertino play. Careful listening should reveal that the tutti plays the same or essentially the same

Concerto grosso dominated orchestral music in the baroque era.

Bach's *Brandenburg* Concerto no. 2 reveals a fast-slow-fast structure.

In the *Brandenburg* Concerto no. 2, the concertino consists of the violin, oboe, flute, and trumpet.

Formal cohesion is created by the ritornello.

material each time it enters—*A* or *A'*. Also, each member of the concertino plays *B* or *B'*. This formal process has the special name **ritornello.** In the case of the *Brandenburg* no. 2, both the tutti and the concertino have unique ritornellos. The repetitive nature of the ritornello process creates formal cohesion and unity. But it is only one way of creating formal cohesion.

A large number of concerto grosso movements have ritornello structures, but also contain a variety of formal types. Moreover, there is diversity in both the roles and the positions of tutti and concertino. In contrast to the *Brandenburg* no. 2, some movements lead with the concertino and follow with the tutti. In other movements the concertino passages may be of equal length to the tutti passages; in still others, some of the concertino passages may be quite protracted. In short, a great diversity of internal workings and structure are possible within the general framework of baroque concerto grosso movements.

Baroque concerto grosso movements show diversity in internal workings and structure.

But we left the first movement in midstream, at the point where all four members of the concertino had entered the action.

The remainder of the movement consists essentially of a series of varied repetitions of the tutti's material. These repetitions have the following rhythm:

The concertino's material has the rhythm:

The slow and fast movements are in direct contrast.

The slow movement provides a dramatic textural contrast to the first movement: the tutti and the concertino trumpet are silent, and the movement is carried by the other three concertino instruments and the basso continuo. The continuo provides the harmonic backdrop and the slow but constant atomic rhythm, over which the violin, oboe, and flute weave an intricate contrapuntal web.

The trumpet heralds the opening of the concluding fast movement. Here, in contrast to the first movement, the tutti is silent until each of the concertino members has entered the texture.

Vivaldi was the most prolific composer of the concerto grosso.

The most prolific composer of the concerto grosso was Antonio Vivaldi (ca. 1675–1741). Approximately 450 of his concerti are extant, of which many are solo concerti. These solo concerti have a concertino consisting of only one instrument. Particularly charming is a set of four programmatic concerti called *The Seasons,* published about 1725. Each of the four has the standard fast-slow-fast arrangement of movements, and each is prefaced by a sonnet: the first to spring, the second to summer, the third to autumn, and the last to winter. The program and structure of the first movement of the "Spring" concerto reads as follows:

Opening tutti ritornello	Spring has come back again, and joyously
Concertino	The birds salute him with their merry song;
Tutti ritornello followed by some new material	And streams, by zephyr's gentle breath set free,
	With a sweet murmur swiftly flow along.
Tutti ritornello followed by agitated material	With veils of darkness covering the sky,
	Come thunder and lightning, to proclaim him king;
Tutti ritornello with concertino	But when their fury's spent, and passes by,
	Sweetly once more the birds are heard to sing.

Trio Sonata

The **trio sonata,** a multimovement work usually written for two solo instruments plus basso continuo, was the dominant form of chamber music in the baroque era. (**Chamber music** calls for a few instruments rather than an entire orchestra, and is designed for intimate surroundings, such as one's home, rather than a concert hall.) The trio sonata was developed in the mid-seventeenth century and raised to a high artistic level by, among others, Arcangelo Corelli (1653–1713), and later in the era by Handel, J. S. Bach, Georg Philipp Telemann (1681–1767) and others.

In the closing years of the seventeenth century, Corelli published four volumes of trio sonatas. The third of these, Opus 3, contains twelve trio sonatas, most of which follow the four movement plan: slow-fast-slow-fast. Generally speaking, the slow movements tend to be homophonic and the fast movements contrapuntal.

The Trio Sonata in F Minor, op. 3, no. 9, for two solo violins and basso continuo, is a particularly lovely example of the genre. The keyboard part of the basso continuo is played on an organ. The figured bass of the opening measures of the initial movement is provided here so that you can appreciate how the keyboard player fleshes out the harmony and adds appropriate improvisation by interpreting the numbers and symbols.

George Frederick Handel (1685–1759)

Johann Sebastian Bach (1685–1750)

The trio sonata was the dominant form of chamber music in the baroque era.

Trio sonatas often show the slow-fast-slow-fast movement plan.

The keyboard player fleshes out the harmony in Corelli's Trio Sonata in F Minor, op. 3, no. 9.

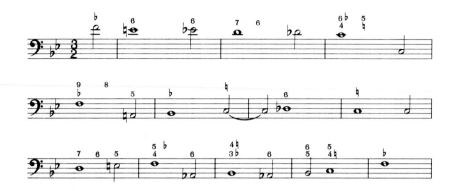

Handel's Trio Sonata in F Major, op. 2, no. 5, exhibits mixed solo instruments and a fifth movement—a gigue.

Handel's Trio Sonata in F Major, op. 2, no. 5, for flute, violin and continuo (published 1731), is a fine example of the late baroque trio sonata. The composer mixed his solo instruments, a common procedure in the late baroque, and combined a woodwind with a string. You will notice that in contrast to the earlier Corelli sonata, Handel's sonata has five movements, the last of which is a dance called a gigue. The keyboard member of the continuo is played on a harpsichord. Notice that the other member of the continuo, the cello, has a very active part in the texture and is not restricted merely to presenting the bass line.

Harpsichord with elaborate decoration

Keyboard Music

There were several kinds of keyboard instruments in use during the baroque, but by far the most popular were the harpsichord and the organ. The history of the harpsichord dates back to the fifteenth century, but the widespread use of the instrument and the creation of a body of literature for it did not develop until the seventeenth century. In the late baroque, both the mechanics of the instrument and the music composed for it reached a zenith. In fact, to today's audiences the harpsichord is probably the instrument that sounds the "most baroque."

The harpsichord reached its zenith in the baroque era.

Baroque composers were fond of arranging various kinds of dances for harpsichord. Usually such dances were grouped into a collection and termed a **suite** or a **dance suite** for harpsichord. The binary structure of most baroque dances, as discussed in chapter 3, is an *AABB* design. The core of the dance suite consisted of four dances with contrasting tempos and/or meters: **allemande** (moderate tempo, duple time), **courante** (moderate tempo, triple meter), **saraband** (slower tempo, triple meter) and **gigue** (lively tempo, usually in 6/8).

In the baroque, dance suites were arranged for harpsichord.

Most of the dances in a baroque suite have binary structure.

Later in the baroque, this basic core of dances was expanded to include other dances and sometimes an opening movement that was not a dance, the **prelude.** Examples of this type of baroque suite for harpsichord are found in the six English Suites and the six French Suites, both by J. S. Bach.

Throughout the baroque, composers of keyboard music expressed a special fondness for variations (see chapter 3), either a theme with variations or a set of improvisatory melodic variations over a ground bass. An example of the latter type is found in Henry Purcell's *Variations for Harpsichord,* sometimes called *Variations On A New Ground Bass* (no. 38 in *Masterpieces of Music Before 1750*).

The other important baroque instrument, the organ, has been a part of music making for a very long time. In the course of its history, it has undergone numerous changes in size, mechanism, and basic sound. The baroque was witness to a major change in the organ: it became larger, more powerful, more versatile, and tonally richer than any of its ancestors. The marvels of this instrument were matched by a body of organ music which, in the opinion of many, is unparalleled in the history of Western art music.

The organ was another important baroque keyboard instrument.

A variety of organ music was produced by many composers during the baroque era. The toccata and the fantasia were flashy, virtuosic types of organ music written with no set form. They contained something of the spirit of improvisation, whereas the fugue was much more rigorously structured and usually more sombre in mood. The chorale prelude was another important type of organ music that was raised to the highest artistic level by J. S. Bach.

Organ improvisation was popular in baroque.

GENRES OF VOCAL MUSIC

The opera, oratorio and cantata emerged as vocal genres during the baroque era.

The baroque created and developed three large-scale genres of vocal music with instruments: opera, oratorio, and cantata. These have proven to be enduring, for composers throughout the baroque, the classical era, and the nineteenth and twentieth centuries have continued to produce them. The elements that these three have in common are solo singing in the form of recitatives and arias, small ensemble numbers for a duet or trio of singers, choruses, and orchestra.

Opera

Opera blends music and drama.

The most dramatic musical genre, the **opera,** emerged in the late baroque era. It has undergone numerous changes throughout its history, but regardless of the time, the place, or the composer, opera has always been the synthesis of drama and music intended for the stage. The visual aspect of the genre cannot be overestimated; the full impact of an opera can only be experienced by witnessing a performance. Obviously this cannot be produced in the format of a book and we are thus at a disadvantage in our effort to fully understand what opera is and how it works. However, we can profitably explore some aspects of opera that will be useful when we actually attend opera performances.

The largest structural component of an opera is an act; acts are composed of numerous scenes.

The operatic structure On the largest structural level, an opera, an essentially secular genre, is divided into a number of acts. In the middle baroque the standard was five acts, and in the late baroque the standard was three acts. Each act is comprised of a variable number of scenes, usually two or three, though acts with several scenes were not unusual in the baroque. A scene is a unit in which a character may be introduced and developed, some new facet of the story may be presented, or a given scene may be presented for more or less purely musical reasons.

The libretto is the text of an opera.

The text of an opera is called a **libretto** and is normally written by someone other than the composer—the librettist.

The story, the characters, and the music develop simultaneously.

The opera composer and his librettist (the author of the opera text) must constantly be aware of the flow of three basic lines: the story line, the line of character development and the musical line. The drama or story line must have some innate interest and must unfold at an appropriate pace or the audience will become disinterested. The characters must continue to evolve and develop to assure audience involvement with them. Not everything that happens in an opera is the equivalent of a hit song, but there must be enough vocal "treats" along the way to satisfy the strictly musical palate. And it becomes an even more complicated and difficult undertaking to make sure that one of these three lines doesn't steal the limelight from the others.

The composer must also be concerned with the arrangement of the musical forces—solos, small ensembles, chorus, and orchestra. Working within the limits imposed by the libretto, the opera composer strives for an agreeable mixture of these forces and tries to avoid long stretches in which only one is present.

Solo singing in the opera   There are two basic types of solo singing in opera: **recitative** and **aria.** The word recitative suggests singing in the manner of a recitation, and indeed the typical recitative from baroque opera is such. Recitative tends to be wordy, syllabic, and loaded with information about the characters and the unfolding story. Frequently it is musically static, and the audience's attention is focused more on the text than on the melodic line. In contrast, the aria—the songlike phenomenon—is very active musically. It may be greatly embellished and may traverse a wide vocal range. An aria may revolve around a very few lines of text or single words that are repeated. The story line may stand still when this happens, but its pace will pick up again in an ensuing recitative.

Recitative singing provides much of the opera's story line.

An aria is musically active.

Opera history   The oldest examples of opera are products of early seventeenth century Florence, Italy. A group of Florentine noblemen called the Camerata were responsible for the creation of opera. In 1602 a Camerata composer, Giulio Caccini (ca. 1550–1618), published a collection of songs under the title *Le Nuove musiche.* The title was well-chosen, for the style of Caccini's music was new and contrasted sharply with the late Renaissance choral contrapuntal style of Palestrina. It consisted of solo singing with very minimal homophonic accompaniment called monody. The operas of Caccini and the other Camerata composers were completely monodic; there was no ensemble, chorus, or orchestra.

Their fascination with classical antiquity led the Camerata quite naturally to the production of librettos based on Greek mythology. They were particularly interested in the drama and in the clear, affective, uncluttered presentation of the text. In their opinion, word painting and counterpoint interfered with such a presentation. Here, in part, is what Caccini said in the preface of *Le Nuove musiche:*

The first operas were based upon subject matter drawn from Greek mythology.

> [I was] convinced . . . with the clearest reasons not to follow that old way of composition whose music, not suffering the words to be understood by the hearers, ruins the conceit and the verse . . . a laceration of the poetry. . . . I have endeavored in those my late compositions to bring in a kind of music by which men might, as it were, talk in harmony, using in that kind of singing . . . a certain noble neglect of the song. . . .

The first operatic masterpiece, *Orfeo*, was composed by Monteverdi.

Orfeo blends solos, choruses, small ensembles, and orchestra.

What the Camerata lacked was a truly expert composer, one thoroughly grounded in the craft and techniques of musical composition and possessing a fertile musical and dramatic imagination. Such a composer was Claudio Monteverdi (1567–1643). His earliest opera *Orfeo* is generally regarded as the first operatic masterpiece.

Based on the Greek myth of Orpheus and Euridice, *Orfeo* was first performed at Mantua in 1607. Unlike the operas of the Camerata, Monteverdi's *Orfeo* skillfully blended solo singing with choruses, small ensembles, and an orchestra of about forty players. It is a musical palette of great richness and diversity, as is evident in act III (the whole act contains but one scene).

The setting is the entrance of the underworld where Orfeo has come, guided by Speranza, the goddess of hope. He is in search of his beloved Euridice. Orfeo sings a recitative in syllabic style with basso continuo accompaniment. He is answered by another recitative sung by Hope (Speranza). Notice how gloom pervades Hope's recitative. In Orfeo's next recitative we learn that he must continue his pursuit without the company of Hope.

Charon is introduced next, and with him a new vocal range. He is a bass, while Orfeo (tenor) and Hope (alto) are high voices. At the conclusion of his recitative the orchestra plays the prelude to Orfeo's extended aria which follows. This is a strophic aria with a variety of instrumental accompaniments. It should be immediately obvious that the style of the aria, "Posente spirto," is markedly different from the recitatives: it is fancier, more elaborate, and imbued with virtuosity. Clearly the aria is the center of gravity in this act.

After another statement from Charon, Orfeo sings an active and impassioned recitative that approaches the quality of an aria. The act concludes with a fatalistic statement from the chorus. Again, the chorus adds an ingredient to the mix of musical forces employed by Monteverdi.

In the seventeenth century, opera spread from Florence across Europe and to England.

French opera combined drama and ballet.

French opera featured an overture made up of one slow and one fast section.

Operatic forms   Opera rapidly gained popularity, and during the seventeenth century spread over western Europe and England. In many of these nations the opera developed unique characteristics.

A distinctly French brand of opera called **tragedie lyrique** was developed in the 1670s under Jean Baptiste Lully (1632–87). In Lully's operas, the French dual loves of drama and ballet became central features. Lully also created an orchestral preface called a French overture for his operas. Other composers were attracted to this and the French overture was widely employed later in the baroque era as the frontispiece of operas as well as a separate orchestral piece. The French overture consisted of two sections: the first was slow, majestic, and in dotted rhythms, the second was livelier and imitative. An example of French overture is found in Lully's *Alceste*.

The British imported Italian opera but developed their own operatic style in the English language. The central composer of English opera was Henry Purcell (1659–95), whose masterpiece is the short opera *Dido and Aeneas* (1689). The work begins with a French overture, and contains a lovely aria called "When I am Laid in Earth," which occurs near the opera's conclusion.

The central composer of English opera was Purcell.

Italian opera continued to change, and during the period 1700–1725 evolved into a highly formalized type called **opera seria.** Almost without exception the subject matter of opera seria was drawn from classical antiquity. Particularly favored were those stories or legends in which there are two pairs of lovers and a minimal number of secondary characters. Attention was thus focused on individual characters caught in dramatic situations; in musical terms the attention was focused on solo singing. Small ensemble numbers were few and the chorus, if there was one at all, played a very minor role. In essence, then, an opera seria consisted of a sequence of arias connected by recitatives and embellished with an occasional ensemble. The opera seria was always presented in three acts with one, two, or three scenes per act.

The highly formalized opera seria focused on individual characters, downplaying the chorus.

Unquestionably the central features of an opera seria, and the most popular with the audience, were the incredible singers. The art of singing in **bel canto** (beautiful singing) style was raised to an unprecedented height. The primary vehicle for the singer was a special type of aria called **da capo aria.** The da capo aria is a three-part form *ABA* in which the repetition of *A* is greatly embellished by the singer.

A da capo aria is in *ABA* form.

Act I, scene 2, from Handel's *Alcina* (1735) illustrates how these forces work together. Alcina, the enchantress, capable of turning people into wild beasts or rocks, is infatuated with Ruggiero. Ruggiero is similarly infatuated with Alcina, though he is betrothed to Bradamante. Ruggiero has been evading Bradamante for some time, and Bradamante, disguised as her own brother Ricciardo, has come with her tutor, Melisso, to search for her lost lover. The story, though farcical, provides an excellent vehicle for the singers to display their voices and a variety of passions.

In this scene there are five arias, four of which are da capo arias; one for Oronte, another character in the opera, two for Alcina, and two for Ruggiero (whose part is often sung by a female despite the fact that Ruggiero is a male character). The remainder of the scene is given to connective recitative accompanied only by basso continuo. Notice how the recitatives move the story line and seem to build or lead directly to the arias. Notice also that the orchestral accompaniment to each aria revolves around a single idea. This is, of course, a reflection of Handel's involvement with the *Doctrine of Affections.*

Handel's *Alcina* (act I, scene 2) offers a variety of arias.

An anti-chamber to Alcina's apartments

Ruggiero

Vo cercando la bella cagion delle mie pene;
vieni, deh! vieni a me, caro mio bene!
Bramo di trionfar
sol per piacer d'amor,
ma non contento ancor
m'agita l'alma.
Bramo di trionfar, ecc.
Suol gloria accompagnar
un generoso ardor,
ma senza amor il cor
non può aver calma.
Bramo di trionfar, ecc.
La cerco in vano, e la crudel non torna.

Ruggiero

I go in search of the lovely cause of all my woes;
come, oh come to me, my dearest dear!
I long to triumph
only for the pleasure of love,
but all unsatisfied yet
my heart aches within me.
I long to triumph, etc.
Glory should attend
a noble passion,
but, lacking love, my heart
cannot rest in peace.
I long to triumph, etc.
I seek her in vain, and the cruel woman does not return.

Oronte

(Nuovo inganno si trovi; un geloso amator all'altro giovi.)
Senti, Ruggiero, senti; e credi ai sguardi, alla mentita frode d'Alcina tua?

Oronte

(entering: to himself)
(Let us contrive a new deceit; one jealous lover may console another!)

(to Ruggiero)

Listen, Ruggiero, listen; do you believe the false glances and the lying impostures of your Alcina?

Ruggiero

Così favella Oronte?

Ruggiero

Can Oronte speak thus?

Oronte

Così. Tu sol non sai, che chiudon queste selve mille amanti infelici, conversi in onda, in fredde rupi, in belve?

Oronte

He can. Are you the only one who does not know that these woods harbour thousands of unfortunate lovers changed into waves, cold rocks and wild beasts?

Ruggiero

Io so ben di quai lacci per me la strinse amore.

Ruggiero

I know full well with what strong fetters Alcina is bound for love of me.

Oronte

Il laccio è sciolto.

Oronte

Those fetters are loosed.

Ruggiero

Me sol ama e desia.

Ruggiero

She loves and longs for me alone.

Oronte

Va, che sei stolto; Ricciardo è l'idol
suo.

Ruggiero

Già di lui s'invaghì?

Oronte

Lui solo adora: e per lui cangeratti
in belva ancora.
Semplicetto! a donna credi?
Se la vedi,
che ti mira,
che sospira,
pensa e di':
ingannar potrebbe ancor.
Semplicetto! a donna credi? ecc.

Ruggiero

Ah! infedele, infedel! Questo è
l'amore?

Alcina

Mio tesoro, mio ben, anima mia!
chiami Alcina infedele?

Ruggiero

Sì, chè lo sei, crudele. Va, Ricciardo
t'attende; egli a' tuoi prieghi qui
volse il piè; quivi per te dimora.

Alcina

Alla costanza mia così favella il tuo
core crudele? E pur ti son fedel, e
pur son quella.

Sì; son quella,
non più bella,
non più cara
agli occhi tuoi;
ma se amar
tu non mi vuoi,
infedel, deh! non mi odiar, ecc.
Sì! son quella, ecc.

Oronte

Go to, how stupid you are!
Ricciardo is her idol.

Ruggiero

Has she fallen enamoured of him so
soon?

Oronte

Him alone she adores: and on his
account will change you, too, into
a wild beast.
Simpleton! Do you put your trust in
woman?
If you observe
that she looks at you
and sighs,
think to yourself and say:—
She, too, could prove false.
Simpleton! Do you put your trust in
woman? etc.

(Oronte withdraws, as Alcina
suddenly appears.)

Ruggiero

(reproachfully, to Alcina)
Oh, false, fickle woman! Is this,
then, love?

Alcina

My beloved, my treasure, my soul!
Do you call Alcina false?

Ruggiero

Yes; for you are, unkind woman!
Go, then; Ricciardo awaits you. He
is coming hither at your request; he
delays here, for your sake.

Alcina

Can your cruel heart speak thus to
my constancy? Yet I am true to you
and just the same as I have always
been.
Yes, I am just the same,
No longer beautiful,
no longer dear
in your eyes;
yet, if you do not wish
to love me, faithless man,
at least, then, do not hate me, etc.
Yes, I am just the same, etc.

(Alcina retires.)

Bradamante
Se nemico mi fossi, potresti peggio far?

Ruggiero
Rival mi sei, t'odio, Ricciardo.

Bradamante
Odii il german diletto della tua Bradamante?

Ruggiero
E perciò t'odio ancor.

Bradamante
Perfido amante, tu così mi dispreggi?

Ruggiero
Forse d'amor vaneggi?

Bradamante
Indegno amante!

Ruggiero
Che favelli? ed a chi?

Bradamante
Mirami, altero: Bradamante così parla a Ruggiero.

Ruggiero
Bradamante favella? Bradamante in tal arme? Regina, sei tradita.

Melisso
Eh! non è quella.

Bradamante
Sì: va della tua maga, a espormi all'ira.

Melisso
Ruggier, non l'ascoltar.

Bradamante
(entering; to Ruggiero)
If you were my enemy, could you do me greater wrong?

Ruggiero
You are my rival, I hate you, Ricciardo.

Bradamante
You hate the beloved brother of your Bradamante?

Ruggiero
For that I hate you the more.

Bradamante
False-hearted lover, do you scorn me so?

Ruggiero
Love it is perhaps that makes you talk so wildly?

Bradamante
Unworthy lover!

Ruggiero
What is that you say? And to whom?

Bradamante
Look at me, disdainful man. Bradamante speaks thus to Ruggiero.

Ruggiero
Bradamante speaks? Bradamante thus clad in armour? Great Queen, you are betrayed.

Melisso
(who has entered in time to overhear these last exchanges)
Nay, it is not she!

Bradamante
(mortified and angry: to Ruggiero)
Yes, go on; go to your enchantress and expose me to her anger.

Melisso
Do not listen to him, Ruggiero.

Ruggiero
So che delira.

La bocca vaga,
quell'occhio nero,
lo so, t'impiaga;
ma è fida ancora;
chi t'innamora
per te non è.
La bocca vaga, ecc.
Va, che sei stolto;
cangia pensiero!
Piace quel volto,
ma datti pace,
non è per te,
va, va, stolto, va,
va, che sei stolto, va, ecc.
La bocca vaga, ecc.

Melisso
A quai strani perigli n'espone il tuo
parlar.

Bradamante
Nell'altrui mal, facile è il dar
consigli.

Morgana
Fuggi, cor mio, ti affretta! Al geloso
Ruggiero concesse alfin
l'innamorata maga in belva di
cangiarti.

Bradamante
Va lo ritrova, e digli che Alcina non
desio, che amarla non saprei: che
ardo per altro volto.

Morgana
Io volo, è 'l mio.

Bradamante
Dia l'inganno ristoro al mio gran
duolo.

Ruggiero
I know he is raving.
(to Bradamante)
Those lovely lips,
that black eye,
wound you, I know;
but she is faithful still;
she with whom you are in love
is not for you.
Those lovely lips, etc.
Go to, how stupid you are!
Come to your senses.
You love that face,
but rest assured
it is not for you.
Get along with you, stupid,
go to; how doltish you are! etc.
Those lovely lips, etc.

(Ruggiero goes out.)

Melisso
(reproachfully, to Bradamante)
To what fantastic dangers your wild
speech exposes us!

Bradamante
(bitterly)
How easy it is to advise in another's
distress!

(Melisso departs.)

Morgana
*(entering precipitately; to
    Bradamante)*
Fly, my love, make haste! To please
the jealous Ruggiero the infatuated
sorceress has finally consented to
change you into a wild beast.

Bradamante
Go and find him, and tell him that I
do not desire Alcina. I could not
love her: I burn for another face.

Morgana
I fly. It is mine!

Bradamante
May the deception allay my great
suffering.

Alcina

Tiranna gelosia dell'amato Ruggier
tormenta il core, e pur solo per lui
mi strugge amore.
Tornami a vagheggiar,
te solo vuol amar
quest'anima fedel,
caro mio bene, caro! ecc.
Tornami a vagheggiar, ecc.
Già ti donai il mio cor;
fido sarà il mio amor;
mai ti sarò crudel,
caro mio spene, ecc.
Tornami a vagheggiar, ecc.

*(Both depart in different
    directions.)*

Alcina

(returning)
Tyrant jealousy torments my
beloved Ruggiero's heart, and yet it
is for his sake alone that I am
consumed with love.
*(to Ruggiero, who returns at this
    moment)*
Oh, woo me once again,
you alone would
my true heart love,
my treasure, my dear one! etc.
Oh, woo me once again, etc.
I have given you my heart once
already;
my love will be true
and I shall never prove unkind,
my dearest love, etc.
Oh, woo me once again, etc.

*(A Gavotte, Sarabande, Menuet
    and second Gavotte round off
    the Act.)*

For more than a generation the English public eagerly supported Italian opera seria. In fact, it would be difficult to exaggerate its popularity. Handel and other composers rode the wave of this popularity, but late in the 1720s the affections of the audience began to shift to an emerging brand of opera—comic opera (discussed in chapter 6). Before long, opera seria was no longer in vogue. It could not withstand the competition from the new opera. At this time Handel became very active as a composer of oratorios.

Oratorio

The **oratorio,** though a concert piece rather than a staged work, has some elements in common with opera: recitatives and arias, small ensemble numbers, and orchestra. As we have seen, the chorus played a very minor role in opera seria, but in the oratorio the chorus became a central feature. Unlike the opera, the oratorio does not have a plot or characters per se, but it does utilize a central theme.

In the 1720s the English lost interest in Italian opera seria.

Elements of the oratorio are: recitatives, arias, small ensemble numbers, and orchestra.

Messiah   Handel's most renowned work, and one of the best known works in the entire history of Western art music, is the oratorio *Messiah* (1742). *Messiah* is an extended work for vocal soloists, chorus, and orchestra. It is more in the nature of a narrative than a drama, having fifty-three individual numbers. The piece is divided into three large parts and is based on the Old and New Testament texts. There is no story line per se, but each of the three parts develops a theme.

The first part deals with the coming of Christ and with the manifold glory of God. The general spirit is one of rejoicing. The second part concerns the crucifixion of Christ. Its mood is darker, in sharp contrast to part one. The third part revolves around the theme of humanity's redemption through Christ.

There are twenty choruses in *Messiah*. It is obvious that Handel devoted much of his talent to these choruses, just as he had to the arias in his operas. Handel did, however, include a number of beautiful arias in this work, also.

Messiah begins with a stately French overture and immediately proceeds to a recitative and aria for tenor.

> Recitative: Comfort ye, comfort ye my people, saith your God. Speak comfortably to Jerusalem, and cry unto her that her warfare is accomplished, that her iniquity is pardoned. The voice of him that crieth in the wilderness, Prepare ye the way of the Lord, make straight in the desert a highway for our God.
>
> Aria: Every valley shall be exalted, and every mountain and hill made low; the crooked straight, and the rough places plain.

Most of the recitatives in this work are, like this first one, adorned with orchestral accompaniment, not just the basso continuo. This has a softening effect that seems appropriate, given the nature of the text. The aria is truly an exaltation and Handel makes the most of the word "exalted," by spinning a fine melismatic web over it each time it occurs.

The chorus makes its triumphal entrance in no. 4 on the text "And the glory of the Lord shall be revealed." It is a vigorous and powerful chorus that alternates between imitative and homophonic textures. There is a dramatic and deafening silence just before the last words are sung. Elsewhere in the first part there are arias for bass, alto, and soprano, but there is nothing more compelling than the choruses, especially no. 12, "For Unto Us a Child is Born," with its virtuosic lines and stirring tempo.

The choruses from part two provide an explicit contrast to the joyful mood of part one. Listen in particular to no. 24, "Surely he hath borne our griefs." Notice the extreme, wrenching dissonances that occur on the words "grief," and "He was wounded for our transgressions, He

Handel's *Messiah* is an example of an oratorio.

was bruised for our iniquities." But the gloom that pervades this section is dispelled completely with the final number of that part, no. 44, the famous "Halleluia" chorus.

The overriding optimism of the work is nowhere more obvious than in the lovely aria for soprano that opens part three—"I know that my Redeemer liveth."

Cantata

A cantata has characteristics of both opera and oratorio.

In some respects a **cantata** resembles both opera and oratorio since it contains arias, recitatives, small ensemble numbers, a chorus, and an orchestra. Some secular cantatas even resemble opera in terms of story line and character development; sacred cantatas, however, do not. Like oratorio, but unlike opera, the cantata (both secular and sacred) is not intended for the stage, nor is it divided into acts and scenes. Generally speaking, the cantata is a shorter work than an oratorio. *Messiah,* for example, lasts more than two hours, whereas the average cantata may last from twenty to forty-five minutes.

J. S. Bach composed both church and secular contatas.

Of the many church cantatas composed by J. S. Bach, about 200 have survived from all stages of his musical career—from his earliest compositions for the Lutheran church, to those he composed late in life. Many of his church cantatas make extended use of a chorale (see chapter 11) and for that reason are called chorale cantatas. A **chorale** is a hymn melody (and text) used in the Lutheran worship service. A **chorale prelude** is a composition for organ based on a chorale melody.

Ein' feste Burg ist unser Gott   Cantata no. 80, *Ein' feste Burg ist unser Gott (A Mighty Fortress is Our God)* is a chorale cantata. There are eight numbers in this cantata and part of the chorale (melody and text) is used as the substance of numbers 1,2,5, and 8.

CANTATA NO. 80:
EIN' FESTE BURG IST UNSER GOTT
(Text by Luther; Melody by Crüger for the Reformation Festival)
1. Choral Motet

Ein' feste Burg ist unser Gott,	A stronghold sure is God our Lord,
ein' gute Wehr und Waffen;	Whose strength will never fail us;
er hilft uns frei aus aller Not,	He keeps us free from all the horde
die uns jetzt hat betroffen.	Of troubles that assail us.
Der alte böse Feind,	Our ever evil foe
mit Ernster's jetzt meint,	Would fain work us woe,
gross Macht und viel List	With might and deep guile
sein grausam Rüstung ist,	He plans his projects vile,
auf Erd' ist nicht seinsgleichen.	On earth is not one like him.

2. Choral Duet (Soprano, Bass)
Soprano

Mit uns'rer Macht ist nichts getan,	Standing alone are we undone,
wir sind gar bald verloren.	The Fiend would soon enslave us;
Es streit't für uns der rechte Mann,	But for us fights a mighty One
den Gott selbst hat erkoren.	Whom God has sent to save us.
Fragst du, wer er ist?	Ask ye, who this be?
Er heisst Jesus Christ,	Christ Jesus is He,
der Herre Zebaoth,	Lord God of Sabbaoth,
und ist kein andrer Gott,	There is no other God;
das Feld muss er behalten.	He can and will uphold us.

Bass

Alles, was von Gott geboren,	Every soul by God created,
ist zum Siegen auserkoren.	Has by Christ been liberated
Wer bei Christi Blutpanier	They who Jesus' standard bear,
in der Taufe Treu' geschworen,	To His service dedicated,
siegt im Geiste für und für.	All will in His victory share.

3. Recitativo (Bass)

Erwäge doch, Kind Gottes die	Thou child of God,
so grosse Liebe,	Consider what complete devotion
da Jesus sich mit seinem	The Savior showed for you
Blute dir verschriebe,	In His supreme atonement,
womit er dich zum Kriege wider	Whereby He rose triumphant
Satans Heer und wider Welt	Over Satan's Horde, and human sin
und Sünde geworben hat.	And error and all things base.
Gib nicht in deiner Seele	Let not, then, in your being,
dem Satan und den Lastern statt!	The Evil One have any place.
Las nicht dein Herz,	Let not your sins
Den Himmel Gottes auf der Erden,	Convert the Heaven there within you,
Zur Wüste werden,	Into a desert.
Bereue deine Schuld mit Schmerz,	Repent now of your guilt in tears,
dass Christi Geist	That Christ the Lord
mit dir sich fest verbinde.	To you be fast united.

4. Aria (Soprano)

Komm in mein Herzenshaus,	Come dwell within my heart;
Herr Jesus mein Verlangen.	Lord Jesus, I adore Thee.
Treib' Welt und Satan aus,	Bid evil all depart
und lass dein Bild in mir erneuert prangen.	And let Thine image ever shine before me.
Weg, schnöder Sündengraus!	Out, sin, how base thou art!
weg, weg.	Begone away, away.

5. Unison Chorale (Soprano, Alto, Tenor, Bass)

Und wenn die Welt voll Teufel war

Though fiends appear on every hand

Und wollten uns verschlingen,
so fürchten wir uns nicht so sehr
es soll uns doch gelingen.
Der Fürst dieser Welt
wie saur er sich stellt,
tut er uns doch nichts,
das macht, er ist gericht't,
ein wörtlein kann ihn fällen.

All eager to devour,
We need not fear; we can withstand
And baffle all their power.
The Arch-Fiend of all,
Shall not us appall,
His might is laid low,
He cannot strike a blow;
One Word from God will fell him.

6. Recitativo (Tenor)

So stehe denn bei Christi
blutgefärbter Fahne,
O Seele, fest,
und glaube, dass dein Haupt dich
nicht verlässt,
ja, dass sein Sieg auch dir
den Weg zu deiner Krone bahne.
I ritt freudig an der Krieg!
Wirst du nur Gottes Wort
so hören als bewahren,
so wird der Feind gezwungen
auszufahren,
dein Heiland bleibt dein Heil
dein Heiland bleibt dein Hort.

So take thy stand with Jesus'
blood-be-spattered banner,
O soul of mine,
And trust thee ever in His power
divine!
Yea, He will lend His might
To gain for thee thy crown of glory.
Go joyous forth to fight!
If thou but hear God's Word
And do as He command thee,
No foe, however mighty can
withstand thee,
Salvation now is sure,
Thy refuge is secure.

7. Duet (Alto, Tenor)

Wie selig sind doch die,
die Gott im Munde tragen,
doch sel'ger ist das Herz,
das ihn im Glauben trägt.
Es bleibet unbesiegt
und kann die Feinde schlagen,
und wird zuletzt gekrönt,
wenn es den Tod erlegt.

Blessed is he who praises God,
Whose Words will sanctify him;
More blessed still is he
Who bears Him in his heart.
With Him will grace abound
Nor can the foe come nigh him;
At last will he be crowned,
When death shall set him free.

8. Chorale

Das Wort sie sollen lassen stahn
und kein Dank dazu haben.
Er ist bei uns wohl auf dem Plan
mit seinem Geist und Gaben.
Nehmen sie uns den Leib,
Gut, Ehr', Kind und Weib,
lass fahren dahin,
sie haben's kein Gewinn;
das Reich muss uns doch bleiben.

The Word of God will firm abide
Against our foes assailing,
For He will battle on our side,
An Ally never failing.
Tho' they take from me here
All that I hold dear
I will not complain,
Their vantage will be in vain,
God's might is all-prevailing.

A basic theme of Cantata no. 80 is the conflict between good and evil; one's struggle with the temptations of evil and the power and eventual triumph of God in one's life.

Number 1: Using the chorale tune and the first verse of the chorale text, Bach created a magnificent, intricately detailed musical tapestry for chorus and orchestra. It is a big, imposing number that reflects the might and majesty of God. Notice that Bach provides a free and florid treatment of the chorale tune, sometimes augmenting its note values, sometimes adding musical embroidery of his own invention.

The structure of both tune and text is *AAB*. The two *A* parts of the text speak of God as a stronghold, a liberator of earthly troubles. The *B* part of the text speaks of Satan in vivid terms. The *A* and *B* parts, then, present the sense of conflict in the text.

Number 2: Sopranos sing the second stanza of the chorale, speaking alternately of Satan (the fiend) and Christ, once more staging the conflict. A very active and florid bass solo that speaks of liberation and victory acts as an anchor for this number. Notice that the orchestral accompaniment revolves around a single, initially stated figure.

Number 3: A bass soloist sings a reflective recitative accompanied only by basso continuo, in this case organ and cello. The text dwells on the devil and human sin, and is in a sense, a warning.

Number 4: A modified da capo aria for soprano and continuo follows the admonition in the preceding number. The text responds to the admonition, commanding evil and sin to depart. In this and the preceding numbers, notice that the original chorale tune is absent.

Number 5: The chorale tune makes a triumphant reentry in this number, as does the orchestra. The text is aggressive and defiant of Satan.

Number 6: The texture and mood change dramatically in this number. Here the text is resolute. The recitative is sung by a tenor, and we are aware that Bach has carefully mixed his musical forces and vocal types.

Number 7: This is a small ensemble number, a duet for a high male voice and a low-register female voice. The mood of the text is pious and reflective.

Number 8: This is a straightforward, unadorned setting of the chorale tune sung to the last verse of the chorale text. It is likely that, when Bach lived, the entire congregation would have joined the choir in singing this number.

SUMMARY

Our study of the baroque era began with a look at its position in history. The baroque experienced the rise of the Enlightenment and its successful challenge of Absolutism. This major struggle between old and new marked the beginning of the modern democratic nation state. At first termed "baroque" to emphasize its wild, undisciplined nature, the arts of this period now carry the title as a stylistic label.

Baroque art, exemplified by the works of Rubens, show a sweeping, spiraling quality barely contained by the canvas. Figures are robust, muscular, and animated.

The baroque composer felt an obligation to express the various states of the human soul. These can be expressed through means that became characteristics of baroque music. The most important of these characteristics are functional harmony, basso continuo, and figured bass. Stylistic ingredients include drama, activity, ornamentation, and virtuosity. These are found in both the orchestral and vocal music of the period.

The baroque era produced several genres of instrumental music: the concerto grosso, the trio sonata, and keyboard music. Concerto grosso, the dominant form of orchestral music, was a multi-movement piece, featuring a small group of soloists called concertino, alternating with a larger group of instruments called tutti. A basso continuo completed the group. J. S. Bach's *Brandenburg* Concerto no. 2 is a good example.

The trio sonata, the dominant form of chamber music in baroque, was a multi-movement work featuring two solo instruments and a basso continuo. Corelli's Trio Sonata in F Minor, op. 3, no. 9 was our example.

Keyboard music, both harpsichord and organ, flourished during the era. Harpsichord music featured dance suites while organ music focused on the toccata, the fantasia, the fugue and the chorale prelude.

Three large-scale genres of vocal music were created during the baroque: opera, oratorio, and cantata. All three genres include the elements of solo singing in recitatives and arias, small ensembles, choruses, and orchestra.

In opera, several acts are divided into scenes that present a story line through music and drama. Simultaneously, the story, the music, and the characters are developed. Early opera focused on Greek mythology. During the baroque period, the opera developed in the hands of the Italians, French, and British.

The baroque oratorio was a concert piece with the chorus as the central feature. The oratorio also developed a theme. Our example was Handel's *Messiah.*

The cantata resembled both the opera and the oratorio. The cantata is usually a shorter work than the oratorio. J. S. Bach composed both church and secular contatas.

By now, you should feel quite familiar with many elements of baroque—its historical significance, its artistic characteristics, and its musical genres.

KEY TERMS

musical recipes	dance suite	aria
basso continuo	allemande	tragedie lyrique
figured bass	courante	opera seria
concerto grosso	saraband	bel canto
concertino	gigue	da capo aria
tutti	prelude	oratorio
ritornello	opera	cantata
trio sonata	libretto	chorale
chamber music	recitative	chorale prelude

THINKING ABOUT IT

This is the first of several chapters in which we deal with the concept of style. Be sure you can adequately describe baroque style and list its characteristics. Above all, be sure that you can hear these characteristics in the musical examples included in this chapter. Your ability to identify stylistic baroque features will eventually facilitate your understanding of style in other eras of music and allow you to compare and contrast one style with another.

It is also important to know the types of music written during the baroque era, not only for the purposes of this course, but for future involvement with art music. The term concerto grosso should suggest certain things to you and bring forth a set of expectations—what the musical forces will be, who will play what and when, how many and what types of movements there will be. Similarly, the terms, suite, trio sonata, opera seria, and cantata should be suggestive and develop a set of expectations and predictions.

Knowledge of baroque genres will tell you *what* is being played, knowledge of style will tell you *how* it is being played, and an understanding of the *Doctrine of Affections* will tell you *why* the music is the way it is.

6

MUSIC IN THE PRECLASSIC ÆRA

Interior of a rococo castle

SOUNDS OF THE CHAPTER

C. P. E. Bach
Fantasia in C Minor
Symphony in B Minor ♪

J. C. Bach
Symphony in D Major, op. 18, no. 1 ♪

J. S. Bach
French Suite in D Minor ♪

Couperin
"Le Croc-en-jambe" ♪

Stamitz
Symphony in D Major

MUSICAL STYLES IN THE PRECLASSIC ERA

The preclassic era roughly spanned the years 1720–70. This period was witness to many changes—social, aesthetic, philosophical, and artistic—and to the collapse of the baroque world.

The preclassic period followed the baroque.

During this period, a number of stylistic movements evolved, and with some reshaping, many characteristics of these styles became part of the classical Viennese style that blossomed from roughly 1770–1810. The first of these contributing movements was essentially a French phenomenon known as **rococo.**

Rococo

Louis XIV died in 1715 after a reign of more than half a century. Politically, his death signaled the end of the absolute monarchy in France. Psychologically, the death of Louis forced both the aristocracy and the citizenry to consider the future without their father figure. Artistically, the Sun King's death heralded the decline of baroque ideals in France. The dramatic opulence, virtuosity, and passion of royal baroque art began to crumble as rococo gained popularity with its refinement, grace, wit, simplicity of texture, and a reduction from monumental to more human and natural proportions.

With the death of Louis XIV came the end of baroque.

Rococo introduced refinement, grace, and wit.

The heir to the throne was Louis's seven-year-old great-grandson, Louis XV. However, the child could not assume command of the government until 1723, when he became of legal age. During the interim (1715–23), the government was run by a board of regents, headed by Philip, Duke of Orleans. This period is known as the Regency.

The spirit of rococo began to imprint itself on French culture during the Regency. Louis XV, influenced by Philip, encouraged the popularity of rococo, rather than the baroque his great-grandfather endorsed.

Rococo exhibits the quests for personal liberty and pleasure.

Two dominant trends evident in the French rococo are the quest for pleasure and the quest for personal liberty. Both Philip and Louis XV espoused this hedonistic trend as they were men of weak and dissolute character whose appetites for pleasure exceeded their sense of responsibility toward the country and the people. In fact, their disinterest in governing the country was a contributing factor in the revolution that occurred in the late eighteenth century.

The great palace of Versailles epitomized the grandeur of the French baroque and stood as a visible symbol of the power and majesty of the Sun King for whom it was built. The fact that Versailles was situated eleven miles from Paris presented not only a physical gap between

Rococo exterior

the king and his people, but also symbolized the psychological chasm between them.

Philip left all of the baroque grandeur of Versailles behind when he ascended the throne and reestablished the court in Paris. He was a city man, and the style of painting, decoration, and music that flourished around him was charming, elegant, tasteful, and lighthearted. His style was aristocratic, but not regal; snobbish, but not pompous. His tastes and ideas were refined and clever, but not profound.

The rococo was an age of collectibles. Sea shells displayed in delicate glass cases, porcelain figurines, and snuff boxes were subtly and tastefully displayed in the drawing room. There was also evidence of the love of nature and the out-of-doors as the picnic and the "outing" are common motifs in some of the best paintings from the rococo. This love of nature was not passionate, but rather a delight in nature and a desire

Many rococo paintings show a delight in nature.

Fig. 6.1
The decorative rococo

to be comfortable with it. Gardens were neatly trimmed and often formed into unnatural shapes, reversing the usual order of art imitating nature. The decoration of the interior of the houses typically featured vines, small birds, and butterflies. It appeared as though efforts were made to make outdoors look like indoors, and indoors look like outdoors—the garden filled with furniture, the house filled with plants.

Watteau was the central French painter during the rococo period.

The decorative panel shown in figure 6.1 is by Jean Antoine Watteau (1684–1721), the central French painter of the time. Notice the out-of-doors motif and the use of vegetation to frame the lady and gentleman. Note, too, that the lady and gentleman are beautifully, ideally proportioned. They weigh considerably less than their baroque counterparts.

The Grand Ball—an elegant ball in the rococo.

This *was* an age of ladies and gentlemen; an age in which proper manners and good taste were highly valued. The coquette, the flirtatious, and the risqué were elements of this era, evidenced by the many suggestive seminude paintings, and the behavior of many an aristocrat.

Women occupied a new and important position during the rococo period. They were responsible for the creation of the *salon,* an intimate gathering of educated men and women where fine conversation and the exchange of ideas were encouraged. Later in the century, when Madame Pompadour became the mistress of Louis XV, her impeccable taste and refinement formed a lasting influence on French culture.

Women made an impact on intellectual and social development during the period.

Rococo music reflected many characteristics of the era. The central composer of the French rococo was Francois Couperin (1668–1733). He composed several sets of **ordres** (suites) for the harpsichord, or in French, *le clavecin.* Many individual pieces from these *ordres* have fanciful, playful titles, such as the names of women or the names of moods or states of mind. One piece from the twenty-second *ordre* has the title "Le Croc-en-jambe" or "The Dirty Trick." Its playful mood, light texture, short-breathed melody, and delicate ornamentation, identify it as a product of the French rococo.

Couperin was the central composer of French rococo.

Ordres **are suites written for the harpsichord.**

Madame Pompadour—a
dominant figure in the French
rococo.

The Victoria and Albert Museum

A Party in the Open Air, J. A.
Watteau

Bildarchiv Preussischer Kulturbesitz

Fig. 6.2

Fig. 6.3

Fig. 6.4

The music from this period displays a clear preference for homophonic rather than contrapuntal, and light rather than dense textures. Careful listening to this Couperin piece should reveal that the melody is made up of short phrases that are easily sung, despite the delicate ornamentation. Figure 6.2 illustrates the basic outline of the first phrase of the melody in unadorned form. Figure 6.3 shows us the phrase as Couperin notated it, complete with markings for the ornamentation. Figure 6.4 illustrates the "realization" of the ornamentation, or how the piece actually sounds.

Rococo musical texture is homophonic and light.

Style Galant

The light, elegant style of music from the rococo was not limited to France. A more general term for this musical style is **style galant.** It can be used interchangeably with rococo as a stylistic label for much of the music from the 1720s to the 1750s, and even later.

The terms "rococo" and "style galant" are interchangeable.

The Minuet, Tiepolo

Museo de Artes Decorativas ·

J. C. Bach's pieces are examples of style galant.

J. C. Bach Johann Christian Bach (1735–82), the youngest son of J. S. Bach, composed music that typifies the style galant. He was invited to London in 1762 to take the position of music master to the court. He produced a large number of symphonies and concertos in the style galant, and beginning in 1765, became coproducer of a very successful series of public concerts. His own works were frequently featured in these concerts, resulting in his becoming an enormously popular composer in both Britain and on the continent.

His Symphony in D Major, op. 18, no. 1, first movement, provides an excellent illustration of the temper and ambience of the style galant.

Style galant music was composed for the listener's pleasure.

In the 1750s a British journalist wrote: "More and more people are turning to the delightful art of music." The statement may at first seem silly, but on reflection it suggests some important points. For one thing, it informs us that music was regarded as delightful at this time. This information agrees with a basic tenet of the style galant: it is designed to please.

The masses had access to style galant music.

Secondly, the statement suggests, by inference, that music was no longer the exclusive property of the noble and wealthy. Increasingly, it became a public art with "more and more people turning to it." A rising middle class, economically bolstered by the industrial revolution in England and elsewhere in Europe, could now afford to participate in and learn about art music. In a real sense the masses were being liberated from a cultural prison. They were free to partake of a kind of music that in earlier times was either denied them or beyond their ability to understand, and hence, enjoy. Beginning in 1725 with the **concerts spirituels** in Paris, public concerts became common in many European metropolitan centers.

Public concerts became popular in England and France.

Empfindsamer Stil

There were also centers of creativity scattered about Europe where gifted young composers and musicians clustered to create new, nonbaroque styles of music. The galant was but one of these styles. Some composers found the style galant too limiting, too facile, and lacking in natural, human qualities. The Germans in general, and Carl Philipp Emanuel Bach in particular, were purveyors of a style that leaned heavily on sentiment, even sentimentality. This style emerged in the 1750s and took the German name **empfindsamer stil,** the "sensitive style," and was filled with weeping motives, sighs, fluctuations in tempo, and flights of emotional improvisation. C. P. E. Bach (1714–88), the older brother of J. C. Bach, was for a time an exponent of this sensitive style. His Fantasia in C Minor, K. 475, is an excellent example of *empfindsamer stil.* Note the abrupt changes in mood, tempo, and activity.

The Germans created a sentimental style of music termed *empfindsamer.*

Sturm und Drang

A few years before the eruption of the American Revolutionary War, another preclassic style developed in Europe, again principally in Germany. It was an emotional, sometimes violent style called **Sturm und Drang** ("Storm and Stress"). This style attempted to revitalize music, scourging it of rococo pleasantness and *empfindsamer stil* melancholy. It emphasized crunching dissonance, minor keys, and jagged themes that contrasted sharply with more lyrical ones. Counterpoint, which played such a minimal role in both galant and *empfindsamer* styles, became an important feature of *Sturm und Drang* style. C. P. E. Bach's Symphony in B Minor, written in 1773, twenty years after his Fantasia in *empfindsamer stil,* is a good example of the fiery and passionate *Sturm und Drang* style.

Another offering of Germany at this time was *Sturm und Drang* style music.

Sturm und Drang was in direct contrast with rococo and *empfindsamer* styles.

The middle decades of the eighteenth century experienced a multitude of forces and counterforces. J. S. Bach and Handel, the supreme masters of the late baroque, lived into the 1750s. Other vestiges of baroque style and aesthetics survived and were favored by a segment of the population. To them, it was as if nothing were changing or nothing of consequence was developing. But things were changing, and two of J. S. Bach's own sons, each in his own way, figured prominently in these changes. Further changes were yet to come in the eighteenth century, brought about by Joseph Haydn (1732–1809) (born in the midst of the style galant), Wolfgang Mozart (1756–91) (whose birthdate coincides with the development of the *empfindsamer stil*), and Ludwig van Beethoven (1770–1827) (born as the *Sturm und Drang* movement was taking shape).

While J. S. Bach adhered to the baroque style, his two sons personified these new directions of music.

MUSICAL STYLE AS A REFLECTION OF CULTURE

Music, then as now, did not operate in a vacuum. The changes in musical style and content that occurred in the eighteenth century, the preclassic era, reflect and complement various changes in the larger cultural context.

The American Revolution (1776) and the French Revolution (1789) represent the dramatic quest for personal liberty that, as mentioned earlier in this chapter, was a dominant trend throughout most of the eighteenth century. The philosophical basis of this trend is traceable to a number of studies, treatises, and ideas that fall under the broad umbrella of "The Enlightenment," discussed in chapter 5. Two words—rational and natural—were at the core of this intellectual movement. The French Encyclopedists created a monumental 35-volume work that investigated the whole field of knowledge. In the process, virtually everything, including religious doctrines and authority at all levels, was reassessed in the light of reason. Reason was king, and rationalism was proclaimed:

> A new way of life, entirely factual, to be lived in the light of nature and reason, in political freedom, religious tolerance, and emancipation from the shakles of metaphysics.

Voltaire and Montesquieu were leading forces in the rationalist camp. They and other rationalists decried the "unnatural" authority of organized religion and the "unenlightened" monarchy in France. Rousseau deviated from pure reason into the realm of "naturalness." In his *Social Contract* (1762), Rousseau declared that people are born free, and that the state must serve the interests of the individual. Civilized society was, for him, the archenemy of the human soul, and he called for "a return to nature," the fountainhead of true humanity.

Just after the midcentury, there was a rediscovery of, or at least a renewed interest in, the artistic models of classical antiquity. These models were the most rational and the most natural to the enlightened mind.

The Symphony

The orchestra, as stated earlier, developed during the baroque era. It was used to accompany large-scale vocal works such as operas, oratorios, and cantatas. Composers also produced a strictly instrumental repertoire for it, including the concerto grosso, which was the dominant form of baroque orchestral music. During the preclassic era, the orchestra maintained this role in opera, oratorio, and other forms of sacred music. With some modifications, the concerto also flourished during the classical era.

The Enlightenment influenced both the baroque and the preclassic eras.

Voltaire and Montesquieu led the movement toward rationalism.

Rousseau called for a return to nature.

The orchestra maintained a position of importance during the preclassic era.

Most notably, however, preclassical composers and musicians laid the groundwork for the supreme accomplishment of the classical era, the **symphony.**

The fully-developed classical symphony of the late eighteenth century did not appear overnight. It was the result of an evolutionary process that began in the early years of the century—first in Italy, then in Vienna, Mannheim, Berlin, Paris, London, and elsewhere. Composers of various nationalities were a part of this process. Giovanni Sammartini (1701–75), Alessandro Scarlatti (1659–1725), Matthias Georg Monn (1717–50), Georg Christoph Wagenseil (1715–77), Johann Stamitz (1717–57), William Boyce (1710–79), Francois Joseph Gossec (1734–1829), C. P. E. Bach, J. C. Bach, Luigi Boccherini (1743–1805), and others. But the uncontested masters of the classical symphony were Haydn, Mozart, Beethoven, and Schubert.

The Mannheim School Johann Stamitz was the leading force of the Mannheim school of symphonists. This school, founded in the 1740s, produced compositions and performances that developed a widespread reputation for excellence. In terms of ensemble (ability to play together) and expressiveness, the Mannheim court orchestra became the model for other European orchestras.

One of the distinguishing features of this orchestra was its skill in performing **crescendos** and **decrescendos.** A crescendo (◁══ in musical notation) is a gradual, systematic increase in volume. Thus, instead of moving directly from *p* to *f* in the dramatic baroque manner the increase in volume was achieved gradually—in an orderly, well-mannered way. A decrescendo (══▷), the opposite of a crescendo, is a gradual decrease in volume. It is recorded that audiences literally rose from their chairs in the excitement of a crescendo and had their breath taken away with a decrescendo.

Stamitz himself wrote over seventy symphonies, and those in the Mannheim circle composed hundreds of symphonies from the years 1740–60.

The Mannheim orchestra was small by today's standards, probably numbering about thirty-eight to forty-five players, including, in addition to the string family, two players of the flute, the oboe, the French horn, and the bassoon.

Stamitz's Symphony in D Major (actually called *Sinfonia a 8*) is in four movements: presto, andante, minuetto, and prestissimo. He was very innovative, since the majority of preclassic symphonies, including some of the early ones by both Haydn and Mozart, had but three movements.

The groundwork for the symphony was laid during the preclassic era, and it developed through an evolutionary process.

Haydn, Mozart, Beethoven, and Schubert are the master composers of classical symphony.

The Mannheim court orchestra was the model for its time.

A crescendo indicates an increase in volume, while a decrescendo indicates a decrease in volume.

Stamitz, unlike many preclassical composers, wrote symphonies in four movements.

SOUND AND SENSE: *Preclassic Symphony*

Title: Symphony in D Major

Composer: Stamitz

A Closer Look:

First Movement

The first movement of the Stamitz *Sinfonia* in D Major is the longest and most dramatic. Its form suggests sonata-allegro without achieving that status; some development exists, but there is no real development section and no *bona fide* recapitulation. Instead of the *A*-bridge-*B* layout of a real sonata form, this work presents a series of thematic scraps linked together. Notice that the movement begins with three "hammer strokes" by the orchestra, that a long dramatic crescendo connects *b* to *c,* and a brief section of imitative counterpoint leads to *e.*

a—hammer strokes, *a* repeated
b—French horns enter, builds to:
cccc'
d—dominant key, more lyrical gesture, *d* repeated
Bridge containing bits of imitative counterpoint
e—oboes, *e* repeated

These thematic scraps then reappear in this order: *bd'adeebb*
$$d$$

Second Movement

The slow movement in 4/4 is essentially homophonic and is scored only for the strings. This movement also presents a series of short thematic bits: *abcd,* which is then repeated nonliterally.

Third Movement

The third movement is a minuet, the texture is homophonic, and, as expected, the meter is 3/4. The form of this movement is diagramed at the section and the subsection:

A (minuet)	*B* (trio)	*A* (minuet)
aabb	*ccdede*	*ab*

Notice that the trio section features the woodwinds—first the oboes, then the French horns.

Fourth Movement

The last movement is the shortest and the fastest. It has the simple structure:

A—wide ranging theme
B—more lyrical theme
A'
B'

The Berlin School Carl Philipp Emanuel Bach was the premier composer of the Berlin school that flourished at about the same time as the Mannheim school. Bach's Symphony in B Minor, mentioned earlier in connection with the *Sturm und Drang* movement, deserves another, more detailed, listening at this point. The work is in three movements (there is no minuet) as were many symphonies at this time. It is scored for strings and continuo. The continuo existed in the symphony well into the eighteenth century, although it appeared more out of habit than out of necessity. It no longer served any real purpose, and, in time, disappeared entirely.

C. P. E. Bach was the foremost composer of the Berlin school.

The preclassic symphony featured a continuo.

♪ **SOUND AND SENSE:** *Berlin School*

Title: Symphony in B Minor
Composer: C. P. E. Bach
A Closer Look:

First Movement
As you listen, notice that the first movement, like that of the Stamitz *Sinfonia,* is the longest and weightiest, and contains a string of small thematic bits, not a large *A* theme and a contrasting *B* theme. Each of the small thematic bits presented in the exposition has a different emotional character:

a—limpid
b—furious
c—soaring
d—playful
e—weeping and dissonant
f—angry
g—lyrical
h—sad, weeping

Pockets of rather stern counterpoint appear later in the movement.

Second Movement
The second movement commences without pause. Its thematic materials are lyrical and the harmonic language is at times aggressively dissonant. This creates a rather haunting effect, far too passionate and emotional for the style galant. This work is solidly in the *Sturm und Drang* style.

Third Movement
The concluding movement begins with an angry outburst, then continues with a great deal of counterpoint.

The Vienna School was a contemporary of the Mannheim and the Berlin schools.

The Vienna School   The symphonic school at Vienna is geographically and musically closest to Haydn's background. Several stylistic elements at various times commingled in the symphonies from the school, laying the groundwork for what would eventually become, in the hands of the mature Haydn, the Viennese classical style. The pure classical symphony was a mixture of some galant characteristics, some *empfindsamer stil, Sturm und Drang* characteristics, a stabilized orchestra, and the slow but certain expansion of the genius of Haydn.

SUMMARY

We've termed the period from about 1720–75 the preclassic era. The baroque was in retreat while the first signs of the Viennese classical era were emerging. The preclassic era was one of transition in politics, philosophy, and the arts. This transition was shaping eighteenth century Europe.

The rococo style, which developed in France under King Louis XV, showed a refinement, a naturalism and a simplicity of texture not seen in the baroque. The paintings of the period's greatest painter, Jean Antoine Watteau, exude a comfort with nature and the propriety of the age.

Rococo music, sometimes termed style galant, is exemplified by the compositions of Francois Couperin. This music shows homophonic, light texture superimposed with ornamentation. The European masses were exposed to style galant through public concerts offered in several metropolitan centers. J. C. Bach's Symphony in D Major, op. 18, no. 1, is a good example of style galant.

Rococo was only one style of music popular during the preclassic era. A German sentimental and emotional style, *empfindsamer stil,* was popularized by C. P. E. Bach in the 1750s.

In the 1770s the *Sturm und Drang* (Storm and Stress) style emerged. In contrast to the other preclassic styles, *Sturm und Drang* features dissonance, minor keys, counterpoint, and jagged themes. Just listen to C. P. E. Bach's Symphony in B Minor.

As the philosophers of the time expounded upon the enlightenment doctrines of reason and social contract, the composers were in the earliest stages of developing the classical symphony. Schools of symphonists grew up in both Mannheim and Berlin, Germany, and in Vienna, Austria. The Mannheim court orchestra, however, became the European model.

We'll continue our investigation into the evolution of the symphony in the next chapter.

KEY TERMS

rococo	concerts spirituels	symphony
ordres	*empfindsamer stil*	crescendo
style galant	*Sturm und Drang*	decrescendo

THINKING ABOUT IT

A good way to distinguish the late baroque style from rococo style is to listen again to the Couperin "Le Croc-en-jambe" and then to the "Allemande" from J. S. Bach's French Suite in D Minor. Notice that the Couperin is almost entirely homophonic and that its theme is expended in short little bursts. The Bach, on the other hand, always seems to have some inner part moving, creating the illusion of counterpoint. The theme is long and spiraling.

How would you characterize the differences between the Rubens painting in chapter 5 and the Watteau painting, *A Party in the Open Air,* in this chapter? Think in terms of texture, colors, subject matter, physique of the characters in the two paintings. How do the changes in art coincide with changes in musical styles?

7

Banks of the Schiavone, Canaletto

SOUNDS OF THE CHAPTER

J. S. Bach
Brandenburg Concerto no. 2

Beethoven
Quartet, op. 18, no. 1
Piano Concerto no. 1
Piano Concerto no. 4
Sonata no. 12, op. 26
Sonata no. 14, op. 27, no. 2
Symphony no. 1
Symphony no. 3, *Eroica*

Gay and Pepusch
The Beggar's Opera

Handel
Alcina
Trio Sonata in F Major ♪

Haydn
Quartet, op. 3, no. 5
Quartet, op. 33, no. 3
Quartet, op. 50, no. 1–6
Quartet, op. 54, no. 1–3
Quartet, op. 76, no. 1–6

Quartet, op. 77, no. 1–2
String Quartet, op. 20, no. 5
Symphony no. 10 in D Major
Symphony no. 45, in F♯ Minor, *Farewell*
Symphony no. 94, *Surprise*
The Creation
The Seasons

Mozart
Cosi fan tutte
Don Giovanni
K. 16
Piano Concerto no. 17 in G Major
Sonata in B♭
Symphony no. 26
Symphony no. 40 in G Minor ♪
Symphony no. 41, K. 551, *Jupiter*
The Magic Flute
The Marriage of Figaro
Violin Concerto in A Major

The term "classical," when used in music, has a specific meaning.

The terms "classic" and "classical" must be approached with some caution. These terms have been used in so many different ways that confusion about their meaning can arise. For example, we speak of a classic joke, a classic beauty, a classic novel, and we also speak of classical antiquity, the classical era, and classical music. There are, however, distinctions to be made between the various uses of the terms.

Since the early Renaissance the arts of the ancient Graeco-Roman civilizations have been considered models of superiority; hence the title, classical antiquity. We might expect, then, that any succeeding era described as classical would manifest an affinity to the arts of classical antiquity. This is true of some architecture and literature of the later eighteenth century, but in virtually no way does the music of the classical era resemble that of classical antiquity. Nor is it true that the arts of the late eighteenth century are superior to those of other eras simply because they are labeled classical. Not every classical symphony is "a classic," nor is it necessarily superior to a symphony from the nineteenth or twentieth centuries.

The music of the classical era, however, does not resemble the music of classical antiquity.

The confusion is further compounded by the Western world's tendency to label all music other than popular, jazz, or folk as classical music. Many large record companies issue popular music on one label and classical music on another. These companies also cater to a rock market, a jazz market, and a classical music market. But this does not infer that a record label or a particular market is devoted exclusively, or even primarily, to music from the classical era. They merely use the term classical in a much larger sense: it encompasses all art music, including that from the classical era.

All music conveniently categorized as "classical" is not from the classical era.

THE SYMPHONY IN THE CLASSICAL ERA

Figure 7.1 diagrams the number, order, and character of movements in the typical classical symphony.

The shapes suggest the character of the movements. In terms of what is called "musical weight," the first movement is the heaviest. It is normally the longest of the four movements, contains proportionately more of the most profound ideas, and has the most involved development. The slow second movement provides lyrical balance for the drama of the first movement. The third movement, the dance (minuet and trio), is in some respects the least complicated. The presence of the minuet

Fig. 7.1

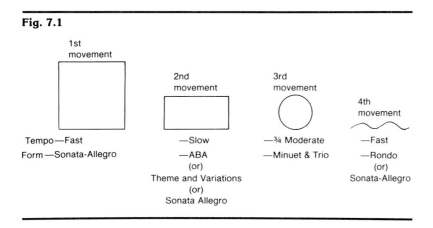

1st movement
Tempo—Fast
Form—Sonata-Allegro

2nd movement
—Slow
—ABA
(or)
Theme and Variations
(or)
Sonata Allegro

3rd movement
—¾ Moderate
—Minuet & Trio

4th movement
—Fast
—Rondo
(or)
Sonata-Allegro

proved to be a valuable tool for eighteenth century audiences. Its famil-iarity encouraged them to feel more comfortable with the complete sym-phony. Because it was a familiar element, it is diagramed here as a comfortable round shape. The squiggly line representing the final move-ment indicates this is the shortest of the four movements and is often playful in mood.

The tempo of the first movement is reasonably fast, although not so fast as to violate the classical sense of good taste. Similarly, the slow second movement is not too slow. Irrational exaggerations of anything, including tempos, may have suited the baroque ideal, but were avoided in the classical age. The minuet, or third movement, again moves at a moderate tempo. The last movement usually takes a tempo just a little faster than that of the first movement; if the first movement is allegro, the last movement is likely to be presto.

Haydn in particular was fond of prefacing his late symphonies with a brief, slow introduction. This solemn frontispiece leads directly to the first movement proper.

FRANZ JOSEPH HAYDN

Haydn (1732–1809) was born into a peasant family at Rohrau in southern Austria. This inauspicious birth hardly suggests the magnitude of his destiny. When he died seventy-seven years later, Haydn was unques-tionably regarded as the greatest composer of his time. This fame and success as a composer, however, were not easily won.

Haydn's formal education ended when he left the Cathedral of St. Stephen in Vienna at the age of sixteen. For about the next twelve years, he scratched out a meager existence in Vienna, primarily as a street mu-sician.

The final movement of the classical symphony is the shortest.

The relative tempo of each movement has been standardized.

Franz Joseph Haydn
(1732–1809)

The Esterhazy Estate

At the age of twenty-nine, Haydn was employed by the wealthy and artistically discriminating Esterhazy family. He took up residence at the family palace in Eisenstadt, Austria, where he remained for the next thirty years. Haydn worked in virtual isolation, away from the mainstream of musical activities in Vienna and other important centers.

Haydn's responsibilities while in the Esterhazy employ were very demanding. He was expected to compose and rehearse music for the court orchestra, for chamber music, for the opera theater, and for the chapel, as well as to manage administrative tasks. Despite all this, Haydn had complete liberty to compose and experiment as he wished. He learned by trial and error the effects and procedures that were successful and discarded those that were not. Slowly, steadily, Haydn mastered the craft of composition and learned to harness and channel his enormous creativity.

Haydn achieved fame and glory during his lifetime.

These years of experimentation, growth, and self-fulfillment were rewarding eventually. Haydn spent the last twenty years of his life basking in the sunshine of worldwide acclaim. His works were performed widely, resulting in Haydn's being much celebrated, honored, and sought after.

Haydn's Compositions

Haydn's output was prolific: he composed 104 symphonies, 83 string quartets, 52 piano sonatas, 2 major oratorios—*The Creation* and *The Seasons*—operas, church music, concertos, and chamber music. The symphonies were written throughout his creative years and so serve as a vehicle to trace both Haydn's development as a composer and the metamorphosis of the symphony from its playful galant beginnings to its magnificent classical arrival.

Haydn's symphonies trace the development of his talents and the metamorphosis of the genre.

Haydn's Symphony no. 10 in D Major was probably composed during his first eighteen to twenty-four months at the Esterhazy palace, from 1761–62. Its demeanor, size, and scope are completely galant in style. The orchestra numbers about twenty players (four each of first and second violins, four violas, two cellos, and two basses, two flutes, and two French horns). This early work follows the three-movement format: fast-slow-fast. The entire symphony is only about twelve minutes in length, roughly half that of most of Haydn's mature classical symphonies.

Haydn's earliest symphonies had only three movements.

Haydn wrote about forty-three symphonies during his first ten years at the Esterhazy estate. All except one of these are in major keys. These works all stay within the general limits of the style galant, although Haydn continued to experiment, expand, and move steadily in the direction of the four-movement format.

Style galant characterizes Haydn's early symphonies.

A major stylistic shift is evident in the next six symphonies (nos. 44–49). Here Haydn is in the midst of his *Sturm und Drang* years. Many of these symphonies are in minor keys and contain some striking dissonances. The thematic content also reveals some violent contrasts. Typically, a *Sturm und Drang* theme is either very energetic and angry or it is quiet and introspective. Established forms, such as the sonata-allegro, are sometimes twisted out of their customary shapes in these *Sturm und Drang* symphonies.

Haydn's Symphony no. 45 in F♯ Minor (1772), subtitled *Farewell,* illustrates several of these features. It is composed in four movements, fast-slow-minuet-fast, all of which are in sonata-allegro form except the minuet.

Haydn's symphonies numbered 44 through 49 feature *Sturm und Drang* characteristics.

SOUND AND SENSE: Sturm und Drang *Features*

Title: Symphony no. 45 in F♯ Minor, *Farewell*

Composer: Haydn

A Closer Look:

First Movement

The first movement is the most violent of the four. The exposition begins with several varied repetitions of the *A* theme. This is a jagged, restless theme that stretches over three octaves in the space of eight measures, and contains a great deal of startling interplay between *f* and *p*. Oddly, there is no *B* theme in the exposition, and the lack of one serves to make the *A* theme even more prominent. The angry character of the *A* theme dominates. Stranger still, a *B* theme appears in the middle of the development section. The *B* theme is as melancholy as the *A* theme is violent.

Second Movement

This is quiet and reflective, yet there are many unexpected dissonances and changes of key.

Third Movement

The minuet, normally a mild-mannered movement, has a number of harmonic jolts beginning in the third measure.

Fourth Movement

The presto finale (last movement) begins with a quiet, but furious *A* theme, leading to a contrasting *B* theme that features some pockets of imitative counterpoint. The extended coda that follows has an interesting history. Whether fact or fancy, the story illustrates Haydn's creative genius.

The court orchestra musicians were anxious for a holiday and had been pestering Haydn to speak to the prince on their behalf. Haydn, not wanting to be brash or undiplomatic, refused to do so. Instead, he devised a musical plan to accomplish this end. The coda to the *Farewell* symphony was written so that one by one, the various parts of the orchestra ceased playing. As a player reached the end of his part, he packed up his instrument and exited. Thus, during the coda, the orchestra got smaller and smaller, until at the end there were only two violins left playing. The prince understood the message and is reported to have said: ''I see what you're after—the musicians want to go home! Very well, we'll pack up tomorrow.'' Where words had failed, Haydn's music had succeeded.

The charm of this story does not diminish the character of the coda. Like the rest of the work, it has an urgency, a dissonance not found in Haydn's style galant symphonies.

Sturm und Drang contributed to Haydn's musical maturity.

Haydn's zenith as a symphonist occurred in the 1780s and 1790s.

The creative and emotional storm of the *Sturm und Drang* years waned, but the experience was necessary for the composer's growth. The most beneficial aspects of the experience greatly influenced Haydn's crystallized classical style. The symphonies from the 1780s and 1790s are in this more mature style and reflect Haydn's zenith as a symphonist. The last twelve symphonies (93–104) were commissioned by an entrepreneur named Salomon for a London concert series. Any one of the collection is a model of classical music style.

SOUND AND SENSE: *Classical Style*

Title: Symphony no. 94, *Surprise*

Composer: Haydn

A Closer Look:

The four movements (fast-slow-minuet-fast) are prefaced by a majestic, slow introduction. The work is scored for a full-scale classical orchestra (the usual strings, but in greater numbers than in earlier times, plus two flutes, oboes, bassoons, French horns, trumpets, and timpani).

Introduction and First Movement

The slow introduction is dignified and serious, laced with touching and ponderous dissonance. It is in 3/4 meter, but after a brief pause at the end of the introduction, the meter switches to 6/8, vivace, and the first movement proper begins:

Exposition

A—has the rhythm

bridge—a lengthy one

B—has the syncopated rhythm

C—brief closing theme

Development

Principally, the *A* theme is developed.

Recapitulation

Follows the order of the exposition and has a coda.

Second Movement (Andante, Theme and Variations)

Theme Section
a—eight bars
a'—eight bars, ends with a "surprise" crash
b—eight bars
b—eight bars
First variation—thirty-two bars in length. The violins add a countermelody to the theme.
Second variation—thirty-two bars in length, plus a two-bar bridge. Minor mode and change of character.
Third variation—thirty-two bars in length. The theme moves in quicker note values, thus again changing its character.
Fourth variation—thirty-two bars in length. A triplet figure is introduced.
Coda

Third Movement
A (minuet)-*B* (trio)-*A* (minuet) structure. The trio section features violins and bassoons.

Fourth Movement
Rondo—*ABACA*-coda

WOLFGANG AMADEUS MOZART

Franz Joseph Haydn and Wolfgang Amadeus Mozart (1756–91) met for the first time in the winter of 1781 when Haydn was forty-nine and Mozart was twenty-five. A profound and long-lasting admiration and friendship developed between them, as evidenced by Haydn's remark to Mozart's father:

> Before God and as an honest man, I tell you that your son is the greatest composer known to me either in person or by name. He has taste, and what is more, the most profound knowledge of composition.

By the time of this meeting, Mozart had already been acknowledged as a child prodigy, having played the piano before many European heads of state who adored and coddled the amazing child. But after the joy and success of his childhood, Mozart endured an adulthood haunted by frustration, financial woes, ill health, and a discouraging lack of widespread acclaim for his music.

Even though Mozart and Haydn are often coupled by musical historians, their lives were strikingly different. Hadyn's peasant childhood, youthful years of scuffling, acceptance of a role in the patronage system, and slow, steady artistic growth leading to widespread acclaim vividly contrasts Mozart's life.

Haydn and Mozart were contemporaries on the musical scene in Europe in the late eighteenth century.

Wolfgang Amadeus Mozart (1756–91)

Mozart's acclaim came in his childhood.

Born into a musical and educated (though not wealthy) family, Mozart enjoyed public adulation during his childhood. But his stubborn refusal to conform to the patronage system denied him solid, steady employment, and led to financial ruin. He lived less than half as long as Haydn, and was buried in a pauper's common grave, without ceremony or friends. The bright promise of Mozart's youth was never fulfilled in adulthood.

Mozart's works have been catalogued chronologically by K. numbers.

Mozart's works are catalogued by Köchel or K. numbers, not by opus numbers. Ludwig von Köchel was a nineteenth century author-historian who undertook the chronological cataloguing of all of Mozart's more than 600 works. Each work was assigned a K. number, such as Symphony no. 40 in G minor, K. 550. Though there are exceptions to the rule, generally a high K. number indicates that Mozart composed the work later in his life. K. 550 is thus a late work.

Mozart composed his first symphony at the age of eight or nine.

Mozart wrote his first symphony, K. 16, at the age of eight or nine. This is a miniature galant piece in three movements (fast-slow-fast) that is about eleven minutes in length and is filled with galant charm. It is, of course, a marvel that a nine-year-old child could compose such a piece, but his earliest symphonies are separated from his later work by a wide artistic gulf. You can appreciate the scope of this gulf by listening to the first symphony (K. 16), and then to the G Minor Symphony, K. 550, the first movement of which was discussed in chapter 3.

Mozart was influenced by *Sturm und Drang* at the age of about seventeen.

At the age of 17 or 18 (1773–74) Mozart encountered the *Sturm und Drang* movement. Some of his symphonies from those years reflect the movement's influence. Mozart's no. 26, K. 184, is especially representative of this.

Mozart's *Jupiter* symphony does not reflect his failing health and low spirits of the time.

Mozart's later symphonies, together with Haydn's London Symphonies, are the crowning glory of the late eighteenth century symphony. Symphony no. 41, K. 551, subtitled *Jupiter,* was written during the last few years of Mozart's life when his health was failing rapidly. And yet, this work is filled with youthful energy and sunny spirits.

The third movement of *Jupiter* is outstanding among eighteenth century minuets.

Both the first and second movements of *Jupiter* are in sonata form. The first, as expected, is longer and weightier. The second movement presents a songlike theme, and a *B* theme which, with its touching dissonances, suggests tragedy. The third movement (minuet and trio) is a gem among eighteenth century minuets. The minuet theme consists of a series of short, descending phrases, each starting on a different pitch. When properly performed, the rhythm has an easy, billowing effect, rather than the stiff, pompous character of so many other classical minuets. The fourth movement, also in sonata-allegro form, is larger, more complex, and more dramatic than most symphonic final movements. This last movement is also highly contrapuntal.

Ludwig van Beethoven
(1770–1827)

LUDWIG VAN BEETHOVEN

Ludwig van Beethoven (1770–1827) is probably the most famous of all composers of Western art music. He is also extremely complex in terms of both his personal life and musical compositions. In fact, the image of Beethoven as a lonely genius who accomplished musical miracles in an aggressively individual way is essentially accurate.

Complexity is common to Beethoven's music and personality.

It is not true that Beethoven was a starving, penniless artist who labored in some hovel producing masterworks that only future generations would appreciate. In reality, his music sold very well and afforded him a comfortable living. During his lifetime he was a much-celebrated composer, but, unlike Haydn, was not an approachable person, and so he distanced himself from the adoring musical public.

Beethoven knew and greatly admired the works of Haydn and Mozart; in fact he moved to Vienna for the purpose of studying with Mozart, but that plan was interrupted by Mozart's death. In 1792, Beethoven left Bonn to study with Haydn, but it was not a happy teacher-student relationship, and so it ended quickly. The two composers went their separate ways, but Beethoven never lost his enthusiasm for Haydn's music, and the influence of that master is evident in much of Beethoven's early work.

Haydn's influence is obvious in Beethoven's early work.

Neither Beethoven nor Mozart entered the patronage system.

Beethoven would not consider the patronage system for himself.

Many of Beethoven's most significant works were written after he became deaf.

Beethoven's life spanned the end of the classical era and the beginning of the romantic age; he was influenced by both periods.

Beethoven's early career was nurtured and in part financed by a group of noblemen who recognized the composer's genius. Although Beethoven was grateful for the help, he did not let this association dictate his actions: he refused to enter the patronage system.

As we mentioned before, Haydn was able to accommodate himself to the patronage system, and profited by staying with it for nearly thirty years. Mozart's more temperamental and quarrelsome personality prevented him from fitting into the system. But Beethoven, in contrast to his two great contemporaries, simply *would not* enter the system. Although he realized the patronage system was beneficial for some, Beethoven would not even consider it for himself. On that issue alone he battled against formidable odds—and won decisively. Beethoven's fierce independence of the patronage system, coupled with the fact that he did not fit into any neat stylistic or sociological pigeonholes, helps explain his reputation as a complex personality.

In the late 1790s and the early years of the nineteenth century, a malady that had been stalking Beethoven for several years finally caught up with him: Beethoven realized that he was becoming deaf. A more devastating affliction for a composer is hardly imaginable, nor is it imaginable for a person who cannot hear to compose music. And yet, the majority of Beethoven's most monumental works, many of which are numbered among the richest musical treasures we possess, were written in the silence of deafness. Once more, Beethoven had triumphed against formidable odds.

Classifying Beethoven's Compositions

Beethoven lived the first half of his life in the eighteenth century, so by the time he became a young man, the classical style was fully formed. By the time he had reached middle age, nearly all of the philosophical bases and many artistic manifestations of nineteenth century romanticism had appeared. Since Beethoven's music is a product of his lifetime experiences, it is difficult to classify it as classical, romantic, both, or neither.

A fine sense of proportion and balance, a mastery of the developmental process, and the creation of large, organically solid edifices are characteristic of musical classicism. Inasmuch as Beethoven was a consummate master of these, he is a classical composer. Romanticism is characterized by wizardry in the expression of emotions and subtle nuances of mood, the musical presentation of ideals and programs, and the harnessing of an expanding functional harmony. Beethoven was equally masterful of these, and so can legitimately be called a romantic.

Still, Beethoven does not conform to these hallmarks of the eighteenth and nineteenth centuries. The man and much of his music transcend chronological and stylistic boundaries. As a result, Beethoven's music must be examined as a unique entity, only generally related to one style or another.

Beethoven's Symphony no. 1 (1798?) is the most Haydnesque of the nine symphonies he composed. But his Symphony no. 3 (subtitled *Eroica*, 1803) is the epitome of those characteristics of classicism listed previously. At the same time, the work completely transcends all previous conceptions of a symphony.

Beethoven's compositions, while exhibiting characteristics of both classical and romantic music, also reflect a unique style.

Beethoven's *Eroica* set new standards for symphony.

SOUND AND SENSE: *Musical Classicism*

Title: Symphony no. 3, *Eroica*

Composer: Beethoven

A Closer Look:

Symphony no. 3 has the standard number and order of movements found in classical music: fast-slow-dance-fast. Its structure is created from a few, rather than a profusion, of ideas. The process of development, so important to the classical style, is fully realized.

But the work extends beyond the limits of the late eighteenth century classical symphony. The length of *Eroica* is atypical of a classical symphony. Usually, a classical symphony will run about twenty-five minutes; *Eroica* is nearly twice that length. Another difference is the replacement of the courtly minuet of the classical symphony with a rough-and-ready peasant dance called a **scherzo.** No lady in a long, flowing gown could possibly dance to the tempo of this scherzo. And the codas to the first, second, and particularly fourth movement, are greatly protracted. They amount almost to additional development sections.

First Movement

The first movement, in sonata-allegro form, begins after two loud and vicious hammer strokes. The *A* theme is comprised of three subthemes that are interrelated. Notice that the subthemes can be reduced to simple triads. Members of the triads to which these themes are reducible are marked here with an x.

Similarly, the *B* theme is comprised of three subthemes, one of which, *e,* is also triadic.

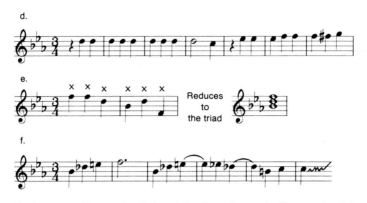

The long exposition section that contains these themes is diagramed as follows:

A					
a	*a*	*a*	*a*	*b*	*c*
in the cellos	in the woodwinds	marked by syncopation	key of E♭, then C minor, then A♭		

B			
d	*e*	*f*	*a'*
in clarinets, then violins, then woodwinds	derived from the triadic natures of *a,b,c*	includes a passage of extreme dissonance	

The long development section that follows is charged with energy and violence; the *a* theme is ripped apart note from note. Toward the middle of the development there is a fugal section; this is followed by an extended passage of shattering dissonance that raises the listener to a state of near frenzy and leaves little doubt that the composer is enraged. The supreme tension finally reaches a peak and collapses into a quiet section that provides the necessary antidote to the preceding violence.

This diagram serves as a road map through the battlefield of the development section:

a'—the theme is twisted slightly out of shape
b—appears accompanied by some figuration in the violins
a—is presented four times in succession beginning each time on a different note:
     C C♯ D E; this series of entrances generates tremendous power
a—is further developed as it is combined with *c*
b—is developed
fugal section
shattering dissonance

b—(the antidote) note the change of orchestration that creates a complete change of mood

a—further and new development

b—more of the antidote

a—is dismantled as its pitches are torn, one by one, off the torso of *a*. Finally there is but one pitch left quivering in the violins.

Recapitulation

Before the orchestra can conclude the development section on the V_7 chord, a solo French horn enters with *a* on the tonic chord. The juxtaposition of the orchestra's V_7 and the horn's I chord creates an odd harmonic jolt that may at first sound like an error by Beethoven. But it is not a mistake; Beethoven intended the jolt. This moment provides us with the first clue that the French horn has a special and symbolic role to play in the *Eroica* symphony. The horn is the symbol of the hero. Notice that when the rest of the orchestra is content to linger in the ashes of the development, the French horn pulls it out of the development and into the recapitulation wherein the battered *a* theme is reconstructed. After only a few measures into the recapitulation, the *a* theme is restored to its original shape, using the French horn for its voice. The remainder of the recapitulation parallels the order of events in the exposition.

Coda

Perhaps one of the things that most startled the early nineteenth century audience was the length and character of the coda. No longer a mere musical "stop sign," in Beethoven's hands it is prolonged and assumes the character of an additional development where new facets of the *a* theme are revealed. Notice the prominence of the French horn in the coda, also.

Second Movement

The slow movement—Marcia funebre (funeral march)—is solemn and dramatic. It is cast in a very large *ABA* form with an extensive coda. The *A* sections are in C minor, and the *B* section in C major. The principal themes from these sections are, like those of the first movement, easily reduced to triads.

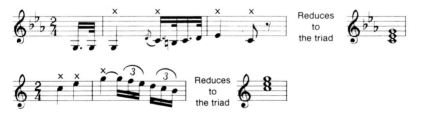

Third Movement

The third movement is a scherzo, having the form *A* (scherzo)-*B* (trio)-*A* (scherzo). The theme of the trio is also triadic. Notice that the trio is played by the French horns, the voice of the hero.

Fourth Movement

After a brief dramatic flourish, the last movement quickly proceeds to a set of seven variations based on the triadic theme

and its bass line.

A long, brilliant coda featuring the French horn concludes the movement and the work.

Eroica captures the essence of classicism while foreshadowing romanticism.

The *Eroica* is a landmark composition. It appears to be the essence of musical classicism; providing a final glorious exclamation point to that noble creation of the eighteenth century—the symphony. But simultaneously, the piece is an example of a newly emerging style—musical romanticism—with all its echoes of heroism, symbolism, formal and emotional expansiveness, and the urge to interrelate in a close and unmistakable way all the parts to the whole.

A typical late eighteenth century symphony is a collection of four agreeable movements. For a symphony of this kind, any minuet and trio (provided it is in the appropriate key) can serve as the third movement; one minuet can be substituted for another without damaging the integrity of the symphony as a whole. This is not true of the *Eroica,* where no such substitutions can be made. These specific four movements belong together; they share thematic, rhythmic, and instrumentational interconnections that are critical to the sense of the whole work. Each of the movements has its being, makes sense, and is in part explained by the others. Beginning with the *Eroica,* the symphony acquired a narrative sense, and every major symphonist who came after Beethoven in the nineteenth century employed this as a starting premise.

THE CONCERTO

The concerto was an important part of the legacy bequeathed by the baroque to succeeding ages. Composers of the classical era were quick to claim this inheritance and to remodel it to conform to their own tastes and needs.

    The new age made use of the basic three-movement plan (fast-slow-fast) of the old concerto grosso, but replaced the concertino (with its usual complement of two, three, or four performers) with a single soloist—one violin, one piano, or some other solo instrument. Thus, whereas in the baroque the genre is referred to as the concerto grosso, in the classical era it is called a **concerto**—a piano concerto, a violin concerto, or a horn concerto.

    The classical composers, so fascinated with the sonata-allegro, put the form to use in the concerto. Typically, the first movement of the concerto was cast in this form. Immediately, though, a problem arose: How should the materials of the exposition section be distributed between the orchestra and the soloist? Who gets to play what, and when? Should the orchestra be allotted the *A* theme and the bridge, and the soloist be given the *B* theme? Or should this be reversed? The ingenious solution was found in the double exposition.

Mozart's Concertos

As previously explained, the exposition section in a sonata form is repeated literally. However, in the double exposition of the concerto, the repetition is nonliteral. When listening to the first movement of Mozart's Piano Concerto no. 17 in G Major, K. 453, notice that the orchestra alone plays the exposition in its entirety once. But instead of the expected verbatim repetition of the exposition, the soloist enters and, with the cooperation of the orchestra, performs a varied repetition of the exposition. This is a **double exposition.** It was an ingenious, aesthetically satisfying, and well-mannered solution to the problem. Neither soloist nor orchestra felt slighted; both were allowed to deal with the entire substance of the exposition.

    In the classical concerto, the orchestra and the soloist share the development and recapitulation. At the end of the recapitulation, and before the coda, a special section played only by the soloist occurs. This section is called the **cadenza.** In the cadenza, the soloist improvises and develops one or more themes from the movement. Often (but not always) the cadenza concludes with a trill or series of trills. The trills are a signal to the orchestra that the soloist is ready to finish the improvisation and is requesting the orchestra's cooperation in playing the coda that ends the first movement.

> The classical composers reshaped the baroque concerto to fit their own needs.

> The concerto grosso evolved into the concerto of the classical age.

> The first movement of the concerto was usually in sonata-allegro form.

> Double exposition was also utilized.

> The classical concerto features a solo between the recapitulation and the coda called the "cadenza," a solo improvisation.

SOUND AND SENSE: *Classical Concerto*

Title: Piano Concerto no. 17 in G Major, K. 453

Composer: Mozart

A Closer Look:

First Movement

First Exposition—Orchestra
A (playful)-bridge-*B* (lyric)-bridge-*C* (quiet)

Second Exposition—piano and orchestra
A-bridge-*B'*-bridge-*C*

Development
Many changes of key and of mode

Recapitulation
A (in violins)-bridge-*B* (mainly in piano)-*C*
Cadenza—piano alone, ends with a long trill

Coda
Orchestra rejoins piano

Second Movement
The middle movement is in song form, *ABA'*-coda, and is filled with gentleness and melancholy reminiscent of *empfindsamer stil,* but without any shallowness.

Third Movement
The concluding movement consists of a set of variations on a simple, folklike theme. This is the kind of variation in which the theme itself is varied. Notice, too, how Mozart varies his performing forces. The movement is diagramed as follows:

Theme section—*aabb* (orchestra)
First variation—*aabb* (piano with light orchestral accompaniment)
Second variation—*aabb* (piano and woodwinds)
Third variation—*a* (woodwinds)
             a (piano)
             b (woodwinds)
             b (piano)
Fourth variation—*a* (strings and winds shift to minor)
             a (piano)
             b (strings and woodwinds)
             b (piano)
Fifth variation—*a* (full orchestra, shift back to major mode)
             a (piano)
             b (full orchestra)
             b (piano)

Bridge leading to an extended coda. Variations continue.

Now is an appropriate time to listen to Mozart's Violin Concerto in A Major, K. 219, and to any of his four horn concertos.

Beethoven's Concertos

Beethoven's Piano Concerto no. 1 was composed in 1798 when Beethoven was better known as a concert pianist than as a composer. Frequently, Beethoven performed the work in public, dazzling audiences with his playing, particularly his ability to improvise in the cadenzas of piano concertos. The form of his Piano Concerto no. 1 is very straightforward, beginning with a fast movement in a clearcut, though lengthy, sonata form, followed by a quiet and lyrical slow movement, and a fast third movement in rondo form.

> **Beethoven performed his Piano Concerto no. 1 in public, dazzling his audience with the cadenza.**

The great length of the work is the most obvious departure from the classical norm; the first movement alone is nearly as long as entire late eighteenth century concertos. When listening to the first movement, notice the double exposition with its three distinctly different themes, the lengthy development, and the standard recapitulation. The cadenza grows to monumental proportions, and systematically calls into play each of the dominant themes. It also features an elaborate set of trills near the very end.

Beethoven broke new ground with his Piano Concerto no. 4 (1805), for the first movement begins, not with the orchestra, but with the soloist who gently enunciates the dominating theme of the movement. Only after the initial statement from the soloist does the orchestra enter. Later in the nineteenth century, this procedure of soloist followed by orchestra was so prevalent that it became the norm.

> **Beethoven began his Piano Concerto no. 4 with a solo.**

THE STRING QUARTET

During the classical era, the string quartet became the dominant form of chamber music. Like the symphony, the string quartet slowly evolved during the preclassic period and finally assumed its classical shape in Haydn's hands.

> **The string quartet was the dominant form of chamber music in the classical era.**

Appreciation of the string quartet is often an acquired taste, since it lacks the pizzazz of the full orchestra and the dazzle of soloistic music. Many audiences find the magic of the string quartet genre is slow to materialize, but once the taste is acquired, the appetite is insatiable.

> **An appreciation for the string quartet is often acquired over time.**

Haydn's Early Quartets

Haydn's first string quartets were written several years before his first symphonies. The earliest of these are in true galant style, and some may, in fact, be arrangements of other instrumental pieces written while he was a street musician in Vienna. These quartets are lighthearted, essentially homophonic, and harmonically subdued. Some are in three movements, some in four, and some in five. As with Haydn's symphonies, it

> **Haydn's first string quartets were composed before he began to write symphonies.**

Haydn rehearsing a string
quartet

**Haydn's string quartets
evolved from style galant
through *Sturm und Drang*
to pure classicism.**

**Opus 3 is a good example
of Haydn's style galant
string quartet.**

**In Haydn's early string
quartets, the first violin
dominates the second
violin, viola and cello.**

is possible with the quartets to trace his evolution as a composer and to
monitor his changes from galant, to *Sturm und Drang,* to pure classicism.

Many of Haydn's string quartets were composed and published
in sets of six. Thus, Opus 1 contains six individual quartets: Opus 1,
no. 1; Opus 1, no. 2, and so on. Opus 3, no. 5 was probably written in
the middle 1760s, when Haydn had already composed a dozen or more
quartets. This work is not indicative of his early efforts, but is, nonetheless, still solidly entrenched in the style galant.

Opus 3 has four movements (fast-slow-dance-fast). The first
movement is cast in a miniature sonata-allegro form; the charming second movement is in the form of a serenade, the dance movement is a
standard minuet-trio-minuet, and the last movement is a playful rondo.
The whole quartet is only about eleven minutes in length. This order and
number of movements became the standard in the classical era; notice
that it corresponds precisely with the classical symphony. In this quartet, as in most of Haydn's early ones, the first violin is clearly dominant,
and the second violin, viola, and cello serve primarily as accompaniment.
But with time and experience, Haydn learned to integrate the four instruments equally.

Haydn's *Sturm und Drang* Quartets

Haydn composed the String Quartet, op. 20, no. 5 (1772) in the midst of the tumultuous *Sturm und Drang* years. The same kind of passion, dissonance, and raw energy we found in the *Farewell* symphony of the *Sturm und Drang* years are evident in this quartet, too. *Sturm und Drang* works deviate from classical models in some forms and the order of movements. Such is the case with this work: it has the standard four movements, but in the order fast-dance-slow-fast.

SOUND AND SENSE: Sturm und Drang *Quartet*

Title: String Quartet, op. 20, no. 5

Composer: Haydn

A Closer Look:

The first movement is in sonata form but is somewhat misshapen. The opening *A* theme is followed by a bridge that modulates to the proper key for the *B* theme, but before we hear the *B* theme, *A* appears again in the new key. The development section is followed by the recapitulation in which the second statement of *A* does not appear. The movement concludes with a long, complicated coda that amounts to an additional development section.

   The minuet is also in the principal key of the work (F minor). Here, there is none of the galant charm. Instead, there is a brooding, agitated quality. The mood brightens a little in the trio section, but is more bittersweet than cheerful.

   The slow movement, adagio in 6/8, is dominated by a single theme that is played against a succession of countersubjects, producing some jarring dissonances and several unexpected twists in the harmony.

   The last movement is an angry-sounding fugue filled with stern, serious counterpoint. The movement is much too serious and rigorous for rococo ears.

Haydn's Later Quartets

With the six quartets, Opus 33 (1781), Haydn arrived at the threshold of string-quartet mastery. Now listen to Opus 33, no. 2 in its entirety, for here, fully formed, is the classical string quartet that Haydn worked thirty years to perfect. Other important purely classical quartets by Haydn that deserve listening attention include Opus 50 (six quartets), Opus 54 (three quartets), Opus 76 (six quartets), and Opus 77 (two quartets).

Haydn's Opus 33 exemplifies his fully matured classical string quartet.

Mozart's Quartets

The early string quartets of Mozart are, like those of Haydn, mostly in the style galant. But in the 1780s Mozart, again like Haydn, began to produce purely classical string quartets of the highest quality. The last ten quartets include a set of six that Mozart composed in 1783–85 and dedicated to Haydn. Mozart said it was from Haydn that he first learned the art of string quartet writing. Any of this group of six will serve as a model for Mozart's mastery of the classical string quartet.

Mozart mastered the classical string quartet after first composing in style galant.

Beethoven's Quartets

Beethoven began composing string quartets at the height of the classical period.

Beethoven documented the difficulty he had composing the first theme of Opus 18, no. 1.

The earliest of Beethoven's string quartets (the six quartets of Opus 18) date from 1798–99, and were thus composed at a time when musical classicism was in full bloom. Beethoven kept track of various musical ideas in sketchbooks, of which several are extant. One of these sketchbooks reveals the difficulty he had and the numerous trials and errors he had to endure in order to create the first theme of Opus 18, no. 1. When listening to the theme, it seems to have been composed with ease, but the numerous entries in the sketchbook indicate this was not the case.

The first movement is the longest and is dominated by this theme that caused Beethoven such grief. The second movement is slow and has an air of tragedy about it. The third movement is a scherzo-trio-scherzo. And the last movement is an allegro in rondo form.

PIANO SONATA

Once the piano rose to prominence, it replaced the harpsichord as the primary keyboard instrument.

Piano music has these advantages: range, sustenance of sound, versatility, power, and ability to blend well with other instruments.

During the classical era a body of music was created for the piano—the piano sonata.

Piano sonatas were not in demand.

The piano was invented in the early eighteenth century, but did not come into real prominence and widespread use until the second half of that century. When it did arrive, however, the piano quickly displaced the harpsichord as the primary keyboard instrument. Composers devoted their energies to creating a repertoire of solo and ensemble music for it.

The reasons for the piano's popularity are many. As its name *pianoforte* (Italian for "soft and loud") implies, the instrument can produce a range of volume levels, something the harpsichord cannot do. The piano also can sustain sounds, whereas the sounds produced by a harpsichord decay and disappear quickly. The piano is a versatile and powerful instrument. It is so powerful that it can be heard over an entire symphony orchestra, making the piano concerto possible. Since the instrument blends well with other instruments, classical composers developed a rich body of chamber music involving the piano. Finally, the piano is a fine solo instrument, worthy of the body of solo music created especially for it during the classical era: the piano sonata.

Since the vogue for solo piano recitals did not develop until the second quarter of the nineteenth century, there was no demand to create solo sonatas in the classical era. Nevertheless, Haydn, Mozart, Beethoven, and others composed piano sonatas. Perhaps they did so for their private entertainment, for those who commissioned them, or out of a love for and fascination with the marvelous new instrument. Regardless of their motivation, Haydn wrote fifty-two sonatas, Mozart nineteen, and Beethoven thirty-two.

Haydn's Sonatas

The earliest Haydn sonatas date from the 1760s and, for the most part, are lightweight homophonic works consisting of three or four movements in the style galant. Some of the sonatas from the 1770s are in minor keys, and have other *Sturm und Drang* characteristics. Increasingly, the tendency was toward a three-movement plan, fast-slow-fast, and no dance movement. The last of Haydn's sonatas, some of which were written during his final productive years, are models of classical grace and inventiveness. These are the Haydn sonatas most frequently heard in recitals today.

Mozart's Sonatas

All of the Mozart piano sonatas were written from 1774–89, and all are in three movements. This music is so rich and diverse that it is difficult to pick a single favorite or even to say what constitutes a "typical" Mozart piano sonata. The Sonata in B♭, K. 333 (1778) is but one of many exquisite examples of Mozart's sonatas. The first and second movements of this sonata are in sonata-allegro form; the last movement is a rondo.

Beethoven's Sonatas

Throughout the nineteenth and twentieth centuries, Beethoven's piano sonatas have been among the most widely performed. In terms of technical and performing difficulty, they range from pieces suitable for gifted amateur piano students, to works so devilishly difficult that they nearly defy performance. Stylistically, they range from classical to romantic to those which transcend all stylistic labels and enter a kind of mystic realm. The thirty-two sonatas are as diverse in terms of overall shape: some are in four movements, some in three, some in two, and no. 13 has but one movement with frequent internal changes of tempo and mood. Variation also exists in the order of movements in Beethoven's sonatas. Even more so than with Mozart, it is not easy to identify a "typical" Beethoven sonata.

The Sonata no. 12, op. 26 (1800–1801), the first movement of which was encountered in chapter 3, is an appropriate listening selection. Opus 26 has four movements: andante-scherzo-funeral march-allegro.

Haydn's sonatas evolved from style galant through *Sturm und Drang* to classical.

All of Mozart's piano sonatas are in three movements.

Beethoven's piano sonatas are among the most popular.

The thirty-two Beethoven sonatas vary widely in both style and shape.

SOUND AND SENSE: *Sonata*

Title: Piano Sonata no. 12, op. 26

Composer: Beethoven

A Closer Look:

First Movement

The first movement consists of a theme with five variations. The opening segment of the theme is simplicity itself, stressing repeated notes.

Second Movement

This movement, scherzo-trio-scherzo, is propelled almost entirely by a simple rhythm.

Third Movement

The third movement, entitled "Marcia funebre sulla morte d'un Eroe" ("Funeral march on the death of a hero"), is related to the second movement of the *Eroica* symphony. This movement has the shape *ABA*. The *A* sections are in the minor mode, and the *B* section shifts to the major mode. This is similar to what occurs in the second movement of the *Eroica*. This movement, too, is dominated by one rhythm—in this case, a dotted rhythm.

Fourth Movement

Rondo form: *ABACA*.

During the years 1800–1801, Beethoven composed his most popular sonata, *Moonlight Sonata* (Sonata no. 14, op. 27, no. 2). However, many people know only the first movement of this work.

This haunting movement is effective in and of itself, which accounts for its popularity, but its full impact is lost when it is taken out of the context of the whole sonata. The three movements that comprise the sonata span an incredible emotional range. The first movement has the mysterious, brooding quality, foiled perfectly by the gentle, quietly playful second movement. The third and last movement, with its agitation and fire, presents another facet in the emotional spectrum.

SOUND AND SENSE: *Sonata*

Title: Piano Sonata no. 14, op. 27, no. 2

Composer: Beethoven

A Closer Look:

First Movement

The first movement has a tightly knit *ABA*-coda form. The triplets that serve as an accompanimental figure in the *A* sections rise in the texture of the *B* section and become the thematic material.

Second Movement

This movement introduces a complete change of mood and is propelled by the rhythm. The movement takes the form of a minuet-trio-minuet, but the mood and ambience are unlike the standard eighteenth century minuet.

Third Movement

The last movement is in sonata-allegro form:

Exposition
A—quick and agitated
Bridge
B—lyric theme with agitated accompaniment
Bridge
C—bravura

Development

Recapitulation

Coda

OPERA

The attitudes and tastes of the preclassic era differed greatly from those of the baroque. It is not surprising that the baroque opera seria, with its virtuosic musical style and the pompous gods and goddesses of its contrived plots, could not survive in the breezy atmosphere of the new age. The opera seria was a perfect vehicle for the royal baroque age, but the democratically-oriented Enlightenment called for a more accessible musical style, and more down-to-earth characters and plots.

The opera seria fit the style of the baroque age, but was not suitable for the classical age.

Comic Opera

After the opera serias of Handel and his generation, Mozart assumed a position of importance in opera history. But between the decline of opera seria and the rise of Mozart's ideal, the most important development was the creation of **comic opera.** Although its origins were humble, it caught the public's fancy rapidly and soon displaced opera seria all over Europe.

Comic opera was an important element in the development of the opera.

There were, in fact, several national forms of comic opera: in Italy it was called opera buffa; in France it was called opéra-comique; in Germany, Singspiele; and in England, ballad opera. By the middle of the eighteenth century, all of these types were alive and flourishing.

Recall that an opera seria has three acts, interspersed with long intermissions during which the audience visited, dined, played cards, and conducted business. Some composers developed the idea of supplying light musical entertainment to fill these intermissions. Increasingly, this entertainment was organized into acts. Thus the evening consisted of the three acts of the opera seria plus the two acts of the light entertainment, called **intermezzo.** The opera seria consisted of: Act I, (act 1) Intermezzo, Act II, (act 2) Intermezzo, Act III. When the intermezzo was extrapolated from this context and given individual attention, the comic opera was born.

In opera seria, the intermezzo was light entertainment organized into two acts; the comic opera grew out of the intermezzo.

The Beggar's Opera   The most famous and widely performed ballad opera is *The Beggar's Opera,* written and compiled in 1728 by John Gay and Johann-Christoph Pepusch. This short comic opera does not concern gods and goddesses; instead street people are its characters: highwaymen, jailers, pimps, and trollops. Spoken dialogue is interspersed with ballads or popular songs. Clearly, bel canto is inappropriate for this style; indeed, virtuoso singers would be hopelessly out of place in this opera. Unlike opera seria, this music with its more mundane content, was very accessible to the public at large.

During the first act of *The Beggar's Opera,* two of the main characters, Peachum and his common-law wife, are enraged at the news of the marriage of their daughter, Polly. They sing the following ballad text:

Comic opera themes were popular with the general public.

> Our Polly is a sad slut! nor heeds what we have taught her.
> I wonder any man alive will ever rear a daughter!

Comic opera featured ballads.

The characters, plot, and language definitely bespeak the commoners.

The Merging of Comic and Serious Opera

The Beggar's Opera and other similar pieces are distinct opposites of opera seria; they are an unmistakable, perhaps shocking reaction against it. But in the later decades of the eighteenth century, some composers reworked the comic opera to conform to some of the conventions of more highbrow opera. These composers believed that arias, recitatives, and ensemble numbers could be absorbed into the fabric of comic opera and would enrich their works. They also determined that comic opera need not be slapstick, nor even truly comic, but that serious subject matter and characters could be employed.

Eighteenth century composers were able to create a compromise between opera seria and comic opera.

Several of the operas of Mozart, including *The Marriage of Figaro, Don Giovanni, Cosi fan tutte,* and *The Magic Flute* synthesize the comic and the serious. These operas, so rich with marvelous music, are also credible dramas with real characters who emerge, come to life, and develop personalities.

Several of Mozart's operas illustrate that compromise—*Don Giovanni,* for example.

Mozart's **Don Giovanni**   The very first scene of *Don Giovanni* (1787) illustrates that the story line, character development, and music are artistically excellent.

DON GIOVANNI

Atto I	*Act One*
Scena I	*Scene I*
Piazza. Da un lato il Palazzo del Commendatore; dall'altro una locanda.—S'appressa l'alba.	*(A Garden. Night.)*

Leporello

(indi Don Giovanni e Donna Anna.)
Notte e giorno faticar,
Per chi nulla sà gradir;
Piòva e vento sopportar,
Mangiar male e mal dormir.
Voglio far il gentiluomo,
E non voglio più servir;
Nò, nò, nò, non voglio più servir.
Oh che caro galantuomo:
Vuol star dentro colla bella,
Ed io far la sentinella!
Voglio far il gentiluomo,
E non voglio più servir,
Nò, nò, nò, non voglio più servir.
Ma mi par, che venga gente,
Non mi voglio far sentir, Ah!
(Entra Don Giovanni, e Donna Anna.)

Leporello

(wrapt in a dark mantle,
  impatiently pacing to and fro
  before the steps to the palace)
On the go from morn till night,
Running errands, never free,
Hardly time to snatch a bite;
This is not the life for me.
I would like to play the master,
Would no more a servant be,
No, no, no, no, no, no,
I would a master be.
(facing the palace)
What a difference between us!
Warm you lie in arms of beauty
While I freeze on sentry duty;
I would like to play the master,
Would no more your servant be,
No, no, no, no, no, no,
I would your master be.
What was that? We're in for trouble.
This is not the life for me,
No, no, no, no, no,
This is no life for me.
(Hides himself. Enter Donna Anna,
  holding Don Giovanni firmly by
  the arm.)

Anna
Non sperar, se non m'uccidi,
Ch'io ti lasci fuggir mai.

Giovanni
Donna folle, indarno gridi!
Chi son io tu non saprai.
(Taci, e trema al mio furore.)

Anna
Scellerato!

Giovanni
Sconsigliata!

Anna
Genti, servi! Al traditore!
Come furia disperata
Ti saprò perseguitar.

(Esce Donna Anna.)

Donna Anna
No, you won't, you shan't escape
me!
I will never let you go!

Don Giovanni
(trying to conceal his features)
Do not scream! You'll wake the
household.
Kiss me, dear, and let me go!
Now! Now let me go.
*(almost hissing; covering his
     mouth)*
Stop that noise or I shall hurt you.
Stop, I tell you!
(seizing her roughly)

Must I hurt you?

Donna Anna
No, you won't, you shan't escape
me,
I shall never let you go.
Fire and murder! Save me! Seize
him!
Fire and murder! *(freeing herself)*
Try to stop me!
(turning to the palace)
Help me! Save me!
From my unrelenting fury
You shall never get away.
From my unrelenting, my avenging
fury
You shall never get away.
Fire and murder! Try to stop me!
Save me! Help me!
*(During this action the
     Commendatore enters, hastily,
     a torch in his left hand, a sword
     in his right. Seeing the
     Commendatore approach, she
     runs into the house.)*

Giovanni
(Questa furia disperata
Mi vuol far precipitar.)

*(Don Giovanni, il Commendatore,
    Leporello.)*

Leporello
(Che tumulto! oh, ciel, che gridi)
Il padron in nuovi guai!
(Sta a veder ch'il malandrino
Mi farà precipitar.)

Commendatore
Lasciala, indegno;
Battiti meco.

Giovanni
Va, non mi degno
Di pugnar teco.

Commendatore
Così pretendi
Da me fuggir?

Commendatore
Battiti!

Giovanni
Misero! Attendi,
Se vuoi morir.

*(Si battono—il Commendatore
    cade)*

Don Giovanni
From her unrelenting fury
I had better get away.
Stop, I tell you!
I shall hurt you.
How am I to get away?
*(He haughtily confronts the
    Commendatore.)*

Leporello
Master cursing, the lady screaming,
How am I to get away?
Well, we're in a pretty pickle;
How am I to get away?
Yes, we're in a pickle this time,
Yes, a very pretty pickle,
And I cannot get away
From this pretty pickle this time,
And I think that I can say
For this pretty pickle this time
There will be the deuce to pay!

Commendatore
Where is the villain? Draw, sir, and
fight me!

Don Giovanni
No! Pride forbids me to draw on
greybeards.

Commendatore
Faint-hearted coward! I challenge
you.

Don Giovanni
Force me not!

Commendatore
Draw, I say!

Don Giovanni
Force me not!
(draws his sword)
Dotard, on guard, then!
Your death is near.
*(He strikes the torch out of the
    Commendatore's hand. The
    Commendatore attacks. They
    fight and the Commendatore
    falls mortally wounded.)*

Leporello
(Potessi almeno
Di quà partir.)

Leporello
If I could only get out of here!
*(The moon rises slowly; lights
    appear in the palace windows;
    great excitement within;
    servants hasten with torches
    behind the closed gates.)*

Commendatore
Ah soccorso! Son tradito.
L'assassino m'ha ferito,
E dal seno palpitante
Sento l'anima partir.

Commendatore
Ah, I'm wounded! Ah, I'm dying!
God, protect my child from evil!
From this mortal scene of sorrow
My immortal soul must fly.
(He dies.)

Giovanni
Ah, già cade il sciagurato,
Affannoso e agonizzante;
Già dal seno palpitante
Veggo l'anima partir.

Don Giovanni
Ah, he's fallen! Ah, he's dying!
Paying dearly for his folly.
On this world of love and beauty
He must close his aged eye.
*(Servants return with Don Ottavio
    and hasten with him from the
    street into the palace.)*

Leporello
(Qual misfatto! qual eccesso!
Entro il sen dallo spavento
Palpitar il cor mi sento—
Io non so che far, che dir!)

Leporello
Who has fallen? Who is dying?
How I shiver, how I shudder!
Rooted to the spot by terror,
I can neither move nor cry.

Recitative

Giovanni *(Sotto voce)*
Leporello, ove sei?

Don Giovanni *(softly)*
Are you there, Leporello?
*(He sheathes his sword and dons
    his cloak.)*

Leporello
Son quì per mia disgrazia, e voi—

Leporello
I only wish I wasn't. Are *you* there?

Giovanni
Son quì.

Don Giovanni
Of course.

Leporello
Chi è morto—voi, o il vecchio?

Leporello
Are you a ghost? Is *he* one?

Giovanni
Che domanda da bestia! Il vecchio!

Don Giovanni
What an imbecile question! He's
done for.

Leporello
Bravo! Due imprese leggiadre:
sforzar la figlia ed ammazzar il
padre!

Giovanni
L'ha voluto suo danno.

Leporello
Ma Donn'Anna cos'ha voluto?

Giovanni
Taci! Non mi seccar, vien meco—se
non vuoi qualche cosa ancor tu—
(Minacciandolo)

Leporello
Non vo' nulla, Signor! Non parlo
più.
*(Partono. Donna Anna, Don
      Ottavio, e Servi con fiaccole.)*

Anna
Ah, del padre in periglio in soccorso
voliam!

Ottavio
Tutto il mio sangue verserò, se
bisogna. Ma dov'è il scellerato?

Leporello
Bravo! Pretty good for one evening.
To rape the daughter and then
skewer the father!

Don Giovanni
He compelled me; I had to.

Leporello
And Donn'Anna . . . also
compelled you?

Don Giovanni
Silence! No more from you.
Remember, *(threatening to strike
him)* you can join the old man if
you wish.

Leporello
From now on I'll be dumb as any
     fish.
*(Exeunt. Donna Anna enters; she
      agitatedly descends the steps
      with Don Ottavio and servants
      bearing torches.)*

Donna Anna
Quick! His life is in danger. We
must come to his help.

Don Ottavio
(raising his drawn sword)
I will defend him. I will save him or
perish.
But I see and hear no one.

Donna Anna
I fear some evil.

Recitative and Duet

Anna
In questo loco. *(Vedendo il corpo di
suo padre.)* Ma qual mai s'offre, oh
Dei, spettacolo funesto agli occhi
miei! Padre mio! Mio caro padre!

Ottavio
Signore!

Donna Anna *(seeing the corpse)*
What, O God, do I see! What
spectacle of horror appears before
me! *(sinks down beside the body)*
It can't be! Not my father ! *(throws
herself upon the corpse)* Speak to
me, father!

Don Ottavio
Who did this?

Anna

Ah, l'assassino mel trucidò! Quel sangue, quella piaga—quel volto tinto e coperto del color di morte! Ei non respira più—fredde le membra! Padre mio! Caro padre! Padre amato! Io manco—io moro!

Ottavio

Ah soccorrete, amici, il mio tesoro! Cercatemi, recatemi qualche odor, qualche spirito. Ah non tardate! Donn'Anna, sposa, amica! Il duolo estremo la meschinella uccide.

Anna

Ahi!

Ottavio

Già riviene! Datele nuovi aiuti.

Anna

Padre mio!

Ottavio

Celate, allontanate agli occhi suoi quell'oggetto d'orrore. Anima mia! Consolati, fa core!

Donna Anna

Ah, the assassin has struck him down! He's wounded! Look, he's bleeding! So silent, so still and so unnaturally pallid! *(Don Ottavio offers to raise her; she refuses.)* So icy to the touch, breathing no longer! *(She rises.)* Tell me, father, that I'm dreaming! Answer me, father! *(She reels.)* Have mercy! Have pity!
(Don Ottavio supports her, and leads her to the stone seat.)

Don Ottavio *(to the servants)*
Help! Do not stand there gaping, but help your mistress! Bring smelling salts immediately. Go at once, get some brandy. Be quick, I tell you! Donn' Anna! Dearest! Beloved! O Grace of Heaven, let her not die of sorrow!
(A maid hurries into the palace and returns immediately with a smelling-bottle which she offers to Donna Anna.)

Donna Anna

Ah!

Don Ottavio

Look, she's stirring! Give her a sip of brandy!

Donna Anna *(with a deep sigh)*
Let me dream it.

Don Ottavio *(to servants)*
And quickly! Remove this blood-be-spattered body! She musn't see it again. *(Serving-men raise the Commendatore, and bear him into the palace.)* Wake, Donna Anna! I love you! Be comforted!

Duet

Anna

Fuggi, crudele, fuggi!
Lascia che mora anch'io!
Ora ch'è morto, oh Dio!
Chi a me la vita diè!

Ottavio

Senti cor mio, deh senti!
Guardami un solo istante!
Ti parla il caro amante.
Che vive sol per te!

Anna

Tu sei, perdon, mio bene!
L'affanno mio, le pene!
Ah, il padre mio dov'è?

Ottavio

Il padre lascia, o cara!
La rimembranza amara:
Hai sposo e padre in me!

Anna

Ah, vendicar, s'il puoi,
Giura quel sangue ognor!

Ottavio

Lo giuro agli occhi tuoi.
Lo giuro al nostro amor!

Donna Anna (springing up, and
    repulsing Don Ottavio as if
    insane)

Heartless tormentor, leave me!
Leave me to die beside him.
Cold is he now and lifeless
Who gave my life to me.

Don Ottavio

Hear me, dear heart, Donn' Anna,
Turn to your faithful lover
Whose heart is in your keeping,
O turn your eyes to me!

Donna Anna

(perceiving her error and giving
    Don Ottavio her hands)
Let me once more embrace him.
Once more! Once! Father! My
father!
(approaching the spot where the
    Commendatore fell)
But where, O where is he?

Don Ottavio

Donn' Anna, weep no longer.
Time will abate your sorrow.
Your husband and father I'll be.

Donna Anna

Gone! Forever! O where, O where is
he?

Don Ottavio

Weep no longer!
Time will abate your sorrow.
Both husband and father,
Both husband and father I'll be.
(Donna Anna stands with lofty
    demeanor opposite Don
    Ottavio.)

Donna Anna

Ah! Will you swear to avenge him?
Blood must for blood be poured.

Don Ottavio

(raising his hand as for taking an
    oath)
I swear it. I swear it.
By the eyes I love, I swear it.
I swear it on my sword.

A 2
Che giuramenti oh Dei!
Che barbaro momento!
Fra cento affanni e cento
Vammi ondeggiando il cor!
(Partono)

Donna Anna
Though cunning as the serpent
He fly from retribution,
Our righteous wrath shall find him,
Blood shall for blood be poured.
Blood for blood is calling.
Vengeance!
No ocean deep shall hide him
Nor subterranean cavern;
Our righteous wrath shall find him,
Death be his just reward,
At last his just reward.

Don Ottavio
Though cunning as the serpent
He fly from retribution,
Our righteous wrath shall find him,
Blood shall for blood be poured.
I swear it! By love I swear it. I swear
it on my sword.
No ocean deep shall hide him
Nor subterranean cavern,
Our righteous wrath shall find him,
Death be his just reward.
*(Exeunt slowly into palace. The
curtain falls rapidly.)*

Mozart develops the characters quickly.

This scene is about twelve minutes in length. During that brief span, five different characters, a soprano, a tenor, a baritone, and two bass voices are all introduced. Each is sharply drawn, unique. Leporello is a manservant who, it is clear, is accustomed to abuse and is afraid of his own shadow. The music that Mozart creates for him has a comic air. But to an attentive listener, it becomes clear that he is not a simple buffoon, but rather a bitter, cynical person who would surely turn on his master if only he could. He says, "I would like to play the master, would no more your servant be."

All facets of Don Giovanni's character are not exposed in this one scene, but it is obvious that he is ruthless and cruel.

Donna Anna's complicated personality begins to unravel in this opening scene. Though certainly in this first scene she appears to hate Don Giovanni, eventually there is some doubt as to her true feelings toward him. Some of her comments to her fiancé, the weakling, Don Ottavio, indicate some uncertainty about her love for him.

The musical forces are distributed so as to provide maximum variety:

Aria—bass
Recitatives
Trio—soprano, baritone, bass
Recitatives
Trio—baritone, two basses
Recitatives
Duet—soprano and tenor

Mozart's music provides diversity.

The story moves as briskly as the character development and music: an alleged rape, a fight, a murder, and a vow of vengeance are all packed into the short scene.

The story line holds the interest of the audience by moving quickly from incident to incident.

SUMMARY

The classical era was dominated by three powerful and distinctly different personalities: Haydn, Mozart, and the young Beethoven. It is principally from the works of these three composers that our perception of musical classicism is formed. At the root of this classicism is a sense of proportion and balance, a mastery of the developmental process, and the creation of large, organically solid edifices out of few musical raw materials. These large edifices took the shape of the symphony, the concerto, the string quartet, the piano sonata, and the opera.

The symphony of the classical era was in four movements, with each movement designed to perform a specific function and to carry a certain musical weight. Haydn's symphonies clearly reflect his evolution as a composer. His early works are in style galant, his next symphonies exemplify *Sturm und Drang* influence, and his compositions from the 1780s reveal him at his zenith as a classical symphonist.

Mozart composed his first symphony at an early age. He, like Haydn, began writing in three movements. Later, however, he fell under the influence of *Sturm und Drang,* and by the time he had reached his twenties was writing some of the most beautiful classical symphonies ever created. Beethoven, unlike the other two, never settled into the purely classical pattern. His symphonies exuded characteristics of the classical and romantic eras, but transcend them both.

The concerto emerged in the classical era, but had evolved from the baroque concerto grosso. The classical concerto featured one solo instrument to partake in the repetition of the exposition and to add improvisation. Beethoven, not stylistically confined to the classical era, composed concertos that deviated from the classical norm as standardized by Mozart.

The string quartet was the dominant form of chamber music in the classical era. It assumed its classical form in Haydn's hands, and was masterfully developed by Mozart and Beethoven.

Once the piano achieved prominence in the second half of the eighteenth century, the classical composers created a body of solo music to feature the instrument's qualities. The piano sonatas of Haydn evolved over time, revealing the stages of his musical development. Mozart's sonatas show a wide diversity of styles while Beethoven's piano sonatas transcend all stylistic labels.

The classical era witnessed the birth of a new type of opera. The popularity of the baroque opera seria declined in favor of a light, down-to-earth opera that had evolved from the intermezzo. The first comic operas included simple themes, spoken dialogue and ballads or popular songs. Later in the eighteenth century, Mozart and other classical composers reworked the comic opera to create credible drama and more sophisticated music. These composers created a middle ground between the extremes of opera seria and the early comic opera.

KEY TERMS

scherzo	cadenza
concerto	comic opera
double exposition	intermezzo

THINKING ABOUT IT

It is important to have a solid understanding of the major genres of the era. Using the text, your notes, and recorded examples, answer the following questions.

1. What is a symphony? What are some of the differences between a style galant symphony and Haydn's *Surprise* symphony?
2. What are the differences between the Bach *Brandenburg* Concerto no. 2 and the Mozart piano concerto discussed in this chapter?
3. What are the differences between Handel's Trio Sonata in F Major (see chapter 5) and the Mozart Piano Concerto no. 17, K. 453?
4. How is a dance suite different from a piano sonata?
5. Contrast the scene from Handel's opera *Alcina* (chapter 5) with the scene from Mozart's *Don Giovanni* discussed in this chapter.

8

MUSIC
IN THE
AGE OF
ROMANTICISM

Forest of Fountainbleu, Jean-Baptiste-Camille Corot

The National Gallery of Art, Chester Dale Collection, 1962

SOUNDS OF THE CHAPTER

Beethoven
Symphony no. 3
Symphony no. 5
Symphony no. 6 ♪
Symphony no. 9

Bellini
Norma

Berlioz
Roméo et Juliette ♪

Bizet
Carmen

Borodin
In the Steppes of Central Asia ♪

Brahms
Intermezzo, op. 118, no. 2 ♪
Symphony no. 2 ♪

Chopin
Étude, op. 10, no. 3
Étude, op. 10, no. 5 ♪
Polonaise in A♭ Major, op. 53 ♪
Preludes
Twenty-Four Preludes, op. 28

Donizetti
Lucia di Lammermoor

Dukas
L' Apprenti Sorcier (The Sorcerer's Apprentice)

Grieg
Piano Concerto in A Minor

Liszt
Années de Pèlerinage (Years of Pilgrimage)

MacDowell
Woodland Sketches

Mendelssohn
Fingal's Cave
Songs Without Words
Symphony no. 4, *Italian*
Violin Concerto in E Minor

Mozart
Symphony no. 40 ♪

Mussorgsky
Night on Bald Mountain
Boris Godunoff

Puccini
La Bohème

Rossini
Il barbiere di Siviglia (The Barber of Seville) ♪

Schubert
An die Musik
Die Schöne Müllerin (The Miller's Beautiful Daughter)
Die Erlkönig
Moments musicaux
Die Winterreise (The Winter's Journey)

Schumann
Kinderscenen
Papillons
Piano Concerto in A Minor ♪

Strauss
Also sprach Zarathustra
Till Eulenspiegels lustige Streiche (Till Eulenspiegel's Merry Pranks)

Tchaikovsky
Symphony no. 6

Verdi
Rigoletto

Wagner
Der fliegende Holländer (The Flying Dutchman)
Der Ring des Nibelungen
Lohengrin
Tristan und Isolde

"Romantic" is the stylistic label applied to the philosophy and the arts of the nineteenth century.

The term "romantic" had different connotations during the nineteenth century than it does in the twentieth. To us, the word romantic conjures visions of moonlight and soft music. But romantic is also the stylistic label applied to the arts and philosophy of the nineteenth century.

The nineteenth century artist had a strong personal relationship with nature. We can see this in the writing of those who shaped romantic philosophy, the canvases of the great nineteenth century landscape painters, the poetry, and the music of the nineteenth century romantics. These people were not content merely to observe nature. For them, there was a sort of mystical bond that existed between the earth and the soul. Self-discovery and inner peace resulted from this communion with nature.

Self-discovery and inner peace resulted from the nineteenth century artist's relationship with nature.

The following lines by Phillip Otto Runge exemplify this special relationship between artist and nature:

> When the sky above me abounds with countless stars, when the wind rushes through the wide space . . . when above the woods the sky turns red; the valley steams and I fling myself upon the grass under the glittering drops of dew, each leaf and each blade of grass teems with life, the earth lives and stirs beneath me, all resounds together in a single chord, then the soul jubilates aloud and soars into the boundless space around me, and there is no below and no above, no time, no beginning and no end. . . .

(Phillip Otto Runge, 9 March, 1802)

The mystery of nature is reflected in the artistic works of the nineteenth century.

The romantic also loved the mystery of nature. The darkness of the night or the dense, sun-forsaken forest where shapes and images are either invisible or blurred, were often integrated into the arts of the time. These environments unleashed the imagination and stimulated the creativity of the artist, sometimes producing works considered macabre or horrifying. The reading public of the nineteenth century, whose numbers had swelled with the spread of public education, devoured the literature of the romantics. Mystery stories (such as Mary Shelley's *Frankenstein*), novels set in faraway, exotic places, or historical tales (especially from the Middle Ages) were particular favorites.

The nineteenth century romantic studied the past.

The expansive spirit of the romantic was attracted to, and sometimes tortured by, the attempt to achieve the unattainable—to comprehend infinity. Some romantics sought to achieve this by searching into the past. In Germany, particularly, the nineteenth century was an age of historicism that mined the past in search of cultural roots. This search was beneficial in terms of the literature produced: the first German dictionaries were compiled, along with important collections of German folklore and tales, such as the tales compiled by the brothers Grimm.

This journey into the past could be interpreted as an attempted escape from the present. And the concurrent fascination with utopia and the infinite confirms this escapist theory. Indeed, the nineteenth century was a troubled and frightening time. The old rationalist order of the eighteenth century had begun to decay, and there were few reliable clues about what would replace it. It is understandable that people sought stability, even if this meant backtracking into the past or speculating about the future.

This situation, together with the romantics' interest in nature, resulted in the romantic notion that "There is no longer any above or below, no longer any beginning or end," but rather a continuity in which "Everything is in tune with everything." Let's now take a look at the music of the romantic era to see how this philosophy applies.

MUSIC: LANGUAGE OF THE SOUL

Music occupied a very important position in the romantic era. To the romantic, words were the language of the intellect, but music was the language of the soul. Painting provided the clearest vision of the exterior, but music provided the clearest vision of the interior—the world of emotions, the heart, and the soul. The intangible, invisible nature of music made it the most expressive of the arts, and its awesome power intoxicated the romantic mind. The romantics believed that words somehow limited experiences, but music had the power to break the shackles of these limitations and to free the imagination and emotions to realize an experience completely. Whereas painting and poetry were descriptions of an experience, music and the experience were nearly one and the same thing.

Integration of Music with the Other Arts

Even some romantic poets recognized this critical difference and suggested that all the arts should "aspire to the mysterious condition of music." Several romantic composers, however, did not restrict themselves to music, but undertook literary endeavors as well. Schumann, Berlioz, Mendelssohn, and Wagner were authors as well as composers. Schubert, Brahms, and others created a vast repertoire of solo songs because of their personal fascination with words. So although music was the most appropriate romantic vehicle, the other arts were also attractive to the composers, and helped to define or enhance their work.

An urge to blend the arts was a natural outgrowth of this situation. Program music, discussed in chapter 4, reached an unsurpassed level in the romantic age as a result of this movement to synthesize the arts. (As

The romantic period was one touched by escapism.

The people of the romantic era sought stability.

Romanticism influenced all of the arts.

Music was the best means for expressing the soul of romanticism.

Music was the most expressive of the arts in the romantic era.

Several romantic composers wrote literature also.

A movement to synthesize the arts arose in the nineteenth century. Mendelssohn attempted this type of synthesis in *Fingal's Cave.*

you recall, words were provided with the music to ensure full audience appreciation of the work.) Remember, too, that Mendelssohn was displeased with his composition, *Fingal's Cave,* because it had too much counterpoint (a strictly musical phenomenon) and too little of the smell of salted cod and whale blubber (things that can be perceived through visual images and words). To him, the desired synthesis of the sonorous, the visual, and the verbal arts failed to materialize in this piece.

The nineteenth century was an age of extremes and paradoxes. No experience was too small or too subtle to escape the attention of the romantic artist, nor was any so vast that the artist feared trying to express it. Thus, the nineteenth century composer created on the one hand, the art of the miniature, like the piano preludes of Chopin, some of which last less than a minute, and the brief *Moments Musicaux (Musical Moments)* of Schubert. Yet, the nineteenth century was also the age of gigantic works when some symphonies were four or five times the length of their classical counterparts. In fact, some of Wagner's music dramas lasted nearly six hours!

Romantic composers created musical pieces of various lengths.

THE COMPOSERS

Many of the works performed by modern symphony orchestras, chamber ensembles, opera companies and solo recitalists are products of the nineteenth century. In fact, art music audiences of today listen to far more music composed during the nineteenth century than from any other time period. Nineteenth century music is not necessarily superior; rather, sociological, practical, and even political concerns endowed it with a popularity unexceeded in these other musical periods.

Much of the art music we hear today was created during the nineteenth century.

Nineteenth century artists were believed to possess a greater depth of feeling than ordinary mortals, and presumably their ability to express their thoughts and ideas was somehow inspired. For this reason, the composer and the virtuoso performer were regarded as wizards or prophets. They were heroes in an age that sought heroes. A great wealth of music issued from the romantic age and many of these revered composers—some of the highest artistic genius, as well as some with more modest talent—contributed to this musical treasure chest. A list of some of the most prominent composers of the nineteenth century follows. Good, informative biographies of most of these composers are available, so they are discussed here as a group. Biographical details are provided only if they affected the musical examples discussed here.

Composers and performers were considered heroes of the romantic era.

Hector Berlioz (1803–69) French
Georges Bizet (1838–75) French
Alexander Borodin (1834–87) Russian
Johannes Brahms (1833–97) German
Frédéric Chopin (1810–49) Polish
César Franck (1822–90) Belgian
Edvard Grieg (1843–1907) Norwegian
Franz Liszt (1811–86) Hungarian
Edward MacDowell (1861–1908) American
Gustav Mahler (1860–1911) Austrian
Felix Mendelssohn (1809–47) German
Modest Mussorgsky (1835–81) Russian
Giacomo Puccini (1858–1924) Italian
Sergei Rachmaninoff (1873–1943) Russian
Gioacchino Rossini (1792–1868) Italian
Franz Schubert (1797–1828) Austrian
Robert Schumann (1810–56) German
Richard Strauss (1864–1949) German
Peter Tchaikovsky (1840–93) Russian
Giuseppe Verdi (1813–1901) Italian
Richard Wagner (1813–83) German

How many of these names do you recognize?

This extraordinary group of composers brought to nineteenth century romanticism a diversity of cultural backgrounds, temperaments, and artistic creeds. Some, like Chopin, Liszt, Mendelssohn, and Rachmaninoff, were virtuoso performers in addition to being composers. Others, like Berlioz, never mastered a musical instrument, though he was and still is regarded as a master orchestrator. It was mentioned earlier that some romantic composers were active in literature or journalism fields; others, Schubert, for instance, found verbal expression difficult, yet he is among the most significant and prolific song composers of the romantic era.

Verdi and Wagner were primarily opera composers; Chopin wrote almost exclusively for the piano. Borodin and Mussorgsky added the flavor of the exotic East to the pool of nineteenth century music. Rossini continued the Italian tradition of bel canto singing in his operas; Brahms and Franck, each in his own way, continued and expanded the contrapuntal traditions of northern Europe. Tchaikovsky's lovely and personal harmonic language stayed within the bounds of functional harmony; Liszt, Wagner, and Mahler composed works that almost entered the realm of keyless music.

The Romantic composers had diverse backgrounds and talents.

Each composer developed his own specialty.

Hector Berlioz (1803–69)

Johannes Brahms (1833–97)

Frédéric Chopin (1810–49)

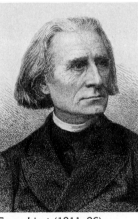

Franz Liszt (1811–86)

Felix Mendelssohn (1809–47)

Franz Schubert (1797–1828)

Robert Schumann (1810–56)

Giuseppe Verdi (1813–1901)

Richard Wagner (1813–83)

Many of these composers knew each other or knew each other's music. Schumann actively supported the music of young composers, particularly Brahms, about whom he said in print, "Hat's off, gentlemen, a genius." Liszt supported, conducted, and to some extent funded, performances of Wagner's music. Schumann and Brahms were close personal friends but Wagner and Brahms, largely due to Wagner's temperament, were bitter enemies.

Several of these contemporaries knew of each other's works.

The accomplishments of some of these composers are even more incredible considering their tragically short lives. Chopin died of consumption at the age of thirty-nine; Mendelssohn, whose life was otherwise happy and comfortable, died of exhaustion at thirty-eight; Mussorgsky died of alcoholism at forty-six; Schubert died of venereal disease at only thirty-one; and Schumann died in an insane asylum at forty-six.

Many romantic composers died at an early age.

THE SYMPHONY IN THE NINETEENTH CENTURY

A singular symphonic ideal did not exist after Beethoven began working with the form. Instead, there were several different symphonic ideals. For example, Beethoven's Symphony no. 5 demonstrated that the Viennese developmental approach was still a viable and powerful symphonic ideal. On the other hand, the *Eroica* symphony demonstrated that this same ideal could be broadened to include a philosophical program laden with symbolism. Symphony no. 6 *(Pastoral)* created a new symphonic ideal, one of whose bases was descriptive program music. The final movement of Beethoven's last symphony, Symphony no. 9, has extensive parts for vocal soloists and chorus with lines from Friedrich Schiller's *Ode to Joy.* Thus, the choral symphony was established as yet another symphonic ideal. All of the great nineteenth century symphonists employed one or another of these symphonic ideals as a point of departure for individual experimentation. Some of those ideals and the composers' interpretation thereof are examined here.

Many different symphonic ideals existed.

Classical Orientation

Mendelssohn's Symphony no. 4 (subtitled *Italian*), composed from 1831–33, exemplifies the nineteenth century symphony that is modeled on the classical symphony perfected by Haydn, Mozart, and Beethoven. Mendelssohn created the colorful harmonic language of *Italian,* but the general shape of the symphony, the developmental process, and the manipulation of simple, effective thematic materials are rooted in classicism. The *Italian* symphony has the standard classical four movements: fast-slow-minuet-fast.

Mendelssohn's *Italian* symphony is rooted in classicism.

SOUND AND SENSE: *Nineteenth Century Symphony*

Title: Symphony no. 4, *Italian*

Composer: Mendelssohn

A Closer Look:

The first movement is in sonata-allegro form and 6/8 meter. The principal thematic materials, arresting in and of themselves, are derived from manipulations of the long (♩) and short (♪) note values of 6/8 meter as illustrated in figure 8.1. This simple, yet ingenious, manipulation of minimal materials are indicative of Mendelssohn's classical orientation.

Notice in this symphony that the orchestra is moderately sized and that the texture is generally light and airy, much like Mozart's. The development section is extensive and features a fugal section, after which activity quiets down. The onset of the recapitulation is extremely rapid, and this is succeeded by a lengthy coda.

The quiet second movement (andante), diagramed here, is in ternary form, and, like the first movement, prominently features clarinets and oboes.

A	*B*	*A*
aabba	cd	a'b'da-coda

The third movement is not, strictly speaking, a minuet, but its character and personality are closer to a minuet than to a scherzo. It has the form: *A* (minuetlike), *B* (trio, featuring French horns), *A'*, and then a partial repetition of *B* that serves as a coda.

Mendelssohn has been called the "romantic classicist," meaning that his classical background, training, and general disposition are those of an eighteenth century classicist. But this classicism was fanned by the flames of nineteenth century romanticism. His romantic inclinations are evident in the last movement of the *Italian* symphony. In that movement, the drama and fire of romanticism are evident. Although the main key of the symphony is A major, Mendelssohn switched to the darker minor mode, ending in the key of A minor for this movement. The last movement is a saltarello—a sixteenth century Italian dance.

Fig. 8.1

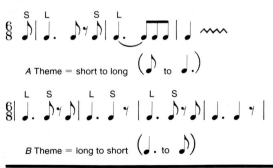

Brahms and classicism The structural and developmental principles of the classical symphony were continued and greatly expanded later in the nineteenth century by Johannes Brahms. Early in his career, Brahms was considered a radical composer, but when he tempered that radicalism and unleashed the power of his innate classicism, he found his true personality as a composer. This, however, did not occur until later in Brahms's musical career.

In awe of Beethoven's symphonies, Brahms was reluctant to try his own hand at composing one. Indeed, he waited until he was forty-three years old to write the first of his four symphonies.

Brahms's classical orientation is not immediately apparent in his symphonies. His music sounds far too full to be termed such. In fact, Brahms's harmonic language is more exotic than Mendelssohn's, and is even laced with painful dissonances. But these dissonances assume a softer quality with repeated listening. This harmonic language has been described as "autumnal."

In contrast to Mendelssohn's work, Brahms's textures are very dense and an inner part is always in motion. Mendelssohn's airy orchestral textures are reminiscent of Haydn and Mozart, but the density of Brahms's textures could not be mistaken for those of Haydn and Mozart. Mendelssohn's *Italian* symphony is about the same length as a late Haydn symphony; the symphonies of Brahms are about twice that length.

Once we see beyond the lush harmonic language, the dense textures, and the great length of Brahms's symphonies, we see a composer who is a master of the sonata form, counterpoint, and the developmental process. And like Haydn (and Mendelssohn), Brahms created organic themes out of small units of material. Ultimately, Brahms is considered a thoroughly romantic composer who mastered and adhered to classical principles of structure and organization. His Symphony no. 2 serves to illuminate this.

Brahms composed symphonies in the classical style.

Brahms's harmonic language has been described as "autumnal."

Brahms's symphonies show a dense texture.

Brahms was a romantic composer who had mastered classical structure and organization.

♪ SOUND AND SENSE: *Romantic Symphony*

Title: Symphony no. 2

Composer: Brahms

A Closer Look:

Symphony no. 2 has four movements: fast-slow-dance-fast. The first movement is cast in a very large, but clear-cut, sonata form. In this movement, and in fact, in Brahms's sonata forms in general, not one *A* theme and *B* theme are found in the exposition, but rather several themes under *A* and several under *B*. These themes form theme groups: the *A* theme group and the *B* theme group.

Before proceeding to a diagram of the movement, look at the *A* theme group of this movement. Notice in figure 8.2 that each of the themes evolves from an initial

Fig. 8.2

descending half step (marked by brackets); this is the seed from which these themes grow in organic fashion. The themes are unique but are obviously very closely related to one another.

Exposition

A Theme Group

a1	bridge	a2	a3	bridge
French horns	trombones	high violins, then woodwinds	woodwinds	
b1	b1	b2	b3	b1
cellos	woodwinds	dotted rhythm loud (ff)	low strings syncopated accompaniment	strings

(Brahms indicates that the exposition is repeated. Some recordings, however, do not honor this repeat, but go instead directly to the development section.)

Development

An extended fugal section is followed by a brief section filled with sharp dissonance that is played by the low brass.

Recapitulation

The recapitulation closely follows the order of events in the exposition. The movement then concludes with a lengthy coda based mostly on theme *a1*.

The second movement (adagio) is cast in a large song form—*ABA*—and demonstrates Brahms's considerable skill with counterpoint.

The third movement has the shape that was favored by several late nineteenth century symphonists: *A* (scherzo)-*B* (trio)-*A'* (scherzo)-*B'* (trio) *A''* (scherzo). This constitutes an elongation of the usual scherzo-trio-scherzo plan of the earlier nineteenth century.

The last movement is the fastest of the four. It is in sonata-allegro form and features an *A* theme that has a folklike quality.

Program Symphony

Pathétique   Tchaikovsky's Symphony no. 6 *(Pathétique)* is different from Brahms's Symphony no. 2 in both conception and result. Though it is a symphony and has four movements, *Pathétique* otherwise has little connection with the classical symphony model.

In February of 1893, Tchaikovsky wrote to his nephew, saying:

> On the way to Paris last December the idea for a new symphony came to me, this time a symphony with a program, but a program that will remain an enigma to all. Let them guess for themselves; the symphony will be called merely 'Programmatic Symphony' [6]. But the program is indeed permeated with subjectiveness, so much so that not once but often, while composing it in my mind during my journey, I shed tears.

It is clear from the music itself as well as from these words, that this is not a descriptive program symphony. Rather, the program is philosophical or subjective in character. The subtitle, *Pathétique,* does not mean pathetic, but is translated as pathos, the Greek term for suffering. Tchaikovsky was a man haunted by self-doubt and given to self-pity. The subtitle, as well as Tchaikovsky's personal problems, may be a clue to the meaning of the program.

Pathétique begins with a slow, moody introduction, in which the bassoon is the principal voice. The introduction moves immediately to the first movement proper: allegro and sonata form. An *A* theme is introduced in the exposition, after which a bridge leads to a change of tempo (andante) and to the *B* theme. Oddly, the *B* theme is so compelling and is repeated so often in the course of this movement that it completely overshadows the *A* theme. It is as if Tchaikovsky wanted to save the best theme for last. This is not a classical procedure, and there is something even more unclassical about this sonata form. There is a so-called development section, but there is no real development in *Pathétique.* There are merely repetitions, primarily of the lovely *B* theme.

The developmental process lies at the foundation of the classical or the classically oriented symphony. Haydn, Mozart, and Beethoven, as well as Mendelssohn and Brahms, created themes that were capable of being developed for their symphonies. Such themes became even more fascinating and multidimensional as they were developed. In a sense, these themes acquired their full personalities and potential only after being developed. This is true of theme *A* of the first movement of Mozart's Symphony no. 40, and also of the *A* theme (first movement) of the *Eroica* symphony.

Tchaikovsky's Symphony no. 6 does not resemble a classical symphony.

In *Pathétique* the *B* theme overshadows the *A* theme.

Liberty Leading the People by
Frederick Eugene Delacroix—a
heroic theme.

**The dominant theme in
Pathétique needs no
development.**

This is not the case, though, with the dominant theme (the *B* theme) of the first movement of Tchaikovsky's *Pathétique.* It is a theme so complete and self-contained that it requires no development; in fact, any conceivable development of it would detract from, rather than add to, its personality and potential. It is a melody that would suffer a great loss if it were dissected or forced to compete with a countermelody in a contrapuntal environment. The ⅄ ♪♪♪ | ♩ | , which dominates the first movement of Beethoven's Symphony no. 5, was made for and purposely designed for development. It has been suggested that this is a kind of musical seed whose flowering is achieved only through development. In contrast, Tchaikovsky's theme is already a flower. Since Tchaikovsky started with a flower rather than a seed, there was neither the necessity for nor even the possibility of a germinating (developmental) process. Continuing along this line, we might think of a classical theme and its development as a phenomenon in a state of becoming, whereas Tchaikovsky's theme is in a state of being.

**The tempo, meter, and form
in the second movement of
Pathétique depart from the
classical model.**

Tchaikovsky further departs from classical models by using an allegro rather than a slow tempo in the second movement of *Pathétique.* The movement is in the rare 5/4 meter throughout, and is cast in a large song form *(ABA)*. It is dominated by two full-blown themes, and contains virtually no counterpoint.

The third movement begins with scherzolike material (though it is not in 3/4). This leads to a much longer section that is dominated by a loud and forceful march theme. (As in the first movement, the second theme dominates.) The scherzolike material returns briefly, but is then completely overshadowed by the march for the remainder of the movement.

The last movement is slow (adagio). This represents yet another departure from a classical model. This movement has an *ABA* form with coda. Both the *A* and *B* themes have an air of tragedy about them. Since they are the concluding statements of the symphony, they may perhaps be clues to the overriding quality of Tchaikovsky's unspoken program.

The third movement of *Pathétique* is dominated by a march theme.

Choral/Dramatic Symphony

A number of nineteenth century composers emulated Beethoven in his ninth Symphony and incorporated the human voice into the once instrumental symphony. In doing so, they broke with classical tradition and transformed the symphony into a romantic phenomenon—the **choral** or **dramatic symphony.**

Some Romantic composers followed Beethoven's lead in creating choral symphonies.

Roméo et Juliette   Hector Berlioz's profound interest in Shakespeare and literature in general undoubtedly affected the creation of *Roméo et Juliette* (Romeo and Juliet) (1839). The work is scored for a large symphony orchestra plus chorus and vocal soloists, and has the following formal divisions:

Berlioz composed a symphony based upon Shakespeare's *Romeo and Juliet.*

Part 1
1. Introduction: Tumult and strife; the Prince intervenes (orchestra).
2. Prologue: Three sections for chorus and vocal soloists with orchestral accompaniment.

Part 2
1. Romeo alone; his sadness (orchestra).
   Concert and ball; fete at the Capulets (orchestra).
2. Calm night; the young Capulets, as they leave, sing recollections of the ball music (chorus with orchestra).
3. Love scene between Romeo and Juliet (the orchestra).
4. Queen Mab or the Dream Sprite (orchestra, scherzo).

Part 3
1. Funeral march for Juliet (chorus and orchestra).
2. Romeo at the tomb of the Capulets (orchestra).
3. Finale (bass solo, two choruses, and orchestra).

Berlioz abandoned the classical four-movement plan.

Obviously, the basic classical four-movement plan, fast-slow-dance-fast, is discarded in favor of three large parts that contain various subparts. A drama is presented here, told in part by words and voices, and in part by the wordless orchestra. The work is long and complicated, but some idea of how these various forces work together is gained by examining Part 2. (Time permitting, you should listen to the work in its entirety, from start to finish.)

In Part 2, no. 1, Romeo is alone with his thoughts: thoughts that are reflected in the orchestra's music. Eventually the tempo quickens and ballroom music begins to intrude and then to dominate the scene. This leads to no. 2, where the chorus sings strains of the dance music as they disappear into the late night. The chorus sings:

Ohé! Capulets—bonsoir, bonsoir!	Ho ho! Capulets, good-night all!
Cavaliers, au revoir!	Gentlemen, farewell!
Ah! Quelle nuit, quel festin!	Ah! what a night, and what
Bal divin!	A glorious ball!
Que de folles paroles!	What mad, enchanting talk!
Belles Véronnaises	Oh, girls of Verona,
Sous les grands mélèzes,	Can't you go now and dream of love
Allez rêver de bal et d'amour,	Under the evergreens till dawn?
Allez rêver d'amour	Go dream of love
Jusqu'au jour!	Til dawn,
Tra la, la la la la, la le ra la!	Tra-la, la la la la . . .

The famous love scene between Romeo and Juliet then follows (Part 2, no. 3). Significantly, Berlioz directs the orchestra to recount this part of the story. Although the words between Romeo and Juliet in this scene are among the most famous in the English language, Berlioz relies upon the power of the wordless orchestra to convey the meaning. A cello is prominently featured in an impassioned solo, answered by a flute—the voices of Romeo (cello) and Juliet (flute). Toward the end of this section there is some activity involving cello and flute that suggests the excitement of heartbeats. The section then ends very quietly.

Berlioz chose a cello and a flute to represent the voices of Romeo and Juliet in the love scene.

Queen Mab is depicted by the orchestra in Part 2, no. 4. Berlioz described this section to his friend, the poet, Heinrich Heine:

. . . Queen Mab in her microscopic car, attended by the buzzing insects of a summer's night and launched at full gallop by her tiny horses, fully displayed to the Brunswick public her lovely drollery and her thousand caprices. . . . You, the poet of fairies and elves . . . know only too well with what slender thread their veil of gauze is woven, and how serene must be the sky beneath which their many-colored tints sport freely in the pale starlight.

Part 2, no. 4 has the form scherzo-trio-scherzo, so structurally, it is not too far removed from Beethoven's model. The orchestration is quiet and dazzling throughout. The close resemblance that exists between the music and Berlioz's programmatic basis is strikingly apparent when listening to the movement.

TONE POEM

The **tone poem** (or symphonic poem) was the special contribution to the field of orchestral music by some nineteenth century composers. The juxtaposition of the words "tone" and "poem" suggests once again the romantic's desire to synthesize the arts. The tone poem is usually a one-movement piece for orchestra, and is usually programmatic.

> **The tone poem resulted from the romantic composers' attempt to synthesize the arts.**

There is no set form or length for a tone poem. Some are cast in a loose sonata form, and many are cast in "homemade" forms (forms that are freshly invented by the composer to accommodate the program behind the tone poem). Some tone poems are only about eight minutes in length, while others last an hour or more.

Franz Liszt is generally credited with the invention of the tone poem in the 1840s, but many other composers in the nineteenth and twentieth centuries were attracted to the genre. Two tone poems, one by the Russian composer, Borodin, and one by Richard Strauss, are examined in this section. These provide a good idea of how a tone poem functions.

> **Liszt is usually credited with the invention of the tone poem.**

♪ SOUND AND SENSE: *Tone Poem*

Title: *In the Steppes of Central Asia*

Composer: Borodin

A Closer Look:

Borodin provided the following program for this haunting tone poem.

> Out of the silence of the sandy steppes of Central Asia come the sounds of a peaceful Russian song. Along with them are heard the melancholy strains of Oriental melodies, then the stamping of approaching horses and camels. A caravan, accompanied by Russian soldiers, traverses the measureless waste. With full trust in its protective escort, it continues on its long journey in a carefree mood. Onward the caravan moves. The Songs of the Russians and those of the Asiatic natives mingle in common harmony. The refrains curl over the desert and then die away in the distance.

The musical structure of this tone poem is simplicity itself; it is one of the homemade forms mentioned earlier. Two themes, *A* (introduced by a clarinet) and *B* (introduced by an English horn), are presented. These themes recur and eventually are combined contrapuntally. In the background cellos and violas perform a plucking figure suggestive of footsteps. Here is a graphic illustration of the order and content of this work after a brief, mysterious-sounding introduction played by high strings and flute:

A—clarinet, answered by French horn
Footsteps—low strings
B—English horn
A—clarinet, answered by French horn
A—full orchestra
Footsteps
B—English horn and cellos
B—violins answered by violas and cellos
A & B—combined contrapuntally; *A*-oboe, *B*-violins
A & B—combined contrapuntally; full orchestra
A—fragmented in French horn, clarinet, English horn, oboe
A—solo flute

Curtain of Trees by Millet—a romantic attachment to nature

The Louvre

Richard Strauss' *Till Eulenspiegels lustige Streiche (Till Eulenspiegel's Merry Pranks)* (1894) is another example of a tone poem.

Till Eulenspiegel is a legendary character of the fourteenth century who delighted in playing devilish practical jokes. Strauss's imaginative orchestration brings Till to life and carries the audience through four of his escapades until he is apprehended by an angry mob, taken to court, sentenced, and hanged. Till is identified throughout by two musical motifs called **leitmotifs.** A leitmotif is a brief musical gesture which is associated with a character or an object in a tone poem or other dramatic musical form. A leitmotif may consist of a short strand of melody or even a single sonority.

The first leitmotif is played by a French horn and traverses a wide range; the second leitmotif is played by a clarinet. The two motifs show us both the irksome and ornery sides of Till's personality.

Richard Strauss used leitmotifs to characterize the personality of Till Eulenspiegel.

SOUND AND SENSE: *Tone Poem*

Title: *Till Eulenspiegels lustige Streiche*

Composer: Richard Strauss

A Closer Look:

The tone poem begins gently—like the unfolding of events in a novel. It's as if a grandfather were slipping into a comfortable chair to read a story to a child. Several statements of leitmotif no. 1 follow. After a climax and a pause, leitmotif no. 2 is introduced.

Here the story begins. Till takes off on horseback and rides recklessly through a marketplace, knocking over tables and wares. But before anyone can catch and punish him for his mischief, he rides away. He then imitates a priest delivering a mock-serious sermon, rips off his disguise and vanishes, once more, leaving a bewildered congregation behind. Next he makes advances on a young country maiden (a solo violin sings an amorous song that concludes with a long descending slide). Once more he disappears. He converses with a group of stuffy professors (imitated by honking bassoons). When he has had enough of their company, Till sticks out his tongue at them and rides away, singing a playful ditty. Finally he is apprehended. After the hanging, the gentle atmosphere of the beginning returns. However, the spirit of Till returns to haunt the crowd as heard in leitmotif no. 1. The piece ends on a happy note—Till Eulenspiegel in the end is triumphant.

The information presented here will be useful in following the events of *Till Eulenspiegels lustige Streiche*. Notice that *A* (or variants of *A*) recurs several times in the course of the piece, giving the work a loose rondo structure.

Introduction

A—Till appears: leitmotif no. 1, French horn; leitmotif no. 2, clarinet.

B—Till rides off on horseback and upsets the marketplace.

A'—Leitmotif no. 2: Till departs after a sneer; quick note values on woodwinds.

C—Till, disguised as a priest, delivers a mock-serious sermon; low strings, then flute, then violins carry the thematic material of this brief section. At the end, Till rips off his disguise; full orchestra.

A''—Leitmotif no. 2: Till departs after scorning the congregation.
D—The romance: violins play a simple theme, and a little later horns and trumpets imitate the fluttering of his heart; section concludes with the long violin slide.
A'''—Leitmotif no. 2: Till departs once more.
E—The stuffy professors are imitated by squawking bassoons. Till sticks out his tongue (nasty-sounding trill by woodwinds) and leaves, singing a playful, folklike tune.
A—Leitmotif no. 1, French horn.
F—Till is apprehended and sentenced to hang: drum rolls and low brass. Till, with the noose around his neck, twice mocks the crowd: leitmotif no. 2.
Till's death squeal: mutilated version of leitmotif no. 2. Return to the mood and substance of the introduction. Boisterous conclusion.

Nineteenth century tone poems vary in length and nature.

The nineteenth century bequeathed a rich body of orchestral tone poems. Some of these are long and serious in nature, such as Strauss' *Also sprach Zarathustra (Thus Spake Zarathustra)*, the dramatic opening of which was used as the soundtrack for the movie *Planet of the Apes.* Other tone poems are more playful and entertaining, like Paul Dukas's *L'Apprenti Sorcier (The Sorcerer's Apprentice)* and Mussorgsky's *Night on Bald Mountain.*

SOLO MUSIC FOR THE PIANO

The piano was an important instrument in the nineteenth century.

Nineteenth century advances in piano construction and quality vested in the instrument thunderous power and also enabled it to play the subtlest and most delicate nuances. The piano became an instrument for both virtuosos and amateurs—for the large concert hall and the intimate drawing room. And it was useful in churches, schools, and social clubs.

Romantic composers were attracted to the piano's versatility and expressive power.

Because of its versatility and expressive power, the piano was the romantic instrument par excellence. The instrument was also a positive factor in the economic climate of the nineteenth century. In London, Vienna, and elsewhere in Europe, piano factories were established that employed craftsmen and laborers in significant numbers. As the demand for tutoring of amateurs increased, more teachers joined the work force. The music publishing industry also benefited from the increased interest in the piano, since instruction books for the amateur pianist were in demand.

Because of this fascination with the piano, a demand for piano music of a high quality arose. Composers such as Chopin, Liszt, Schumann, and many others fulfilled this need.

In the nineteenth century the formal solo piano recital became an institution.

Each of these changes contributed to the nineteenth century establishment of the formal solo piano recital as an institution.

Liszt at the piano with friends: Mussot, Victor Hugo, George Sand, Berlioz, Rossini, and Countess D'Agoult.

Piano Sonata

Two major branches of nineteenth century solo piano music developed: the **sonata** and the character piece. Several of the era's major composers wrote piano sonatas, such giants as Schubert, Chopin, Liszt, and Brahms. The piano sonatas were generally long and complex pieces in two, three, or four movements, and were technically very demanding.

Piano sonatas of the nineteenth century are generally long, complex, and technically demanding.

Character Piece

The other branch of solo piano music, the **character piece,** embraces a much wider variety of music. The typical character piece is shorter and less complicated than the piano sonata. Often, character pieces were published in groups or collections, and frequently had fanciful and programmatic titles. Schubert's *Moments musicaux,* Chopin's Polonaises and Preludes, Brahm's Intermezzos, Mendelssohn's *Songs Without Words,* and Schumann's *Kinderscenen (Scenes From Childhood)* and *Papillons* are all collections of character pieces.

Character pieces are shorter and less complicated than piano sonatas.

There is no set length or structure for a character piece.

There is no prescribed length for a character piece. Chopin's Ballades last from eight to ten minutes, while seven of his Twenty-Four Preludes last less than a minute each. There is also no definite formal structure for a character piece, though the great majority are cast in straightforward two- or three-part forms. The emotional content of these nineteenth century character pieces ranges from stormy and dramatic, to quiet and introspective, to playful. These character-piece traits are especially evident in the following works by Chopin, Liszt, MacDowell, and Brahms.

Character pieces vary greatly in mood.

Chopin conveys an emotional message in each of his preludes.

Prelude Chopin composed the Twenty-four **Preludes,** op. 28 during the years 1836–39. These short pieces traverse a wide emotional range and most successfully deliver the emotional message in a very limited span of time. Prelude no. 1 in C Major consists of little more than two phrases, that together last only about forty-five seconds. And yet, despite its brevity, the prelude is a complete and satisfying musical experience. Notice, then, the contrasting qualities of the following preludes: Prelude no. 4 in E Minor (brooding), Prelude no. 7 in A Major (simple and delicate), Prelude no. 20 in C Minor (solemn and majestic), and Prelude no. 21 in B♭ Major (lyrical with a touch of drama near the end).

Chopin turned the Polish polonaise dance into an important type of piano music.

Polonaise Chopin also reshaped the **polonaise,** a dance of Polish origin, into an elegant and important musical phenomenon. His eleven polonaises were fashioned as character pieces but on a larger scale than his preludes. They are longer and more structurally involved, and employ internal contrasts of theme and mood. Polonaise in A♭ Major (sometimes called *Heroic*) is an excellent introduction to the genre. It is cast in a large multi-sectional form with the following subdivisions.

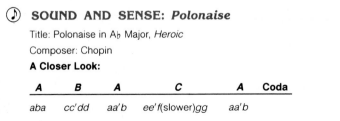

♪ **SOUND AND SENSE:** *Polonaise*

Title: Polonaise in A♭ Major, *Heroic*
Composer: Chopin
A Closer Look:

A	*B*	*A*	*C*	*A*	Coda
aba	*cc'dd*	*aa'b*	*ee'f*(slower)*gg*	*aa'b*	

Étude   The **étude** (study) was another type of character piece developed by Chopin and Liszt. As well as being superior music, each of the Chopin etudes presents a specific technical problem for the pianist. The pianist encounters many such problems in his or her effort to master the instrument—difficulties in playing **legato** (smoothly) or **staccato** (playing the notes crisply), in playing extended passages of octaves in the right or left hand, or in moving rapidly from one part of the keyboard to another.

An étude is a type of character piece written for piano.

♪ SOUND AND SENSE: *Études*

Title: Twelve Études, op. 10

Composer: Chopin

A Closer Look:

Chopin said the following about his Twelve Études, op. 10.

> In writing my études I tried to put not only science but also art into them. Since a virtuoso must practice for a long time, he should be given exercises in which he will find proper food for his ears and his soul lest he be bored to death. I am disturbed because there are no beautiful exercises for beginners. A virtuoso has everything open to him; when he is bored by exercises, he can reach out for the most beautiful music. But a poor fellow who cannot play anything except exercises, whose fingers are as though tied, needs beautiful exercises that will save him from becoming disgusted with music. I have tried to write something of this kind, but I haven't been successful, because for the beginner anything is too difficult.

The Étude, op. 10, no. 3 in E Major is a simple three-part form that is diagramed: *AABA*.

Étude, op. 10, no. 5 in G♭ Major *(Black Key Etude)* addresses the problem of playing octaves rapidly in the right hand. Its form is: *ABCA*-coda.

Franz Liszt wrote a vast number of character pieces, including three sets of works called *Années de Pèlerinage (Years of Pilgrimage)*. These character pieces are more explicitly programmatic than those by Chopin. Two pieces from the first set are descriptive of water: "Au lac de Wallenstadt" ("By the lake of Wallenstadt"), and "Au bord d'une source" ("By the side of a spring"). In both of these short pieces, Liszt magically captures the rippling effect of water: a dreamy atmosphere for "Wallenstadt" and a playful atmosphere for "By the side of a spring." The form of Wallenstadt is a simple *ABA'*-coda with a rippling figure in the accompaniment throughout the piece. The form of "By the side of a spring" is *A*-bridge-*A'*-bridge-*A''*-bridge-*A'''*-coda, a theme with variations.

Liszt's character pieces are more explicitly programmatic than Chopin's.

Schumann's *Kinderscenen* capture the spirit of childhood.

Among the best known sets of character pieces is Robert Schumann's *Kinderscenen (Scenes From Childhood).* Schumann originally composed more than two dozen of these pieces, but selected only twelve of them to make up this set. Each of these twelve has a brief descriptive title. Schumann did not intend the *Kinderscenen* for virtuoso pianists, but neither are they for children. The pieces are touching because Schumann has captured the spirit, the innocence, and joy of childhood, not because they detail childish behavior.

It is said of Schumann that he carried something of his childhood with him throughout his life. As we grow into adulthood most of us tend to forget the special joy and wonder of childhood. It is left to an artist such as Schumann to help us remember. That is the real accomplishment of the *Kinderscenen.*

"Traumerei" ("Dreaming"), no. 7 in the set, has sometimes been distorted through overly sentimental arrangements. Nevertheless, in the context of this collection of pieces, it loses none of its appeal when played well.

Listen now to *Kinderscenen.* The pieces are short and should not present any problems.

The American MacDowell composed character pieces focusing on nature.

The American composer Edward MacDowell (1861–1908) was also active in the production of character pieces for the piano. Best known among MacDowell's short character pieces for piano is a set of descriptive nature pieces called *Woodland Sketches.*

♪ SOUND AND SENSE: *Character Pieces*

Title: Intermezzo, op. 118, no. 2

Composer: Brahms

A Closer Look:

Brahms composed many works in the vein of characteristic pieces, though his are not overtly programmatic nor do they bear descriptive titles. The Intermezzo, op. 118, no. 2 (composed 1892–93) is an excellent example of Brahms's lyrical, moody, and contrapuntal style of characteristic piece. It is diagramed as follows:

A	*B*	*A*
aabc	*ddee'*	*a'bc*

THE CONCERTO

Concertos were created during the nineteenth century in response to the public's enchantment with virtuoso pianists. The compositions provided the opportunity for the experts to display their extraordinary talents. Chopin, Liszt, Rachmaninoff, and other composer-pianists often performed their own concertos in public. Mendelssohn, Brahms, Tchaikovsky, and Grieg contributed piano and violin concertos for other virtuosos to perform. The nineteenth century also produced important concertos for viola, cello, clarinet, and other solo instruments, but the greatest and most numerous concertos were written either for piano and orchestra or for violin and orchestra. Of these, the important piano concertos outnumber those for violin. Two piano concertos and one violin concerto are examined here.

Piano concertos were composed for performance by virtuoso pianists.

Concertos were written for piano, violin, viola, cello, clarinet and other solo instruments.

Piano Concerto

Schumann was, in some aspects, the most romantic composer, and among the most tragic figures of the nineteenth century. In addition to his musical gifts, he had a genuine flair for literature and poetry, and as a youth was trained in the legal profession. This variety of interests, each holding an equal attraction, and thus demanding an equal commitment, created mental stress which led to self-abuse. In his zeal and dedication to become a concert pianist, Schumann fashioned a leather device to stretch the reach of his fingers. The device left one of his fingers permanently maimed.

Schumann was dedicated to poetry and literature as well as to music.

In his literary works and in his musical scores, Schumann frequently referred to three fictitious persons: Eusebius, the dreamer; Florestan, the fiery revolutionary; and Raro, the knowledgeable arbiter of disputes between Florestan and Eusebius. Florestan and Eusebius conducted their disputes in print, but it is also likely they waged torturous warfare in Schumann's mind. His thoughts were torn between those of a dreamer and those of a reactionary. These conflicting emotions influenced Schumann's music.

Schumann's music reveals the composer's inner conflict.

It is easy and erroneous to go too far in reading these conflicting personalities into some of Schumann's works. On the other hand, it would be a mistake to ignore Florestan and Eusebius altogether, for it seems clear that in a sense they are parts of the unwritten programmatic basis of some of Schumann's music.

♪ SOUND AND SENSE: *Piano Concerto*

Title: Piano Concerto

Composer: Schumann

A Closer Look:

Schumann's Piano Concerto is cast in the standard three movements: fast-slow-fast. Originally it consisted only of the first movement, but was later expanded to three movements at the insistence of Schumann's wife, Clara, a well-known keyboard virtuoso and one of the great women of the nineteenth century.

The first movement is in sonata form (without the double exposition of the eighteenth century concerto); the second movement is in a large three-part form—*ABA'*; the last movement is in sonata form and recalls the *A* theme from the first movement. The first movement is examined here in greater detail.

First Movement

The movement begins with a loud, dramatic cascade of full chords on the piano. (Notice the soloist leads.) This outburst is brief and moves quickly to the orchestra's statement of the *A* theme (in A minor, the principal key of the piece).

The soloist then continues the theme, thus far creating the structure: introduction, *A* in the orchestra, *A* in the piano. An extended bridge passage shared by orchestra and soloist follows which leads to the key and the location of an expected *B* theme. However, the piano plays the *A* theme, but in the key of C major. In another extended bridge passage, the piano has a dialogue, almost like a conversation, with first the oboe, then the clarinet. Toward the end of the exposition the mood and character of the music change as a marchlike closing theme for the whole orchestra is introduced. This closing theme has the aggressiveness associated with Florestan.

The development section has two parts and is split almost exactly in half. The first half creates an Eusebian dreamlike atmosphere, and the piano and clarinet resume their intimate conversation. But with a crash from Florestan, the dream is interrupted and the remainder of the development up until the last few measures is more militant and aggressive.

The recapitulation begins quietly with a statement of *A* in the woodwinds and another statement of *A* in the piano. A little later the mood brightens and the orchestral fire leads to a statement of the *A* theme, this time in the major mode. Once more, piano, clarinet, and oboe resume their private conversation, after which the aggressive closing theme from the exposition reappears and carries the piece to the cadenza. Notice that in the cadenza Schumann makes systematic use of the entire range of the keyboard. The cadenza ends with the conventional trill, after which the coda ends the movement in heroic fashion.

Edward Grieg's Piano Concerto in A Minor (1868) possesses both similarities and contrasts in relation to Schumann's Concerto. The Grieg concerto, like the Schumann, has the standard three-movement format: fast-slow-fast.

SOUND AND SENSE: *Concerto*

Title: Piano Concerto in A Minor

Composer: Grieg

A Closer Look:

The first movement is in the sonata form (without the double exposition) and, like the Schumann Concerto, begins with a dramatic flourish by the pianist.

When listening to this movement, notice that the exposition is rather conventional. It presents two themes of sharply contrasting character: *A* is dramatic, *B* is lyrical. The abbreviated development section features more repetitions of the themes than it does real development of them. These themes, like those in the Tchaikovsky *Pathétique* symphony, are self-contained and are unsuitable for the developmental processes. The recapitulation closely adheres to the order of events in the exposition. The cadenza is a focal point in this movement; it is long, dramatic, and resembles a display of bravura. The movement is diagramed here.

Dramatic opening gesture with piano

A—orchestra

A—piano

Bridge—piano and orchestra, playful in character

B—cellos

B—piano, a lengthy crescendo leads to the development

Development

Concludes with the dramatic opening gesture and leads to the recapitulation

Recapitulation

A—piano

Bridge—piano and orchestra, playful in character

B—orchestra

B—piano

Brief orchestral statement leads to the cadenza

Cadenza—soloist

Coda

The second movement contains two alternating themes: a lyrical one, first introduced by the orchestra, and a more animated one, introduced by the soloist.

The last movement is cast in a very large *ABA'* form, in which there are dramatic differences between *A* and *B*. The opening *A* section has a quick tempo and features a folklike theme played first by the soloist and then elaborated upon by both the orchestra and the soloist. The tempo slows markedly and the texture changes drastically as the *B* section enters. It begins with a lovely flute melody accompanied by strings. The piano then picks up and elaborates on the *B* theme. The *A'* section is marked by the return of the folklike theme from *A,* the original tempo is restored, and the movement concludes with a brilliant, flashy coda.

Violin Concerto

There were also a number of violin virtuosos during the nineteenth century. Romantic composers, in response to these virtuosos' demands for music, wrote violin concertos. The Concerto in E Minor, by Felix Mendelssohn (1844) ranks among the best of these. Two major features of this concerto are the compelling thematic materials and its unusual structure.

SOUND AND SENSE: *Violin Concerto*

Title: Violin Concerto in E Minor

Composer: Mendelssohn

A Closer Look:

Mendelssohn's Concerto in E Minor has three movements, which is in itself conventional, but the work is made unusual by the absence of any pauses between the movements. The first movement is connected to the second by a long-held note in the bassoon and a modulation that is accomplished in the span of only a few measures. The second movement is connected to the third movement by means of an intervening brief allegreto movement. In this ingenious manner, Mendelssohn achieved the romantic ideal of the interconnection of all the parts to the whole. In the diagram of the first movement, notice another departure from formal convention. The cadenza is in the "wrong" place; it occurs before, rather than after, the recapitulation.

In some areas, however, Mendelssohn adhered to the classical orientation of his *Italian* symphony. The textures are generally light and airy and do not introduce extra voices that create thickness or density. He also pursued the classical tradition, creating a wealth from a limited fund of materials. With Mendelssohn a development section is still very much a development section. The themes, particularly the first theme of the first movement, and the dominating theme of the second movement, are among the most romantically-inspired themes Mendelssohn ever created.

The first movement is in sonata form and is diagramed as follows:

First Movement

Exposition

A—the soloist expands and embroiders upon A

A—the orchestra

Bridge—this, too, is expanded and almost acquires the status of a subsidiary theme

B—woodwinds, answered by the soloist who expands this theme in virtuoso fashion

Development

A, B, and the bridge "theme" are thoroughly developed. The texture becomes thin and the activity moderates near the end of the development section. Then, quite unexpectedly, the soloist proceeds to play an extraordinarily difficult cadenza.

Cadenza

Recapitulation

Follows the order of the exposition, but is shorter

Coda

Lengthy and filled with virtuosic fireworks played by the soloist

The long-held bassoon note mentioned earlier now enters.

Second Movement

The second movement is in *ABA'* form. The *B* theme contrasts sharply with the lovely, simple *A* theme. As this movement ends, the short allegretto section that serves as a connecting link to the third movement follows without warning.

Third Movement

The last movement is in sonata form though it has the playfulness of a rondo finale. Two bouncy themes are passed between the soloist, clarinets, flutes, and the entire orchestra. The soloist is once again required to play with incredible virtuosity.

ART SONG

The strong attraction poetry held for many romantic composers led quite naturally to the creation of a significant body of songs in the nineteenth century. In art music, the solo song with piano is usually called art song to distinguish it from popular, folk, or other types of song. Schubert, Schumann, Brahms, and other German composers were particularly adept at setting German romantic poetry to music. The special name for German art song is **Lied,** pronounced *leed* (plural—Lieder). A Lied is, then, a short lyrical song for solo voice with piano. Sometimes the piano serves as accompaniment, but very often the piano assumes a role nearly equal in importance to that of the voice.

Lieder composers were attracted to many romantic texts and to a bewildering mixture of good as well as poor poetry. Some of the poets whose lines were immortalized by Schubert and other fine Lieder composers would likely be forgotten if their poetry were examined on its own merits.

Some composers created songs from whole sets of poems related to each other by the development of a character or a central theme. Sets of this kind are called **song cycles.** Schubert wrote over 600 Lieder, included among which are two major song cycles—*Die Winterreise (The Winter's Journey)* and *Die schöne Müllerin (The Miller's Beautiful Daughter).* The examination of only a few of Schubert's many Lieder exposes the range of subject matter, emotional content, and musical content this composer's work spans.

The art song was a product of the nineteenth century composer's fascination with poetry.

A Lied is a short lyrical song for solo voice with piano.

Romantic composers based their Lieder on German poetry.

An die Musik

Schubert composed music for the following poem by Franz von Schober:

An die Musik

Du holde Kunst, in wieviel grauen
  Stunden,
Wo mich des Lebens wilder Kreis
  umstrickt,
Hast du mein Herz zu warmer Lieb'
  entzunden,
Hast mich in eine bessre Welt
  entrückt!
Oft hat ein Seufzer, deiner Harf'
  entflossen,
Ein süsser, heiliger Akkord von dir,
Den Himmel bessrer Zeiten mir
  erschlossen,
Du holde Kunst, ich danke dir dafür!

To Music

O sublime art, in how many gray
  hours,
when the wild tumult of life
  ensnared me,
have you kindled my heart to warm
  love,
have you carried me away to a
  better world!
Often a sigh, escaped from your
  harp,
a sweet, solemn chord from you,
has opened the heaven of better
  times for me—
o sublime art, I thank you for it!

Goya's *Bobabilicon*—a dark
side of romanticism.

The Metropolitan Museum of Art, Harris Brisbane Dick Fund, 1924

**Schubert's *An die Musik*
reveals simplicity and
unexpected harmonies.**

Schubert set the poem as a simple, strophic Lied, the second strophe beginning with the words "Oft hat ein Seufzer" ("Often a sigh"). When listening to this Lied, notice the marvelous simplicity of the melody. The gently pulsating piano figure established in the two-measure introduction runs uninterrupted throughout the song, and for all of its simplicity, it, in conjunction with the gently moving bass line, creates gripping dissonance and unexpected harmony. It is never harsh, but is imbued with a dignified and understated strength that underscores the heartfelt, gentle power of the melody and the sentiment of the text.

Die Erlkönig

**Schübert's *Erlkönig*
conveys drama and tragedy
through the Lied format.**

Die Erlkönig, based on a text by Goethe, is both dramatic and tragic, resulting in a different sort of Lied. The vocalist sings the parts of the four characters who populate this little drama: the narrator, the father, the Erlkönig, and the son.

Goethe's text is derived from the legend of the Erlking (the king of the elves) whose touch is fatal. In the *Erlkönig,* the victim is the son. Schubert ingeniously differentiates the four characters by creating a tone of voice and harmony that is unique to the individual. The son's fear and anxiety is conveyed by the music he sings while accompanied by a dissonant harmony. The father's voice and music reflect his desire to calm the son. The Erlkönig pleads and tantalizes, and this is also reflected in the music. A rushing triplet figure in the bass line of the piano part appears several times during the course of the song to heighten the tension and drama.

Read the entire text of the *Erlkönig* before listening to the song. The text is as follows:

Erzähler
Wer reitet so spät durch Nacht und Wind?
Es ist der Vater mit seinem Kind;
Er hat den Knaben wohl in dem Arm,
Er fasst ihn sicher, er hält ihn warm.

Vater
Mein Sohn, was birgst du so bang dein Gesicht?

Sohn
Siehst, Vater, du den Erlkönig nicht?
Den Erlenkönig mit Kron' und Schweif?

Vater
Mein Sohn, es ist ein Nebelstreif.

Erlkönig
Du liebes Kind, komm, geh mit mir!
Gar schöne Spiele spiel' ich mit dir,

Manch bunte Blumen sind an dem Strand,
Meine Mutter hat manch gülden Gewand.

Sohn
Mein Vater, mein Vater, und hörest du nicht,
Was Erlenkönig mir leise verspricht?

Vater
Sei ruhig, bleibe ruhig, mein Kind:
In dürren Blättern säuselt der Wind.

Erlkönig
Willst, feiner Knabe, du mit mir gehn?
Meine Töchter sollen dich warten schön;
Meine Töchter führen den nächtlichen Reihn
Und wiegen und tanzen und singen dich ein.

Narrator
Who rides so late through night and wind?
It is the father with his child;
He folds the boy close in his arms,

He clasps him securely, he holds him warmly.

Father
My son, why do you hide your face so anxiously?

Son
Father, don't you see the Erlking?

The Erlking with his crown and train?

Father
My son, it is a streak of mist.

Erlking
Dear child, come, go with me!
I'll play the prettiest games with you.
Many colored flowers grow along the shore;
My mother has many golden garments.

Son
My father, my father, and don't you hear
The Erlking whispering promises to me?

Father
Be quiet, stay quiet, my child;
The wind is rustling in the dead leaves.

Erlking
My handsome boy, will you come with me?
My daughters shall wait upon you;

My daughters lead off in the dance every night,
And cradle and dance and sing you to sleep.

Sohn	Son
Mein Vater, mein Vater, und siehst du nicht dort Erlkönigs Töchter am düstern Ort?	My father, my father, don't you see there The Erlking's daughters in the shadows?

Vater	Father
Mein Sohn, mein Sohn, ich seh' es genau: Es scheinen die alten Weiden so grau.	My son, my son, I see it clearly; The old willows look so gray.

Erlkönig	Erlking
Ich liebe dich, mich reizt deine schöne Gestalt; Und bist du nicht willig, so brauch' ich Gewalt.	I love you, your beautiful figure delights me! And if you are not willing, then I shall use force!

Sohn	Son
Mein Vater, mein Vater, jetzt fasst er mich an! Erlkönig hat mir ein Leids gethan!	My father, my father, now he is taking hold of me! The Erlking has hurt me!

Erzähler	Narrator
Dem Vater grauset's, er reitet geschwind, Er hält in Armen das ächzende Kind, Erreicht den Hof mit Mühe und Not; In seinen Armen das Kind war tot.	The father shudders, he rides swiftly on; He holds in his arms the groaning child, He reaches the courtyard weary and anxious: In his arms the child was dead.

OPERA

The development of opera in the nineteenth century was influenced by nationalism.

Several different kinds of opera developed in the nineteenth century. These differences are traceable in part to the swelling tide of nationalism which, after midcentury, became an increasingly visible and powerful force in Europe. The Russian group, including Mussorgsky and Glinka, produced operas on a colossal scale utilizing the native tongue as well as subject matter from Russian history and legend.

Mussorgsky's *Boris Gadunoff* is probably the greatest nineteenth century Russian opera.

The greatest of these Russian operas is Mussorgsky's magnificent *Boris Godunoff* (1874). Some sense of its power and of Mussorgsky's earthy musical style and imaginative flair with orchestration is gained from listening to the "Coronation Scene" (scene ii of the Prologue).

Opéra-comique continued to flourish in the nineteenth century. It became increasingly more serious, though, in terms of both subject matter and musical style. It did, however, retain the element of spoken dialogue.

The French developed another opera type at this time called the grand opera. The grand opera (which contained no spoken dialogue) was big and spectacular and usually drew upon historical or epic subject matter for its plots.

But all of the grand operas and opéras-comique were overshadowed by the greatest French opera of the nineteenth century, Georges Bizet's *Carmen* (1875). As it was originally conceived, *Carmen* was technically an opéra-comique since it contained spoken dialogue. These spoken lines were later converted to sung recitative (by another composer) so that *Carmen* could be performed in the grand opera hall. But *Carmen* is not a typical representation of either grand opera or opéra-comique. It is a work unto itself. Its subject matter is both tragic and "realistic."

In terms of influence, staying power, and widespread public appeal, the Italians and the Germans were the leaders in nineteenth century opera. The consummate master of the Italian operatic ideal was Verdi, although he did not control the field. Early in the nineteenth century Rossini, Donizetti, and Bellini contributed masterpieces such as *Il barbiere di Siviglia (The Barber of Seville), Lucia di Lammermoor,* and *Norma.* And very late in the century, Puccini led the Italian tradition to new areas with masterworks of verismo (the nineteenth century Italian interpretation of realism) such as *La Bohème.* Despite these composers' monumental work, Giuseppe Verdi remained the central composer of Italian opera.

The German opera and the German operatic ideal were very different from the Italian counterparts, mainly because German music at this time was dominated by one composer: Richard Wagner created an operatic revolution in Germany.

Wagner's early operas, such as *Lohengrin* (1846–48) and *Der fliegende Holländer (The Flying Dutchman)* (1841) contained such typical elements of opera as arias, recitatives, and chorus.

After the mid-1800s, however, Wagner created an entirely new kind of musical-dramatic work. For these works, he dropped the name opera and adopted the new generic title—music drama. *Tristan und Isolde* (1857–59) and the *Der Ring des Nibelungen* (1853–74) (which contains four individual works) are music dramas. This music drama is the embodiment of the German operatic ideal of the second half of the nineteenth century.

In France, opéra-comique became more serious in subject matter and style.

The French grand opera was a product more spectacular than opéra-comique.

The greatest nineteenth century French opera was *Carmen.*

The Germans and Italians were leaders in the development of nineteenth century opera.

Verdi dominated Italian opera.

In Germany, Wagner ignited an operatic revolution.

The genre created by Wagner is called music drama.

Nineteenth century Italian opera focused on the singers.

Italian Opera

Italian and German operas differed from each other in many aspects. At the heart of the Italian ideal was the aria—the special song that enraptured audiences. No matter how neatly an aria fits into a story line, it has a tendency to call attention to itself. This tends to stop the flow of the drama, particularly if the aria is followed by thunderous applause from the audience. To the Italians, opera was still a vehicle for singers and singing.

Aside from the overture and other special numbers, the orchestra in an Italian opera functioned essentially as accompaniment to the singers. It rarely called attention to itself and never interfered with or detracted from the singers on the stage. Sometimes the orchestra was so secondary that Wagner was prompted to say that the Italians "treat the orchestra like a big guitar," rather like an ump-chunk-chunk, ump-chunk-chunk accompaniment.

The aria "Quando rapito in estasi," in Donizetti's opera *Lucia di Lammermoor,* demonstrates the memorable quality of melodic line, the virtuosic demands on the singer, and the minimal, accompanimental role of the orchestra. The text to this aria (and the text to the momentary interruption by Alisa) appears below.

Lucia
Quando, rapita in estasi
del più cocente ardore,
col favellar del core
mi giura eterna fe,
in estasi del più cocente ardore,
ecc.
gli affanni miei dimentico,
gioia diviene il pianto . . .
Parmi che a lui d'accanto
si schiuda il ciel per me, ecc.

Alisa
Ah! giorni d'amaro pianto
ah! s'apprestano per te!
Si, giorni, ecc.
Ah! Lucia, ah! desisti.

Lucia
Ah! Quando rapito in estasi,
ecc. . . .

Lucia
When, transported in an ecstasy
of most ardent passion,
with heartfelt words
he swears to love me ever,
in an ecstasy of most ardent
passion, etc.
I forget my cares,
tears turn to joy . . .
It seems that at his side
the gates of heaven open to me,
etc.

Alisa
Oh, days of bitter weeping
lie in store for you!
Yes, days, etc.
Oh, draw back, Lucia!

Lucia
Ah! When, transported in an
ecstasy, etc. . . .

Arias such as this and small ensemble pieces are called **set numbers.** In the Italian ideal, arias and ensemble numbers are joined by connective recitatives. In opera of this kind, smaller set numbers are joined to create larger structural entities. It becomes obvious when listening to these operas that they are not simply music added to a libretto (text), but that the small sets and larger entities are very carefully and logically constructed. It is only through such skillful control that the music, text, and story can produce maximum impact.

Il barbiere di Siviglia   Rossini's *Il barbiere di Siviglia (Barber of Seville)* (1816) is among the finest, if not *the* finest, of comic operas from the nineteenth century, and perhaps of all time. The opening scene of the opera reveals Rossini's musical and comedic gifts and, at the same time, exemplifies the compactness of the overall structure.

Briefly, the dramatic situation of the scene is as follows: Count Almaviva has contracted Fiorello and a group of musicians to help him serenade Rosina, with whom he is secretly in love. They meet just before dawn under her balcony window. When the count realizes that Rosina is not going to appear, he decides to pay off the bumbling musicians and call it a night. A hilarious episode ensues as the musicians, who cannot stop thanking the count for his generosity, do not leave. As they continue to make a racket, the count is beside himself. Finally they do leave and the wonderful character, Figaro—the Barber of Seville, enters.

It would have been easy to dismiss the musicians after their failure to arouse Rosina. Many another composer and dramatist would have done just that. It would be, after all, a convenient and dramatically justifiable thing to do. But Rossini and his librettist took this ordinary situation and transformed it into wonderful slapstick comedy.

Figaro turns out to be an unforgettable character, not so much because of the words he utters, but because of the quality of the vocal line Rossini has developed for him. Figaro is something of a braggart and know-it-all, in love with the sound of his own voice. Notice how he holds certain high notes, celebrating the sound of his voice. Despite these human failings, Figaro is still a likable character. The music persuades us to befriend Figaro.

Count Almaviva, however, is depicted as a bumbling fool who seems to have no control over his own destiny, despite the fact that he is a nobleman. Frustrated by his ineffectiveness, he requests Figaro's aid in solving his problems. This can be interpreted as a thinly veiled political statement on Rossini's part: the aristocracy hasn't brains enough to take care of itself.

Set numbers are the arias and the small ensemble pieces.

Rossini's *Barber of Seville* may be the finest comic opera of all time.

Figaro is an unforgettable figure in the *Barber of Seville.*

Rossini's opera carries a political statement.

Here is the text, translation, and formal analysis of the opening part of Act I, scene i. Notice that the three sets are joined by connective recitative.

ACT I
SCENE i

A Square in Seville.
Set 1:

It is daybreak outside Dr. Bartolo's house. Preceded by Fiorello and a band of musicians, Count Almaviva appears.

Fiorello
Piano, pianissimo,
senza parlar,
tutti con me
venite qua.

Musicians
Piano, pianissimo,
eccoci qua.

Fiorello
Venite qua.

Musicians
Eccoci qua.

Fiorello
Piano.

Musicians
Piano.

Fiorello
Venite qua.

Musicians
Eccoci qua.

Fiorello
Tutto è silenzio;
nessum qui sta,
che i nostri canti
possa turbar.
Tutto è silenzio, ecc.

Almaviva
Fiorello . . . 01à . . .

Fiorello
Signor, son qua.

Almaviva
Ebben! . . . gli amici?

Fiorello
Softly, softly now,
without a word,
all of you
come here with me.

Musicians
Quiet as anything,
here we are.

Fiorello
Come here.

Musicians
Here we are.

Fiorello
Don't make a sound.

Musicians
Not a sound.

Fiorello
Come here.

Musicians
Here we are.

Fiorello
All is quiet;
no one's about
to disturb
our serenade.
All is quiet, etc.

Almaviva
Fiorello . . . hey . . .

Fiorello
I'm here, my lord.

Almaviva
Well? What about your comrades?

Fiorello
Son pronti già.

Almaviva
Bravi, bravissimi,
fate silenzio;
piano, pianissimo,
senza parlar.

Musicians
Piano, . . .
. . . pianissimo, . . .

Fiorello
Senza parlar, . . .

Almaviva
Piano.

Musicians, Fiorello
. . . senza parlar

Fiorello
Venite qua.

Almaviva, Musicians, Fiorello

Senza parlar, piano piano, senza
parlar.

Fiorello
They're quite ready.

Almaviva
Good fellows, splendid!
Hush now,
be very quiet,
don't breathe a word.

Musicians
Hush, . . .
. . . hush now, . . .

Fiorello
Not a word, . . .

Almaviva
Hush.

Musicians, Fiorello
(variously)
. . . not a word.

Fiorello
Come here.

Almaviva, Musicians, Fiorello
(severally and variously)
Not a word, hush now, not a word.

Set 2:

Almaviva

Ecco ridente in cielo
spunta la bella aurora,
e tu non sorgi ancora?
E puoi dormir così?
Ah!
Sorgi, mia dolce speme,
vieni, bell'idol mio;
rendi men crudo, oh Dio,
lo stral che mi ferì.
Oh sorte! già veggo
quel caro sembiante:
quest'anima amante
ottene pietà!
Oh istante d'amore!
Felice momento!
Oh dolce contento
che egual, no, non ha! ecc.
Ehi, Fiorello?

Almaviva
(singing)
Lo, smiling in the heavens
the lovely dawn breaks forth,
whilst you are not yet risen;
how is it you can sleep so?
Ah!
Arise, my sweet content,
come, my pretty adored;
oh Cupid, render less unkind
the arrow that has wounded me.
Oh, fortune, I see
that dear image now:
grace is vouchsafed
this loving heart!
Oh, moment of love!
Happy moment!
Oh, sweet content
that has no equal! etc.
Hey, Fiorello?

Connective Recitative:

Fiorello
Mio signore . . .

Fiorello
My lord . . .

Almaviva
Di', la vedi?

Almaviva
Say, can you see her?

Fiorello
Signor no.

Fiorello
No, my lord.

Almaviva
Ah, ch'è vana ogni speranza!

Almaviva
Oh, how vain are all my hopes!

Set 1':

Fiorello
Signor Conte, il giorno avanza . . .

Fiorello
My lord, day is breaking . . .

Almaviva
A che penso? che farò?

Almaviva
What am I thinking of? What shall I
do?

Tutto è vano . . . Buona gente!

All is in vain . . . Good fellows!

Musicians
Mio signor . . .

Musicians
My lord . . .

Almaviva
Avanti, avanti.

Almaviva
Come here.
*(giving his purse to Fiorello, who
    proceeds to pay off the
    musicians)*

Più di suoni, più di canti,
più di suoni
io bisogno ormai non ho.

No more playing, no more song;
of music
I have no further need.

Fiorello
Buona notte a tutti quanti,
più di voi che far non so.
Buona notte, buona notte, ecc.

Fiorello
Goodnight, one and all,
I've no more use for your services.
Goodnight, goodnight, etc.

Concerted Passage:

Musicians
Mille grazie, mio signore, del . . .
. . . favore, dell'onore.

Musicians
A thousand thanks, my lord, for
your . . .
. . . favour and the honour.

Almaviva
Basta, basta!

Almaviva
That'll do, that'll do!

Musicians
Mille grazie, . . .

Musicians
A thousand thanks, . . .

Almaviva
Non parlate, . . .

Almaviva
Don't talk, . . .

Musicians

. . . mio signore, . . .

Almaviva

. . . ma non serve, . . .

Musicians

. . . del favore, . . .

Almaviva

. . . non gridate.

Musicians

. . . dell'onore.

Musicians

Ah, di tanta cortesia
obbligati in verità!
Oh, che incontro fortunato!
È un signore di qualità! ecc.

Fiorello

Zitti, zitti! che rumore!
Maledetti, via di qua!
Ve', che chiasso indiavolato!
Ah, che rabbia . . .
Oh, che rabbia che mi fa! ecc.

Almaviva

Maledetti! Andate via!
Ah, canaglia! Via di qua!
Tutto quanto il vicinato
questo chiasso sveglierà, sì, ecc.

Almaviva

Basta! basta!

Fiorello

Zitti . . .
. . . zitti!

Musicians

Grazie!

Fiorello

Oh che rabbia che mi fa!

Musicians

. . . my lord, . . .

Almaviva

. . . it's quite unnecessary, . . .

Musicians

. . . for your favour, . . .

Almaviva

. . . don't shout.

Musicians

. . . and the honour.

*(singing all together, though often
      at odds with one another, with
      much repetition)*

Musicians

For so much kindness
much obliged, I'm sure!
Oh, what a lucky meeting!
He's a real gent! etc.

Foirello

Shut up! What a noise!
Curse you! Get out of here!
Look here, what a confounded din!
Oh, what a rage . . .
what a rage they've put me in! etc.

Almaviva

Damned fools! Be off!
What a rabble! Get out of here!
This shindy will raise
the entire neighbourhood, it will!
etc.

(And so on)

Almaviva

That's enough, for heaven's sake!

Fiorello

Shut up, . . .
. . . do shut up!

Musicians

Thanks!

Fiorello

Oh, what a rage they put me in!

Almaviva
Ah maledetti, andate via,
ah, canaglia, via di qua!

Fiorello
Zitti zitti, ecc.

Almaviva
Maledetti, ecc.

Musicians
Ah, di tanta cortesia, ecc.

Almaviva
You infernal nuisances, be off,
get out, you dogs!

Fiorello
Oh, do shut up, etc.

Almaviva
Damned fools, etc.

Musicians
For so much kindness, etc.

(They continue in the same strain.)

Connective Recitative:

Almaviva
Gente indiscreta!

Fiorello
Ah, quasi con quel chiasso
importuno tutto quanto il
quartiere han risvegliato.
Alfin sono partiti!

Almaviva

E non si vede!

Figaro's Voice
La lala lalalalalalala!

Almaviva
Chi è mai quest' importuno?
Lasciamolo passar.
Sotto quegli archi, non veduto,
vedrò quanto bisogna; già l'alba
appare e amor non si vergogna.

Almaviva
*(having at last got rid of the
  musicians)*
No sense of discretion . . . the
fools!

Fiorello
With their ill-timed clamour
they've almost woken
the entire neighbourhood.
At last they've gone!

Almaviva
(looking up at the window)
And she hasn't appeared!

Figaro's Voice
La lala lalalalalalala!

Almaviva
Who is it now? Confound it!
Let's wait till he's gone by.

(hiding)

Hidden under these arches,
I'll be able to see all I want;
it's daybreak already and love has
no need to blush.

Set 3:

Figaro
La ra la le ra la ra la!
Largo al factotum
della città, largo!
La ran la, ecc.
Presto a bottega,

Figaro
(coming down the street)
la ra la le ra la ra la!
Room for the town's
factotum, make way!
La la la, etc.
Hasten to the shop

che l'alba è già, presto!	for it's morning already, quick!
La ran la, ecc.	La la la, etc.
Ah che bel vivere,	Oh what a fine life!
che bel piacere	What fun
per un barbier	for a first-class
di qualità!	barber!
Ah bravo, Figaro,	Oh bravo, Figaro,
bravo, bravissimo, bravo!	fine fellow, bravo!
La ran la la, ecc.	La, la, la, etc.
Fortunatissimo,	You're a lucky
per verità, bravo!	man indeed, bravo!
La ran la la, ecc.	La la la, etc.
Fortunatissimo, ecc.	You're a lucky, etc.
La ran la la, ecc.	La la la, etc.
Pronto a far tutto,	Ready for anything,
la notte il giorno	day and night
sempre d'intorno,	always on the go,
in giro sta.	here, there and everywhere.
Miglior cuccagna	A better livelihood
per un barbiere,	for a barber,
vita più nobile,	a nobler life,
no, non si dà.	no, there is none!
La la ran la, ecc.	La la la, etc.
Rasori e pettini,	Razors and combs,
lancette e forbici,	lancets and scissors,
al mio comando	ready to hand,
tutto qui sta.	everything's here.
Lancette e pettini,	Lancets and combs,
lancette e forbici, ecc.	lancets and scissors, etc.
V'è la risorsa,	There are the perks
poi, del mestiere	of the job, too,
colla donnetta . . .	with the young ladies
col cavaliere . . .	and with the young gentlemen . . .
colla donnetta, la la la, ecc.	With the young ladies, la la la, etc.
col cavaliere, la la la, ecc.	with the young bloods, la la la, etc.
Ah che bel vivere, ecc.	Oh what a fine life, etc.
Tutti mi chiedono,	Everyone calls for me,
tutti mi vogliono,	everyone wants me,
donne, ragazzi,	ladies, lads,
vecchi, fanciulle.	old men and girls.
Qua la parrucca . . .	Here my wig . . .
Presto la barba . . .	Quick a shave . . .
Qua la sanguigna . . .	I must be bled . . .
Presto il biglietto . . .	Quickly this letter . . .

Italians also became
masters of the small vocal
ensemble.

Verdi's *Rigoletto* features a
masterful quartet.

***Small vocal ensemble:* Rigoletto**   The Italians also showed a preference for and became the masters of the small vocal ensemble, such as the sextet and the quartet. One of the most memorable of these is found in Act III, scene i, of Verdi's tragic masterpiece *Rigoletto* (1851). The scene begins with some recitative that leads eventually to a strophic aria called "La donna e mobile," then to a duet, and after more recitative, to the spectacular quartet. The text and stage directions that follow will guide you through the action and enable you to envision what is happening and what is on the mind of each of the people in the scene. Gilda has been in love with the Duke, but doesn't know until this scene that the Duke is an evil man, despite her father's, Rigoletto's, warnings.

The Duke and Maddalena, upon whom he tries to make advances, are inside a run-down road house. Gilda and Rigoletto are able to observe his actions through a hole in one of the walls. Thus, two members of the quartet are inside (Duke and Maddalena), and two are outside (Gilda and Rigoletto).

Notice how Verdi develops each of the characters through song in the quartet. The Duke continues singing in his arrogant and lecherous manner. Maddalena is skittish. Gilda is broken-hearted and her melodic line is full of weeping and wailing. Rigoletto sings in a state of controlled anger.

La sponda destra del Mincio. A sinistra è una casa a due piani, mezzo diroccata, la cui fronte, volta allo spettatore, lascia vedere per una grande arcata l'interno d'una rustica osteria al pian terreno, ed una rozza scala che mette al granaio, entro cui, da un balcone senza imposte, si vede un lettuccio. Nella facciata che guarda la strada è una porta che s'apre per di dentro; il muro poi è sì pieno di fessure, che dal di fuori si può facilmente scorgere quanto avviene nell'interno. Il resto del teatro rappresenta la deserta parte del Mincio, che nel fondo scorre dietro un parapetto in mezza ruina; di là dal fiume è Mantova. È notte. Gilda e Rigoletto inquieto, sono sulla strada. Sparafucile nell'interno dell'osteria, seduto presso una tavola, sta ripulendo il suo cinturone senza nulla intendere di quanto accade al di fuori.	The right bank of the Mincio river. Left, a two-storied house, half fallen into ruin. On the ground floor, the interior of a rustic wineshop beyond an arcade. A rough stone staircase leads to a loft above, with a balcony. The outer wall facing the audience is without shutters, and a cot inside is clearly visible. Downstairs, in the wall of the house facing the road, there is a door, opening inward. The wall itself is so full of cracks and holes that whatever takes place within is clearly visible. The rest of the stage represents the deserted fields along the Mincio, which runs behind a ruined parapet in the background. Beyond the river, Mantua. It is night. Gilda is in the road, with Rigoletto, who is obviously tense. Sparafucile, seated at a table in the wineshop, is cleaning his swordbelt. He is unaware of what is taking place outside.

Recitatives:

Rigoletto
E l'ami?

Rigoletto
And you love him?

Gilda
Sempre.

Gilda
Even now.

Rigoletto
Pure
Tempo a guarirne t'ho lasciato.

Rigoletto
Yet
I have given you time to forget.

Gilda
Io l'amo.

Gilda
I love him.

Rigoletto
Povero cor di donna! Ah, il vile
infame! Ma ne avrai vendetta, o
Gilda.

Rigoletto
Poor woman's heart! Ah, the
scoundrel! You shall be avenged, o
Gilda.

Gilda
Pietà, mio padre—

Gilda
Have pity, my father—

Rigoletto
E se tu certa fossi
Ch'ei ti tradisse, l'ameresti ancora?

Rigoletto
And if you were sure that he is
unfaithful, would you still love him?

Gilda
Nol so, ma pur m'adora.

Gilda
I do not know, but he adores me.

Rigoletto
Egli?

Rigoletto
He?

Gilda
Sì.

Gilda
Yes.

Rigoletto
Ebbene, osserva dunque.

Rigoletto
Well, then watch carefully.

*(l a conduce presso una delle
fessure del muro, ed ella vi
guarda.)*

*(He leads her to an opening in the
wall. She looks through into the
wineshop.)*

Gilda
Un uomo
Vedo

Gilda
I see
A man.

Rigoletto
Per poco attendi.

Rigoletto
Wait a moment.

*(Il Duca, in assisa di semplice
ufficiale di cavalleria, entra
nella sala terrena per una porta
a sinistra.)*

*(The Duke, wearing the uniform of
a cavalry officer, enters the
room on the ground floor
through a door, left.)*

Gilda
(trasalendo)
Ah, padre mio!

Gilda
(startled)
Ah, father!

Duca

(a Sparafucile)
Due cose e tosto—

Sparafucile
Quali?

Duca
Una stanza e del vino.

Rigoletto
(Son questi i suoi costumi!)

Sparafucile
(Oh, il bel zerbino!)

(Entra nella stanza vicina.)

Duke

(to Sparafucile)
Two things—and quickly.

Sparafucile
What things?

Duke
A room and some wine.

Rigoletto
(These are the fellow's habits!)

Sparafucile
(Oh, the gay blade!)

(He goes into an adjoining room.)

Strophic Aria:

Duca
La donna è mobile
Qual piuma al vento,
Muta d'accento, e di pensier.

Sempre un amabile
Leggiadro viso,
In pianto o in riso, è menzognero.

La donna è mobile ecc.
E sempre misero
Chi a lei s'affida,
Chi le confida, mal cauto il core!

Pur mai non sentesi
Felice appieno
Chi su quel seno, non liba amore!

La donna è mobile ecc.

Sparafucile

*(Rientra con una bottiglia di vino e
    due bicchierl che depone sulla
    tavola: quindi batte col pomo
    della sua lunga spada due colpi
    al soffitto. A quel segnale una
    ridente giovane, in costume di
    zingara, scende a salti la scala:
    il Duca corre per abbracciarla,*

Duke
Oh, woman is fickle
As a feather in the wind,
Simple in speech, and simpler of
mind.

Always the lovable,
Sweet, laughing face,
But laughing or crying, a false face,
be sure.

Oh, woman is fickle etc.
Oh, the poor devil
Who gives himself up to her,
And if he trusts her, there goes his
heart!

Yet no man can feel
Quite fully content
Unless, in her arms, he drinks to
Love's health!
Oh, woman is fickle etc.

Sparafucile

*(He returns with a bottle of wine
    and two glasses, which he puts
    on the table. Then, with the butt
    of his sword, he strikes twice
    against the ceiling. At this
    signal, a buxom young woman
    in gypsy costume comes
    running down the stairs. The*

ma ella gli sfugge. Frattanto Sparafucile, uscito sulla via, dice a parte a Rigoletto:)

Duke tries to greet her with a kiss, but she eludes him. Meanwhile Sparafucile has gone out into the road, he speaks softly to Rigoletto:)

È là vostri'uomo? Viver dee o morire?

Is that your man? Shall he live or die?

Rigoletto
Più tardi tornerò l'opra a compire.

Rigoletto
I'll come back later to conclude our business.

(Sparafucile allontana dietro la casa verso il fiume. Gilda e Rigoletto rimangono sulla via, il Duca e Maddalena nel piano terreno.)

(Sparafucile moves off, around the house to the rear, in the direction of the river. Gilda and Rigoletto remain in the road. The Duke and Maddalena, Sparafucile's sister, are together in the wineshop.)

Duet:

Duca
Un di, se ben rammentomi,
O bella, t'incontrai.
Mi piacque di te chiedere
E intesi che qui stai.
Or sappi chi d'allora
Sol te quest'alma adora.

Duke
One day, if I remember rightly,
I met you, pretty girl.
I asked someone about you
And was told you live here.
Let me say that ever since then,
I have abjectly adored you.

Maddalena
Ah! ah!—e vent'altre appresso

Le scorda forse adesso?
Ha un'aria il signorino
Da vero libertino.

Maddalena
Ah! ah! And the twenty more since then,
Do you forget them now?
I think my fine young man
Is a bit of a libertine.

Duca
(per abbracciarla)
Si—un mostro son—

Duke
(trying to kiss her)
Yes—I'm a monster—

Recitative:

Maddalena
Lasciatemi,
Stordito.

Maddalena
Leave me alone,
You fool.

Duca
Ih, che fracasso!

Duke
Ho, what a hubbub!

Maddalena
Stia saggio.

Maddalena
Behave yourself!

Duca
E tu sii docile,
Non farmi tanto chiasso.
Ogni saggezza chiudesi
Nel gaudio e nell'amore.
(Le prende la mano.)
La bella mano candida!

Maddalena
Scherzate, voi signore.

Duca
No, no.

Maddalena
Son brutta.

Duca
Abbracciami.

Maddalena
Ebro!

Duca
D'amore ardente.

Maddalena
Signor, l'indifferente,
Vi piace canzonar?

Duca
No, no, ti vo'sposar.

Maddalena
Ne voglio la parola—

Duca
(ironico)
Amabile figliuola!

Rigoletto
*(a Gilda che avrà tutto osservato
    ed inteso)*
E non ti basta ancor?

Gilda
Iniquo traditor!

Maddalena
Ne voglio la parola.

Duca
Amabile figliuola!

Rigoletto
E non ti basta ancor?

Duke
And you be sweet.
Don't make such a fuss.
The end of all wisdom lies
In the joy of loving.
(He takes her hand.)
Your pretty white hand!

Maddalena
You are joking, sir.

Duke
No, no.

Maddalena
I'm ugly.

Duke
Kiss me.

Maddalena
You're drunk!

Duke
With love.

Maddalena
My cynical friend,
You like to joke, don't you?

Duke
No, no. I want to marry you.

Maddalena
I want your word of honor—

Duke
(ironic)
Lovable child!

Rigoletto
*(to Gilda, who has seen and heard
    all)*
Haven't you seen enough?

Gilda
Wicked traitor!

Maddalena
I want your word of honor.

Duke
Lovable child!

Rigoletto
Haven't you had enough?

The Quartet:

Duca

Bella figlia dell'amore
Schiavo son dei vezzi tuoi;
Con un detto, un detto sol
tu puoi
Le mie pene consolar.
Vieni e senti del mio core
Il frequente palpitar.
Con un detto sol
tu puoi
Le mie pene consolar.

Duke

Fairest daughter of love,
I am a slave to your charms;
With a word, one word, you have
the power
To quiet all my anguish.
Come, feel the wild beating
Of my lovesick heart.
With one word you have the power

To quiet all my anguish!

Maddalena

Ah! ah! rido ben di core,
Che tai baie costan poco;
Quanto valga il vostro gioco,
Mel credete, so apprezzar.
Sono avvezza, bel signore,
Ad un simile scherzar.

Maddalena

Ah! ah! That is really laughable—
How cheap such talk is, really.
What all this stuff is worth,
Believe me, I know exactly.
I am quite used by now, sir,
To foolish jokes like this.

Gilda

Ah, così parlar d'amore
A me pur l'infame ho udito!

Infelice cor tradito,
Per angoscia non scoppiar.

Gilda

Ah, to speak of love in such a way!
The scoundrel spoke so once to
me!
O wretched heart, betrayed,
Do not break for sorrow.

Rigoletto

(a Gilda)
Taci, il pianger non vale;
Che'ei mentiva or sei sicura.
Taci, e mia sarà la cura
La vendetta d'affrettar.
Pronta fia, sarà fatale;
Io saprollo fulminar.

Rigoletto

(to Gilda)
Be silent, weeping is useless now.
You are convinced he was lying—
Be silent, and I shall move at once
To hasten our revenge.
It will be quick, it will be deadly,
And I shall know how to strike.

Verdi was not only a great composer, he was also a man of the theater with an uncanny sense of effective drama. The stories of several of his operas are based on works by great literary figures such as Shakespeare and Victor Hugo. Unquestionably, he was well-acquainted with fine drama, but ultimately, the power of his operas is derived from the music. To simplify a difficult matter, it can be said that for the Italians, Verdi among them, music was the culmination of expression. The drama and other elements were important, but music was the essence of opera.

The music is the most important element in nineteenth century Italian opera.

German Opera: Wagner's *Gesamtkunstwerk*

Wagner said, "The error in opera lies in the fact that a means of expression, namely music, has been made the object, while the object of expression, namely the drama, has been made the means." In other words, Wagner felt that the ultimate expression of the opera was the drama, and music a means to that end. In his view, the Italians created "the error in opera" with their interpretation.

Given Wagner's bias toward drama, you might expect that his musical interest and abilities were limited. On the contrary, Wagner was not only a gifted musician, but an influential one as well. His ideas about opera and his use of harmony and leitmotifs profoundly influenced the course of music in the last half of the nineteenth century and beyond. Not just opera, but symphonic music as well, was affected by Wagnerian practices.

Wagner theorized about and then put into practice what we now recognize as the ultimate synthesis of the arts—a unification of music, drama, poetry, dance, architecture—to which Wagner gave the German name **Gesamtkunstwerk.** Wagner believed that drama, as a central part of a total art work (or *Gesamtkunstwerk*), revealed the innermost feelings and beliefs of the culture. Wagner was not dealing in terms of a simple comedy or tragedy. The *Gesamtkunstwerk* revealed the thoughts and aspirations of a culture. The most direct and compact mode of drama, Wagner believed, is myth. Wagner's music dramas, then, used myth—Teutonic mythology—as the vehicle for revealing a culture to itself.

Arias, recitatives, and ensemble numbers were purged from Wagner's music drama because they were too one-dimensional and got in the way of the continuous unfolding of the drama. Wagner opted instead for endless or **infinite melody.** This infinite melody was supported by an ever-active orchestral accompaniment which constantly revealed additional information about a particular character. In fact, there are times in Wagner's music dramas when the orchestra nearly overpowers the singers, making it almost impossible to hear the text. However, when this occurs the emotions and the sense of the text are unequivocally established before the orchestra assumes command. Thus, it really doesn't matter that all of the words are not discernable.

Toward the middle of his career, Wagner discarded the term opera for his stage productions, and instead used the term **music drama.** His music dramas incorporated all of the elements just described.

Tristan und Isolde   Act II, scene ii of Wagner's music drama, *Tristan und Isolde,* features a lengthy, powerful love duet between the two principal characters. Below is the text of the opening portion of that duet. As you listen to the example, note the role of the orchestra and how

---

Wagner's practices greatly affected German opera and symphonic music.

Wagner succeeded in his attempts to synthesize the arts.

Wagner utilized myth as a vehicle for revealing elements of German culture.

Wagner replaced the aria and ensemble numbers with "infinite melody."

In some of Wagner's music the orchestra assumes command.

different it is from its Italian counterpart. Note also that absence of anything resembling either aria or recitative, and the presence of continuous, infinite melody in the voice parts.

SCENE ii

Tristan
Isolde! Geliebte!

Isolde
Tristan! Geliebter! Bist du mein?

Tristan
Hab' ich dich wieder?

Isolde
Darf ich dich fassen?

Tristan
Kann ich mir trauen?

Isolde
Endlich! Endlich!

Tristan
An meiner Brust!

Isolde
Fühl' ich dich wirklich?

Tristan
Seh' ich dich selber?

Isolde
Dies deine Augen?

Tristan
Dies dein Mund?

Isolde
Hier deine Hand?

Tristan
Hier dein Herz?

Isolde
Bin ich's? Bist du's? Halt' ich dich fest?

Tristan
Bin ich's? Bist du's? Ist es kein Trug?

Beide
Ist es kein Traum?
O Wonne der Seele, o süsse, hehrste,
kühnste, schönste, seligste Lust!

Tristan
Ohne Gleiche!

Tristan
Isolde! Beloved!

Isolde
Tristan! Beloved! Are you mine?

Tristan
Do I hold you again?

Isolde
Can I embrace you?

Tristan
Can I believe it?

Isolde
At last! At last!

Tristan
Here on my breast!

Isolde
Is it really you I feel?

Tristan
Do I really see you?

Isolde
These your eyes?

Tristan
These your lips?

Isolde
This your hand?

Tristan
This your heart?

Isolde
Is it I? Is it you? You in my arms?

Tristan
Is it I? Is it you? Is it no illusion?

Both
Is it no dream?
O rapture of my soul, sweetest, highest,
brightest, loveliest, blissful joy!

Tristan
Unparalleled!

Isolde
Überreiche!

Tristan
Überselig!

Isolde
Ewig!

Tristan
Ewig!

Isolde
Ungeahnte, nie gekannte!

Tristan
Überschwenglich hoch erhabne!

Isolde
Freudejauchzen!

Tristan
Lustentzücken!

Beide
Himmelhöchstes Weltentrücken!
Mein! Tristan! Mein! Isolde!
Mein und dein! Ewig, ewig ein!

Isolde
Wie lange fern! Wie fern so lang!

Tristan
Wie weit so nah! So nah wie weit!

Isolde
O Freundesfeindin, böse Ferne!

Träger Zeiten zögernde Länge!

Tristan
O Weit' und Nähe, hart entzweite!

Holde Nähe! Öde Weite!

Isolde
Im Dunkel du, im Lichte ich!

Isolde
Supreme treasure!

Tristan
Supreme joy!

Isolde
For ever!

Tristan
For ever!

Isolde
Unimagined, unknown!

Tristan
Overflowing, sublime!

Isolde
Overwhelming joy!

Tristan
Entrancing bliss!

Both
Highest Heaven's oblivion of the world!
My Tristan! My Isolde!
Mine and thine! One for ever and ever!

Isolde
How long apart! How far apart so long!

Tristan
How far when near! How near when afar!

Isolde
O foe to friendship, spiteful distance!
Dragging length of sluggish hours!

Tristan
O distance and nearness, harshly divided!
Blessed nearness, tedious distance!

Isolde
You in the darkness, I in the light!

Leitmotifs

Wagner unified his lengthy music dramas through leitmotifs.

Wagner found that his most effective means of unifying these tremendously long music dramas was through the use of leitmotifs. A leitmotif is a brief musical gesture that is associated symbolically with a character, object, or idea, so that when the leitmotif is sounded it brings to mind that with which it is symbolically associated. Thus, the character, object or idea need not be present on the stage when the orchestra plays the leitmotif, the audience's attention will be focused on the appropriate character, object, or idea.

A leitmotif may be a melodic phrase, a motive, or even a mere chord. Leitmotifs occur frequently throughout a music drama, and a typical Wagnerian music drama will contain dozens of such leitmotifs. Usually the orchestra plays the leitmotifs, but occasionally they are sung. Once more this points to the very important role of the orchestra in this operatic ideal.

Der Ring des Nibelungen   Wagner's longest work is the set of four music dramas that make up *Der Ring des Nibelungen (The Ring of the Nibelungen)* (1853–74): 1) *Das Rheingold,* 2) *Die Walküre,* 3) *Siegfried,* 4) *Götterdämmerung.* Each of these music dramas presents its own leitmotifs, and some leitmotifs from earlier sections of the *Ring* are carried over into later ones.

Figure 8.3 presents a set of leitmotifs and the text to the introduction of *Die Walküre.* You will find numbers at the ends of some lines; these numbers correspond to the list of leitmotifs. For example, at the

Each leitmotif is associated with one particular character, object, or idea.

In Wagner's *The Ring of the Nibelungen,* leitmotifs appear throughout the set of four music dramas.

Fig. 8.3

end of Siegmund's first speech the numbers 3 and 1 appear. This means
that during Siegmund's speech, leitmotifs 3 and 1 are heard in the orchestra. Act I begins with an orchestral depiction of a storm that is subsiding. Leitmotif 1 is the "storm" motif. Leitmotif 2 appears a little later
in this orchestral introduction, and is called the "storm spell" motif. Leitmotif 2 is carried over from *Das Rheingold* into *Die Walküre*.

ACT I
SCENE i

*The interior of Hunding's dwelling.
In the middle of the room is a
great ash tree, whose branches
grow through the roof. It is
evening; a thunderstorm is just
subsiding.*

Siegmund

Wess' Herd dies auch sei,
hier muss ich rasten. *(3,1)*

Siegmund

*(entering hastily and sinking
    wearily down beside the fire)*
Whose hearth this may be,
here I must rest. *(3,1)*

Sieglinde

Ein fremder Mann!
Ihn muss ich fragen.
Wer kam in's Haus
und liegt dort am Herd? *(3)*
Müde liegt er
von Weges Müh'n:
schwanden die Sinne ihm?
wäre er siech? *(4)*
Noch schwillt ihm der Atem;
das Auge nur schloss er;
mutig dünkt mich der Mann,
sank er müd' auch hin.

Sieglinde

(in the doorway of an inner room)
A stranger!
I must question him.
Who is it that came in
and is lying by the hearth? *(3)*
He lies there weary
and travel-worn—
is he unconscious,
is he ill? *(4)*

*(looking more closely at
    Siegmund)*

He is still breathing;
he has fallen asleep.
He looks to me a brave man,
though he is now so exhausted.

Siegmund
Ein Quell! ein Quell!

Siegmund
Drink! Drink!

Sieglinde
Erquickung schaff' ich. *(3,4)*
Labung biet' ich
dem lechzenden Gaumen:
Wasser, wie du gewollt. *(3,5)*

Sieglinde
I'll bring you refreshment. *(3,4)*

*(She fetches a horn filled with
    water.) (4)*

Here is something
for your parched mouth—
the water you called for. *(3,5)*

*(Siegmund drinks, and as he gives
her back the horn, he fixes his
eyes on Sieglinde with growing
interest.)*

Siegmund

Siegmund

Kühlende Labung
gab mir der Quell, *(4)*
des Müden Last
machte er leicht;
Erfrischt ist der Mut,
das Aug' erfreut
des Sehens selige Lust: *(4)*
wer ist's, der so mir es labt? *(4)*

The draught has given me
cooling relief, *(4)*
the burden of my weariness
is lightened;
my courage revives,
my eyes enjoy
the pleasure of sight: *(4)*
who is it that has so restored me?
(4)

Sieglinde

Sieglinde

Dies Haus und dies Weib
sind Hundings Eigen;
gastlich gönn' er dir Rast:
harre bis heim er kehrt! *(3)*

This house and this woman
belong to Hunding;
as a guest he will grant you rest:
wait until he comes home. *(3)*

Siegmund

Siegmund

Waffenlos bin ich:
dem wunden Gast
wird dein Gatte nicht wehren.

I am unarmed:
your husband will not rebuff
a wounded guest.

Sieglinde

Sieglinde

Die Wunden weise mir schnell! *(3)*

Quick, show me your wounds! *(3)*

Siegmund

Siegmund

Gering sind sie,
der Rede nicht wert;
noch fügen des Leibes
Glieder sich fest.
Hätten halb so stark wie mein Arm
Schild und Speer mir gehalten,
nimmer floh' ich dem Feind;
doch zerschellten mir Speer und
Schild. *(1)*
Der Feinde Meute
hetzte mich müd',
Gewitter-Brunst
brach meinen Leib;
doch schneller als ich der Meute,
schwand die Müdigkeit mir: *(3)*
sank auf die Lider mir Nacht,
die Sonne lacht mir nun neu. *(4)*

They are but slight,
not worth speaking of;
my limbs are
in good trim.
Had shield and spear but held out
half as well as my arm,
I should never have fled from the
foe;
but spear and shield were shattered.
(1)
The enemy's horde
harried me to exhaustion,
the force of the storm
wore me out;
but quicker than I fled from the foe,
my weariness has fled from me: *(3)*
night closed on my eyelids,
now the sun smiles on me anew. *(4)*

Sieglinde

Des seimigen Metes
süssen Trank
mög'st du mir nicht verschmäh'n.
(4)

Siegmund

Schmecktest du mir ihn zu? *(5)*
Einen Unseligen labtest du—
Unheil wende
der Wunsch von dir! *(4)*
Gerastet hab' ich
und süss geruht:
weiter wend' ich den Schritt.

Sieglinde

Wer verfolgt dich, dass du schon
fliehst?

Siegmund

Misswende folgt mir
wohin ich fliehe;
Misswende naht mir
wo ich mich neige: *(5)*
dir Frau doch bleibe sie fern!
Fort wend' ich Fuss und Blick.

Sieglinde

So bleibe hier!
Nicht bringst du Unheil dahin,
wo Unheil im Hause wohnt! *(6,4,6)*

Siegmund

Wehwalt hiess ich mich selbst:
Hunding will ich erwarten.

Sieglinde

Perhaps you will not refuse
a sweet draught
of honeyed mead? *(4)*

Siegmund

Will you taste it first? *(5)*

*(After Sieglinde has sipped the
    drink, Siegmund takes a long
    draught.) (5,3)*

You have restored an unfortunate
man—
I would avert
misfortune from you! *(4)*
I have enjoyed
a good rest,
now I must wend my way farther.

Sieglinde

Who pursues you, that you must
flee?

Siegmund

Ill-luck follows me
wherever I fly;
ill-luck draws near
wherever I stop: *(5)*
may it stay far from you!
I will turn aside both step and
glance.

Sieglinde

No, stay here!
You cannot bring misfortune
where misfortune dwells already!
(6,4,6)

Siegmund

Wehwalt [Woeful] was what I named
myself:
I will await Hunding.

SUMMARY

Romanticism is the name given to the movement that dominated philosophy and the arts in the nineteenth century. At the core of romanticism was the desire to create a strong, personal bond with nature, and to express the self-discovery and inner peace resulting from that bond. In many cases, this expression demanded a synthesis of several art forms. This synthesis was duly expressed by the gifted romantic composers who were often masters of poetry and literature as well.

The romantic composers adapted classical music genres to the nineteenth century ideal while also developing genres unique to the times. The symphonies of Mendelssohn and Brahms reveal a classical orientation while the symphonies of Tchaikovsky and Berlioz go beyond the classical form to the program approach. The choral symphony and the tone poem were products of the nineteenth century. Both genres dramatically illustrate the romantic fascination with a synthesis of the arts. Liszt, Borodin and Strauss were masters of the tone poem.

The piano was very important to the romantic age. Piano music was in great demand and Chopin, Liszt, Schumann, and others filled that need with piano sonatas and character pieces written for piano. The polonaise and the étude were types of character pieces born in the romantic era. Concertos, too, were composed for piano as well as for violin, viola, and other solo instruments.

The art song resulted when romantic composers set German poetry to music. The German art song is termed "Lied." We considered Lieder composed by Schubert.

The opera existed in many forms in the nineteenth century. Italian opera, as characterized by Verdi, focused on the singer, while the German opera, as transformed by Wagner into the music drama, put special emphasis on mythic drama and the role of the orchestra.

KEY TERMS

choral (dramatic) symphony	polonaise	song cycle
tone (symphonic) poem	étude	set number
leitmotifs	legato	*Gesamtkunstwerk*
sonata	staccato	infinite melody
character piece	Lied	music drama
prelude		

THINKING ABOUT IT

In the classical era there was a symphonic ideal in which the character, number, and order of movements within the symphony were relatively standardized. Compare the classical symphony to the nineteenth century symphonies discussed in this chapter. Was there a singular symphonic ideal in the romantic era? Thinking back (or perhaps relistening) to certain examples in this chapter, how would you characterize a tone poem? What could have led the romantics to invent such a thing as the tone poem?

What are some of the differences in the operatic ideal of Wagner and the Italian operatic ideal exemplified by Verdi and Rossini?

9

THE ROOTS OF TWENTIETH CENTURY MUSIC

Three Musicians, Picasso

The Philadelphia Museum of Art: The A. E. Gallatin Collection

SOUNDS OF THE CHAPTER

Barber
Adagio for String Orchestra ♪

Bartók
Music for strings, percussion and celesta
Fourth String Quartet
Out of Doors suite

Berg
Wozzeck ♪

Cage
*Concerto for Prepared Piano and
  Orchestra*
4' 33''
HPSCHD
Imaginary Landscape no. 4

Copland
Appalachian Spring
Music for the Theatre

Debussy
"Brouillards," *Preludes*, Book II ♪
Danse bohémienne ♪
Images
"La Flute de Pan"
La Mer
"Nuages," *Nocturnes*
Pelléas et Mélisande
*Prélude à l'Après-midi d' un faune
  (Prelude to the Afternoon of a Faun)*

Honegger
Jeanne d' Arc au bûcher
Le Roi David (King David)
Pacific 231

Ives
"At the River"
Concord Sonata
Fourth Symphony
"General William Booth Enters Heaven"
Holidays symphony
The Unanswered Question ♪
Universe Symphony
Variations on "America"

Milhaud
*La Création du Monde (The Creation of
  the World)*
*Le Boeuf sur le Toit (The Bull on the
  Roof)* ♪

Mozart
Symphony in G Minor, K. 550 ♪

Prokofiev
Third Piano Concerto in C Major, op. 26

Satie
Desiccated Embryos
Flabby Preludes
Gymnopédie no. 1
Parade ♪
Second to Last Thoughts
Three Pieces in the Form of a Pear

Schönberg
Pierrot Lunaire ♪
Suite for piano

Stockhausen
*Gesang der Jünglinge (Song of the
  Youths)*

Stravinsky
*Le Sacre du Printemps (The Rite of
  Spring)*
Octet
Petrushka
Symphony in C
The Firebird

Webern
Five Movements for string quartet

"Columbia the Gem of the Ocean"
"Nearer My God to Thee"
"Shall We Gather at the River?"
"Turkey in the Straw"

Historically, the listening repertoire of a given audience was limited by time, place, and economics. People listened mainly to the new music of the day: baroque audiences listened to music composed in that era, audiences in the classical era listened to classical music, and so on. Even in the nineteenth century, when there were revivals of earlier kinds of music, the listening public focused on the works of the romantic composers.

However, twentieth century art music is unique in this respect. We listen to proportionately less music written in our own century than we do to music written in previous eras. Why is this true? In order to answer this question, we need to focus on technological advancements that have resulted in our diverse musical environment.

THE EVOLUTION OF TWENTIETH CENTURY ART MUSIC

Presently, we have available to us more music, and more kinds of music, than ever has been the case before. We can, if we wish, listen to music of the Renaissance, of the Pygmies of the Ituri Forest, or of J. S. Bach, Vivaldi, Mozart, Beethoven, Mahler; our choices are nearly limitless. We enjoy this diversity of music largely due to the development and refinement of the phonograph, magnetic tape, and other mass communication devices, but several musical developments were equally influential.

From the middle of the seventeenth century to the beginning of this century, functional harmony (tonality) was an identifiable and unchallenged musical reality. Music—virtually *all* music—was written in a key. Thus, despite the idiosyncrasies of individual composers throughout the baroque, classical, and romantic periods, tonality remained a constant in Western art music. It was so deeply ingrained and so much a part of our musical conditioning and expectations that when, in the early twentieth century, some composers began to abandon tonality, the audience was either unable or unwilling to comprehend this new music.

Although some composers adhered to the structure established in earlier eras, some twentieth-century composers experimented heavily. Composers either remained within the boundaries of tonality (though generally their music became more dissonant), abandoned it temporarily, or discarded it permanently. Some composers continued to write symphonies, string quartets, and piano sonatas, while others created new

Historically, people heard only the music of their own era.

We are exposed to music written in previous eras.

The availability of various types of music is due mainly to technological advancement.

Tonality was a constant in Western art music until the twentieth century.

The twentieth century has been a period of musical experimentation.

forms and experimented with previously unexplored instruments and instrumental ensembles. Toward the middle of the twentieth century, some composers began to tap the reservoir of electronically generated sound. Still others explored the visual and spatial parameters of music, suggesting at least a partial redefinition of music. And still other composers explored the outer limits of improvisation and entered the realm of "chance" operation.

Twentieth century musical activity is analogous to a volcanic eruption where streams of lava shower in all directions. Our century, at least from a contemporary viewpoint, has produced not one broad musical style, but many different styles having few or no apparent interconnections. This situation has made it difficult for audiences to grasp the total concept of today's music. Audiences and serious students of art music sense a fundamental stylistic unity in the music of other eras, but a basic and perplexing disunity exists in twentieth century music.

Twentieth century art music has moved in many directions, producing various styles and disunity.

Despite the fact that, overall, twentieth-century music differs from earlier music in terms of harmony, themes, form, and instrumentation, its diversity includes a spectrum of deviation. Some works *are* tonal and *do* employ themes and forms that are similar to those of previous eras. Others, as stated earlier, are at the opposite end of the spectrum and are unlike any predecessor. And between these two poles, a middle ground of vaguely familiar work exists. This area has the potential of becoming a bridge of comprehension for audiences confused by the array of twentieth century music.

Three degrees of familiarity are apparent in twentieth century art music: direct correspondence with an earlier era; reminiscence with another era; total uniqueness.

MUSICAL TRENDS AT THE TURN OF THE CENTURY

Several dominant musical trends and movements are presented in this chapter. These are representative of one of the three "familiarity" categories mentioned in the preceding paragraph. The trend or movement will either correspond directly to one of another era, will be reminiscent of one, or will be totally unique from any musical counterpart.

Impressionism

The early twentieth century was an age of "isms" in the arts. The earliest of these was impressionism, a movement that began in painting in the 1870s. Later the term was carried over into the field of music.

The central painters in the impressionist movement were Claude Monet, Pierre Auguste Renoir, and Edgar Degas. Although each had a unique artistic style, they are associated because of their similar treatment of color and light, and also because of their purposeful disregard

Impressionism began in painting with Monet, Renoir, and Degas.

A twentieth century image

Impressionist painters recreated the mood and atmosphere of a scene, not the image itself.

of photographic reality. Notice in Monet's painting (fig. 9.1) an object that resembles a woman in a pastoral setting. The faithful photographic representation of the scene was not a concern of Monet's; the mix and flow of colors, the play of light upon them, and the urgency to capture the magic and the atmosphere of the moment were his concerns. The reality of the scene is not obliterated, but it is somewhat distorted. This is a purposeful distortion, however, for the painting is not really "about" the woman or the setting; it is more "about" the mood and the atmosphere of the scene.

Debussy captured impressionism in music.

Debussy's *Danse bohémienne* is characteristic of piano music of the late nineteenth century.

Impressionist music—Debussy It is always risky and rarely fruitful to try to draw direct parallels between two different art forms. Nevertheless, some musicians and scholars have found analogies between impressionist painting and certain works by Claude Debussy (1862–1918), and these analogies are not without some validity. To understand Debussy's music, let's listen to two of his many works for piano. The first, *Danse bohémienne* (1880), is an early work composed several years before Debussy formulated his impressionistic style.

Danse bohémienne is a piano piece like countless others written in the late nineteenth century. Despite its charm, the piece alone would not ensure Debussy's position as a master. Notice that *Danse bohémienne* has a very clear-cut *ABA*-coda design, is solidly in a key, and is in

Fig. 9.1
Impressionist painting: *Woman Seated Under the Willows* by Monet.

The National Gallery of Art, Chester Dale Collection, 1962

Claude Debussy
(1862–1918)

2/4 meter. There is also a clear division of labor between the two hands: the right-hand plays the melody (which, you will notice, is singable and memorable) while the left-hand plays an accompaniment.

In contrast, listen to Debussy's "Brouillards" from Preludes, second book (1910–13). What is the form of this piece? Does it sound as if it is definitely in a key? What meter is it in, and can you sing a melody? In terms of texture, is there an unmistakable division of labor between the right- and the left-hand?

The formal structure of *Danse bohémienne* is predictable and conventional. For example, the return of the *A* section is not surprising. But practically nothing about the structure of "Brouillards" is predictable: the events in the piece do not seem to connect with one another,

Brouillards is impressionistic.

The key, the meter, and the texture are not readily apparent in Brouillards.

Debussy's impressionist music reflects the experimentation of the twentieth century.

Debussy's atmosphere pieces are unconventional.

Debussy combined standard musical practices with twentieth century innovations.

The symbol A+ designates a nonliteral repetition of a section plus the introduction of new material.

but merely succeed one another. It is evident only after repeated listenings that this order of events is purposeful, not accidental. A clear sense of tonic and dominant does not emerge from the harmony. The chords are not violently dissonant, yet the key the piece is in is not well-defined. The key is not obliterated, but is veiled.

The piece is in 4/8 meter, but this is not immediately apparent when listening to the work. In the place of melody, fragments of thematic material are presented, yet these don't constitute a theme in the conventional sense. The fragments materialize and then disappear in the texture. The texture is not divided into melody and accompaniment; rather, the right-hand and the left are interwoven in such a way that each plays an equal role. Thus, in form, rhythm, harmony, melody, and texture, Debussy departed from the norms of his immediate background. Notice how Debussy's music reflects the dawning of a new era—the era of twentieth century music.

Every so often a composer comes along who has a special touch with orchestration. Debussy was such a composer. His major orchestral works—*La Mer, Prélude à l'Après-midi d' un faune, (Prelude to the Afternoon of a Faun), Images,* and the three *Nocturnes,* all possess a touch of magic.

Debussy's wonderfully atmospheric piece, "Nuages," was introduced in chapter 4. Listen to the piece again, this time concentrating on a different perspective and taking into consideration the context of twentieth century musical practice. "Brouillards" suggests the possibility of an unconventional formal structure in Debussy's works. For instance, Debussy's works can be analyzed in terms of sections, but a major difference exists between his sectional forms and the sectional forms of earlier composers. Some of Debussy's content, for example from section *A,* is likely to appear in some guise in section *B.* This shared content creates a situation where there are no sharply defined differences between the various sections of the same piece; the lines between the sections are blurred. Debussy was also fond of repeating sections, but at the same time introducing new material in the repetitions. This practice creates both old and new sections simultaneously.

In diagraming forms in baroque, classical, and romantic works, the symbol *A'* has been used to indicate a nonliteral repetition of *A.* In Debussy's music, the *A'* is either inaccurate, or at best, incomplete. In his music those repeated sections having new and significant material are better designated *A+.*

Listen to the piece just to take in its sound and mood before proceeding to the Sound and Sense. Once you have heard the piece, study the formal diagram, and with it in hand, listen to "Nuages" once again.

SOUND AND SENSE: *Twentieth Century Sectional Form*

Title: "Nuages" from Three *Nocturnes*

Composer: Debussy

A Closer Look:

A—Introduces a gently floating figure played on clarinets and bassoons, followed by a mysterious figure played on the English horn (this is a terse, fragmentary figure so typical of Debussy). The floating figure is repeated, this time by the string section, and the English horn fragment is stated twice more.

B—Begins with a dark, slow, ascending figure stated by the lower woodwinds. Behind this figure, the strings restate the floating figure from *A*—this is an instance of shared content mentioned earlier.

A+—Repeats the English horn fragment two more times. The floating figure is stated by the strings, this time, however, the violas and cellos add a soft plucking backdrop. Toward the close of this section, a solo viola introduces a new theme-fragment, thus creating the need for an *A+* rather than a simple *A'*.

C—A new theme is introduced by flute and harp. Although this theme seems to have no conventional sense of direction, it is long and shapely enough to be a genuine melody.

Coda—Is introduced by the English horn figure. The piece ends slowly and very quietly.

The success of this piece owes a great deal to Debussy's masterful orchestration. It would be a very different piece, and far less successful, if it were to be played on a piano instead of by an orchestra. Debussy employed a large orchestra that never rises to full voice; in fact, there is only one measure marked *f* (the last measure of the *B* section). The remainder of the piece is marked *mp* or softer. The size and potential power of the orchestra is not disguised, but Debussy subtly restrains this coiled power.

Through orchestration, Debussy created the illusion of space and distance. Just at the close of the first English horn statement in the *A* section, listen carefully for the low, rumbling tympani (marked *ppp*) and the simultaneously-sounding violins far, far above. The same illusion of space is evident later in the *A* section as the English horn figure is restated under the floating figure in the violins. The French horns add another spatial dimension, for they seem to be sounding from a distance. With this illusion of space, listen again to the entire *C* section.

Symbolism

A literary movement called **symbolism** (another early twentieth century "ism") developed in Paris shortly after impressionism. The symbolist poets and playwrights were fascinated by the raw materials of language—words—and the sonorous qualities of them. Their poetry often consisted of words that were carefully selected and strung together because of the way they sounded, rather than because they made syntactical sense. The symbolist poets were willing to distort syntax in order

Symbolist poets and playwrights focused on words rather than meaning.

Art Nouveau: Tiffany lamp

to expose the sheer beauty of words and the symbolic references evoked by them.

Debussy's music shows the influence of symbolism.

Debussy was attracted to the ideas and aesthetics of the symbolists, several of whom were his close friends. His only opera, *Pelléas et Mélisande,* is based on a text by symbolist Maurice Maeterlinck, and *Prélude à l' Après-midi d' un faune (Prelude to the Afternoon of a Faun)* was inspired by a text by another symbolist, Stéphane Mallarmé.

Symbolist poetry was especially attractive to Debussy. This is a suggestive art, one that hints and suggests rather than one dealing with concrete descriptions of things and ideas. Typical ingredients of symbolist poetry include a sense of mystery, veiled eroticism, potential danger, and fear. There are also frequent evocations of an ancient decaying world—often the world of classical antiquity. The poetry is subtle and refined, but rarely is it dramatic or heroic.

Symbolist poetry is subtle, mysterious, erotic, and carries an unspoken element of danger and fear.

Some of these qualities of symbolist poetry are evident in the poem ''La Flute de Pan'' by Pierre Louÿs, another friend of Debussy's. Debussy set this strange, enigmatic poem to music. When listening to the song, notice how perfectly Debussy's vocal line and piano part fit the mysterious mood of the text, shown here.

Debussy set symbolist poetry to music.

"La Flute de Pan"

Pour le jour des Hyacinthies,
I m'a donné une syrinx faite
De roseaux bien taillés,
Unis avec la blanche cire
Qui est douce à mes lèvres comme
 le miel.
Il m'apprend à jouer, assise sur ses
 genoux;
Mais je suis un peu tremblante.
Il en joue apres moi, si doucement
Que je l'entends à peine.
Nous n'avons rien à nous dire,
Tant nous sommes près l'un de
 l'autre;
Mais nos chansons veulent se
 répondre,
Et tour à tour nos bouches
S'unissent sur la flûte.
Il est tard;
Voici le chant des grenouilles vertes
Qui commence avec la nuit.
Ma mère ne croira jamais
Que je suis restée si longtemps
A chercher ma ceinture perdue.

"The Flute of Pan"

On this day of Hyacynthus,
He has given me a pipe made
Of well-cut reeds,
Joined together with white wax
That is as sweet as honey on my
 lips.
He teaches me to play while I sit on
 his knees;
But I tremble just a little.
He plays it after me so softly
That I can hardly hear him.
We have nothing to say,
So close are we to one another;

But our songs want to harmonize,

And gradually our lips
Are united on the flute.
It is late;
Here is the chant of the green frogs
That begins with the night.
My mother will never believe
That I stayed out so long
In search of my lost belt.

A great deal is suggested in this poem, but little that is concrete is divulged; the whole episode is bathed in mystery. The poem is also vaguely erotic, and the words "I tremble just a little," hint at some undefined fear. Pan, the half-man, half-beast creature from classical antiquity, is in modern times associated with music (his flute), but in mythology is also supposed to have had the power to incite irrational fear in others (our word *pan*ic is derived from this side of Pan's personality). Thus, Louÿs aptly introduced this element of fear in his poem.

"La Flute de Pan" exhibits the characteristics of symbolist poetry.

As mentioned earlier, there was a school of impressionist painters united by similar ideas about painting. At the same time, a circle of symbolist authors evolved because they, too, felt a kinship in literary convictions. These two groups of artists found a common aesthetic ground. The impressionist artists distorted photographic reality; the symbolist authors distorted syntactical reality. The impressionist painters were fascinated by the raw materials of painting—color and light; the symbolists were enthralled by the raw material of literature—words.

Impressionist painters and symbolist poets came together on common aesthetic ground.

No school of impressionist/ symbolist musicians evolved.

Debussy had a profound influence on many twentieth century composers.

Unlike these artistic areas, no similar circle or school of music was established in Paris. Debussy was the sole musical representative of the impressionist/symbolist faction, and most of his closest friends were painters or poets, not composers. But Debussy's musical style had a profound influence on younger, contemporary composers and on composers of succeeding generations. Principal among these were the Frenchman Maurice Ravel (1875–1937), the American composer Charles Griffes (1884–1920), and the Englishman Frederick Delius (1862–1934). Some aspects of Debussy's harmonic practices and his orchestration impressed many other composers and even affected American popular music, especially movie music beginning in the 1940s.

Expressionism

The chaotic, mean, and ugly state of the world during the opening years of the twentieth century was partly responsible for the emergence of an artistic movement called **expressionism.** Expressionist writers such as Franz Kafka (1883–1924) described the horrifying destruction of European civilization in their publications. These works were capable of exposing raw nerves, and expressing the horror, emotionalism, terror, pain, and agony felt by humanity. Expressionism survived into the mid-twenties, reacting against the horror and inhumanity of World War I.

Expressionism reflected the horror of World War I and its aftermath.

Expressionist writing, painting, and music were created to reveal the unpleasant truth of human existence.

Expressionism, whether in literature, painting, or music, did not attempt to create beauty. It strove rather to express the unvarnished and terrible truth of human existence. Where impressionism viewed the world objectively and covered it with a beautiful, sensuous surface, expressionism looked at the world subjectively from the inside out.

The three principal exponents of musical expressionism were Austrians.

Schönberg   The principal exponents of musical expressionism were Arnold Schönberg (1874–1951) and two other Austrian composers who were once his students: Alban Berg (1885–1935) and Anton Webern (1883–1945).

Schönberg's expressionist music evolved over time.

The fertile, innovative mind of Arnold Schönberg led his style through several evolutionary stages. As a young man his style showed the influence of Brahms and Wagner. But in the first and second decades of the twentieth century, he produced a number of atonal expressionistic works. And in the 1920s Schönberg developed—literally invented—a new method of organizing pitches: the twelve-tone system. This system, and expansions of it, have had far-reaching implications on twentieth century music. Its principles and methodology have been adopted, in varying degrees, by hundreds of European and American composers since World War II.

In the early twenties Schönberg invented the twelve-tone system.

Schönberg's *Pierrot Lunaire* (1912) is the quintessential expressionist work. Based on twenty-one poems by Albert Giraud, the work is scored for a small instrumental ensemble and voice. The activity of the voice in this work has become a trademark of musical expressionism. Schönberg wrote this part not to be sung in the conventional manner of singing, nor to be spoken as in dramatic recitation, but to partake of both singing and speaking. This type of vocal utterance is called **Sprechtstimme.** *Sprechtstimme* is not as lovely as singing nor as dramatic as speech can be, but its position between the two endows it with a peculiarly evocative and highly-charged emotionalism. The text to the first poem of *Pierrot Lunaire* appears here.

Arnold Schönberg (1874–1951)

MONDESTRUNKEN

Den Wein, den man mit Augen
    trinkt,
Giesst Nachts der Mond in Wogen
    nieder,
Und eine Springflut überschwemmt
Den stillen Horizont.

Gelüste, schauerlich und süss,
Durchschwimmen ohne Zahl die
    Fluten!
Den Wein, den man mit Augen
    trinkt,
Giesst Nachts der Mond in Wogen
    nieder.

Der Dichter, den die Andacht treibt,
Berauscht sich an dem beilgen
    Tranke,
Den Himmel wendet er verzückt
Das Haupt und taumelnd saugt und
    schlürft es
Den Wein, den man mit Augen
    trinkt.

MOONDRUNK

The wine that only eyes may drink

Pours from the moon in waves at
    nightfall,
And like a springflood overwhelms
The still horizon rim.

Desires, shivering and sweet,
Are swimming without number
    through the flood waters!
The wine that only eyes may drink

Pours from the moon in waves at
    nightfall.

The poet, by his ardor driven,
Grown drunken with the holy
    drink—
To heaven he rapturously lifts
His head and reeling slips and
    swallows
The wine that only eyes may drink.

Much of the music composed by Schönberg and his two students during the early decades of the century is marked by extreme dissonance and by feverish emotionalism. Tonality (functional harmony) was abandoned in this music, so it is often referred to as **atonal.**

Expressionist music exhibits extreme dissonance, emotionalism, and atonality.

Webern   Webern's *Five Movements* for string quartet (1909) is an excellent introduction to his stylistic traits as well as to the realm of musical expressionism. The five movements are extremely brief: movements two and four are each only thirteen measures long, but each presents an extraordinary amount of emotional intensity and range of emotions. Every

Webern's music is charged with emotional intensity and mood change.

phrase, every motive, almost every note creates an emotional impact, so condensed are these emotions. When listening to movement one, notice how quickly and drastically the moods change. On a higher structural level, notice the radical difference in mood and atmosphere as movement one progresses into movement two.

Berg composed an expressionist opera—Wozzeck, the story of one man's tragic existence.

Berg's **Wozzeck**　Alban Berg's *Wozzeck* (1921) is a monumental work of the later stages of musical expressionism and ranks among the greatest and most powerful operas of the twentieth century. It consists of three acts, each having five scenes, in which the grizzly story of Wozzeck unfolds, a man in the process of a complete mental, moral, and spiritual disintegration. Wozzeck, an underling in the army, is hounded and abused by his superiors. He is humiliated by his common-law wife, Marie, whom he murders at the peak of his insanity. In his madness Wozzeck returns to the rural lake that is the scene of his crime. He wanders out into the lake, which he believes has turned to blood, and drowns.

The small child of Wozzeck and Marie is left behind to find his own tragic way in the world. In the final scene of the opera, Wozzeck's orphan is playing on a homemade stick horse. His playmates rush to him and say: "Hey, you . . . your mother is dead." In one of the classic understatements in the history of opera, the scene ends—or perhaps we should say it disappears quietly, almost sweetly.

The complete text to act III, scenes ii and v, is shown here. Ideally you should listen to the entire opera with text in hand. If, however, time is limited, these two scenes at least introduce you to the work and to the vocal, harmonic, and orchestral practices of Berg at this stage in his career.

The Holy Face, Rouault

National Museum of Modern Art, Paris

ACT III
Scene ii

(Waldweg am Teich. Es dunkelt. Marie kommt mit Wozzeck von rechts.)

Marie
Dort links geht's in die Stadt. 's ist noch weit. Komm schneller!

Wozzeck
Du sollst dableiben, Marie. Komm, setz' Dich.

Marie
Aber ich muss fort.

(Forest Path by a pool. Dusk is falling. Marie enters with Wozzeck, from the right.)

Marie
The town lies over there. It's still far. Let's hurry!

Wozzeck
You must stay awhile, Marie. Come, sit here.

Marie
But it's getting late.

Wozzeck

Komm. *(sie setzen sich)* Bist weit gegangen, Marie. Sollst Dir die Füsse nicht mehr wund laufen. 's ist still hier! Und so dunkel.—Weisst noch, Marie, wie lang' es jetzt ist, dass wir uns kennen?

Marie

Zu Pfingsten drei Jahre.

Wozzeck

Und was meinst, wie lang' es noch dauern wird?

Marie

(springt auf)
Ich muss fort.

Wozzeck

Fürchst Dich, Marie? Und bist doch fromm? *(lacht)* Und gut! Und treu! *(zieht sich wieder auf den Sitz; neigt sich, wieder ernst, zu Marie)* Was Du für süsse Lippen hast, Marie! *(küsst sie)* Den Himmel gäb' ich drum und die Seligkeit, wenn ich Dich noch oft so küssen dürft! Aber ich darf nicht! Was zitterst?

Marie

Der Nachttau fällt.

Wozzeck

(flüstert vor sich hin)
Wer kalt ist, den friert nicht mehr! Dich wird beim Morgentau nicht frieren.

Marie

Was sagst Du da?

Wozzeck

Nix.

(Langes Schweigen. Der Mond geht auf.)

Marie

Wie der Mond rot aufgeht!

Wozzeck

Come! *(They sit down)* So far you've wandered, Marie. You must not make your feet so sore, walking. It's still, here in the darkness.—Tell me, Marie, how long has it been since our first meeting?

Marie

At Whitsun, three years.

Wozzeck

And how long, how long will it still go on?

Marie

(jumping up)
I must go!

Wozzeck

Trembling, Marie? But you are good? *(laughing)* and kind! and true! *(He pulls her down again on the seat; he bends over her, in deadly earnest)* Ah! How your lips are sweet to touch, Marie! *(kisses her)* All Heaven I would give, and eternal bliss, if I still could somtimes kiss you so! But yet I dare not! You shiver?

Marie

The night dew falls.

Wozzeck

(whispering to himself)
Who cold is, you who shiver, will freeze no more in cold morning dew.

Marie

What are you saying?

Wozzeck

Nought!

(A long silence. The moon rises.)

Marie

How the moon rises red!

Wozzeck
(zieht ein Messer)
Wie ein blutig Eisen!

Marie
Was zitterst? *(springt auf)* Was
willst?

Wozzeck
Ich nicht, Marie! Und kein Andrer
auch nicht!
*(packt sie an und stösst ihr das
Messer in den Hals)*

Marie
Hilfe!
*(sinkt nieder. Wozzeck beugt sich
über sie. Marie stirbt.)*

Wozzeck
Tot!
*(richtet sich scheu auf und stürzt
geräuschlos davon)*

Wozzeck
(He draws a knife)
Like a blood-red iron!

Marie
You shiver? *(She jumps up)* What
now?

Wozzeck
No-one, Marie! If not me, then no-
one!
*(He seizes her and plunges the
knife into her throat)*

Marie
Help!
*(She sinks down. Wozzeck bends
over her. She dies.)*

Wozzeck
Dead!
*(He rises to his feet anxiously, and
then rushes silently away)*

Funfte Szene
Scene Five

*(Strasse vor Mariens Tür. Heller
Morgen. Sonnenschein. Kinder
spielen und lärmen. Mariens
Knabe auf einem Steckenpferd
reitend.)*

*(In front of Marie's door. Bright
morning. Sunshine. Children are
playing and shouting. Marie's
child is riding a hobbyhorse.)*

Die Spielenden Kinder
Ringel, Ringel, Rosenkranz,
Ringelreih'n!
Ringel, Ringel, Rosenkranz Rin . . .

*(unterbrechen Gesang und Spiel,
andere Kinder stürmen herein)*

Children
Ring-a-ring-a-roses, all fall down!

Ring-a-ring-a-roses, all . . .

*(They stop, and other children
come rushing on)*

Eins Von Ihnen
Du Käthe! . . . Die Marie . . .

Zweites Kind
Was is?

Erstes Kind
Weisst' es nit? Sie sind schon Alle
'naus.

One of These
Katie! . . . Marie . . .

Second Child
What is it?

First Child
Don't you know? They've all gone
out there.

Drittes Kind	**Third Child**
(zu Mariens Knaben)	*(to Marie's child)*
Du! Dein Mutter ist tot!	Hey! Your mother is dead.

Mariens Knabe	**Marie's Child**
(immer reitend)	*(still riding his horse)*
Hopp, hopp! Hopp, hopp! Hopp, hopp!	Hop, hop! Hop, hop! Hop, hop!

Igor Stravinsky (1882–1971)

Zweites Kind	**Second Child**
Wo is sie denn?	Where is she now?

Erstes Kind	**First Child**
Draus' leigt sie, am Weg, neben dem Teich.	Out there, on the path by the pool.

Drittes Kind	**Third Child**
Kommt, anschaun!	Let's go and look!
(Alle Kinder laufen davon.)	*(All the children run off)*

Mariens Knabe	**Marie's Child**
(reitet)	*(continues to ride)*
Hopp, hopp! Hopp, hopp! Hopp, hopp!	Hop, hop! Hop, hop! Hop, hop!
(zögert einen Augenblick und reitet dann den anderen Kindern nach.)	*(hesitates a moment, and rides off after the other children.)*

Stravinsky's Early Works

Igor Stravinsky (1882–1971) is the most honored and celebrated composer of the twentieth century. His works have all been recorded and have been performed all over the world. Countless articles, books, and special studies have been written about him, his life, and music. He is unquestionably one of the giant figures in twentieth century art music and his influence on composers is incalculable.

Stravinsky is a major twentieth century composer.

In the course of his long, productive career, Stravinsky's personal style continuously evolved and changed. This evolution can be categorized into three distinct style periods: the early works—up to about 1917; the middle, or "neoclassic" period—up to about 1951; and the late works, created during the last twenty years of his life. On the surface, each of the three styles sounds unique. However, one aspect of Stravinsky's creativity is obvious in all three. Each has the same uniquely powerful rhythm. This rhythm is especially effective in dance pieces, as evidenced by the popularity of Stravinsky's work in this musical genre.

Stravinsky's art music shows three distinct styles.

All three of Stravinsky's styles have powerful rhythm.

Stravinsky rehearsing *The Rite of Spring.*

Petrushka   Stravinsky burst upon the Parisian musical scene with the production of three ballets that established him as a luminary in the musical world: *The Firebird* (1910), *Petrushka* (1911), and *Le Sacre du Printemps (The Rite of Spring)* (1913). All three are scored for a very large orchestra, all have story lines based on Russian folklore, and all employ Russian folk melody.

Stravinsky's ballets are based upon Russian folklore and feature Russian folk melodies.

SOUND AND SENSE: *Ballet*

Title: *Petrushka*

Composer: Stravinsky

A Closer Look:

The setting of *Petrushka* is a fair, and the time framework is a single day. The ballet is divided into four scenes. In the first scene, a showman appears with his three puppets—Petrushka (a clown), a beautiful ballerina, and the evil but fascinating Moor. The showman charms his puppets to life with his flute. To the astonishment of a gathering crowd, the puppets jump down from the stage and begin to dance.

In the second scene, Petrushka, who has become the most human of the puppets, is in his cell. Here, the audience is made aware of Petrushka's humanlike emotions: he bitterly resents the showman, but falls in love with the ballerina. The scene ends as Petrushka, in frustration, hurls himself at a portrait of the showman.

Scene three takes place in the Moor's cell. A love scene between the ballerina and the Moor is interrupted by Petrushka's arrival. Petrushka is beaten and thrown out.

The final scene occurs in the evening at the end of the day's festivities. Petrushka is killed by the Moor, and his corpse lies in the street as it begins to snow. But Petrushka's ghost appears above the stage, threatening and thumbing his nose at the showman.

The following is a listening guide for the first scene:

A—The atmosphere of the fair is conveyed—sparkling, shimmering orchestration. A leaping motive in the flute enters periodically and sails over the rest of the texture.

B—The full orchestra plays (homophonically) a bright, energetic Russian tune that has the rhythm:

This accompanies the performance of a group of slightly drunk, prancing merrymakers.

C—A stroke on the tympani announces the arrival of the showman. A few bars later, the leaping motive from *A* reappears.

D—A few bars after the *A* repetition, the tempo slows and two twittering flutes call attention to an organ grinder and a street dancer. The organ grinder plays on.

E—The street dancer plays a triangle and dances to a popular tune played by flutes and clarinets. The tune disappears briefly and then returns. Intermittently, the leaping motive from *A* returns. Then there are varied repetitions of *CABAA*, culminating in a big climax that is followed immediately by a long roll on the drums. This completes the first large section of this scene. It runs directly into the concluding portion.

F—After a brief introduction, a playful flute solo is heard—this is the showman playing his flute. After a short but brilliantly orchestrated episode, the flute, with three little strokes, brings the puppets to life.

G—A fast Russian dance is played by the full orchestra. The tune has the rhythm:

Notice that the piano is an active member of the orchestra, and although it plays a solo later in this section, it is not treated as a soloist with orchestra, but rather as a legitimate member of the orchestra. This was a new role for the piano, one which held great attraction for later composers.

At the beginning of the second scene, after an introduction of a few measures, two clarinets play a theme-fragment. Notice that something sounds peculiar. This peculiarity stems from the fact that the clarinets are playing in two different keys at the same time. The first clarinet plays the theme-fragment (which has come to be known as Petrushka's theme) in the key of C, while the second clarinet plays it in the key of F♯. This type of music, performed simultaneously in two different keys, is called **bitonality.** (Music written in three or more simultaneously sounding keys is called **polytonality.**) In the history of music there are isolated examples of bitonality and polytonality, but these practices were not widely used until the early twentieth century. Thus, they are considered harmonic innovations of our century.

Innovative Bartók

Béla Bartók (1881–1945) had several musical careers: he was a pianist, a teacher, an important folk music collector of his native Hungary as well as elsewhere, was active in music education, and was one of the giant composers of the twentieth century.

Collecting and studying folk music was not a hobby for Bartók; it was a scholarly and musical passion. Many of his compositions reflect this passion, for they abound with Hungarian folk melodies and rhythms.

Bartók's music did not enjoy widespread popularity during his lifetime, but since the end of World War II, his popularity has grown dramatically. His string quartets, six in number and composed from 1909–39, are now regarded as among the greatest written during the twentieth century. They are popular the world over, and are frequently recorded by various string quartet groups.

The Fourth String Quartet (1928) is not a typical string quartet, but is a work unto itself. The work does, however, present some features that are typical of Bartók's style. The harmonic language is at times extremely dissonant, but generates excitement and interest rather than repulsion. The thematic materials are either drawn directly from folk sources or are newly composed by Bartók and resemble folk song. Many of his themes are compact and limited to a narrow range; they revolve around relatively few pitches and intervals. The sense of color is very pronounced in his work. Color refers to the harmony and special effects Bartók draws from the instruments. Notice that in one movement in this quartet, there are several types of pizzicatos, including one in which the fingernail causes the string to snap against the wooden neck of the instrument, producing a percussive sound. Bartók also requires the players to strum their instruments like guitars.

Bitonality describes music performed simultaneously in two different keys.

If music is played in more than two keys at the same time, it's called polytonality.

Bartók was active in diverse areas of music.

Bartók's compositions reflect his scholarly interest in Hungarian folk music.

Bartók's string quartets are considered among the greatest of the twentieth century.

The Fourth String Quartet typifies Bartók's style.

Bartók's style includes: dissonance, folk themes, colorful harmony, pizzicatos, and unique rhythms.

Bartók's rhythm Bartók's rhythms are as individual and unique as are Stravinsky's. The peculiar yet fresh flow of many of Bartók's rhythms are also derived from Hungarian folk music. The meters in this type of music are different from the regular meters of Western European music. For example, the 9/8 meter is normally beat and felt in three beats of three eighth notes each:

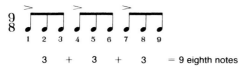

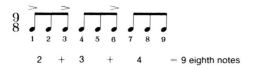

But in Bartók's music, the accents are likely to produce different groupings of eighth notes, and hence an entirely different feel for the 9/8 meter:

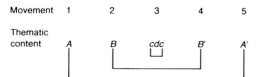

Bartók's structure Bartók is one of the most ingenious and innovative twentieth century composers in terms of musical structure. The large-scale structure of the Fourth String Quartet is as follows:

Movement	1	2	3	4	5
Thematic content	A	B	cdc	B'	A'

The diagram reveals the symmetrical shape of the five-movement piece. The outer movements (one and five) are similar because they share variations of the same material. The inner movements (two and four) also share the same material and are thus closely related. The central movement (three) is not linked to another, but notice that it, too, has the symmetrical shape *cdc.*

Be aware that the outer movements of this work are contrapuntal (counterpoint is a central ingredient in Bartók's music). The inner movements have the character of the scherzo, and in terms of texture, are opposites of each other: the second movement is muted and legato (smooth, connected playing), while the fourth movement presents a wide variety of pizzicato playing. Both of these movements proceed at a breathtaking pace. The central movement, on the other hand, is very

Many of Bartók's rhythms are derived from Hungarian folk music.

Bartók's accents create a unique feeling in common meters.

Béla Bartók (1881–1945)

Symmetrical shape is common in Bartók's movements.

Counterpoint is central to Bartók's music.

slow and mysterious. Its c sections feature cello solos with obvious folk or gypsy music roots. These solos are played against a soft, dissonant background of long-held notes on the other three instruments. The d section is a night music episode for which Bartók is famous. (Remember the movement called "The Night's Music" from Bartók's *Out of Doors* suite we met in chapter 4?) The chirping of birds and the zinging and twittering of insects are given full and magical voice in this d section.

Music for strings, percussion and celesta   Bartók's Music for strings, percussion and celesta (1937) has found a permanent place in the repertoire of many major symphony orchestras. It is one of the earliest major works to feature and realize the potential of the percussion family. Concertgoers who are turned off by "dissonant music" are attracted to this work, even though it abounds with dissonance. There is much more in the work that is fascinating, haunting, and compelling.

In this work, two string orchestras are played against a third body of instruments consisting of celesta, xylophone, harp, tympani, other percussion instruments, and piano, which is used mainly for its percussive effects in a manner similar to Stravinsky's use of the piano in *Petrushka*. There are four movements in the piece, each of which develops a different mood. However, there are some general similarities between movements one and three and two and four. The structure of interrelationships is very complex, such that a detailed explanation of them at this point would be less useful than broad comments about some of the salient features of the work. With the following comments in mind, listen to the piece several times.

The first movement is a fugue, the subject of which is long and full of short chromatic twists and turns. It is confined to the range of a perfect fifth and is thus very compact. There are twelve successive statements of the subject, each one beginning on a different pitch. The arrival of the twelfth entry marks the climax of the movement. Having arrived at that point, Bartók inverted the theme (turned it upside down), and in another series of staggered entries, returned it to the original starting pitch, A. At that point, the celesta enters for the first time. The plan of this movement is diagramed in figure 9.2.

The mood of the second movement is entirely different in character. Some of the featured thematic material is reminiscent of folk music, but is treated in a saucy, playful manner and moves in and out of passages of extreme dissonance. Notice that the piano is used in a percussive, barbarous way and that there are extended solo passages for the tympani. The movement is in a sonata form, although this may not be immediately obvious. The exposition presents the energetic A theme on

Bartók is famous for his night music episodes.

Bartók's Music for strings, percussion and celesta is one of the first major works to feature the percussion instruments.

Bartók uses the piano for percussive effect.

The first movement of the piece is a fugue.

The celesta enters at the end of the first movement.

The second movement is in sonata form.

Fig. 9.2

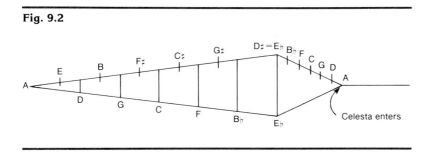

Celesta enters

the piano. Later, a loud strike on the tympani ushers in the skittish *B* theme on the violins. The development section, the longest part, introduces a new theme that becomes the basis for another fugue. An extended passage for tympani signals the recapitulation, which is considerably different from the exposition.

In the third movement, the night music atmosphere returns. Special features of the movement include tympani **glissandos** (sliding from one pitch to another), another gypsylike theme in the low strings, an extended passage in which the celesta creates an atmosphere rather like a gauze of pure color, without the benefit of anything resembling a real theme. The whole movement is, in fact, given over to washes of color and the atmosphere of the nighttime. The movement ends as it began—quietly and mysteriously.

Folk song elements are present in the last movement. There are also exact repetitions of the fugue subject of the opening movement. Again, the piano is used in a percussive manner. Near the end of this final movement, the music quiets down momentarily, and then concludes with a furious rush.

The Music of Ives

The music of American Charles Ives (1874–1954) was virtually ignored until shortly before his death. However, in recent years, a widespread enthusiasm for it has developed and has resulted in numerous performances and recordings of his works. Ives was a rugged individualist who stubbornly clung to his musical-philosophical beliefs and refused to conform in the ways that might have gained him popularity. He was a man who was truly ahead of his time; thus it took the musical public about half a century to catch up with and recognize the nature and the quality of his music.

The third movement features night music.

The term "glissandos" describes the method of sliding from one pitch to another.

Folk song appears in the final movement.

Charles Ives (1874–1954)

Ives, in the spirit of
Thoreau, was a rugged
individualist.

The individualist   Among Ives' heroes was Henry David Thoreau, the American transcendentalist writer, who was himself a rugged individualist. A few lines from Thoreau's *Walden* aptly describe Ives:

> Why should we be in such desperate haste to succeed and in such desperate enterprises? If a man does not keep pace with his companions, perhaps it is because he hears a different drummer. Let him step to the music which he hears, however measured or far away.

Ives believed that, because he would be forced to conform or compromise in order to "succeed" in music, his creative powers would suffer if he were to make music his career. Instead, he elected to pursue a career in life insurance and proved to be very successful at it. He composed in the evenings and on weekends, working at an upright piano in the attic of his home in Danbury, Connecticut. In the seclusion of this environment, Ives exercised his freedom to create many kinds of music: tonal, atonal; sacred, secular; and music for voices and various instrumental ensembles. Ives was also an experimenter: he wrote bitonal and polytonal works before such things were current in Europe, and retuned a piano in quarter tones (that is, intervals smaller than the minor second); he also used tone clusters that are batches of adjacent pitches. He envisioned, but purposely did not complete, a gigantic work called the *Universe Symphony* (conceived in 1910). The three sections of the symphony were to represent the "formation of the waters and mountains"; the "earth, evolution in nature and humanity"; and "heaven, the rise of all to the spiritual." The work was to have been performed by a number of choruses and orchestras spread out over various mountains and valleys. Such was the incomparable imagination of this gentle New England man at the turn of the century.

Ives composed many kinds
of music and experimented
with bitonality and
polytonality.

Ives conceived of a major
work entitled "Universe
Symphony."

Ives' patriotism and
religious zeal are reflected
in his compositions.

Ives was a patriotic American and a deeply religious person, though not in any orthodox sense. This may account for the fact that many of his works quote patriotic songs, hymn tunes, and other songs native to America. These quotations are sometimes misunderstood by those not familiar with Ives' character and philosophy, and so appear humorous. Ives did have a very active sense of humor, but generally the quotations from well-known tunes were not employed for their comedic value.

Many familiar tunes were
woven by Ives into new
musical fabrics.

The tunes and the fresh environments Ives created for them were important to the substance of his music. Ives said that in music it is not so much what happens, but the way it happens. You can expect to hear "Turkey in the Straw," "Nearer My God to Thee," "Columbia the Gem of the Ocean" (one of Ives' particular favorites, used in several different pieces), and many other tunes as you acquaint yourself with his music. But keep in mind the importance of the way these tunes occur, not simply that they do occur.

It is important to note,
however, *how* these tunes
are incorporated in the
composition.

"The Fourth of July"   "The Fourth of July" is the first movement of a larger piece called *Holidays* symphony. As a young boy, Ives had been thrilled by two marching bands, each playing a different piece, coming toward each other from opposite directions. The young Ives was situated at the point where the two bands converged. The clash of the two oncoming bands was pure excitement to him. Again, it was not so much what happened, but the way it happened.

"The Fourth of July" is a musical recollection of that experience. After a quiet beginning, the piece develops into a free fantasy on "Columbia the Gem of the Ocean" and some other tunes. Toward the close of the movement there is a passage of tremendous excitement, clashing rhythms, and roaring dissonance. This passage ends as abruptly as it began and the soft murmuring strings carry us off into the evening on a fourth of July many years ago.

Included among his other major works are the *Concord* Sonata (for piano), Fourth Symphony (for which Ives suggests using two conductors), *The Unanswered Question* (heard in chapter 4), *Variations on "America"* (for organ), and over a hundred songs. His output was not prolific, but failing health and perhaps lack of recognition contributed to the fact that after 1921 he composed very little.

Of Ives' collection of songs, the most dramatic is "General William Booth Enters Heaven." One of the most charming is "At the River," Ives' unique adaption of the old hymn "Shall We Gather at the River?"

Ives' "The Fourth of July" was inspired by a childhood experience involving two marching bands.

The dissonance is reminiscent of the two bands coming together, each playing a different song.

Ives did not produce a large number of compositions.

MUSIC BETWEEN THE WARS

Dadaism

> Honor can be bought and sold like the arse. The arse represents life itself like potato-chips, and all you who are serious-minded will smell like cow's dung. Dada alone does not smell: it is nothing, nothing, nothing. It is like your hopes: nothing.

This quotation is from one of the numerous "Manifestos" published by various dadaist groups early in the twentieth century.

Is it a joke? If so, it's not particularly funny—strange maybe, but not humorous. Is it serious? If so, it is a grim, nihilistic view of life. That is the most enigmatic thing about the curious movement called dada: we can never be sure whether it was intended to be funny or serious or perhaps both.

No one can be sure of the exact intent of the dada movement, but it was a reaction against the horrors of World War I.

After World War I, many movements were spawned in Europe.

Futurism advocated the overthrow of the present establishment and its replacement with a machine civilization.

Dadaists reflected the insanity of humankind rather than advocated further destruction.

The dadaist movement did inspire some of the music of Erik Satie.

Satie, an eccentric, captured the dadaist spirit in his compositions.

Consider the titles of Satie's works.

In the years surrounding World War I, several strange, short-lived movements developed that were partly artistic and partly political in nature. The horror, slaughter, and scope of World War I shook European civilization to its very roots. Because of this war, there was reason to believe that humankind had become a race of mad dogs. Out of revulsion, and as a reaction against this state of affairs, these movements were spawned.

Some of the movements, futurism, for example, preached violence, anarchy, the overthrow of all institutions and conventions, and the establishment of an entirely new civilization based on action and the adoration of machines. The movement called for a music created from the sound of machines, rattles, scrapers, and other noisemakers.

Dadaism, too, grew out of the ashes of World War I, but it was a less violent and more productive movement than futurism. This movement espoused the philosophy that it is better to laugh at the world than to further destroy or lament it; it is better to admit and reflect the insanity of humankind than to pretend that all is at last well. Dada is the French term for hobbyhorse, a purposeless name appropriate for the outrageous antics of the dadaist movement members.

Erik Satie   A body of dadaist music as such is nonexistent, but some music does develop the dadaist spirit of fun. Although he was not an official member of the dadaist movement in Paris, some of the music, as well as the mannerisms, of Erik Satie (1866–1925) captures the spirit of dada.

Erik Satie's behavior has earned him the label "eccentric." He appended his signature with "gentle, medieval musician," and it is said that he wore nothing but gray suits, and that he ate nothing but white foods. His sense of humor, too, was offbeat. He said of himself:

> Ask anyone, and he will also tell you that I am no musician. This is quite true. Since the beginning of my career, I have been a phono-metrographist . . . I measure sound. Phonometer in hand, I blithely weigh all of Beethoven . . . all of Verdi, etc. The very first time I used a phono-scope I examined a medium-sized E♭. I assure you in all sincerity that I have yet to see anything quite as repulsive! . . . On my phono-scale, a common F♯ attained the weight of ninety-three kilograms! (It came from a very fat tenor.) Have you ever heard of the science of cleaning sound? It's filthy, you know.

Even the titles of some of his works are imbued with dadaist nonsensical humor: *Three Pieces in the Form of a Pear, Second to Last Thoughts, Flabby Preludes,* and *Desiccated Embryos,* all composed for

Collection, The Museum of Modern Art, New York, Purchase

piano. The production of his ballet, *Parade,* in 1917, caused a scandal in Paris because of its unorthodox content and presentation. Satie composed the music, Jean Cocteau wrote the scenario, and Pablo Picasso designed the cubist-style sets and costumes. The score calls for a standard orchestra as well as a revolver, roulette wheel, and typewriter.

Given all of this as a background, what can we expect the music to be like? The most astonishing aspect of *Parade's* music is its tameness. Like all of Satie's music, it is essentially simple and consonant. Cocteau said, "We want to create art with an axe." Despite this announced goal, Satie's music is gentle and at times even melancholy. Some of his themes even border on banality and his orchestration is modeled on music-hall sound rather than elegant, polished orchestral sound characteristic of many of his contemporaries. In effect, Satie brought the sounds of the street into the concert hall, a most shocking and revolutionary concept in music. To an audience accustomed to the music of Brahms and Tchaikovsky, Satie's music was shocking, not because it was trenchantly dissonant or wild, but because it struck them as disgustingly and arrogantly cheap.

Satie's ballet, *Parade,* caused a scandal.

Satie's revolution was caused by bringing the sounds of the street into the concert hall.

♪ SOUND AND SENSE: *Dadaist Style*

Title: *Parade*

Composer: Satie

A Closer Look:

Listen to the first few minutes of *Parade*—until the sounds of the gunshots. This will serve as an introduction to Satie's dadaist style. This brief encounter includes the following:

A homophonic statement in the brass, in the form of a slow fanfare
A serene, repetitious tune
A fugue
Another repetitious tune played first by the clarinet, then picked up by other members
  of the orchestra building to a full statement
A vaguely Oriental-sounding section
Ragtime, music hall section
Typewriter solo
The gunshots

Satie's most famous work—*Gymnopédie* no. 1—is not dadaist.

Not all of Satie's music can be called dadaist. For example, his most famous piece, *Gymnopédie* no. 1, is not. Originally written for piano, the piece was later orchestrated by Debussy, and in more recent times has been incorporated into a work by the rock group Blood, Sweat, and Tears. Listen to the original (piano) version first. It may not be profound, but it is delicate and charming, and creates a unique mood.

Satie's music has been more popular recently than it was with his contemporaries.

Young composers influenced by Satie formed a group called "Les Six."

Satie's popularity, though never monumental, has increased with time even though his output was limited. Those elements of his music that were considered banal and cheap by audiences during his lifetime are fresh and touching to contemporary audiences. There was a revival of interest in Satie's music during the late 1960s with the rise of a movement called neo-dadaism. But even before that time, Satie's influence was evident in the works of some young composers known as **Les Six** (the French Six).

The French Six

Three of the six composers were important to twentieth century music.

Only three of the six members of this group had an impact on twentieth century music: Darius Milhaud (1892–1974), Francis Poulenc (1889–1963), and Arthur Honegger (1892–1955). None of them ever studied with Satie, but each profited from his encouragement and guidance. Milhaud, early in his career, and Poulenc to a lesser degree, were influenced by some of Satie's music and by his irreverent attitude toward art music. Honegger, a very capable composer, was less radical in his views and was less directly influenced by Satie.

The French Six, or perhaps more accurately the French Three, produced a handful of sturdy, enduring works that are still performed frequently. Some of their music, however, borders on the trivial.

These three men produced music that is still performed today.

Honegger's best known works are his two dramatic oratorios, *Le Roi David (King David)* (1923), and *Jeanne d' Arc au bûcher (Joan of Arc at the Stake)* (1938), as well as the tone poem *Pacific 231* (1923).

Pacific 231 is the name of a French train. In using a train for the subject, Honegger strayed from the nineteenth century programmatic basis of a tone poem of either a person, an idea, or a scene drawn from nature. Honegger's choice of a train for this purpose is a distinctly twentieth century idea. The short work is a marvel of musical realism, for it effectively captures the sounds, motion, and speed of the train using a conventional orchestra.

Honegger's tone poem *Pacific 231* is an example of twentieth century musical realism.

The piece begins with the train in the station, huffing and puffing, slowly gathering the steam necessary to get the enormous machine into motion. We can actually sense the build up of power. It slowly moves from the station and gradually picks up tempo until it reaches its full speed dashing across the countryside. Then the opposite process begins: the slowing down of the train. Finally it reaches its destination— the station at the other end of the line.

Notice the new "sound effects" Honegger creates with the orchestra. These are essential to the success of the composition. Notice, too, that although there is, by nineteenth century standards, considerable dissonance, the piece does not greatly deviate from the sense of being in a key.

Sound effects created by the orchestra are essential to the success of the piece.

Milhaud   Milhaud was one of the most prolific of contemporary composers. He composed in all the major genres, and incorporated into his own style elements of several kinds of music, including jazz and Latin American rhythms. His most experimental works (and many people believe, his best works) date from his early career. At that time Milhaud was particularly fond of polytonality, especially evident in his *Le Boeuf sur le toit (The Bull on the Roof)* (1919). Milhaud assembled several popular melodies, mostly of Brazilian origin, and separated them from each other by a recurring rondo theme, which also begins the piece. Toward the end of the rondo theme, a flute produces a fragment in one key,

Milhaud, another member of the French Six, incorporated into his style a number of influences.

Polytonality is evident in Milhaud's early works.

followed by a clarinet echoing the fragment in another key. The first Brazilian melody occurs next, the initial phrase of which is solidly in key.
When this phrase is repeated, however, the harmony becomes discord-
ant, as though someone were playing the wrong notes. The notes are,
in fact, correct, but are also in several different keys. The music-hall
sound of the brass and the popular atmosphere of this work suggest that
Milhaud was here influenced by Satie.

**Milhaud incorporated
American jazz into his
ballet, *The Creation of the
World.***

A somewhat more serious but no less experimental work is Milhaud's ballet, *La Création du Monde, (The Creation of the World)* (1924).
In the 1920s several art music composers became fascinated with American jazz and tried to incorporate some of its spirit into their concert
works. Milhaud did this in several of his works, but primarily in this ballet. *La Création du Monde* is also one of the earliest art music works to
extensively use the saxophone.

Neoclassicism

Stravinsky's new style   Igor Stravinsky's tremendous success in the
early years of the century is attributable to the three ballets mentioned
earlier. These, as was explained, relied heavily on Russian folk music,
pounding rhythms, and a huge, colorful orchestra. However, beginning
at the close of World War I Stravinsky changed his style dramatically,
thus confusing the musical world. He abandoned the large orchestra in
favor of small instrumental ensembles, and the thicker, many-toned
chords in favor of leaner harmonies. He also worked more with tonality
and began writing works that were in a key. In the 1920s, 1930s, and
1940s Stravinsky composed sonatas, a violin concerto, a piano concerto, symphonies, and even concerti grossi. In other words, he reverted
to the genres, textures, and tonality of the classical era, and in some
instances, to the baroque era.

**Stravinsky began to
compose a different kind of
music after World War I.**

**Stravinsky's new style
reverted to the genres,
textures, and tonality of
the classical era and the
baroque.**

**The movement that formed
around Stravinsky and his
emulators is called
neoclassicism, but because
of the importance of
baroque elements to this
music, it could have been
termed neobaroque.**

Stravinsky succeeded in bringing a new freshness to these traditional forms and practices. Other composers emulated him, creating
what amounted to a movement. In time, the movement acquired a label—
another twentieth century "ism"—neoclassicism. But the influence of
the baroque on this movement is just as great as the influence of the
classical. Thus the movement could just as easily have been labeled neobaroque.

SOUND AND SENSE: *Classical and Baroque Combination*

Title: *Octet*

Composer: Stravinsky

A Closer Look:

Stravinsky's *Octet* (1923) is a piece in which both classical and baroque elements are welded to create a new musical amalgam. The *Octet* is scored for flute, clarinet, two bassoons, two trumpets, and two trombones. It has two movements, each of which has two parts: "Sinfonia," composed of a slow introduction, and a fugue; and "Theme with Variations," composed of a theme with variations and a finale. The work is in a key, although it contains many dissonances that are further accentuated by this peculiar instrumentation.

First Movement

The introduction is similar to the slow ones Haydn often used in his symphonies. This leads directly into the fugue, a musical process perfected by Bach and other masters from the late baroque.

Second Movement

Stravinsky took the concept of theme with variations, a form favored in both the baroque and classical eras, and reshaped it to conform to his own needs. The theme section is, of course, stated first. This is followed by the first variation that features, among other things, running passages on the bassoons. Then follows the second variation that is marchlike in character. The first variation then returns, which is a departure from baroque and classical norms. A third and fourth variation are followed by another repetition of the first variation. This part of the movement concludes with a fifth variation that contrasts sharply with the others in terms of tempo and mood. The finale follows without pause and has a modified rondo form: *ABAC-coda*. In a classical rondo the form would have concluded with another statement of *A*; Stravinsky omits this and moves directly to a heavily-syncopated coda.

Stravinsky's Symphony in C (1940) (which deliberately alerts us to the fact that the work is in a key) is a prototypical neoclassic work. Based directly on the model of the late eighteenth century symphony, this one has the standard four movements: fast-slow-dance (scherzo)-slow/fast. The slow portion of the last movement is the only structural departure from the classical norm.

Stravinsky's Symphony in C is based directly upon the eighteenth century symphony.

Your knowledge of Haydn and Mozart symphonies should help you recognize the sonata-allegro form of the first movement. There is even a similarity between Stravinsky's *A* theme and the *A* theme (first movement) of Mozart's well-known Symphony in G Minor, K. 550.

Compare Stravinsky's symphony to Mozart's Symphony in G Minor, K. 550.

While Stravinsky was an early and important advocate of neoclassicism, it is inaccurate to name him its inventor. Many composers from the 1920s to the present have produced works that to varying degrees are neoclassic. This does not mean, however, that the music of all

Many twentieth century composers were attracted to neoclassicism.

The works of the neoclassic composers do not sound alike.

Prokofiev's music is considered neoclassical.

Prokofiev identified three basic aesthetic/stylistic lines in his music.

these composers sounds alike. Each was attracted to one or more aspect of neoclassicism: tonality, the genres, themes, forms, or instrumentation. Thus, Stravinsky and Prokofiev could each write a neoclassic piece, but the Stravinsky piece would sound uniquely like Stravinsky, while the Prokofiev work would sound only like Prokofiev.

Prokofiev   Russian Sergei Prokofiev (1891–1953) was another important composer during the years between the wars. Many of his compositions fall into the neoclassical category. In his autobiography (1941), Prokofiev outlined three basic aesthetic/stylistic lines in his music: (1) a lyrical line that is peppered by the lively spirit of the scherzo; (2) a classical line that is a reflection of his love for the music of Beethoven, Haydn, Mozart and others; and (3) a motor line, referring to his frequent use of perpetual motion rhythms. These attributes are obvious in Prokofiev's music. They are, for example, clearly evident in his Third Piano Concerto, C Major, op. 26 (1921).

SOUND AND SENSE: *Neoclassicism*

Title: Third Piano Concerto, C Major, op. 26
Composer: Prokofiev
A Closer Look:

The work has the standard three-movement concerto format: fast-slow-fast. The first movement lacks a cadenza and is in sonata-allegro form.

First Movement

Exposition
Introduction—begins with a lyrical theme in the clarinet, is joined by the strings and
    leads to *A.*
A—this vigorous theme is stated first by the piano and then by the orchestra with
    piano.
Bridge—here, the motor line continues.
B—some heavy piano chords lead to this *B* theme stated first by an oboe. This theme
    has the lyrical scherzo nature mentioned previously.
B'—the piano picks up this theme and bends it out of shape.
Bridge

Development
The *A* theme is developed by strings, piano, and clarinet. The clarinet theme from the introduction is also developed. The development continues in a marchlike section.

Recapitulation
A—stated by the piano as in the exposition.
A'—restated and further developed.
Coda—the *B* theme is not recapitulated.

Second Movement

The second movement, a theme with five variations and coda, presents a theme that is heavily laden with a lyrical scherzo quality. Notice that just as the theme begins to turn sweet, Prokofiev introduces sour dissonance.

The form of the second movement is as follows:

Theme
first variation—stated by the piano
second variation—piano with orchestra, perpetual motion
third variation—fulll chords, very energetic
fourth variation—slow, lyrical, almost dreamlike
fifth variation—faster
Coda—the theme is restated in ornamented form and is filled with driving energy.
However, the movement ends abruptly and quietly.

Third Movement

The third movement begins with a theme in the bassoons that is then extended and developed. Then follows a sarcastic theme played by the piano in alternation with strings and woodwinds. It, too, is expanded and developed. Suddenly and quite unexpectedly a long, lyrical section, dominated by two subthemes, enters. This builds to a romantic climax reminiscent of Rachmaninoff. The movement and the piece conclude with a brilliant extended coda in which the first theme of this movement is prominently featured.

The Americana Composers

During the years between World War I and World War II, several talented young American composers emerged as significant musical figures. This group includes Aaron Copland (b. 1900), Samuel Barber (b. 1910), Walter Piston (1894–1976), Roger Sessions (b. 1896), and Virgil Thomson (b. 1896). These composers were born at the turn of the century, and so are considered children of the twentieth century. Several of them eventually held teaching positions at prestigious American universities and became prominent figures in art music circles in the States. More than a few of these men studied composition in Paris with the legendary composition teacher, Nadia Boulanger (1887–1980), truly one of the great women in the history of Western art music.

Until early in this century, the United States labored under an artistic inferiority complex that made it difficult for American composers to be accepted as serious artists. But this situation began to change and the inferiority complex began to dissipate with the emergence of this group of young Americans. Their composition skills and artistic sensitivities demanded attention.

Important American composers emerged between the wars.

The young American composers—Copland, Barber, Piston, Sessions, and Thomson—were children of the twentieth century.

Not until the twentieth century were American composers accepted as serious artists.

Copland's compositions incorporated distinctly American music and themes.

In time, these composers became a source of national pride. Some of them, most notably Copland, began to experiment with indigenous music and subject matter. Their works incorporated American jazz and folk music, along with distinctly American themes. This experimentation was reflected in the songs, operas, ballets, orchestral music, and movie music these composers created.

The music was consciously composed to have broad appeal.

Copland, Barber, and several others consciously crafted and tailored their musical styles to appeal to a larger audience. Each in a highly individual way created music that was lyrical and energetic without being abrasive.

SOUND AND SENSE: *American Themes*

Title: *Music for the Theatre*

Composer: Copland

A Closer Look:

Copland's *Music for the Theatre* (1925) is composed of a set of five short pieces ranging in length from three to five minutes, and scored for a small orchestra. The pieces are all tonal though there are many effective, pungent dissonant sonorities. This music is not designed to frighten an audience out of its wits with prolonged dissonance and complex counterpoint, but is tastefully designed to appeal to a broad audience. It is intended to sound familiar to an audience that has relatively little acquaintance with art music. The music is "comfortable," yet it does not stoop to cheap musical tricks or to oversimplification. It is possible to detect the influence of 1920s jazz, and some thematic material is reminiscent of folk song.

The first piece, called "Prologue," presents an *A* theme played by the trumpet. The strings enter quietly and provide a cushion for the lyrical *B* theme, played by an oboe. A faster, heavily syncopated and jazzy development section follows, at the conclusion of which the *A* and *B* themes are recapitulated, ending the piece quietly.

The second piece, "Dance," again displays the influence of jazz. Bassoon and percussion play a saucy *A* theme. Muted trumpet and then clarinet pick up a *B* theme to the thumping background of the piano playing an ostinato. *A* and *B* are repeated, and a brief, abrupt coda ends the piece.

"Interlude," the third piece in the set, is the most folklike in quality. The English horn plays an extended melancholy theme that resembles music from an epic western movie. Gradually the strings, the piano, and percussion emerge to form a background as the clarinet picks up the theme and adds to it some blue notes. One by one, other solo instruments enter against the soft, velvety string background. The English horn restates its original solo to end the piece quietly.

"Burlesque," the fourth in the set, sharply contrasts with the preceding piece. It has the form *ABAB*. The *B* theme features a jazzy trumpet that plays against the background of a lazily bouncing accompaniment

The last piece in the set, "Epilogue," restates themes from "Prologue" and "Interlude." The clarinet begins by stating the trumpet theme from "Prologue," though here the mood is very different. The piece and the set end quietly.

Nighthawks, Edward Hopper

Art Institute of Chicago, Friends of American Art Collection

Another notable Copland work is *Appalachian Spring* (1944), a ballet he composed for dancer Martha Graham. The story presented in the ballet is very simple, detailing life in an American pioneer community in the early nineteenth century. The most famous excerpt from *Appalachian Spring* is a set of variations Copland wrote on the folk hymn "Simple Gifts." The work is still performed as a ballet, but the orchestral arrangement is even more popular today.

Copland's ballet *Appalachian Spring* features an American theme and an American folk hymn.

♪ SOUND AND SENSE: *The American School*

Title: *Adagio for String Orchestra*

Composer: Barber

A Closer Look:

Another example of music from the American school is Samuel Barber's *Adagio for Strings* (1938). It is a seven-minute work built on a single theme. This softly undulating theme is long, slow, and haunting. It winds around a few notes, then leaps upward with complete naturalness and effortlessness. The work contains a great deal of counterpoint, but is never fussy or intricate; it, too, seems to evolve and roll with ease. The harmonic language is tonal and soft, though not without sad and touching dissonances.

The theme or variations of it is stated four times before reaching an impressive climax in the high strings. A coda that includes a final shortened statement of the theme then follows. In all but one case there is a clear break between the end of one statement of the theme and the start of the next. Graphically illustrated the structure looks like this:

A	*A'*	*A''*	*A'''*	*A''''*	Climax	Coda
Theme in violins	Theme in violins	Theme in violas	Theme in cellos	Theme in cellos		

The Twelve-Tone System

In 1925 Arnold Schönberg produced the first piece of music composed in its entirety in accordance with the principles of the **twelve-tone system.** He had been formulating the system for some years and had composed a partial twelve-tone work as early as 1923, but the system was not fully formulated until 1925.

Schönberg completed the twelve-tone system in 1925.

What is the twelve tone system? Simply stated, Schönberg's twelve-tone system is a means of organizing pitches to create musical coherence and consistency. As stated previously, there are twelve different pitches normally employed in the music of the Western world.

C C♯(D♭) D D♯(E♭) E F F♯(G♭) G G♯(A♭) A A♯ (B♭) B
1 2   3 4   5 6 7   8 9   10 11   12

The twelve-tone system is a careful, logical method of organizing pitches to avoid tonality.

Schönberg's idea was to relate these pitches only to one another rather than to have them relate to and be subservient to a few pitches and chords. In tonality, pitches and chords are arranged so that they all relate to tonic, dominant, and subdominant, and all ultimately resolve into and relate to the tonic. In a real sense, Schönberg's system released all pitches of their obligations to the tonic and allowed them to become free agents related only to each other. The system is a careful, logical means of avoiding tonality.

No pitch will reoccur until the other eleven have been sounded.

One of the principles of this system is that no single pitch is repeated until all of the other eleven pitches have been sounded. Thus, if the first pitch in a given piece is C, it will not reoccur until C♯, D, D♯, E, F, F♯, G, G♯, A, A♯, and B have been sounded. These pitches can be sounded one at at time, as in melody, or they can be sounded in clusters, that is, chords. Another principle is that melodies and chords that sound similar to melodies and chords found in tonality are avoided.

The tone row is a series of twelve different pitches and their attendant intervals.

The basic building blocks of the twelve-tone system are the **tone row** and versions of it. The tone row is a series of twelve different pitches and their attendant intervals. The row is the basic thematic and harmonic material out of which the music is made. Figure 9.3 shows the row from Schönberg's *Suite* for piano, op. 25 (1925).

If the row is upside-down, the term is inversion.

If the row is backwards, the term is retrograde.

An upside-down and backwards row is termed retrograde inversion.

A group of pitches such as in this row has an intrinsic relationship to certain versions of itself. Such a relationship exists (1) in the upside-down version of the row, (2) in the backwards version, and (3) in the upside down and backwards version. In the twelve-tone system the upside-down version of the row is called the **inversion;** the backwards version is called the **retrograde;** and the upside-down and backwards version is called the **retrograde inversion.** These versions of the row are illustrated in figure 9.4.

Fig. 9.3

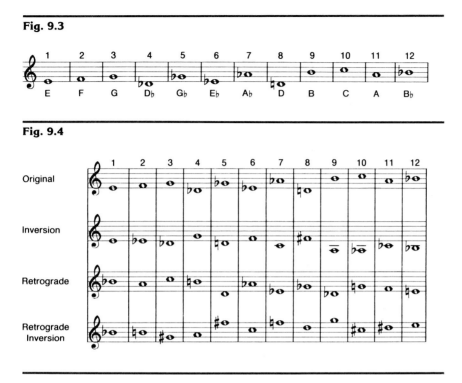

Fig. 9.4

In figure 9.4 the row is referred to as the "original" or simply "O"; it is the original row from which the other versions spring. Notice that this original begins by moving up a half step and then up a whole step, and so on. The inversion begins by moving *down* a half step and then *down* a whole step, and so on. In other words, when the original moves up by a specific interval size, the inversion moves down by that same specific interval size. When the original moves down, the inversion moves up. The retrograde is simply the mirror version of the original: it starts with the last pitch of the row and follows the series backwards to the first pitch of the row. As its name implies, the retrograde inversion is the retrograde in upside-down form.

Any of these four versions can be transposed (moved up or down) to begin on any other pitch. Eleven transpositions are possible for each of the versions. There are, then, $4 \times 11 = 44$ possible versions of the row, the total available pitch material for a given twelve-tone composition.

Listen now to Schönberg's *Suite* for piano. It is composed in the manner of a baroque keyboard suite with the following movements: prelude, gavotte, musette, intermezzo, minuet and trio, and gigue.

The original row is designated "O."

In twelve-tone composition, there are forty-four possible versions of each tone row.

Webern expanded upon Schönberg's system.

Schönberg's system ordered pitches in serial fashion—hence the name **serial music.** His student, Webern, expanded the system by serializing rhythms, dynamics, and timbres, and he also developed a rhythmic language that was startlingly new and different. Webern's approach to pitch and rhythm was highly intellectual, mathematical, esoteric, and above all, musical. His music and ideas had an enormous impact on post World War II serialist composers.

MUSIC AFTER WORLD WAR II

Since about 1950 a flood of new ideas has emerged and many different things have happened in the world of music, both popular music and art music.

The latest developments in music show three common characteristics.

In trying to assess the major developments in art music over the past several decades, at least three things rise to the surface and command our attention: (1) the ''new'' music is a continuation and expansion of earlier musical traditions; (2) electronically-generated sound is used; and (3) there is a fascination with the element of chance.

Contemporary composers are following the lead of early twentieth century composers.

Many contemporary composers have found that their musical needs are best served by following and enlarging upon the paths blazed by composers from earlier in this century, regardless of whether the path is essentially tonal, atonal, serial, or experimental. Today, these men and women are successfully producing music guided by the efforts of their predecessors. Much of the music of Stravinsky, Bartók, Ives, Schönberg and others, that was once so controversial, has become traditional. Some has even been assured a permanent place in the repertoire of Western art music. These early twentieth century traditions, and those from several other eras, are a dominant force in the art music scene today.

Music considered shocking early in the century has now become accepted as a part of art music.

The practices of Schönberg and Webern have been adapted over the years.

The musical practices of Schönberg and Webern, especially, have been adopted by many composers in recent decades. Milton Babbitt (b. 1916) and Pierre Boulez (b. 1925), among others, have been influenced by Schönberg and Webern. Even Aaron Copland and Igor Stravinsky have written twelve-tone works in recent years. Babbitt and others have expanded serialization to rhythm and other parameters of music.

The twentieth century has witnessed unorthodox methods of playing instruments.

Some composers have enlarged the sound resources of conventional instruments and the voice. Beginning in the 1960s, composers sometimes required performers to do unorthodox things with their instruments: a trombonist was asked to take the instrument apart and play on only a part of it; an oboist was required to gently stroke the instrument with a felt mallet; a flutist was instructed to run the fingers rapidly over the keys without blowing into the instrument; a singer was asked

The Detroit Institute of Arts, Founders Society Purchase, Edsel B. Ford Fund and Gift of Edsel B. Ford

Detroit Industry; 1932–33 by Diego M. Rivera

to gurgle and scream instead of sing; and a pianist was required to manually strum the strings of the piano. As early as the mid-1940s, composer John Cage wrote music for prepared piano, which is a piano having bits of metal, glass, rubber, plastic or other articles placed in its strings. At its worst, the prepared piano is cheap and gimmicky, but when performed with taste and skill, the instrument can offer a thrilling array of new sounds. John Cage's *Concerto for Prepared Piano and Orchestra* (1951) reveals the prepared piano at its most beautiful.

Music written for prepared piano is unique to the twentieth century.

The Rise of Electronic Music

Just after the end of World War II several types of electronic equipment were either invented or refined. The ensuing decades saw an increase in such inventions and refinements, so that today we have a fund of highly sophisticated and versatile electronic instruments that have been and are being put to a variety of musical uses.

Electronic music emerged after World War II.

Bringing music to life by capturing it on magnetic tape distinguishes electronic music from every other type.

Twentieth century composers have the option of combining media.

Electronic music is created with magnetic tape, a tape recorder, a sound generator, and a loudspeaker.

All audible sound is the source of music for the composer of electronic music.

Distortion of audible sounds is also used by the electronic-music composer.

Electronic equipment can increase the number of pitches within an interval.

Rhythm also has been drastically affected by electronic equipment.

There is at least one fundamental difference between purely **electronic music** and all other music. Consider how nonelectronic music evolves. The composer invents the musical idea then transliterates the idea into a system of notation that is committed to paper. The composer must then rely on the ability of someone else to read and interpret these notational symbols and transliterate them in yet another way into sounds that are produced by that person's voice or instrument.

In contrast, the composer of electronic music captures the sounds he or she desires on magnetic tape, then plays the tape resulting in the music coming to life. Remember, however, that the composer's role in this process is infinitely more complex than this simple statement suggests.

Some composers create purely electronic music, or music that uses only electronically generated sounds; others create compositions that use both electronically generated sounds and sounds produced by human performers—a mixture of media.

The basic pieces of equipment needed to create electronic music are magnetic tape and a tape recorder, a sound generator, and a loudspeaker. To these, various filters and mixers, which allow the composer to alter the generated sounds, can be added. Literally, anything audible can be captured on magnetic tape, so the composer of electronic music has an enormous resource of sounds at his disposal. The composer can, if he or she wishes, use the sound of thunder, airplanes, traffic, factory whistles, or other environmental noises. In fact, such sounds were the basis of an early form of electronic music called Musique Concrete, which first developed in France in the late 1940s.

The composer may also employ any or all of the infinite variety of sounds that can be produced by a sophisticated electric sound generator. Of course ordinary pitches and the sounds of conventional instruments and voice are still available to the electronic-music composer. If he or she has the right equipment, the composer can alter or distort any sound in limitless ways, and different kinds of sounds can be combined in equally limitless ways.

The smallest standard interval commonly employed in Western music is, as stated earlier, the minor second: c to c♯, for example. But with the proper electronic equipment, forty to fifty individual pitches between c and c♯ can be obtained by the simple rotation of a dial.

Electronic music is no less revolutionary in terms of rhythm. Nonelectronic music measures musical time in terms of beats, meters, and tempos. Electronic music measures time in terms of inches per second of tape, so the notion of beat and meter is of no consequence. An

Sound synthesizer

infinite number of durational values and mind-boggling rhythmic complexities are available in electronic music, plus the composer is not at the mercy of human performers to accurately deliver them.

Some composers, Babbitt among them, celebrate the idea of having absolute control over every aspect of their compositions, including the performance of them. Electronic instruments ensure the composer that his or her works will remain intact, as they were conceived, without the risk of human error during performance. In pure electronic music nothing is left to chance: no one will sing or play out of tune, no one will assume the wrong tempo or fail to properly execute the most intricate rhythms. This may seem cold and impersonal, and there is no denying that in some respects pure electronic music is depersonalized; yet unfailing precision in performance has definite merit.

(As has been seen, pure electronic music differs from all other music in fundamental ways. Therefore, it cannot be interpreted or analyzed according to traditional methods. If we attempt to force electronic music into all of our preconceived musical pigeon holes we will only be frustrated and disappointed.)

Electronic music cannot be analyzed in terms of beat, meter, rhythm, and other traditional elements.

Stockhausen's *Song of the Youths* is a landmark in electronic music.

This piece combines one human voice and eleven different electronically generated sounds.

Stockhausen   Karlheinz Stockhausen (b. 1928) has emerged as a central figure in the field of electronic music. He has written pure electronic works, nonelectronic pieces, and a now-famous composition for voice and electronic instruments called *Gesang der Jünglinge (Song of the Youths)* (1956). This work is generally considered a landmark in the development of electronic music. Listening to the work and understanding its construction leads to the conclusion that it is, among other things, a technological wonder.

Gesang der Jünglinge sounds incredibly complicated, yet the sound materials from which it is constructed are relatively simple: one human voice and eleven different electronically-generated sounds. All of the sounds can be filtered, mixed, and dubbed (recorded over the original sound at different pitches and speeds). Stockhausen began by recording the voice of a youthful choirboy singing and sometimes speaking the following text:

Preiset den Herrn, ihr Werke alle des Herrn;	O all ye works of the Lord, bless ye the Lord:
lobt ihn und über alles erhebt ihn in Ewigkeit. . . .	Praise Him and magnify Him for ever. . . .
Preiset den Herrn, Sonne und Mond;	O ye Sun, and Moon, bless ye the Lord;
preiset den Herrn, des Himmels Sterne.	O ye Stars of Heaven, bless ye the Lord.
Preiset den Herrn, aller Regen und Tau;	O ye Showers, and Dew, bless ye the Lord;
preiset den Herrn, alle Winde.	O ye Winds of God, bless ye the Lord.
Preiset den Herrn, Feuer und Sommersglut;	O ye Fire, and Heat of Summer, bless ye the Lord;
preiset den Herrn, Kälte und starrer Winter. . . .	O ye Cold, and icy Winter, bless ye the Lord. . . .

Stockhausen was less interested in the text being sung in a ''meaningful'' way than he was in the sounds produced by the boy's voice. These individual sounds, which he calls ''phones'' (from phonetics), are blended into the electronic sounds of the work, and some are electronically altered. By means of multiple dubbings, the single voice is made to sound like several voices singing simultaneously. Thus, from one voice comes many different sounds, rhythms, and timbres.

Similarly, the handful of basic electronic sounds are manipulated to yield a rainbow of sounds and timbres.

SOUND AND SENSE: *Electronic Music*

Title: *Gesang der Jünglinge (Song of the Youths)*

Composer: Stockhausen

A Closer Look:

In this composition as in any music, it is critical that we get our bearings, that is, that we have some idea of structure and of activities that take place. With repeated listenings, the differences between the various activities should be apparent. The description and order of these activities is listed below. Notice that in most cases one section of activities is set off from the next by silence. Thus, silence is a unifying factor in this piece.

The piece begins with a fanfare made of electronic gurgles, squeaks, pops, and
   grunts. It ends softly.
Silence
The boy's voice enters next. In the background is a soft accompaniment of new
   electronic sounds. The activity swells to a chord; there is a soft ending.
Silence (very brief)
Multiple voices in counterpoint are heard behind a solo voice. The electronic sounds
   are now more numerous and active. Later, speech develops into singing, but
   then returns to the multiple-voice background. The section ends with a long-held
   note.
Silence
This is a longer section than the others, containing speech, *Sprechstimme,* and
   singing. The electronic sounds create some violent periodic outbursts and some
   hitherto unexplored low notes.
Silence
This section begins with electronic screeches and bird calls. There are snatches of
   solo and of multiple voices, followed by more bird calls and swarming sounds.
Multiple voices are reduced to a solo voice having echo effects. In the background
   there are rattling sounds. Then a solo voice sings against a background of
   silence. Soon the rattling sounds reoccur. Throughout the remainder of this long
   section, listen for thumping sounds that resemble low drums playing an almost
   recognizable tune. A chorus fades in and out and there are patches of speech.
   The section ends quietly.
Silence
Voices are heard far in the distance behind a solo voice and a very animated
   electronic accompaniment.
Silence
A low hum gradually swells and builds to a chorus of humming voices.
Silence
A quick, jerky flourish ends the piece without warning.

Chance Music

The composer of chance music gives up most of the control over the performance of the piece.

The composer who seeks absolute control over all aspects of his or her composition is at the opposite end of the aesthetic pole from the composer of **chance,** or **aleatory, music.** The composer of chance music willfully abdicates some or most of the control over what happens in a given composition. For example, instead of indicating specific notes, rhythms, or dynamics to the performers of the piece, the composer might say to them, "Here are some notes and rhythms. Please play them in any order, at any speed, but play them all very, very softly." Thus the composer's work is part composition in the usual sense of the word, and it is part suggestion. When the performers follow the specific directions and the nebulous suggestions, they create a piece of music that happens by chance. The chances are that the piece will never be the same in any subsequent performances. For the composer, the performers, and perhaps even the audience, this is the desired situation.

A piece of chance music will never sound exactly the same at any two performances.

Some composers use chance throughout the entire process of writing music.

Some composers of chance music have resorted to completely random processes for selecting the materials included in their compositions. The composer collects numbers, forms, and other kinds of information from rolling dice, flipping cards, or throwing darts at tables of numbers. The gathered information then suggests to the composer chords, rhythms, instrumentation, and other elements of the composition.

There are, though, degrees of chance. Some composers use chance in a restricted way, reserving chance for only certain portions of a given composition. Others try to build into the composition as much chance as is possible without a chaotic result.

Composers of chance music differ over the philosophy behind it.

Some people who are active in the field of chance music state that there is no purpose in this type of music. Others attempt an explanation of chance music in philosophical terms, or in vague terms about freeing music from the shackles that have imprisoned it for centuries. Exactly how it is being freed, and precisely how music will improve with this "freedom" are questions that have not yet been adequately answered.

Many composers of chance music are experimenting beyond the realm of music as we know it.

But to give chance or aleatory music its due, it should be said that there are composers in the movement who are honestly and skillfully exploring the outer limits of music. Some venture beyond these limits and into a realm beyond music as we know it, but may find they have to retrace their steps. It is also possible that these explorers may succeed in expanding the limits of music as it now exists.

John Cage is the leader of chance composers.

Cage　The spiritual leader of chance music is John Cage (b. 1912), who first legitimized the use of chance operations in musical composition. In 1951 he wrote (or designed) a piece called *Imaginary Landscape no. 4.* The work requires twenty-four performers and twelve radios; for each radio, one performer rotates the station dial and another performer operates the volume dial. All performers read from written parts and are directed by a conductor.

Obviously *Imaginary Landscape no. 4* can never sound the same twice. The content of the piece is determined by which radio stations are picked up by the twelve different radios during the performance of the piece. The time of day and the geographical location also affect the content. At any performance no one, including Cage himself, can determine the final outcome.

The outcome of a chance music performance can not be predicted.

Four years later, in 1954, Cage "composed" a piece called *4' 33"*. In this piece a person with a watch sits at a piano playing nothing at all for four minutes and thirty-three seconds. The noises of the audience as well as all other audible sounds during the performance are the sound material of the piece. Clearly, it is impossible for *4' 33"* to sound the same way twice.

(To my knowledge there are no recordings of these pieces. In fact, recording a piece that is supposed to be different each time it is performed would be pointless and would run counter to the philosophy on which it rests.)

Other works by Cage use chance operations, but in a more restricted sense. Among the most elaborate of these is *HPSCHD* (1971), which he wrote with Lejaren Hiller, a composer who specializes in computer-generated music. *HPSCHD* consists of fifty-one electronic sound tapes, seven solo compositions for harpsichords, and elaborate slide shows and other visuals. Unlike *4' 33"*, recordings of *HPSCHD* are available.

Cage's compositions are innovations in the field of music.

SUMMARY

From the beginning of the seventeenth century until the twentieth century, functional harmony was the musical constant unifying the compositions of the baroque, classical, and romantic eras. Some twentieth century composers, however, abandoned tonality in favor of experimentation with other musical possibilities. The result was expressionism, the twelve-tone system, electronic music, and chance music. Other composers remained faithful to functional harmony while expressing themselves through impressionism, polytonality, and neoclassicism. Students of twentieth century art music have concluded that the century has produced no one fundamental, stylistic unity, but instead has offered a basic and perplexing diversity.

At the turn of the century, the impressionist movement was dominant in both art and music. Painters such as Monet, Renoir, and Degas created art with the purpose of reproducing a mood rather than an image. Debussy's impressionist music offered undefined illusion as in "Nuages."

Early in the twentieth century, symbolism focused on the beauty of words. Symbolist poets wrote of mystery, eroticism, danger, and fear. Debussy set some of this poetry to music. "La Flute de Pan" is an example. Schools of music did not grow up around these two movements, but Debussy reflected their philosophies in his music and influenced other twentieth century composers through his harmonic practices and his orchestration.

Expressionism was a direct statement about the decline of European civilization in the early decades of the twentieth century. Literary men and women, painters and musicians, used their media to express repulsion at the state of human existence. The atonal music of expressionism was born in Austria at the hands of Schönberg. Atonal music, fueled by dissonance and emotionalism, is exemplified by Schönberg's *Pierrot Lunaire* and Berg's *Wozzeck*.

Many of Stravinsky's works are masterpieces of twentieth century music. Typical of his early pieces is the ballet *Petrushka* scored for a large orchestra and based upon Russian folklore. *Petrushka* features bitonality and polytonality—both within the functional harmony system.

Bela Bartók, like Stravinsky, utilized folk themes and melodies. Counterpoint is central to Bartók's music, but he also features compact themes, unique rhythms, unusual accent patterns, and ingenious structures. His Music for strings, percussion and celesta is a complex piece featuring the percussion family.

American composer Charles Ives experimented in both tonal and atonal music. He, like Bartók and Stravinsky, focused on native folk tunes, but his use of the tunes is unique. The inclusion of folk music is central to his compositions.

The music and movements that emerged between the wars were diverse. The twenties witnessed the development of artistic activity in reaction to the horror and destruction that had just engulfed the world. Dadaism presented a nihilistic view of life while futurism preached violence and anarchy. Many of Erik Satie's works represent dadaism in music through simple consonance and banality. Satie's influence is seen in the experimental compositions of Milhaud, Poulenc and Honegger.

The inclination of Stravinsky, Prokofiev, and other composers of the twenties was to turn to the past for inspiration. In their compositions, neoclassicism flourished, rich with concertos and symphonies. This music actually combined characteristics of the classical and the baroque eras, as in Stravinsky's *Octet*.

It was between the wars that some American composers gained recognition. Copland, Barber, Piston, Sessions, and Thomson—all children of the twentieth century—created a distinctly American art music. Copland in particular featured American folk music and American themes in his works.

At the same time, a musical revolution occurred in Europe with the introduction in 1925 of Schönberg's twelve-tone system. Composers who preferred atonal music were given a means of systematic organization of pitches. No longer would atonal pieces be the work of a few expressionist composers. The tone row is the building block of the twelve-tone system, and forty-four variations of each row are possible. Schönberg's student, Webern, expanded this system and created a collection of serial music.

Post-World War II composers have experimented with the twelve-tone system, serial music, and unique methods of creating sound from traditional instruments, such as the prepared piano. Electronic music has moved to the forefront in the past decades, offering an infinite number of durational values and rhythmic complexities.

An appreciation for chance music has also arisen since World War II. The composer suggests musical activities that can never be duplicated in any two performances. The field of chance music offers a realm of future exploration.

KEY TERMS

impressionism	glissandos	retrograde
symbolism	dadaism	retrograde inversion
expressionism	Les six	serial music
Sprechtstimme	neoclassicism	electronic music
atonal	twelve-tone system	chance (aleatory)
bitonality	tone row	music
polytonality	inversion	

THINKING ABOUT IT

Several different musical/aesthetic "isms" have been discussed in this chapter. What are some basic differences between them? For example, how are the goals and achievements of impressionism different from those of expressionism? From neoclassicism? From dadaism? Which specific pieces of music support your answers?

Compile a list of twentieth century works that are either tonal or have a close relationship with tonality. Construct a second list of works that are clearly not tonal.

10

MUSIC IN THE MIDDLE AGES

Gothic architecture: Notre Dame Cathredral, Paris

SOUNDS OF THE CHAPTER

Machaut
Je puis trop bien
Ma fin est ma commencement
Messe de Notre Dame
S' il estoit nulz

"Victimae paschali laudes"

Historians have called the period from the dawn of Christianity to about 1450 the Middle Ages.

The Middle Ages, or Medieval era, is a label applied to the period from the dawn of Christianity to about 1450. This long period of time has been further subdivided by historians into the "Dark Ages" (the first eight centuries A.D.), the "Age of Charlemagne" (ninth and tenth centuries), the "Gothic Age" (twelfth and thirteenth centuries), and the "Ars Nova" (fourteenth century). All of this vast expanse of time is called the Middle Ages.

But what was it in the middle of? The label "Middle Ages" suggests that it was somehow a less cultivated period than those that preceded (the Graeco-Roman classical period) and followed (the Renaissance). The term further implies that during the Middle Ages, Western civilization either stood still or marked time—a mere valley between the mountaintops of classical antiquity and the Renaissance.

The period comes between classical antiquity and the Renaissance.

In certain respects the early Middle Ages was a "dark" era. Warfare, barbarous invasions, devastated economic and political systems, and the appalling decline in learning and scholarship nearly extinguished the light of civilization. Nearly, but not quite.

The church of the Middle Ages was the center of intellectual activity.

The church of the Middle Ages was the center of scholarship, not just for ecclesiastical matters, but in all fields of knowledge. Most of what is known about life in the Middle Ages has been preserved for us in handwritten manuscripts that were painstakingly prepared by monks and other clergy. Printing was unknown; and books would have been useless except to the literate minority.

The vast majority of people were illiterate.

All music up to the twelfth century was sacred music. Musicians of the early Middle Ages undoubtedly composed secular music also, but there are no manuscripts that confirm its existence. Since the church was the center of literacy and learning, it was the only institution in a position to record (write down) music, musical practices, and theory. Naturally, the clergy recorded only those elements that applied to sacred music.

THE FORMATION OF THE GREGORIAN CHANT

In A.D. 312, Emperor Constantine legitimized Christianity.

In A.D. 312 Emperor Constantine, who had recently converted to Christianity, issued the Edict of Toleration, legalizing the Christian religion. Since Christianity was no longer an underground movement, its membership and influence grew quickly over a large geographical area.

Fig. 10.1

Fig. 10.2

At about this time the Christian church in Rome—the Roman Catholic church—began to organize its worship services. These services included texts (both scriptural and nonscriptural), melodies called **chants,** and various ceremonies that were sanctioned for use in the church. Broadly speaking, all of this was called the **liturgy** of the church, and each sanctioned text, chant, and ceremony was called a **liturgical item.**

In the fourth, fifth, and sixth centuries, the number of these liturgical items grew rapidly. Eventually the number of liturgical items exceeded practicality; there were hundreds, perhaps thousands of designated chants, for example.

Popes and other high officials in the Roman Catholic church decided that a more uniform set of beliefs and practices was needed, and this required a massive reduction and codification of the liturgy. This was accomplished during the papacy of Gregory I, who served from 590–604. In gratitude for his enormous contribution, the melodies of the Roman church have since that time been called **Gregorian chants.** Let us first examine the nature of this music and then see how it was used in the various services of the Roman Catholic church.

The Nature of the Gregorian Chant

The Gregorian chants were entirely monophonic (one line melodies), and were always associated with a text. Church leaders believed that the text was somehow more memorable and meaningful when sung rather than merely spoken.

There are two basic kinds of Gregorian melodies. The first is **static,** with many repeated notes and few melodic leaps (see fig. 10.1). The other type of Gregorian melody is similar to our contemporary ideas of melody. Notice in figure 10.2 that the melody has more of a shape and uses several kinds of melodic intervals.

The Roman Catholic liturgy included texts, chants, and ceremony.

Pope Gregory I codified the liturgical items.

Gregorian chants are monophonic and associated with a text.

One type of Gregorian chant is static.

The other type of Gregorian chant is more melodious.

Fig. 10.3
Music manuscript from the late Middle Ages

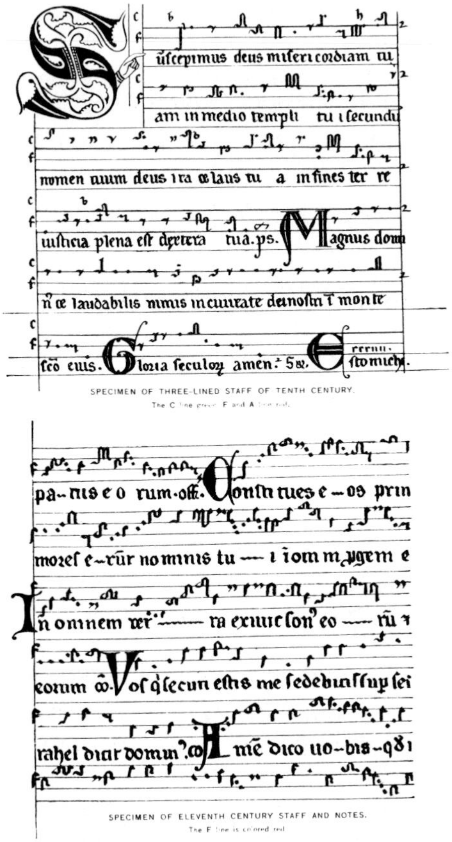

SPECIMEN OF THREE-LINED STAFF OF TENTH CENTURY.
The C line green, F and A drawn red.

SPECIMEN OF ELEVENTH CENTURY STAFF AND NOTES.
The F line is colored red.

Gregorian melodies typically are restricted to a fairly narrow range; many are contained within an octave. They usually proceed by half steps and whole steps, with some larger melodic intervals.

Scholars are still not sure exactly how these melodies operated rhythmically. However, they probably were not metrical according to our understanding of meters. The pitches of the melodies may have been sung in even-note values, they may have been sung in groups of twos and threes, or another method might have been used. Today these melodies are usually notated as even note values without stems, but manuscripts show that a very different kind of notation was used in the Middle Ages. Figure 10.3 shows a page from an eleventh century manuscript. The figures above the text are the notation of the melody.

Gregorian melodies were not metrical.

Today, we notate Gregorian melodies as even-note values without stems.

Church modes Since the mid-seventeenth century the Western world has organized its music according to tonality—music is in a key and in either the major or minor mode. Music in the Middle Ages and the Renaissance, however, was organized somewhat differently: it was modal rather than tonal. In this context, **mode** does not mean simply being in the major or minor mode. Modal music is not in a key, but is in one or another of the church modes. This modal music sounds somewhat different; it seems to lack a sense of progression and direction that emerges from melodies that are in a key.

Each of the eight church modes used in the Middle Ages has a different interval structure, and each has a Greek name—Dorian mode, Phrygian mode, Lydian mode, Mixolydian mode, and so on. In its purest form each mode has only seven different pitches. One of these is called the **finalis,** the pitch on which the melody usually ends, which is similar to the tonic pitch in tonal music. Another common pitch in modal music is called the **reciting tone,** which is similar to the dominant pitch in tonal music.

In summary, Gregorian music is vocal, monophonic, modal, limited in range, and moves in a freely flowing rhythm.

The Integration of the Gregorian Chant with the Mass

During the first several hundred years of its existence the church developed two major types of worship: the Mass and the Canonical or Office Hours.

The **Mass** was a worship service celebrated by priests, bishops and other clergy. Bishops often presided at the Mass in a cathedral, while a priest celebrated Mass for the common people in a parish or neighborhood church. The Mass in the smaller parish church was much less elaborate than those in the cathedral, and so had much less music. Eventually, the cathedrals were opened to congregations, thus exposing more to the music performed there. Since the Gregorian chant in itself comprised the whole of church music in the Middle Ages, it would be difficult to exaggerate its importance at that time.

Ordinary and Proper Today the mass consists of elements that were gradually incorporated over a period of about 1,000 years. The individual parts of the Mass belong to one of two categories: the **Ordinary** or the **Proper.** The Ordinary, as these parts are called collectively, are chanted or spoken at every Mass and their texts never change. For example, the first Ordinary, the Kyrie, is heard near the beginning of every Mass. The Kyrie is recited, and its text is always:

> Kyrie eleison (Lord have mercy)
> Christe eleison (Christ have mercy)
> Kyrie eleison (Lord have mercy)

Music from the Middle Ages is in a church mode rather than in a key.

In the church modes the finalis is similar to our modern tonic pitch, while the reciting tone acts as does our dominant pitch.

Name the characteristics of Gregorian chant.

The Mass is the major Roman Catholic worship service.

Masses celebrated in cathedrals included more music than those offered in parish churches.

The Mass is divided into two parts—the Ordinary and the Proper.

The texts of the Ordinary elements never change, while elements of the Proper vary according to the church calendar.

A Proper item, on the other hand, is so called because its text is appropriately or properly performed only at a specific time of the church year, or on one specific day of the year. For example, certain Proper texts are appropriate only during the Easter or the Christmas season. Text or prayers in honor of a given saint are proper to and read only on that saint's day.

Today the five Ordinary items of the Mass are, in order: the Kyrie, Gloria, Credo, Sanctus, and Agnus Dei. Interspersed within the Ordinary are a number of Proper items. The outline below lists most of the items of the Roman Catholic Mass as it was structured around A.D. 1000. Only those items in lowercase letters were spoken. All other items were sung by the priests or the choir. Notice how important music was in the Mass.

Elements from both the Ordinary and the Proper were set to music.

The Order of the Mass

Ringing of the bells to welcome the priest(s)	
INTROIT (entrance music for the priest[s])	Proper
KYRIE ELEISON	Ordinary
GLORIA (Glory to God in the highest . . .)	Ordinary
Collect (a reading of various prayers)	Proper
A reading from the Bible	Proper
ALLELUIA	Ordinary
SEQUENCE (only used at certain times of year)	Proper
A reading from the Gospel	Proper
Homily (Sermon. Frequently omitted, but when included it was an amplification of the Biblical readings of the day.)	
CREDO (We believe in one God . . .)	Ordinary
OFFERTORY (the collection of the offering)	Proper
Prayers over the Eucharist (the bread and wine)	Ordinary
SANCTUS (Holy, Holy, Holy, Lord . . .)	Ordinary
Other special prayers and sayings	Ordinary
Pater Noster (Our Father)	Ordinary
AGNUS DEI (Lamb of God)	Ordinary
Eucharist (Distribution of communion)	
Other closing prayers	
ITE MISSA EST (the Mass is ended, go in peace)	Ordinary

Fig. 10.4

Let Christians dedicate their praises to the Easter victim.
The lamb has redeemed the sheep; the innocent Christ has reconciled the
     sinners with the Father.
Death and life have fought in wondrous conflict; after death the leader of life,
     living reigns.
Tell us oh, Mary what thou sawest upon the way?
I have seen the sepulchre of the living Christ, and the glory of the rising Christ.
The angelic witnesses, the veil and the garments.
Christ, my hope, has arisen, he goes before his own into Galilee.
We know in truth that Christ has arisen from the dead: be merciful unto us, O
     victorious king: Amen.

The Gregorian chant in figure 10.4 dates from about the year 1000. It is a **sequence**—a liturgical chant proper to the Easter season—and is called *Victimae paschali laudes* (let Christians dedicate their praises to the Easter victim). *Victimae paschali laudes* is one of the most famous and among the most beautiful Gregorian chants. (There are several recordings of the chant, including the one in the anthology *Masterpieces of Music Before 1750* [vol. 1, side 1, band 3].) The translation of the text appears below the notation. The order of the Mass list indicates where the sequence appeared in the Mass.

The sequence *Victimae paschali laudes* is a beautiful example of Gregorian chant.

Medieval monks at prayer and labor

CANONICAL HOURS: PSALM WITH ANTIPHON

Offices or Canonical Hours were not public worship services.

The monk's required private prayers included music.

The other type of worship is the set of eight Offices or Canonical Hours that are celebrated each day by monks in the monasteries. These are devotional services consisting mainly of chants and special prayers. They are celebrated at appointed hours each day and are intended only for the monks, not a congregation.

The life of a medieval monk was austere and demanding: he slept little, labored in the fields and dairies to supply his own sustenance, and otherwise was dedicated to a life of prayer, meditation, and the performance of the Canonical Hours. In fact, one of the Canonical Hours occurred about every three hours, thus affecting all other activities.

The names of the Hours and their designated times of celebration follow:

Matins	late at night
Lauds	at dawn
Prime	6 A.M.
Terce	9 A.M.
Sext	at noon
None	3 P.M.
Vespers	at evening
Compline	before bed time

A certain number of psalms (from the Bible) were sung for each Hour. A special musical form was developed for singing these psalms—**psalm with antiphon.** Textually this consisted of all the verses of a psalm plus a non-Biblical, newly composed verse that amplified the psalm text. This was the antiphon text.

Psalm with antiphon was a required element of each Canonical Hour.

Fig. 10.5

Chorus: Laus Deo, [etc., as above]

The psalm verses were chanted with the static melody mentioned earlier, while the antiphon was chanted in a more melodious style. Scholars believe that, in practice, the antiphon was sung first, followed by the psalm verses, and concluded with the repeat in antiphon.

A performance of psalm with antiphon is available in *Masterpieces of Music Before 1750* (vol. 1, side 1, band 1). Follow the chant in figure 10.5 when listening to the recording.

Fig. 10.6

THE BEGINNINGS OF HARMONY

The earliest documentation of harmony comes from the ninth century.

Organum is the name given to this two-part harmony.

Manuscripts from the ninth century provide the earliest documentation of harmony. These manuscripts describe a two-part harmony called **organum,** which consists of a melody in the lower voice and a duplication of this melody in the upper voice, usually a perfect fifth above the lower line. The two parts generally move parallel to one another.

Historians believe that the anonymous authors of these manuscripts did not invent harmony, but rather they described an existing musical practice.

Harmony changed the nature of Western music.

The invention of harmony is one of the most significant developments in the entire history of music. It created a cataclysmic change in the nature of Western music. From its crude beginnings in the Middle Ages, harmony developed, was ordered in different ways, and has dominated Western music.

Figure 10.6 shows an example of this earliest form of harmony—organum—moving in parallel, note against note in both voices.

The Emergence of Polyphony

Gradually, composers drifted from the dogged parallelism of early organum and developed a freer, more fluid type of harmony. Other kinds of intervals were used, and the two parts of the texture began to move at different speeds, rather than in a note-for-note fashion.

By the twelfth century, organum had expanded into three parts: the lowest part called **tenor** (meaning "held," not to be confused with the male voice classification called tenor); a voice above this called **duplum;** and a higher voice called **triplum.** The music was still modal, but was now polyphonic rather than monophonic.

Prior to the twelfth century composers did not often sign their musical pieces.

As secular music emerged, composers gained recognition for their pieces.

Lengthy compositions from the twelfth century exist and in some cases, the names of the composers are known. Prior to this era, composers rarely signed their compositions, so nearly all earlier music is anonymous. But in the Gothic era—the twelfth and thirteenth centuries—there is evidence of a gradual secularization, and a new awareness that the artistic and creative powers of humans were a source of pride. This sense of self-recognition increased until the Renaissance, in the fifteenth century, when it flourished.

A highly regarded school of polyphonic composition was based at the cathedral of Notre Dame in Paris, where composers such as Léonin and later Pérotin greatly expanded the horizons of harmony. With their contemporaries, they composed a great body of sacred polyphonic music, including a durable and expressive form called the **motet,** the foremost genre of the thirteenth century.

The typical thirteenth century motet had three voices, with the lowest voice usually holding longer note values than the upper two. The upper two voices, consequently, seemed to be moving faster than the lowest voice. Oddly, each voice sang a different text, and it was not unusual for the tenor to have a Latin text while the upper voices had two different French texts. The thirteenth century motet illustrated in figure 10.7 reveals its polytextual and bilingual features, and a recording of it is found in *Masterpieces of Music Before 1750* (vol. 1, side 1, band 10).

The stable, consonant intervals of this harmonic language were the octave, the perfect fifth, and the perfect fourth. Other intervals, such as thirds and sixths, were perceived as dissonances that required resolution. (In the tonal system familiar to us, however, the thirds and sixths are consonants.) If this motet's harmony sounds archaic, it is because of the presence of so many octaves, fifths, and fourths. Although they may not sound dissonant, they do seem rather incomplete.

THE ARS NOVA: PERIOD OF CHANGE

War ravaged France and England throughout the fourteenth century. An economic depression developed early in the century, severely affecting the middle and lower classes with wartime taxes and the loss of lives. Riots and revolts against authority became almost commonplace.

Moreover, the Roman Catholic church, for centuries the undisputed authority in both religious and civil dealings, was in jeopardy. The French popes refused to move to Rome, the traditional seat of the papacy, and began to reside at Avignon instead. Toward the end of the century the church was put in the ludicrous position of having to recognize two popes, one in Rome and one in Avignon.

Another factor that contributed to the turmoil in Europe was the bubonic plague. It spread from Italy to France, Spain, England, and elsewhere in the mid-fourteenth century. Some countries lost as much as one-third of the population to the horrors of the black death.

Universities, the arts, the church, and society in general survived the troubles of the fourteenth century, but all were profoundly affected. The stranglehold of the church was broken, and a more secular society was created. Indeed, this was the first truly secular era since the birth of Christianity.

Fig. 10.7

The concept of the artist as creator was born during Ars Nova.

One result of the secularism of the Ars Nova was the interest in honoring people of accomplishment. The notion of "the arts" and the "artist" as understood today were products of the turbulent fourteenth century. Prior to this, the artist was viewed as a craftsman rather than as creator, and was content to work anonymously. This work, whether musical, architectural, or other, was done for the glorification of God, not for the self-fulfillment of the craftsman. Broadly speaking, the people of the medieval era viewed themselves as sinful, wicked creatures, wholly unworthy of praise for their crude work.

However, this medieval attitude began to change in the Ars Nova, and by the dawn of the Renaissance, the conversion to the appreciation of art and artist was complete.

Music of the Ars Nova

During the span of the Middle Ages one, then two, and finally three voice texture was developed.

A single-voice texture was the norm in the Dark Ages, while a two-voice texture was used during the Age of Charlemagne and into the Gothic era. In the Ars Nova, however, a three-voice texture became the norm. Often the lower voice, and sometimes the two lower voices in the texture, were played by various instruments, while the upper voice alone carried the text (similar to an instrumentally accompanied solo song).

Church modes were altered by chromatic pitches.

Harmony began to change too. There was a definite shift to the full triad (root, third, and fifth) and a more liberal use of thirds and sixths as harmonic intervals. Though these were still considered dissonant, the fourteenth century audiences began to take delight in these sounds. Many chromatic pitches were introduced, and the popularity of the church modes began to erode. Music was still modal, but the use of modality decreased until, by the seventeenth century, it was superseded by tonality.

Flexible rhythms appeared during Ars Nova.

Rhythm became more flexible and complex, and a greater variety of note values was introduced. Musical notation underwent dramatic changes—an improvement over eleventh century notation shown in figure 10.3. Figure 10.8 shows a page from a fourteenth century manuscript.

Machaut

Machaut, a priest, a trouvère, and an Ars Nova composer, was celebrated in his own time.

The most celebrated composer of the Ars Nova was the Frenchman Guillaume de Machaut (ca. 1300–1377). Machaut was a visible figure in the fourteenth century, not only as a composer of sacred and secular music, but also as a trouvère and priest. **Trouvères** were groups of scholar-musicians, many of whom were priests, some of them migrants, who wrote a considerable amount of poetry and accompanying music. Some of this secular music has been preserved in manuscript form.

Fig. 10.8
Illuminated manuscript of the fourteenth century

Fourteenth century manuscripts from many parts of Europe contain works by Machaut, and he was held in such high regard that a drawing of his face appears in manuscripts along with his music. Clearly he was not anonymous; he was an honored and celebrated musician.

Machaut is known for introducing some of the most advanced harmonic, rhythmic, and formal musical practices of the Ars Nova. His works exhibit most of the major musical trends of the time.

Fig. 10.9

Nonimitative counterpoint was plentiful in the three-voice texture, but occasionally Machaut and other composers employed imitative counterpoint, which came to dominate music of the Renaissance.

Also characteristic of the Ars Nova were the manipulation of pitches and rhythms in patterns, and the fascination with musical and textual puzzles. This fascination is evident in the use of **isorhythm,** in which patterns of note values are repeated. Figure 10.9 shows (in modern notation) the isorhythmic tenor part from a three-voice motet by Machaut, *S' il estoit nulz.* The repetitions of the pattern of note values are set off by double-bar lines. A recording of the isorhythmic motet is available in the anthology *Historical Anthology of Music in Performance* (vol. 1, no. 44).

Machaut displayed his interest in musical puzzles and his technical prowess in a work called *Ma fin est ma commencement (My End is My Beginning).* In this work, the upper voice of the texture is the exact retrograde of the middle voice, and the second half of the lowest part is the retrograde of its first half. Whether or not this is actually heard in the piece is unimportant. It is, however, the kind of masterful pitch manipulation in which a twentieth century serialist composer would take pride. This work is available in *The History of Music in Sound* (vol. 3, side 1, band 5).

Messe de Notre Dame   The *Messe de Notre Dame* is Machaut's most important sacred work. It is the first polyphonic setting for the Ordinary of the Mass written by a single composer, and it sets the precedent for this type of composition in the Renaissance.

Isorhythm was a feature of some music from the Ars Nova.

Notice the isorhythm in Machaut's composition.

Machaut composed the first polyphonic setting for Mass Ordinary.

Ballade Despite Machaut's renown as a composer of sacred music, he devoted more time to secular music. The trouvères developed a number of fixed forms—specific poetic and musical structures. These fixed forms developed, over the course of time, into rigid poetic-musical structures, such as rondeau, ballade, and virelai, each with a prescribed number of lines and sections.

For example, the **ballade** has the following poetic-musical structure:

Music	A	A	B
text	first verse	second verse	third verse

A good example of the ballade is found in *Historical Anthology of Music* (vol. 1, no. 45); it is Machaut's *Je puis trop bien*. The translation follows:

(1) I can all too well compare my lady
    To the image which Pygmalion made.
(2) It was of ivory, so beautiful, without peer,
    That he loved it more than Jason did Medea.
(3) Out of his senses, he prayed to it unceasingly,
    But the image answered him not.
    Thus does she treat me who makes my heart melt,
    For I pray her ever, and she answers me not.

Notice as you listen that the music is the same for verses 1 and 2, while the music for verse 3 is different.

Trouvères' music featured fixed forms.

One fixed form found in the music of trouvères is the ballade.

SUMMARY

In this chapter we gave consideration to the forces that shaped the Middle Ages. In this period the dominance of the Roman Catholic church tells the story. The majority of the European population was illiterate. Scholarship and intellectual activity was carried on by the clergy. It is in the church that we find the music and the composers.

After Emperor Constantine legitimized the practice of Christianity in A.D. 312, the Roman Catholic worship service, the liturgy, evolved. By the sixth century such a massive number of liturgical items had been created that Pope Gregory I called for their codification. Out of gratitude to him, church leaders named the chants of the church "Gregorian" chants.

A Gregorian chant was entirely monophonic and associated with a text. There were two forms: static and melodic. These melodies occurred within a narrow range. Church modes, rather than tonal keys, were the elements of organization.

Church music was written for two purposes: the Mass and Canonical Hours. Medieval composers created music for the elements of the Proper and the Ordinary of the Mass. These pieces were shared with the congregation. Our example was the sequence entitled, *Victimae paschali laudes,* an Easter-time Proper.

The music composed for the Offices or Canonical Hours was celebrated by the monks. Daily chants required for the monks included the form of psalm with antiphon, a biblical psalm plus a composed verse set to chant.

The invention of harmony in the ninth century caused a major change in Western music. A school of polyphonic composition was located at the Notre Dame cathedral in Paris. This school devised the motet, a three-voice piece with a narrow range of consonance that dominated music in the thirteenth century.

During the fourteenth century, the Ars Nova, the European world experienced a change in focus. Riots and revolts against authority brought an end to the total dominance of the Catholic church and laid the foundation for a new secular society. It was at this time that composers were first viewed as creators motivated by self-fulfillment, rather than as craftsmen in the service of God.

The most celebrated composer of the Ars Nova was Machaut— a trouvère and priest. Machaut composed for the church and for the emerging secular society. He was part of the movement toward more modern forms of harmony and new standards of consonance and dissonance.

The flexible rhythms, the sophistication of musical notation and the emergence of nonimitative counterpoint in the fourteenth century lead us directly to our next discussion—the music and flavor of the Renaissance.

KEY TERMS

chant	reciting tone	tenor
liturgy	Mass	duplum
liturgical item	Ordinary	triplum
Gregorian chant	Proper	motet
static	sequence	trouvères
mode	psalm with antiphon	isorhythm
finalis	organum	ballade

THINKING ABOUT IT

Reflect on the history of musical texture from the dawn of Christianity through the Ars Nova. How would you describe this history, and what sorts of musical examples would you use to illuminate the points you make?

Again, using the entire era of the Middle Ages, how would you summarize the issue of sacred versus secular?

11

Creation, Michelangelo

SOUNDS OF THE CHAPTER

Byrd
Christ Rising Again ♪

Farnaby
Loth to Depart

Gabrieli
Gloria in Excelsis Deo ♪

Gibbons
Pavane Lord Salisbury

Josquin des Prez
Ave Maria ♪
Mass: *Pange Lingua*

Luther
Ein' feste Burg ist unser Gott

Marenzio
S'io parto, moro ♪

Morley
Now Is the Month of Maying ♪

Palestrina
Mass: *Aeterna Christi munera*

Mass: *L'homme arme (The Armed Man)*

Renaissance is a French word meaning rebirth, but is also widely used as a cultural and stylistic label for the fifteenth and sixteenth centuries. The label was applied, however, by nineteenth century historians who concluded that the fifteenth and sixteenth centuries, like classical antiquity, was a peak period of great and noble accomplishments in Western civilization—a veritable mountaintop.

It may be true that these same historians perceived their own age, the nineteenth century, as a cultural and artistic mountaintop, and thus felt an affinity with the Renaissance. The people of the nineteenth century were probably more fully aware of the achievements of the Renaissance than those who actually experienced the Renaissance. Still, there can be little doubt that these people—especially the educated minority—knew that they were living in an extraordinary time, a time of intellectual and artistic magnificence, and that things were changing so dramatically that the world appeared new in many ways. The Renaissance was, after all, the age of Shakespeare, Botticelli, Da Vinci, Michelangelo, Raphael, Titian, Copernicus, Palestrina, and Columbus.

HUMANISM REBORN

If the age was really a renaissance, what was reborn? More than anything else a spirit, known as **humanism,** was reborn in the Western world. The main thrust of the humanistic movement was humanity's pride in itself. This spirit had largely been absent since the collapse of the Graeco-Roman classical civilization. Humanism allowed humankind to celebrate the great thinkers, artists, scientists, and explorers of the period without losing their religious moorings.

In many respects the Renaissance was a secularized era, especially when compared to the God-centered Middle Ages. Still, the abundance of sacred music, religious painting, and the Protestant Reformation dispel the idea that the people of the Renaissance turned their backs on God. However, the so-called Renaissance man—one knowledgeable in many fields—was not submissive, viewing himself as a mere creature. On the contrary, he was a self-confident person who took great pride in his ability to think, reason, and create. This was a positive atmosphere for creative artists and thinkers. Moreover, the presence of an adventuresome spirit in the Renaissance made it possible for humankind to discover literally a "new world."

Nineteenth century historians termed the fifteenth and sixteenth centuries the "Renaissance," a French term meaning rebirth.

Those educated in the Renaissance were aware of the period's enormous intellectual and artistic accomplishments.

The Renaissance produced many extraordinary figures.

A spirit of humanism was reborn.

The church was not abandoned during this period.

The Renaissance man valued thought, reason, and creativity.

The invention of printing in the fifteenth century opened up another kind of world. Printed material was much less expensive than handwritten manuscripts, which resulted in the wide dissemination of all kinds of learning and information. The printed page that is taken for granted today was new in the Renaissance, and caused a dramatic increase in learning and the exchange of information.

The invention of printing caused a revolution in the world of communication.

GENERAL CHARACTERISTICS OF RENAISSANCE MUSIC

Harmony

Music in the Renaissance was still governed by modality rather than tonality, but there was an increased interest in the expressive power of chords. Whereas harmony in the Middle Ages was for the most part an accident of the horizontal lines of the texture sounding simultaneously, harmony in the Renaissance was a conscious attempt to focus on the sheer beauty and emotional force of vertical sonorities (chords).

The Renaissance composer created harmony for beauty and emotional force.

Counterpoint

Despite the increased interest in vertical sonorities, Renaissance composers were the consummate masters of imitative counterpoint. The duality of beautiful harmony and ingenious counterpoint is a hallmark of Renaissance music.

Imitative counterpoint reached its zenith in the Renaissance.

Texture

The standard four-voice texture of the era was similar to modern four-part choral texture: soprano, alto, tenor, and bass. There are many examples of textures with more and fewer than four parts, but the four-part choral texture became a norm in the Renaissance.

Four-voice texture became standard during the Renaissance.

Rhythm

Renaissance rhythm resembles the modern concept of meter, though in some ways the rhythm of Renaissance music seems more pliant and supple. Perhaps this is due to fewer heavy downbeats and strong accents in Renaissance music.

Renaissance rhythm seems quite modern.

SACRED MUSIC

In the Renaissance it also became necessary to make a distinction between two types of music based on religious affiliation: Protestant and Catholic music.

Sacred music of the Renaissance is either Catholic or Protestant.

MUSIC OF THE PROTESTANT REFORMATION

Most widespread religious movements, early in their history, develop a body of music that is used as an adjunct to worship. As we have seen, this was true of the Roman Catholic church at the dawn of the Christian era, when the Gregorian chant was developed for this purpose. The Protestant sects that emerged from the Reformation followed this pattern, too. Various Protestant denominations in the Renaissance—Lutheran, Calvinistic, and Anglican—each produced distinctive musical genres: chorales, metrical psalms, and anthems. Let us now take a closer look at these types of sacred music.

The Protestant denominations that emerged from the Reformation created music for their worship services.

Lutheranism

The Lutheran worship service that developed closely resembled the Catholic Mass, and many parts were sung. As a result, a body of texts and melodies, called **chorales,** was assembled. The texts of some of these chorales were Biblical, but many were newly composed religious verses written in German, rather than the Catholic Latin.

Chorales (text and melody) were written for Lutheran services.

  The chorale melodies came from various sources. Some melodies were borrowed from the fund of Gregorian chant. Martin Luther was a priest in the Roman Catholic church prior to the Reformation, so it was quite natural that he used some familiar music for the Lutheran church. Other chorale melodies were appropriated from secular sources, while still others were newly composed by Martin Luther (who was also a trained musician) and by several of his churchmen.

  Through the Middle Ages and Renaissance, music in the Catholic church was performed more and more by priests and professional choirs of men and boys. The church congregation had little if any opportunity to participate in the performance of music. Martin Luther felt very strongly that the congregation, the lay people, should be actively involved in the new church's music. A simple music was necessary for this purpose since something as complex as a Renaissance motet would have been far beyond the musical capabilities of any congregation. But monophonic chorales were not beyond their means, and these chorales proved to be a powerful and personal means of worship. In time many of the Lutheran chorales were harmonized in four parts—soprano, alto, tenor, and bass—and resembled contemporary hymns.

Luther strongly encouraged lay involvement in church music.

Monophonic chorales were well-suited for congregational singing.

The most famous chorale is *Ein' feste Burg ist unser Gott (A Mighty Fortress Is Our God)*. This melody was composed by Luther himself. Recall that the text of this chorale was discussed in chapter 5 as the basis for a chorale cantata by J. S. Bach. The musical structure of *Ein' feste Burg* is simple: three long phrases with the shape *AAB*. Many German chorales have this form.

A Mighty Fortress Is Our God, like many other German chorales, has an AAB form.

Calvinism

The Frenchman John Calvin was another very important figure in the Protestant Reformation of the early sixteenth century. While Martin Luther's doctrines led to the establishment of a single Protestant sect, Lutheranism, the doctrines and ideas of Calvin were disseminated to several Protestant sects, principally Presbyterianism.

Protestantism splintered further under the impact of John Calvin's doctrines.

Calvin was not trained in music and, unlike Luther, his interest in music as an adjunct to worship was limited. He believed that music should be simple and unemotional. Further, the only texts set to music should be scriptural texts, namely the 150 Psalms of David. The Psalms were translated from the original Hebrew into French, cast in poetic meters, and set to melodies. These are called **metrical psalms** or **psalmody.**

Calvin's preference was for simple, unemotional music.

Psalmody was popularized by the Calvinist sects.

At the urging of some of his advisors, Calvin eventually relaxed his stance on music and allowed the previously monophonic metrical psalms to be composed for four-part harmony. Thus, both Lutheran and Presbyterian churches developed the practice of congregational singing.

Anglicanism

The Anglican church or the Church of England also retained much of the service and ceremony of the Roman Catholic church, including the Mass. From a musical viewpoint, the most significant contribution of the Anglican church was the development of the **anthem.** The anthem was a choral work with an English text performed with or without accompaniment. Typically, the anthem was more complex than a simple four-part chorale, psalm, or hymn, and was designed for a trained choir rather than for congregational singing. It was similar to the Catholic motet in both substance and function. Some anthems used a chorus and one or more soloists. An anthem that included a solo was called a **verse anthem.**

Anglican church anthems were choral works designed for trained choirs rather than congregational singing.

Verse anthems featured solo work.

William Byrd England's greatest composer of the late Renaissance was William Byrd (1543–1623). Although Byrd, a Catholic, wrote a considerable amount of music for the Roman church, he ironically was the acknowledged master of the verse anthem that was composed for use in the Anglican church.

The Catholic William Byrd was the greatest composer of Anglican Renaissance music.

Leda, by the Renaissance master, Leonardo da Vinci

Royal Library, Windsor Castle

In Byrd's verse anthem, *Christ Rising Again,* two soprano soloists alternate with a full chorus, accompanied by a group of string instruments. The text and the layout of this verse anthem are listed below:

Soloists: Christ rising again from the dead, now dieth not.
Choir and soloists: Death from henceforth hath no power upon Him. For in that He died He died but once to put away sin.
Soloists: But in that He liveth He liveth unto God.
Choir and soloists: And so likewise count yourselves dead unto sin, but living unto God.
Soloists: In Christ Jesus our Lord.
Choir and soloists: In Christ Jesus our Lord.

MUSIC OF THE CATHOLIC CHURCH

The Mass

The schism in the Catholic church was healed early in the fifteenth century, and at that time certain composers, particularly in the Netherlands, began to set the Ordinary of the Mass to music. This group of composers included Guillaume Dufay (ca. 1400–1474), Joannes Okeghem (ca. 1430–95), and the Englishman John Dunstable (ca. 1370–1453). Composers from all parts of Europe continued to expand and develop Mass composition in the fifteenth and sixteenth centuries, creating a vast repertoire of magnificent music for the Ordinary of the Mass.

Renaissance liturgical music is rich with counterpoint and chordal harmony.

One of the most important musical/technical advances of the Renaissance was the perfection of imitative counterpoint. This was balanced by the enrichment of chordal harmony, mentioned earlier. Thus, Renaissance music—especially the music written for the Mass—features textures rich with counterpoint and chordal homophony.

Many Renaissance Masses feature popular melodies as building blocks.

Many Masses from the Renaissance are based in part on some preexistent melody, all or part of which is usually found in each movement of the Mass. For example, a Mass entitled *Mass: L'homme armé (Mass: The Armed Man)* is one that had incorporated the popular melody of the same name. Many of the Renaissance composers used this particular melody as a structural building block in composing Masses. Early in the Renaissance Dufay borrowed from it, as did Okeghem. Later, Josquin des Prez used it, and, at the end of the Renaissance, Palestrina. However, *L'homme armé* was but one of many melodies that were used by various composers as building blocks for their mass compositions.

Gregorian melodies often appear in Renaissance Masses.

Palestrina's Mass *Aeterna Christi munera* is based on an old Gregorian melody of the same name. The "Sanctus" from this Mass adheres to the pitches of the old Gregorian melody, while simultaneously incorporting Renaissance imitative counterpoint. The Latin text and the English translation appear below:

Sanctus, sanctus, sanctus,	Holy, holy, holy
Dominus Deus Sabaoth.	Lord God of hosts.
Pleni sunt coeli et terra gloria tua,	Heaven and earth are full of Thy glory;
Hosanna in excelsis.	Hosanna in the highest.

Notice that Palestrina has divided the Sanctus into four sections, reflecting the four lines of the text. There is a clear break between the first and second sections, but the other sections overlap. Each of the four sections begins with an individual motive which is then imitated in each of the other voices in the texture. For example, the first section, which is built on the words "Sanctus, sanctus, sanctus," starts with a rising motive in the sopranos. This motive is then imitated in the altos, then in the tenors, and a little later, in the basses.

Josquin des Prez

Josquin des Prez, known by contemporaries as "The Prince of Music," is generally regarded as the greatest composer of the Renaissance. His Mass *Pange Lingua* is one of his major works. The Gloria from this Mass exemplifies the full range of musical/technical processes that were perfected in Renaissance choral music.

Among the greatest Renaissance composers was Josquin des Prez.

SOUND AND SENSE: *Renaissance Choral Music*

Title: "Gloria" from the Mass *Pange Lingua*
Composer: Josquin des Prez

A Closer Look:

This movement has four-part imitation, along with sections in which Josquin separates the four parts into two pairs. In these pairs the alto line imitates the soprano's theme, while the basses imitate a different theme sung by the tenors. Thus, two pairs of voices simultaneously present and imitate two different themes—a complex process, but one that Josquin handles with apparent ease. There are also homophonic patches that contrast the heavily contrapuntal sections.

Josquin also varies the texture, using one, two, three, or four voices. In this way the texture never becomes monotonous. On the contrary, it is complemented with variety.

Josquin's mastery is more fully appreciated by listening to this movement while studying the following outline. Notice that the piece is divided into several sections, each devoted to a portion of the text.

Text	Activity
Section I	
(Gloria in excelcis Deo)	(Four voices in imitative counterpoint.
Et in terra pax bonae volumtatis.	The voices enter as follows: tenor, bass, soprano, alto.)

Section II

Laudamus te,	(Tenor and bass in imitation.)
Benedicimus te,	(Soprano and alto imitate each other. Bass and tenor imitate each other.)
Adoramus te,	(Tenor and bass imitate each other. Soprano and alto imitate each other.)
Glorificamus te,	(Soprano and alto imitate each other. Tenor and bass imitate each other.)
Gratius agimus tibi	(Soprano and tenor imitate each other. Alto and bass imitate each other.)
Propter magnam gloriam.	(Tenor and bass imitate each other. Soprano and alto imitate each other.)

Section III

Domine Deus, Rex coelistis, Deus Pater omnipotens.	(Soprano and alto alone.)
Domine Fili unigenite Jesu Christe. Domine Deus, Agnus Dei, Filius Patris	(Bass and tenor in imitation. Soprano and alto free, i.e., not in imitation.)

Section IV

Qui tollis peccata mundi,	(Four voices in imitative counterpoint, entering as follows: soprano, alto, tenor, bass.)
Miserere nobis.	(Four voices in chordal homophony.)
Qui tollis peccata mundi,	(Tenor and bass only in homophony.)
Suscipe deprecationem nostram.	(Four voices in chordal homophony.)

Section V

Qui sedes ad dextreram Patris,	(Soprano and tenor in imitation.)
Miserere nobis quoniam.	(Soprano and tenor, then soprano and alto.)

Section VI

Quoniam	(Tenor and bass alone.)
Tu solus sanctus.	(Four voice imitation.)
Tu solus Dominus.	
Tu solus Altimus,	
Jesu Christe.	

Section VII

Cum sancto spiritu in gloria Dei Patris. Amen.	(Soprano and bass in imitation. Tenor and alto in imitation.)

The English translation of the Gloria: (Glory to God in the highest) And peace to His people on earth. We praise Thee, we bless Thee, we worship Thee, we glorify Thee. We give thanks to Thee for Thy great glory. O, Lord God, heavenly King, God the Father almighty. O, Lord, the only begotten son, Jesus Christ. O, Lord God, Lamb of God who takes away the sins of the world, have mercy on us. Thou who takes away the sins of the world, receive our prayer. Thou that sittest at the right hand of the Father, have mercy on us. For Thou alone art holy; Thou alone art the Lord. Thou only art most high, Jesus Christ. With the Holy Spirit in the glory of God the Father. Amen.

The Renaissance Motet

The motet, which became secularized in the late Middle Ages, was refashioned and reunited with the Catholic church in the Renaissance. In the hands of Josquin and many others, the **Renaissance motet** became a serious, large-scale, one-movement work with a sacred Latin text. Many of the features of the Renaissance Mass are also found in the "classic" Renaissance motet: the sections of imitative counterpoint, the homophonic patches, and some diversity in texture. There are also many examples of Renaissance motets based on a borrowed preexisting melody.

All of these features are found in Josquin's motet, *Ave Maria*. Follow the several sections of imitation by consulting the Sound and Sense when listening.

The Renaissance motet shows imitative counterpoint, homophonic patches and diversified texture.

SOUND AND SENSE: *Classic Renaissance Motet*

Title: *Ave Maria*

Composer: Josquin des Prez

A Closer Look:

Notice that in addition to these several sections there are three larger divisions of the work: the first part is in the equivalent of 4/4 meter, the second in 3/4, and the third part returns to 4/4.

4/4 Meter
Section I: Ave Maria gratia pleve.
Section II: Dominus tecum.
Section III: Benedicta tu in mulieribus.
Section IV: Et benedictus fructrus ventris tui, Jesus Christus Filius Dei vivi.

3/4 Meter
Section V: Et benedicta sint beata ubera tua quae lactaverunt regem regum.

4/4 Meter
Section VI: Et Dominum Deum nominum Deum nostrum.

SECULAR MUSIC IN THE RENAISSANCE

The Madrigal

The Italian and the English, or Elizabethan, madrigals were the dominant forms of secular vocal music in the sixteenth century. A **madrigal,** whether Italian or English, is a composition for four to six (occasionally eight) voices, built on a secular text. The most favored subjects of madrigal texts were love, in all its forms, and pastoral settings. Text settings tended to be colorful and graphic; imitation (discussed in chapter 4) was

The dominant form of sixteenth century secular vocal music was the madrigal.

Madrigals were composed for four to six male and female voices.

often utilized. Most madrigals were composed for and performed by men and women of the upper classes. Madrigals were intended for the entertainment and edification of these people.

Italian madrigal   Generally speaking, **Italian madrigals** were more dramatic and emotional than the more lighthearted English madrigal, though there are many exceptions. The expressive and dramatic powers of harmony were utilized in both Italian and English madrigals, and both types used sections of imitative counterpoint.

A fine example of the dramatic Italian style is *S'io parto, moro (This parting kills me),* composed by one of the masters of the genre, Luca Marenzio (1560–99). The text is as follows:

S'io parto i' moro,	This parting now kills me,
E pur partir conviene,	And yet I still must leave thee,
Morrò dunque il mio bene,	I shall die then, my dearest,
E questa mia partita	And this my sad departing
Che mi ti toglie,	That takes me from thee,
Mi torrà la vita.	Takes from me my being.
Dolorosa partita che m'ucci di,	Ah, this cruel departing doth slay me,
Quei che congiuns' Amor	For those whom love hath joined,
Perche divi di?	Ah, how divide them?

Notice the expressive use of dissonance on the word "kills" (first line), and again on "ah" (third line). A clever and subtle use of descriptions (see chapter 4) occurs on the word "divide" (last line), where the steady pulse of the quarter note is suddenly divided into eighth notes. Notice the melancholy feeling in the song—though the text deals with love, it is a tragic, unrequited love. This kind of text is very typical of many Italian madrigals.

Elizabethan madrigal   The arts in general and music in particular flourished during the reign of Elizabeth I (reigned 1558–1603). In fact, her prominent role in the cultural life of England resulted in the label "The Elizabethan Age."

The **Elizabethan madrigal** was based on the Italian madrigal model, but it quickly developed a British personality. Though the Elizabethan madrigals displayed a wide range of subject matter and mood, the most famous type was the lighthearted pastoral variety. Among the most famous of all Elizabethan madrigals is *Now Is the Month of Maying* by Thomas Morley (1557–1603), a pupil of William Byrd. The use of a refrain consisting of nonsense syllables is typical of this kind of Elizabethan madrigal.

Italian madrigals were dramatic and emotional; English madrigals were generally lighthearted.

Marenzio's Italian madrigal, *S'io parto, moro* is a good example of this genre.

Elizabeth I supported the development of the arts in England.

Elizabethan madrigals were popularized by composer Thomas Morley.

This pastoral madrigal is essentially homophonic; the only bits of imitation occur on the refrain "Fa-la-la." The text is:

Now is the month of Maying,
When merry lads are playing,
Fa la la.
Each with his bonny lass,
Upon the greeny grass,
Fa la la.
The Spring clad all in gladness
Doth laugh at Winter's sadness,
Fa la la.
And to the Bagpipes sound,
The Nymphs tread out their ground,
Fa la la.
Fie then, why sit we musing,
Youth's sweet delight refusing?
Fa la la.
Say dainty Nymphs and speak,
Shall we play barley break?
Fa la la.

William Shakespeare

Recently there has been a renewed interest in the sixteenth century madrigal, and a number of professional and amateur performing groups have been formed for the purpose of performing this music.

Interest in Elizabethan madrigals has increased recently.

Keyboard and Instrumental Music

During the Renaissance, the harpsichord emerged as an important keyboard instrument, though the full realization of its possibilities did not occur until later, in the baroque era. Many of the English madrigal composers were also active in producing music for the harpsichord or its English equivalent, the virginal. Included in the group of English virginalist composers are William Byrd (ca. 1540–1623), Thomas Morley, Orlando Gibbons (1583–1625), Giles Farnaby (ca. 1560–1640), and John Bull (ca. 1563–1628). The majority of their compositions were sets of variations and Renaissance dances arranged for the keyboard.

The harpsichord rose in importance during the Renaissance.

An example of variations for virginal is Giles Farnaby's *Loth to Depart,* a popular sixteenth century melody. A recording of it is found in *Masterpieces of Music Before 1750,* no. 29. The *Historical Anthology of Music,* no. 179 offers a pair of dances, a pavane and a galliard, in the piece for virginal called *Pavane Lord Salisbury* by Orlando Gibbons.

Sets of variations and Renaissance dances were arranged for keyboard.

Various composers also wrote music for viols, which are stringed instruments of various sizes. (Viols were used to accompany the verse anthem by Byrd, *Christ Rising Again.*) Many genteel English homes had, as a matter of course, a set of viols that were kept in a specially built

Renaissance composers wrote pieces for the viols.

Most Renaissance dance music had the *AABB* structure.

In Venice, pieces were composed specifically for the acoustics of St. Mark's Cathedral.

chest, and used for family entertainment and other social occasions. The viols are the ancestors of the modern string quartet instruments.

Other instruments used in the Renaissance include recorders, shawms, regals, sackbuts, small portable organs, and various drums and hand-held percussion instruments. Most instrumental music was written for dances, and most had the *AABB* structure—the immediate forerunners of the baroque dance suite.

Working in Venice, the famed organist and composer Andrea Gabrieli (ca. 1510–86), along with his equally famous nephew, Giovanni Gabrieli (1557–1612), developed a distinctive, colorful, and expressive style in the late Renaissance. These monumental works, complemented at the time by the spectacular acoustics of Venice's St. Mark's Cathedral, where they were originally performed, often utilized two or more choirs of voices, one or more organs, and an ensemble of brass instruments.

Let us close this chapter on music in the Renaissance by listening to Andrea Gabrieli's *Gloria in Excelsis Deo,* written for four choirs of voices, viols, organs, trumpets and trombones.

SUMMARY

The Renaissance celebrated the rebirth of humanism. In humanistic style, this period of fifteenth and sixteenth century European history produced writers, scientists, artists and composers who altered the course of Western civilization.

The secular world of the Renaissance accommodated the Church and its music. Both sacred and secular music characteristically included these elements: chordal harmony, imitative counterpoint, four-voice texture, and modernized rhythm.

The religious sects that emerged from the Reformation had a profound effect on the sacred music of the period. Martin Luther's emphasis on congregational singing was the impetus for the creation of chorales. The sects based in John Calvin's doctrines developed metrical psalms/psalmody—biblical texts set to simple music. The Anglicans preferred complex choral pieces designed for trained choirs. William Byrd composed many of these anthems. Roman Catholics continued to set the Ordinary of the Mass to music. Renaissance Masses featured various movements of popular melodies, Gregorian melodies enriched with imitative counterpoint, and a refashioned motet form. Josquin des Prez's Masses are very famous.

The dominant form of secular music in the sixteenth century was the madrigal, a composition for four to six male and female voices featuring expressive harmony and imitative counterpoint. Italian madrigals, popularized by Luca Marenzio, were dramatic and emotional, and typically focused on tragic, unrequited love. Elizabethan madrigals were lighthearted, pastoral pieces. One of the most famous composers of this genre was Thomas Morley.

Keyboard and instrumental music were also important in the Renaissance. Variations and dances were composed for harpsichord by madrigal composers while music for organs, trumpets, trombones, and viols was composed for performance in St. Mark's Cathedral, Venice. Renaissance dance music, with *AABB* structure, was played on popular period instruments such as the recorder, shawms, regals, sackbuts, and small portable organs.

I hope that our look at the Renaissance has reinforced in your mind the importance of the period. We have sampled just a bit of this period's offerings.

KEY TERMS

humanism	anthem	madrigal
chorale	verse anthem	Italian madrigal
metrical psalms (psalmody)	Renaissance motet	Elizabethan madrigal

THINKING ABOUT IT

One way to help you understand important advances in Renaissance music is to contrast it with your understanding of Medieval music. Even when done in general terms, this can help bring some important differences into focus. For example, contrast the thirteenth century motet discussed in chapter 10 with the Josquin motet discussed in this chapter. What are the differences in harmony? In the number and kind of voices? In textural activity?

OUTSIDE THE SPHERE OF WESTERN ART MUSIC

12

AMERICAN POPULAR MUSIC TO 1950

Jukebox

SOUNDS OF THE CHAPTER

Arlen
Hooray for What?

Harry Armstrong
"Sweet Adeline"

Barnet
"Cherokee"

Basie
"One O'Clock Jump"

Berlin
As Thousands Cheer
"Easter Parade"
"God Bless America"

Dorsey
"Boogie Woogie"
"Marie"
"Opus One"

Ellington
"Caravan"
"Take the A Train"

Evans
"In the Good Old Summertime"

Fitzgerald
"A Tisket-a-Tasket"

Foster
"Beautiful Dreamer"
"Camptown Races"
"Come Where My Love Lies Dreaming"
"Jeanie with the Light Brown Hair" ♪
"Laura Lee"
"Massa's in the Cold, Cold Ground"
"My Old Kentucky Home"
"Oh, Susanna"
"Old Black Joe"
"Old Folks at Home"
"Ring, Ring the Banjo"
"Way Down Upon the Swannee River"

Gershwin
"I Got Rhythm"
Of Thee I Sing

Goodman
"Don't Be That Way"
"Sing, Sing, Sing"
"Well Get It"

Herman
"Woodchopper's Ball"

James
"Ciribiribin"

Miles/Sterling
"Meet Me in St. Louis, Louis"

Miller
"In the Mood"
"Little Brown Jug"

Porter
"I've Got You Under My Skin"
"Night and Day"

Shaw
"Begin the Beguine"

Thornton
"On the Banks of the Wabash"

Woodworth
"The Old Oaken Bucket"

Work
"Come Home, Father"

"A Foggy Day in London Town"
"April in Paris"
"Argentine Nights"
"As Time Goes By"
"Autumn in New York"
"Avalon"
"Brother Can You Spare a Dime?"

"By the Light of the Silvery Moon"
"Daily Bread"
"Dancing on the Ceiling"
"Don't Blame Me"
"Halleluia I'm a Bum"
"I Wouldn't Trade the Silver in My Mother's Hair"
"If I Ever Get a Job Again"
"In the Shade of the Old Apple Tree"
"Isle of Capri"
"It Happened in Monterey"
"It's Only a Paper Moon"
"I've Got My Love to Keep Me Warm"
"Let Me Wah-hoo, Wah-hoo, Wah-hoo"
"'Leven Pounds of Heaven"
"Little Sir Echo"
"Lord Randall"
"Love Walked In"
"Midnight in Paris"
"Moon of Spain"
"Moon Over Miami"
My Fair Lady
"My Mom"
"My Sweetheart's the Man in the Moon"
"Over the Rainbow"
"Pennies from Heaven"
"Red Sails in the Sunset"
"Shine on Harvest Moon"
"Song of India"
"The Lord's Prayer"
"The Merry-Go-Round Broke Down"
"The Mother Song"
The Music Man
"What Are Little Girls Made Of?"
"You Call It Madness, But I Call It Love"
"You! You're Driving Me Crazy"

The changes in American popular music have reflected the changes in the nation itself.

Three distinct styles emerged between 1850 and 1950.

American popular music is often erroneously viewed as a static phenomenon, a music that has remained stylistically constant, exhibiting only minimal change. On the contrary, American popular music has undergone some significant changes that have reflected the cultural changes of the culture at large.

From the 1850s through the 1950s, no fewer than three styles of popular music are evident. The songs of Stephen Foster exemplify the first of these styles, the genteel tradition of the mid-nineteenth century. Later in the century, popular music changed with the rise of the Tin Pan Alley era. And a third dramatic stylistic change occurred around 1930 with the emergence of swing.

THE DISSEMINATION OF AMERICAN POPULAR MUSIC

Music in some form or other has always been an important part of the American tradition. Evidence suggests that the earliest music brought to America was predominantly sacred—mostly psalms and hymns. However, this by no means precludes the probability that the migrating Europeans also brought secular music with them when they immigrated. They must surely have found this secular music enjoyable, and also appreciated it for its nostalgic value.

The first American songs were kept alive by oral tradition.

Nineteenth century sheet music cover

Many early American songs were composed anonymously, disseminated and kept alive through the process of oral tradition. Frequently these songs changed from generation to generation or from location to location, with the changes reflecting the personalities and experiences of the groups who used the songs.

Such songs were actually more legendary than popular. Strictly speaking, they were personal rather than standardized, and they were not commercially oriented. They were, in fact, recomposed as they migrated from place to place, always adapting the personal statement of the bearer of the song. Thus, the anonymous (seventeenth century?) composer of the ballad "Lord Randall" provided the basis for the anonymous nineteenth century composer who rewrote the material into the song "Where Have You Been, Billy Boy?".

The Rise of the Sheet Music Industry

The commercial sheet music business, as well as the Protestant sacred music business, blossomed in America in the early nineteenth century. Publishing houses, catering to the regional tastes of their prospective customers, emerged in larger cities from the East (Boston, New York, Philadelphia and Baltimore) to the Midwest (St. Louis, Chicago, Cincinnati and Milwaukee).

Although printed music had been available for several hundred years, it was not until the middle of the nineteenth century that a large body of printed music was existent—sheet music, freshly composed, intended for commercial purposes, and distributed widely to the American public. Many of the songs by Stephen Foster, Dan Emmett, Henry Russell, and others from the midnineteenth century achieved commercial success, largely because of the sale of sheet music. Despite these successes, the sheet music *industry* did not develop until later in the century, in the late 1880s and 1890s. At that time many song publishers from around the country converged in a district of New York City that came to be known as Tin Pan Alley.

Some American song writers achieved commercial success in the mid-nineteenth century.

The sheet music industry did not emerge in the United States until late in the nineteenth century.

With the rise of Tin Pan Alley many regional publishing houses began to devote more resources to the sheet music industry. The switch was not entirely geographical, for there was a concomitant switch from the diversity of regional song types to an increasingly homogeneous song style.

The sheet music industry flourished during the period from 1890 to 1920, and was then superseded by other, faster modes of dissemination. It was soon clear that the sheet music industry would have to take a back seat to the other media. The radio, the phonograph, and the sound motion picture are all products of the early twentieth century, and by 1930 all three were commercial successes.

Because of these new media, the term popular assumed a magnitude theretofore unknown and perhaps not even dreamed of. Consider, for example, that a song popular in Boston in 1850 or even 1890 may never have been heard by someone living in San Francisco, Denver, or Houston. But a song beamed over the airwaves in 1927 could be heard over all of the 27,850,000 home-owned radio sets in the country. Since the population of the United States in 1927 was only 119,000,000, it was possible, then, for one in four Americans to listen to a given song at the same time.

The radio, the phonograph, and the motion picture gave Americans, from coast to coast, a common music.

Audience Participation

Audience participation was important during the Tin Pan Alley era, as it was prior to that time. Printed music was purchased for performance at home around the family piano. But with the advent of the new media, audiences were forced into a largely passive role. The audience heard popular music over the radio and in the movies, and bought recordings of their favorite popular songs. There was a movement away from active

The new media decreased the importance of participation.

However, Americans did actively participate in popular music through dance.

participation in the performance of music toward a passive acceptance of it. The notable exception to this was in the field of dance, a type of participation that has been a constant in American music.

Dance   Indeed, as the audience became passive in terms of actual performance, interest in dance increased. This interest was manifest in the various dance crazes of the 1920s, such as the Charleston and the Black Bottom, and in the foxtrotting and jitterbugging of the 1930s and 1940s.

Interest in social dancing spawned the creation of dance bands.

By the 1930s the traveling dance bands became an important factor in popular music. By the late 1930s, the big band era was in full bloom, and in cities across the country the big name bands played before large and enthusiastic crowds of dancers.

The movie musical became popular in the twenties and thirties.

Film   The movie musical, an infant in the late 1920s, grew to adulthood at a dizzying pace in the 1930s, and by the close of that decade many of the recognized landmarks of the genre had been produced, attracting millions of viewers.

Musical comedy   The American musical comedy also came of age in the 1930s. By the late 1920s the operetta (and other European forms of musical theater) had begun to decline on Broadway, relinquishing its popularity to the musical comedy. The Broadway audience, typically more affluent and snobbish than the movie and radio audiences, responded to the music of George Gershwin, Cole Porter, Irving Berlin, Richard Rodgers, and Jerome Kern, at the expense of the Europeans—Johann Strauss, Franz Lehar, Victor Herbert, and Gilbert and Sullivan.

Broadway music appealed to the higher socio-economic classes in the 1930s.

THE GENTEEL TRADITION

The genteel tradition describes the life style of middle class Americans in the early nineteenth century.

In the early decades of the nineteenth century, middle-class Americans prided themselves on honest labor, comfortable surroundings, and the cultivation of good manners and taste. This has been appropriately dubbed the **genteel tradition.** A particular kind of popular music was a part of this tradition.

The so-called **parlor song** was performed both in public and at home with the family around the piano in the parlor. Typically, the parlor song consisted of simple, diatonic harmonies that supported equally unpretentious melodies, frequently marked by fermatas on high notes or textually dramatic points. In general, the texts were overly emotional or nostalgic, with such subjects as the homeless, afflicted children, and lost love. There were also many moralizing texts.

Parlor songs featured overly emotional texts.

The text of Samuel Woodworth's "The Old Oaken Bucket" is typical of the sentimental parlor song:

Notice the sentimentality in these examples.

> How dear to this heart are the scenes of my childhood,
> When fond recollection presents them to view,
> The orchard, the meadow, the deep tangled wildwood,
> And ev'ry lov'd spot which my infancy knew.
> The widespreading stream, the mill that stood near it,
> The bridge and the rock where the cataract fell;
> The cot of my father, the dairy house by it,
> And e'en the rude bucket that hung in the well.
>
> The old oaken bucket, the iron bound bucket,
> The moss covered bucket that hung in the well.

Henry C. Work was among the most popular composers of the era. He won fame with texts such as "Come Home, Father":

> Father, dear father, come home with me now!
> The clock in the steeple strikes one.
> You said you were coming right home from the shop,
> As soon as your day's work was done.
> Our fire has gone out, our house is all dark,
> And mother's been watching since tea,
> With poor brother Benny so sick in her arms,
> And no one to help her but me.
>
> Come home! come home! come home!
> Please, father, dear father, come home.
> Hear the sweet voice of the child
> Which the night winds repeat as they roam.
> Oh, who could resist this most plaintive of prayers?
> "Please, father, dear father, come home."

Today this may seem to be the most banal and tacky kind of sentimentality, but it was precisely that which tugged at the heartstrings of the audience of the day. It is vintage genteel tradition.

This music was a part of the genteel tradition.

Stephen Foster

Stephen Foster (1826–64) was born into this tradition, and many of his songs are closely related to it. "Beautiful Dreamer" (1864), "Come Where My Love Lies Dreaming" (1855), and "Jeanie with the Light Brown Hair" (1854) are all songs about departed or unattainable love. "My Old Kentucky Home" (1853), "Way Down Upon the Swannee River," and "Old Folks at Home" (1851) are filled with a nostalgic longing for the past. The other basic type of song that Foster wrote belongs to the minstrel show tradition. "Oh! Susanna" (1848) and "Camptown Races" (1850) are examples of this type.

Stephen Foster (1826–64)

Most of Foster's compositions are melancholy or nostalgic.

Foster's loved one is always idealized.

Quaint expressions are typical of the genteel tradition.

Foster's harmony is often restricted to the primary chords of the key.

Simple melody characterizes Foster's songs.

The melodies are the highlight of Foster's works.

The genteel tradition seems to have died with Foster in the 1860s.

Despite the melancholy nature of many of Foster's songs, all of his compositions are in major keys. His nostalgic songs and his songs of lost or unrequited love are cast in slow or moderate tempos. The subject of love is never treated in a lighthearted or playful manner. "Jeanie with the Light Brown Hair," "Beautiful Dreamer," and "Come Where My Love Lies Dreaming" move at a dignified pace.

Love is earnest and the loved one beautiful: "borne like a vapor on the summer air." She is sweet: "Why has the happy dream blended with thee, Passed like a fleeting beam, sweet Laura Lee?" She is idealized: "Starlight and dewdrops are waiting for thee. Beautiful dreamer, queen of my song, list while I woo thee with soft melody." Anachronistic expressions such as "borne," "thee/thy," "o'er," "e'een," "tis," and "list" are typical of the genteel tradition.

Most of Foster's songs are diatonic to the extreme; the harmony is generally restricted to the primary chords of the key (tonic, subdominant and dominant). "Camptown Races" (1850), for instance, is built entirely on the tonic and dominant chords, save for one measure of subdominant harmony on the words "Gwine to run all day." "Massa's in the Cold, Cold Ground" (1852) uses only tonic, dominant, and subdominant, and "Old Black Joe" (1860) is limited to those three chords except for one chromatic chord just before the close of the second phrase of the song. "My Old Kentucky Home" uses a chromatic chord near the end of phrases one and three but the rest of the harmony is limited to the primary chords. "Jeanie with the Light Brown Hair" and "Beautiful Dreamer" are only slightly more harmonically adventurous.

The melodic style of these songs also bears the mark of simplicity: diatonic whole and half steps comprise most of the melodic intervals. Like the chords that support them, the melodies are amazingly free of chromatic intervals. Some of his most famous tunes are flavored with pentatonicism: "Oh! Susanna" and "Camptown Races" are completely pentatonic; "Ring, Ring the Banjo" (1851) and "Laura Lee" (1851) are mostly pentatonic; and only the middle section of "Old Folks at Home" (1851) is nonpentatonic. The tunes are almost folklike in their simplicity and in their frequent use of pentatonicism.

Foster's true gift was in the realm of melody. For all of their simplicity and lack of drama, these melodies had a beauty that render them memorable to this day.

In retrospect, it seems clear that when Foster died near the end of the Civil War, a whole tradition of American popular music passed away. Shortly thereafter, a new, more brazen style emerged to replace it.

Singing around player piano

THE TIN PAN ALLEY ERA

Foster's songs contrast sharply with the songs that were popular in the Gay 90s—the **Tin Pan Alley** era. Many of these songs were as chromatic as Foster's were diatonic, their harmonic language abounds with chromatically altered chords, quick modulations, and slithering inner parts. The "close harmonies" of these songs were, in contrast to those of Foster, very dissonant and raucous. They were easily adaptable to the barber shop quartet format that was so popular in America near the turn of the century. It is difficult to think of "Sweet Adeline" (1903, Harry Armstrong) without conjuring up the sound and the image of the mustachioed, straw-hatted male quartet. The same is true of "On the Banks of the Wabash" (1898, James Thornton), "In the Good Old Summertime" (1902, George Evans), "Shine On, Harvest Moon" (1904), and dozens of others.

The restlessness of the harmony in these songs may reflect the national economic, industrial, and geographic expansion that was occurring at that time. As has been seen, even the popular music business expanded into an industry during those years. The placid harmonies of Foster's songs belonged to an earlier, more genteel and static time that was disrupted by the Civil War.

Songs from the Tin Pan Alley era also differed from the genteel era in terms of subject matter, idioms, and specific words.

Tin Pan Alley music became the music of the Gay 90s.

The popular barber shop quartet performed the music of Tin Pan Alley.

The restlessness found in popular music reflects the economic upheaval of the period.

Verse and Refrain

The verse and refrain
format was characteristic of
American popular music in
the 1890s.

The verse told the story,
but often only the refrain is
remembered.

In the gay 90s, popular songs adhered to the format of **verse and refrain.** The refrain was roughly analogous to an aria, and the verse was analogous to a recitative that preceded the aria. The function of the verse was to establish the plot and then lead into the more melodious and memorable refrain. With most of these songs it was the verse, not the refrain, that actually told the story of the song. Today when these songs are performed the verse is almost always omitted. Thus, the general public often misinterprets the true nature of many of these songs.

For example, "Meet Me in St. Louis, Louis" (1904, Kerry Miles and Andrew Sterling) is actually a very roguish song, a fact evident not in the refrain that many people know, but in the verse that one rarely hears. The refrain reads as follows:

> Meet me in St. Louis, Louis, meet me at the fair,
> Don't tell me the lights are shining anyplace but there.
> We will dance the Hoochee Koochee,
> I will be your tootsie wootsie
> If you will meet me in St. Louis, Louis,
> Meet me at the fair.

In the verses we learn that the singer of the song is actually a woman who has just left her husband:

> When Louis came home to the flat
> He hung up his coat and his hat,
> He gazed all around, but no wifey he found,
> So he said, "Where can Flossie be at?"
> A note on the table he spied,
> He read it just once, then he cried.
> It ran, "Louis dear, it's too slow for me here,
> So I think I will go for a ride."
> (Refrain)
> The dresses that hung in the hall
> Were gone, she had taken them all.
> She took all his rings and the rest of his things;
> The pictures he missed from the wall.
> "What! Moving?" the janitor said,
> "Your rent is paid three months ahead."
> "What good is the flat?" said poor Louis, "read that."
> And the janitor smiled as he read.
> (Refrain)

Likewise, the verse to "In the Shade of the Old Apple Tree" clarifies the meaning of the song, not evident from merely listening to the refrain. The song is, in fact, a tragedy—the loved one of the person singing the song is buried under the old apple tree. Similarly, the verse to "Sweet Adeline" tells us something that the refrain barely suggests, namely, that the song is about unrequited love.

The lyrics from "In the Good Old Summertime" (1902, Ron Shields and George Evans) are just as saucy as those from "Meet Me in St. Louis, Louis." "You hold her hand, and she holds yours, and that's a very good sign, that she's your tootsie-wootsie in the good old summertime." The tootsie-wootsie is a far cry from the beautiful dreamer. To speak of the loved one as a tootsie-wootsie during the genteel era would have been scandalous. On the other hand, to suggest that the tootsie-wootsie who dances the Hoochee Koochee could ever have been "borne like a vapor on the summer air" would have been laughable in the Gay 90s.

The many "moon" songs of the Gay 90s introduced a number of slang words to the vocabulary of love texts, words such as spoon, swoon, and croon, were used primarily because they rhyme with moon. Such songs as "By the Light of the Silvery Moon" "Shine on Harvest Moon," and "My Sweetheart's the Man in the Moon" replace the dignity and sentimentality of Foster's love songs with a brassiness, even vulgarity. The refrain of "My Sweetheart's the Man in the Moon" is as follows:

> My sweetheart's the man in the moon, I'm going to marry him soon.
> 'Twould fill me with bliss, just to give him one kiss,
> But I know that a dozen I never would miss.
> I'll go up in a great big balloon, And see my sweetheart in the moon.
> Then behind some dark cloud where no one is allowed,
> I'll make love to the man in the moon.
>
> *Second verse:*
>
> Last night when the stars brightly shone, he told me through love's telephone,
> That when we were wed, he'd go early to bed,
> And never stay out with the boys, so he said.
> We are going to marry next June, the wedding takes place in the moon.
> A sweet little Venus, we'll fondle between us,
> When I wed my old man in the moon.

The true nature of the song is revealed in the verse.

Gay 90s musical language is not the refined language of the genteel tradition.

Gay 90s songs introduced slang words into the American vocabulary.

Popular music increased the gap between Americans reared in the genteel tradition and the youth of the 1890s.

Popular music has always been secular music, but with some of the outrageous songs from the 1890s, it appeared even more so. The harmony of these songs, with their self-conscious, almost defiant chromaticism, and the naughty, rebellious quality of their lyrics, evoked indignation from those who had grown up in the genteel tradition. Young people of the time also began to look and dress differently from their elders. This may have been the first of several generation gaps that have occurred in American culture, and popular music definitely contributed to its creation.

POPULAR MUSIC IN THE 1930s

Popular music is certainly perishable; most of it is hastily produced, quickly consumed, and soon forgotten. The audience for popular music in the 1930s had a voracious appetite for songs and a remarkably fickle attitude toward them. The smash hit of a given day usually became tomorrow's nonentity.

The American audience of the 1930s consumed a huge amount of popular music.

A large body of popular music was created in a short time.

To satisfy this insatiable appetite, hundreds of composers and lyricists combined to create about 10,000 published songs during the years 1930–39. That averaged nearly three songs every day, or one song every eight hours, or, to carry the breakdown to an extreme, the thirties witnessed the production of roughly four measures of popular music every sixty minutes—a phrase an hour.

Few of these thirties hits became standards.

The perishability of these songs is demonstrated by their short lifespan—very few have survived the thirties to become what are commonly known as **standards,** or songs that have continued to be performed to the present day. "Night and Day" (1932, Cole Porter), "Easter Parade" (1933, Irving Berlin), and "I Got Rhythm" (1930, George and Ira Gershwin) are examples of standards.

Audiences continued to ignore the verse and focus on the refrain of the song— the verse became dispensable.

Composers and lyricists in the thirties continued to supply the recitativelike verses mentioned earlier, but for the most part performers, and hence audiences, tended to ignore the verse. (One exception is Broadway shows, where the verse had a necessary dramatic function.) For most audiences the refrain was the golden moment; it was the memorable part of the song, and the verse was forgotten. The era of the storytelling song was over, and it became increasingly clear that the verse was dispensable.

Song Forms

Four- and eight-bar patterns were characteristic of popular thirties songs.

Most popular songs from the thirties contain four- and eight-bar phrases in regular patterns. These songs usually fall into three categories: (1) *AABA,* in which each of the four sections contains eight measures for a total of thirty-two measures. The eight-bar *B* section is usually referred

Plate 25

An image from the Great Depression years: gentle and melancholy. Compare it
to the mood of Samuel Barber's *Adagio for String Orchestra* (chapter 9.)

Nighthawks; Edward Hopper; The Art Institute of Chicago, Friends of American Art.

Plate 26
The clean lines, sharply defined shapes, and general sense of precision and balance suggest neoclassicism. See chapter 9 for the discussion of neoclassicism in twentieth century music.

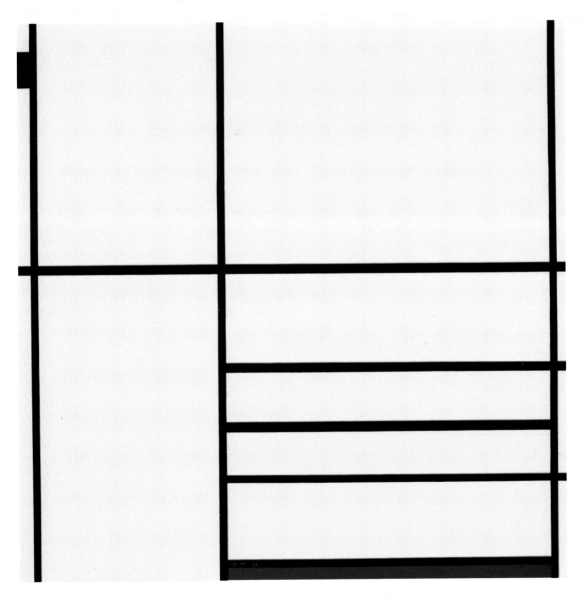

Composition in White, Black, and Red; Mondrian; The Museum of Modern Art, New York, Gift of the Advisory Committee.

Plate 27

A seemingly random pattern of color creates a painting with great energy and density. See the discussions of electronic music and chance music in chapter 9.

Number I; Jackson Pollock; The Museum of Modern Art, New York, Purchase.

Plate 28

The pop art movement of the 1960s has some connection to the dadist movement from the early twentieth century. (See chapter 9.)

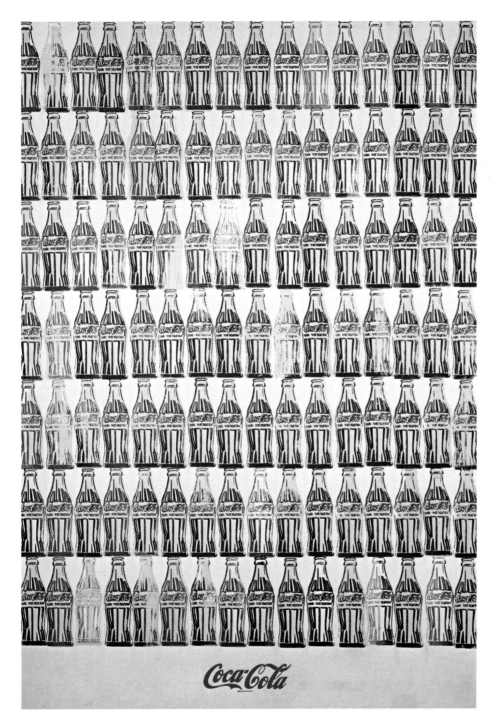

Green Coca-Cola Bottles; Warhol; The Whitney Museum of American Art, New York.

Plate 29
A stained glass window from a Gothic cathedral. (See chapter 10.)

South Rose Window and Lancets; Chartres Cathedral; Art Resource.

Ginevra de' Benci; Leonardo da Vinci; National Gallery of Art; Washington, D.C. Ailsa Mellon Bruce
Fund 1967.

Plate 31

A masterwork by Michelangelo, a luminary of the humanistic Renaissance.

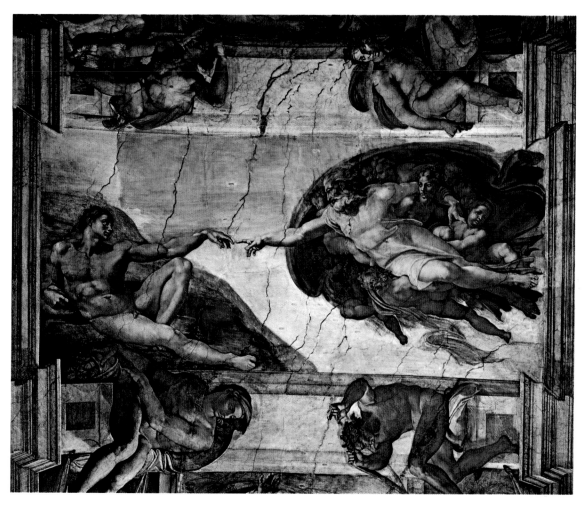

Creation; Michelangelo; Sistine Chapel Ceiling; Art Resource.

Plate 32

An American family in the nineteenth century. (See chapter 12.)

The Sargent Family; American School; National Gallery of Art; Washington, D.C.; Gift of Edgar William and Bernice Chrysler Garbish 1953.

Plate 33
A jukebox from the late 1930s or early 1940s. (See chapter 12.)

Plate 34
The Beatles. (See chapter 13.)

Plate 35
African Musicians.

Plate 36
A Balinese Gamelan Orchestra.

Cole Porter (1893–1964)   George Gershwin (1898–1937)

to as the "release." Most of the songs from the decade have this *AABA* design. (2) *AA* or *AA'*, in which each section contains sixteen bars, again with a total of thirty-two bars. These are the one-idea songs that operate without benefit of a contrasting *B* section. Only about one quarter of the decade's songs are of this type. (3) Songs that encompass a variety of formal designs, ranging from more extended forms such as *AABACA,* to an occasional twelve-bar blues. This category, which is more or less a catch-all for rare formal types, comprises many of the instrumental numbers from the big band era and very few other compositions.

It is obvious, then, that almost all of the songs written in the thirties have either the *AABA* or *AA* form. However, some of the most memorable and popular songs have utilized unconventional forms. For example, many of the songs of Cole Porter, one of the most successful composers in American popular music history, have atypical formal structures: "Night and Day" (1932), or "I've Got You Under My Skin" (1936). Duke Ellington's "Caravan" (1937) has a seldom-used structure, but it, too, has become a standard.

Of course, most of the successful songs used the more common *AABA* format:

"Dancing on the Ceiling" (1930)
"As Time Goes By" (1931)
"Don't Blame Me" (1932)

The majority of popular thirties songs had *AABA* form.

About one fourth of the popular songs had *AA* or *AA'* form.

Very few songs had extended forms.

Cole Porter composed in unconventional forms.

***AABA* form is common to these standard pieces from the thirties.**

"Easter Parade" (1933)
"It's Only a Paper Moon" (1934)
"Red Sails in the Sunset" (1935)
"Pennies from Heaven" (1936)
"I've Got My Love to Keep Me Warm" (1937)
"Love Walked In" (1938)
"Over the Rainbow" (1939)

The longevity of these songs is impressive. Each has been recorded numerous times over the past five decades. However, the vast majority of 1930s songs written in the *AABA* design were permanently discarded by the public very shortly after they were written.

Lyrics

Lyrics in the thirties touched on a wide range of topics.

The lyrics of thirties songs dealt with a fairly diversified range of subject matter. Love, nostalgia, fads, the exotic, the family, and the depression were all topics that sparked the creativity of songwriters.

Love songs remained popular throughout the decade.

Love Although this diversity of subject matter exists, more than half of the songs from the thirties deal with the subject of love. In general, these songs fall into three categories:

1. Love ballads in which the subject of love is treated in a romantic and positive way, as in:

   I'm in the mood for love, simply because you're near me.
   Funny, but when you're near me, I'm in the mood for love.

   I'M IN THE MOOD FOR LOVE. © 1935 (Renewed 1963) ROBBINS MUSIC CORPORATION. All Rights Assigned to CBS CATALOGUE PARTNERSHIP. All Rights Controlled and Administered by CBS ROBBINS CATALOG. International Copyright Secured. All Rights Reserved. Used by Permission.

2. Lighthearted love lyrics—that treat the subject in a more flippant way, as in:

   Three little words, eight little letters
   Which simply mean I love you.

   © 1930 (Renewed) Warner Bros. Inc. All Rights Reserved. Used By Permission.

3. Lyrics dealing with lost or unattainable love, as in:

   Can't go on, everything I had is gone
   Stormy weather, since my man and I ain't together
   Keeps raining all the time.

   STORMY WEATHER by Ted Koehler and Harold Arlen. Used by Permission of ARKO MUSIC CORP. and Copyright © 1933 by Mills Music, Inc. Copyright renewed. Used with permission. All Rights Reserved.

The subject of love was treated in diverse ways.

Certain images from many love ballads of the thirties point unmistakably to escapism. In addition, a number of love lyrics suggest whimsical fancy, in which the adored one (who is quite literally adored) is frequently pictured as an angel. Such is the case with a song from 1939, in which the mere sound of the loved one's voice is enough to produce heavenly choirs:

You speak, and the angels sing
The angels sing the sweetest song I ever heard.

Romantic love was sometimes envisioned as a state of euphoria that borders on sweet madness, as in the song "You Call It Madness, But I Call It Love" (1931). "You! You're Driving Me Crazy" (1930) is more lighthearted, but no less mad.

One also finds romantic love likened to a state of alcoholic haziness:

You go to my head and you linger like a haunting refrain.
I find you spinning round in my brain, like the bubbles in a glass of champagne.

Nostalgia   As with the genteel tradition, nostalgia often figured in songs from the 1930s. Several hundred songs were composed that were little more than reminiscences of the peaceful, happy atmosphere of days gone by. These songs focused on a longing to return to the old homestead in the south, a sentimentality about the tranquility of the mountains, and memories of the old west with its wide open spaces and big sky.

Nostalgia was a popular subject for songs in the thirties.

Oddly enough, many of these nostalgic songs idealizing the deep South or the Southwest were partially influenced by the popularity of cowboy movies throughout the decade. Many of these songs were written by people who lived in New York City or Hollywood, and few had any firsthand knowledge of the settings and people about whom they rhapsodized. Similarly, the audiences who popularized the songs lacked this firsthand knowledge of the subject. Most of the popular music audience did not live in the South or the Southwest. In fact, those two areas of the country stubbornly clung to their own regional music, and shunned popular music for the most part.

The South and Southwest were idealized in song.

Sentimental lyrics also abounded—songs about old rocking chairs, the little church in the valley, an empty saddle, old spinning wheels and wagon wheels, a cabin in the pines, and homes in Georgia, Texas, and the Carolinas.

All of these nostalgic and sentimental songs spoke of a sweetly remembered, but safely irretrievable, past. They were lyrical messages to a confused society that was moving ever more swiftly toward urbanization and industrialization. Little exoticism and no nostalgia were attached to a cement factory, or a conveyor belt, or a typewriter. But the

The past was remembered with longing.

Darkness on the Delta, the Moon Coming over the Mountain, or Heading for the Last Roundup were grist for the romantic mill.

Novelty songs **Novelty songs** represent a relatively small portion of the total songs from the decade. Of all the types of popular songs, novelty songs tend to have the shortest life span. As the fads and crazes that precipitate such lyrics fade and are replaced by new fads, the novelty songs and the fads that spawned them evaporate.

Novelty songs depend upon fads for their existence.

With few exceptions novelty songs were products of Tin Pan Alley. This was one type of song that the sheet music industry could still claim as its own success. The novelty song was supposed to burst on the scene with great force, make its sales in a rush, and then disappear in the wake of the next novelty song. Song writers and publishers surely recognized that novelty songs were not destined to become big money-makers over a long period of time. In a sense, the novelty song was like a joke—it is funniest and most impressive on first hearing, but after that interest wanes.

Novelty songs have a short life span.

Notable among the novelty songs of the thirties were "Let Me Wah-hoo, Wah-hoo, Wah-hoo" (1936), "The Merry-Go-Round Broke Down" (1937), and "Little Sir Echo" (1939). The success of these songs is based in part on a very puerile ingredient: the repetition of nonsense syllables such as wah-hoo, oom-pa-pa, or yoo-hoo—the sorts of nonsense words that amuse children.

The repetition of nonsense syllables is important in novelty songs.

It is impossible to predict the fad of the future.

The silly things that attract the attention of the public are unpredictable, which means what may have amused the public in the 1930s would likely get little or no reaction from audiences of both earlier and later decades.

Exotic songs were popular in the thirties.

Exotic Another important and fairly large body of songs from the 1930s may be categorized as "exotic." Some of these songs could also be included in the category of love songs, a few could be classified as novelty songs, but all of these exotic songs cater to the American fascination with mysterious, distant lands. In fact, most of these songs are identified by a specific location, as noted in the following:

A specific distant land was often the subject of an exotic song.

> "Moon of Spain" (1930)
> "Avalon" (1930)
> "It Happened in Monterey" (1930)
> "Argentine Nights" (1931)
> "Song of India" (1932)
> "April in Paris" (1932)
> "Isle of Capri" (1934)
> "Autumn in New York" (1934)
> "Moon Over Miami" (1935)
> "Midnight in Paris" (1935)
> "A Foggy Day in London Town" (1937)

An examination of the collection of exotic songs from the thirties reveals that the audience and the songwriters were most interested in Hawaii (and by extension, the South Seas), and in Latin America. These two locales seemed to epitomize the idea of the exotic in the mind of the American popular music audience.

Hawaii and Latin America were considered especially intriguing.

Family   There were few devotional songs and songs about family life during the decade. The thirties might be considered an era endowed with artificiality, but this artificiality never encroached on the private domain of family life. Personal family matters, such as a wayward son or daughter, or a father given to gambling or drinking, were not discussed. One finds no "birds in gilded cages" or young women who are "more to be pitied than censured." There were no songs dealing with children begging, "Come home, father," for dirty linen was not aired in public. These were private matters, and either good taste or fear of humiliation prevented discussion of them.

Personal and family issues were not appropriate song topics for thirties.

Since there were few songs that discussed such problems, there were also few songs that offered advice, criticism, or admonition—no didacticism from the soap box.

Very few songs dealt with maternal or deistic subjects, and of those that did, most came across as flat statements, not as exhortations. "The Mother Song" ("M is for the million things she gave me") (1930), "I Wouldn't Trade the Silver in My Mother's Hair" (1932), "Daily Bread" (1931), "My Mom" (1932), "The Lord's Prayer" (1935), " 'Leven Pounds of Heaven" (1931), and "What Are Little Girls Made Of?" (1933) typify and nearly exhaust this repertoire.

Songs dwelling on God and motherhood were almost nonexistent.

Patriotism   The thirties did produce one very popular patriotic song: Irving Berlin's "God Bless America" (1938). This song seemed to give expression to the nation's latent spirit of patriotism, and during the war years this song became the rallying cry of servicemen and civilians alike. The powerful downbeats of its metrical scheme place all the right textual syllables in positions of unmistakable strength: *"God"* . . . A-*"Mer"*-ica . . . *"Love"* . . . *"Home."* The spirit of the song, as well as its important nationalistic flavor, lent itself to the patriotism of the time.

One patriotic song of the thirties did gain widespread popularity—"God Bless America."

The depression   Ironically, very few songs of the time dealt with an obvious, though somber, subject—the Great Depression. "Brother Can You Spare a Dime?" (1932) was the quintessential song dealing with the depression. "Halleluia I'm a Bum" (1932) flippantly spoke of the desperation of the situation, as did "If I Ever Get a Job Again" (1932). George

Very few songs faced the economic reality of the depression.

Gershwin's Broadway musical *Of Thee I Sing* (1931), Berlin's *As Thousands Cheer,* and Harold Arlen's *Hooray for What?* are filled with political barbery, but the vast majority of the songs from the decade make no mention of the depression and its many social and economic problems.

DEFINING SWING

Swing was popularized in the 1930s.

The thirties witnessed a major change in the manner of playing and singing popular music, and during the decade a style of performance developed that remained in vogue until after the end of World War II. Not all of the bands from the era were swing bands, nor were all of the male singers crooners, but swinging and crooning were important developments.

"Swing" and "the swing era" are terms that have been in general use since the 1930s, but some people erroneously assume that swing and the swing era are one and the same thing—that swing flourished exclusively during the swing era.

Swing is an integral part of jazz.

The term **"swing,"** however, has a substantial history: it was a verb used by some of the earliest jazz musicians. Jellyroll Morton described swing as a rhythmic and phraseological action that takes place in jazz. In words and in musical demonstration, Morton eloquently described the process of swing and insisted that without it, jazz was inconceivable.

Swing describes the performance of jazz music.

In simplest terms, swing can be described as a performance practice unique to jazz; more than any other factor, it is the performer's swinging that causes the performance to be labeled "jazzy." Swing is largely a temporal phenomenon, but it also involves a particular kind of musical ambiance. To swing the rhythm of a given tune is to play it with a deliberate disregard for its indicated note values, and to play it with certain accents and inflections that run counter to the direction of its notation.

THE BIG BAND ERA

The "Big Band Era" embraced the years 1932–45.

Because swing has always been a part of jazz the phrase **"swing era"** is misleading; it is too limiting. The swing era embraces the years from about 1932 to 1945, but even as a label for that time period the phrase is not accurate, if considered literally. These were the years during which the big dance bands were a vital part of the American popular music scene, but only some of the bands played swing. For example, the band of Benny Goodman, the "King of Swing," predominantly played swing, while Guy Lombardo played "the sweetest music this side of heaven,"

Not all the big bands featured swing music.

a type of music devoid of swing and having no connection with jazz.

Benny Goodman (clarinet) and band: *sax*—Arthur Rollins, Hymine Shertzen, George Koenig; *trumpet*—Chris Griffin, Jarry James, Ziggy Elman; *trombones*—Murray MacEachern, Red Ballard; *drums*—Gene Krupa

There were dozens of big dance bands operating during the swing era, and depending upon the type of music played, they can be separated into swing bands and sweet bands, or into some part of the vast gray area between the two.

Swing Bands

Some of the best known white swing bands were formed during the mid-to-late 1930s as Benny Goodman, Tommy Dorsey, Glenn Miller, Jimmy Dorsey, and Artie Shaw organized their groups.

The white swing bands performed primarily at dances, but the biggest names among them sometimes had lucrative contracts with radio networks, movies, and of course, the recording industry. Their audiences were usually young (teen and college age), white and middle-income or above. To make themselves marketable, many of these bands (such as those headed by Benny Goodman, Tommy Dorsey, Glenn Miller and Artie Shaw) played a mixture of instrumental swing and popular ballads, though the ballads usually outnumbered the pure swing instrumentals.

This was not true of the black swing bands. Their audiences feasted on a diet much richer in jazz and blues; ballads were of secondary importance.

White swing bands usually played a mixture of instrumental swing and popular ballads.

Black swing bands offered more jazz and blues.

Count Basie In the late 1920s Count Basie was a member of the Kansas City based Bennie Moten band, one of the hottest swing bands of the era. When Basie formed his own band in the mid-thirties, it was built along the same lines as the Moten band. The Basie band played with real drive and energy. Its repertoire included fewer ballads, leaning more heavily on swing blues and riff tunes. One of the most famous arrangements from the entire swing era, and the archetypal riff tune piece, is Basie's "One O'Clock Jump" (1937). This recording became a juke box favorite during the big band era and resulted in nationwide popularity for the Basie band.

The Count Basie band focused on swing blues and riff tunes.

Glenn Miller The most celebrated name to emerge from the big band era is that of Glenn Miller. His tragic and mysterious disappearance on a military flight from England to mainland Europe during 1944, the appeal of his music to the young at heart and to the innocent jitterbuggers of the World War II generation, and the utterly distinctive style and "sound" of his band have contributed to his posthumous image as the grand master of the swing era. For many, Miller's "In the Mood" is alone sufficient to describe, indeed, epitomize an era of American popular music.

Glenn Miller was probably the favorite band leader of the period.

Although many popular music forms have emerged since the demise of the big band era, the abiding popularity of the Miller band clearly demonstrates that an audience of significant number still exists for this music. Miller remains a popular figure, and his music is still a paying proposition.

Miller's music has retained its popularity.

The success of swing bands Some of this success must be attributed to the nostalgia of men and women, now middle-aged, who were attached to this music in the thirties and forties, and who continue to appreciate the musical comfort and stability of the Miller band. The current boon in nostalgia and the curiosity seekers among the younger generation are, doubtless, also a part of the reason for the continuing success of the Miller band. As happens with every generation of music lovers, the fans of swing-era music have clung to "their" music because it is a point of stability for them. As their generation returned from the war to pick up the threads of civilian life, they discovered that popular music was one of many things that had changed or was beginning to change. The sentimental ballads and the big band swing arrangements so familiar during the thirties and early forties were being pushed aside by a younger generation who wanted something else, something that was foreign. The emergence of bebop and progressive jazz in the mid-to-late forties also left them shaking their heads—they could make no sense of it.

Miller's popularity spans two generations of listeners.

As this generation attempted to build careers in the affluent post-war years, and tried to adapt to swiftly changing social patterns and mores, comfort was found in the musical stability represented by the Miller band (and in the many things this kind of music symbolized and represented). Though the world was moving and changing at a rapid pace, Glenn Miller's music was stable, memory-laden, and still interesting.

This phenomenon, however, is not unique to the generation that enjoyed swing music. The musical genre of a particular era will continue to appeal to its audience long after its popularity has waned. Its sound will inspire the memory of youthful confidence and security, of familiarity and consistency in an ever-changing world.

Swing sells Although only fifteen records sold more than 500,000 copies during the thirties, the recording business did very well, largely due to the popularity of the jukebox. Some of the decade's best sellers were swing arrangements that were at the time, and have been ever since, associated with one specific band: Tommy Dorsey's "Marie" (1937), Ella Fitzgerald's "A Tisket-a-Tasket" (1938), Artie Shaw's "Begin the Beguine" (1938), Harry James' "Ciribiribin" (1939), and Glenn Miller's "In the Mood" and "Little Brown Jug" (both from 1939). Similarly, "Well Get It," "Don't Be That Way," and "Sing, Sing, Sing," belong to the Benny Goodman band; "Opus One" and "Boogie Woogie" belong to Tommy Dorsey; "Take the A Train" belongs to Duke Ellington; "One O'Clock Jump" to Count Basie; "Cherokee" to Charlie Barnet, and "Woodchopper's Ball" to Woody Herman.

Sweet Dance Bands

At the opposite end of the spectrum from the true swing bands are those that are unmistakably sweet. This sweet sound was dominated by white bands. Black sweet bands with national reputations were practically nonexistent in the 1930s; there was no call for them by black audiences, and no effective means for them to compete with the white bands for the attention of white society.

Guy Lombardo One of the most commercially successful dance bands ever was that led by Guy Lombardo. His repertoire, style, and arrangements are prototypical of the hotel-style, **sweet dance bands** of the thirties and later. Guy Lombardo's band catered to the fairly affluent, nonswing stratum of society. The band had a sound of its own, characterized by a monochromaticism that never approached raucous or loud. The rhythm section was rather bouncy and metronomic, and the tempos were kept unerringly steady for the dancers.

Nineteenth century sheet music cover

The thirties brought prosperity to the recording business.

Songs popularized by a particular big band were the major sellers in the thirties.

White sweet bands offered an alternative to the swing bands of the thirties.

Guy Lombardo's band typified the sweet band sound.

The sweet bands, like the swing bands, catered to dancers.

The Guy Lombardo band was in the enviable position of having a profitable home base while enjoying nationwide exposure. Dance crowds and ballroom managers were eager to have them perform. Lombardo's enormous popularity bears witness to the fact that swing bands were not the only kind of instrumental ensemble that had an impact on audiences in the 1930s—the popularity of sweet dance music has endured, also.

The national popularity of Guy Lombardo lasted several decades.

SINGING IN THE THIRTIES

Music audiences develop ideals and standards for singers. To some extent audiences dictate how singing should sound and the types of emotional and vocal ingredients that should enter into the singing style. In large measure, audiences are influenced by some particularly electric or novel singer. As the audience changes, as from one generation to the next, the standards and notions about singing often change. A new or different kind of music is usually accompanied by a change in singing styles.

Audience standards for singing tend to change as the style of popular music changes.

There were three distinct singing styles in American popular music of the 1930s: the tenor or "clean" style; the stage or "talking" style; and the crooning or "dirty" style. The tenor and stage styles were vocal traditions from the nineteenth century. Crooning, on the other hand, was a product of the 1930s. During that decade, crooning, which at first appeared to be a mere fad, developed into a genuine tradition and became the dominant style of the time. Its supremacy in popular music remained intact until the mid-1950s with the emergence of rock and roll, when a new style of singing took over.

Singers in the thirties offered three styles: tenor, talking, and crooning.

Tenor or "Clean" Style

The roots of the **tenor style** can be traced to several sources, one being the Irish tenor who sang in a clear, high, and often melodramatic way. This style was exceedingly popular in this country.

The purity or "cleanliness" of vocal quality in the tenor style was usually matched by "clean" lyrics. Typically, the tenor style singer avoided lyrics that dealt with controversial or morally questionable subject matter, such as criticism of traditional values, or drinking and gambling.

Tenor style was clean in quality and subject matter.

The tenor style of singing was particularly popular with middle and older age groups in the thirties—a throwback to the genteel tradition of the early nineteenth century. To the older age groups, this style seemed healthy and wholesome, a buffer against a creeping moral decay that they sensed in the country, and in some types of music. The world was in the process of change and so was the style of American popular music. For many, the tenor style symbolized a return of the good old days, and was a comfort to those who decried or resisted change.

The tenor style reminded thirties listeners of the genteel tradition.

The style also appealed to those who expected to hear evidence of legitimate voice training from their singers. And, unlike the other popular singing styles, the tenor style could claim a filial relationship to "high brow" music, which was also desirable to many.

Talking Style

The **stage** or talking style was a product of the vaudeville stage and night club circuit, both of which were rougher, much less sophisticated forms of theater. The singers from these forms of musical theater were actually more comedians or song and dance men than legitimate vocalists. Since their audiences were often noisy and rowdy, these performers developed voices that had the capacity to "bark" their songs in a somewhat abrasive fashion. It was not their intention to produce beautiful sounds—quite the contrary. Their ranges were limited, their vocal quality was husky, and their delivery was a mixture of genuine singing and rhythmic talking. They set the standard for more recent musical comedy roles such as Harold Hill in *The Music Man* and Henry Higgins in *My Fair Lady.*

The stage or talking style singer also depended on visual effects, such as soft shoe routines. These visual effects added another dimension to the singers' performances and helped to compensate for a lack of vocal prowess.

Jimmy Durante was among the most amusing and successful of the talking style performers.

Crooning or "Dirty" Style

From the birth of the recording industry in the 1870s until the mid-1920s, all songs were recorded through an acoustical process. The performer—Enrico Caruso was an early favorite—had neither microphone nor amplification, but played or sang directly into a recording horn, which activated a stylus that cut the pattern of the sound waves into tinfoil (in the case of cylinder recording) or into wax (in the case of early disc recording). By today's standards the acoustic process is primitive and unsatisfactory. This unsophisticated process is incapable of capturing nuances, soft sounds, a wide range of frequencies and many standard timbral combinations. It was best equipped to record the full-bodied voice, such as Caruso's.

The microphone was introduced to the recording industry in the early 1920s. After 1925, the electric recording with microphone and amplifier replaced the acoustic process, became standardized, and has remained in use to the present day.

The breathy quality of crooning demanded amplification for the singer under most circumstances.

The words "croon" and "crooner" were added to the vocabulary of most Americans in the thirties.

Crooning was a term applied to a particular singing style. The crooner typically sang with half a voice and produced a breathier sound than that of a trained full-voiced singer. Thus, unless the crooner were singing in intimate surroundings, he needed amplification in order to be heard. The microphone became the solution to his dilemma.

An incident reported in *Variety Magazine* in 1931 suggests the extent to which the new term "crooner" was used by the public. Under the headline "Pair of Crooners Crooning Ballads Got Hostess Sore," the report described two men arrested for crooning outside of a young woman's house:

> "They came to my house and remained outside the apartment door. They crooned and crooned . . ." she said.
> "I was in no humor to be crooned for. I was tired and I begged them to leave, but they insisted upon crooning.
> "I then called the cop," stated the hostess.

The crooning style sounded uniquely American.

To identify with crooning was to be with it, or up-to-date. Undoubtedly, the crooner was a symbol of newness, and the sleekness and intimacy of his style clashed with the singing tradition that had dominated the American popular scene for many decades. The crooning style sounded fresh and uniquely American.

Critics of crooning predicted its early demise.

Rudy Vallee was the first well-known singer to croon.

Often in the history of popular music a newly-emerging style or manner of performance is greeted by critics and experts as nothing more than a momentary fad. The advent of crooning in the 1930s was greeted with just such a prediction, since it was a dramatic break with previous popular music practices. The predictions of its early demise, however, did not materialize.

Rudy Vallee was the first well-known singer who was nominally considered a crooner. Vallee was associated with the kind of syncopated orchestra fashionable with New York society in the early decades of this century, and his vocal delivery never overstepped the polite boundaries of that particular style. The blues, which was being brought to the attention of a sizable white audience in the 1920s, had no effect on his singing style, nor was he tempted to swing or "jazz up" his delivery.

Bing Crosby became the epitome of the crooner.

Bing Crosby Bing Crosby did not invent crooning, but his voice became the standard against which all other crooners would be measured. Crosby, unlike Vallee, could make a legitimate claim to a jazz background. The performance practices of the many jazz musicians whom he knew and with whom he worked had a profound impact on his singing style.

Crosby's style closely resembled that of the swing musician. The effortlessness and nonchalance of his delivery, his penchant for imitating

Bing Crosby with Shirley Ross in *Waikiki Wedding,* 1937.

jazz instruments (sometimes with modest improvisational lines and figures), and his ability to swing, imply that his ear was attuned to musicians such as Jack Teagarden, Louis Armstrong, and Bix Beiderbecke.

Moreover, Crosby had a unique quality—humor. Crosby's humor was infectious, but not self-conscious. Though he had the ability to move his audience to tears with a slow, sad ballad, he could put the same audience in a mood of fun and good humor, with his up-tempo pieces. He often accomplished this by caricaturing himself, poking fun at the crooner with all those "Boo boo boo boos."

THE DEMISE OF THE SWING ERA

To paraphrase an important title from the 1930s, the swing era was "gone with the war." The big bands fell on hard times after the war and soon disappeared entirely. The ghost of the big band era was occasionally visible in revivals of the Glenn Miller band and other bands, and in some cases these bands managed to keep their grip on at least a small audience. A significant number of swing musicians either went into studio work, or evolved new styles that were in touch with the changing face of jazz. A few, like Ellington and Basie, somehow managed to keep their bands together. Others left. But for the most part, an era in the history of American popular music was over.

The big bands disappeared after World War II.

SUMMARY

Our study of American popular music has revealed that the period from the mid-nineteenth century through the 1940s was one of great change. During these years American popular music moved through three distinct stages: the genteel tradition, Tin Pan Alley, and swing.

From the colonial days music played a role in the American tradition. It was not until the middle of the nineteenth century, however, when sheet music was commercially distributed, that Americans across the country began listening to the same music. It is at this time that we can begin to identify an American popular music style.

The life-style of the middle-class American in mid-nineteenth century is termed the genteel tradition. Popular music in the form of the parlor song was a part of this tradition. The songs offered simple, diatonic harmony, unpretentious melodies, and nostalgic, sentimental texts. These songs were typically played at home on the family piano. Stephen Foster's music characterizes this style.

In the Gay 90s the mood called for a more dissonant, raucous music—that of Tin Pan Alley. These restless songs featuring saucy verses reflected the economic, social, and political upheaval of the times.

The popular music of the 1930s featured primarily *AABA* and *AA* form. Few songs offered unconventional form. From 1930 to 1939, approximately 10,000 songs were published, ranging in topic from love to nostalgia to the exotic.

"Swing" describes the way much of the thirties music was played. It was popularized by many of the big dance bands such as those of Tommy Dorsey and Glenn Miller. Other bands, including Guy Lombardo's, however, played a "sweet" music that did not swing.

The most popular singing style of the period was crooning. Singers Rudy Vallee and Bing Crosby popularized a breathy style that appealed to audiences across the country. Also popular were the clear tenor style reminiscent of the genteel tradition and the talking style that had developed on the vaudeville stage and in the night club. This style was the abrasive, husky sounding form popularized by Jimmy Durante.

The swing era, which encompassed the musical traditions of the period from 1930 through 1945, died soon after the conclusion of World War II. American popular music would soon after be termed "rock."

KEY TERMS

genteel tradition	standard	sweet dance bands
parlor song	novelty song	tenor (clean) style
Tin Pan Alley	swing	stage (talking) style
verse and refrain	swing era	crooning

THINKING ABOUT IT

It is difficult to single out only a few of the quality compositions from this era because of the vast and diverse collection that exists. Thus, instead of specific Sound and Sense examples, the following list of works from the three major genres is provided. These recordings remain popular enough that locating them should not present a problem. You are encouraged, then, to listen to as many recordings as possible.

From the Genteel Tradition

Songs by Stephen Foster	Nonesuch H 71268 Stereo
Gregg Smith Singers: Songs of S. Foster	Turnabout 34609
An Evening with Henry Russell	Nonesuch H 71338
Songs by Henry Clay Work	Nonesuch H 71317

From the Tin Pan Alley Era

Come Josephine in My Flying Machine	New World Records NW 233
Barber Shop Quartet Favorites	Coral 20012

From the Swing Era

Benny Goodman—Giants of Swing Treasure Chest (3 vols.)	MGM E3788, 89, 90
Duke Ellington: Greatest Hits	Reprise 6234
Brother Can You Spare a Dime?	New World Records NW 270
Rudy Vallee: Heigh Ho, Everybody	Olympic Records OL-7128
The Music Goes Round and Round	New World Records NW 248
Singing Troubadors on the Air	Star-Tone Records ST-206
The Great Big Band Vocalists	Columbia Special; Products CSS 1507
The Original Big Band Hits	RCA R 212227

There are also collections of hits from the thirties and forties by Bing Crosby and by many of the big bands.

13

1960s rock concert

SOUNDS OF THE CHAPTER

Baker
"Jim Dandy"

The Band
The Band
"Like a Rolling Stone"
Music from Big Pink
"The Night They Drove Old Dixie Down"

The Beach Boys
"Fun, Fun, Fun"
"Little Deuce Coupe"
"Surfin' U.S.A."

The Beatles
"A Day in the Life"
"A Little Help from My Friends"
"Being for the Benefit of Mr. Kite!"
"Eleanor Rigby"
"Fixing a Hole"
"Getting Better"
"Good Morning"
"Lovely Rita"
"Lucy in the Sky with Diamonds"
"Polythene Pam"
"Sgt. Pepper's Lonely Hearts Club Band"
"She's Leaving Home"
"Taxman"
"When I'm Sixty-Four"
"Within You, Without You"
"Yesterday"

Berry
"Roll Over Beethoven"
"School Days"

Boone
"Ain't That a Shame"
"I Almost Lost My Mind"
"Love Letters in the Sand"

Brown
"Good, Good Lovin'"
"Please, Please, Please"

Chubby Checker
"The Twist"

Clapton
"Lay Down Sally"

Doggett
"Honky Tonk"

The Doors
"Break on Through"
"Light My Fire"

The Drifters
"Why Do Fools Fall in Love"
"Searchin'"

Dylan
"Like a Rolling Stone"

Fats Domino
"I'm Walkin'"

Franklin
"Satisfaction"
"You Make Me Feel (Like a Natural Woman)"

Haley
"Rock Around the Clock"

Hammerstein
"You Are Too Beautiful"

Hendrix
"Purple Haze"
"The Star Spangled Banner"

Holly
"Peggy Sue"

Jefferson Airplane
"White Rabbit"

Janis Joplin
"Get It While You Can"
"Me and Bobby McGee"
"Piece of My Heart"

The Kingston Trio
"Tom Dooley"

Led Zeppelin
"Stairway to Heaven"

Little Richard
"Good Golly Miss Molly"
"Lucille"
"Tutti Frutti"

McPhatter
"Long Lonely Nights"
"Money Honey"
"The Treasure of Love"

Presley
"Heartbreak Hotel"
"I'm All Shook Up"

Redding
"I've Been Loving You Too Long"
"Try a Little Tenderness"

The Rolling Stones
"Satisfaction"

The Supremes
"Run, Run, Run"
"You Can't Hurry Love"

Tubb
"I'm Walkin' the Floor Over You"

Turner
"Shake, Rattle and Roll"

Weber/Rice
Jesus Christ, Superstar

The Who
Tommy

Willis
"C. C. Rider"

Hair
"Mashed Potatoes"
"The Pony"
"Popeye"
"The Slop"
"Work with Me Annie"

Rock has been America's popular music since the 1950s.

Rock has assumed several styles over the years.

Rock is both an era and a style in American music.

No one musician is responsible for the birth of rock.

Little Richard (b. 1932)

For music that was so often labeled "a passing, obnoxious fad," rock has endured a long time. As public music, one with wide public acceptance and unprecedented commercial success, its life has already exceeded the bounds of an entire generation, and thirty years after its first public splash, its demise is nowhere in sight. Rock music in one form or another has, since the mid-fifties, become the new American popular music.

But rock has not stood still all this time, repeating itself over and over again; instead it has consistently evolved into new and different forms. Thus we cannot speak of *a* rock music, but must instead examine and account for several different branches of rock. Some music mentioned in this chapter has little apparent relationship to what we might call the core of rock—for example, country music and commercial folk music. We must remember, however, that rock not only replaced the kind of American popular music discussed in chapter 12, but was also responsible for freeing the previously rigid boundaries of what Americans accepted as popular music. In this sense rock should be understood both as a style (with many substyles) and as an era in popular music—an era in which a diversity of musical types have flourished. It is important to be aware of this double significance of rock.

It is impossible to determine who invented rock and when: there is no single inventor and no specific date of birth. However, several musicians and events are associated with rock's early years.

A movie called *Blackboard Jungle* featuring Bill Haley and the Comets appeared in 1955 and included a song called "Rock Around the Clock." Haley was a benign, baby-faced, almost middle-aged man with a background in country swing music.

In that same year Little Richard's "Tutti Frutti" was released. Little Richard was a wild young man from Macon, Georgia with a background in gospel music and rhythm and blues.

In 1956 Elvis Presley's million-seller "Heartbreak Hotel" was released. Presley was a surly looking young southerner with a background in country music and white gospel music. His looks, clothes, accent, and attitude were aggressively, even arrogantly, different from his contemporary popular musicians.

Rock was not born during the years 1955–56, nor was it invented by Bill Haley, Little Richard, or Elvis Presley. But *Blackboard Jungle,* "Tutti Frutti," and "Heartbreak Hotel" revealed to the public that a musical, aesthetic, and attitudinal change was taking place. These were the first announcements on a public scale that the attitudes of youths were changing and that the musical impulses to which they responded were very different from those of older generations. The success of this music with teenagers in the mid-to-late fifties was staggering.

Elvis Presley (1935–77)

THE ROOTS OF ROCK

The terms **"rocking and rolling"** and **"rocking and reeling"** are found in black cultural history as early as the first decades of the twentieth century. At that time the terms had both a sacred and a secular connotation. They were used as a kind of exultation in black gospel music, and they were used to describe sexual activity. In both instances the terms seemed to suggest energy, joy, and passion.

"Rocking and rolling" carry black sacred and secular connotations dating to the early twentieth century.

R & B

Sometimes the terms "rock" and "rockin' " appear in the lyrics of a type of black music that emerged in the thirties and forties called **rhythm and blues.** Rhythm and blues (or R & B) is the most immediate and direct ancestor of rock and roll music of the fifties.

R & B emerged in the 1930s and 1940s.

In the thirties and forties the mass white audience listened to the popular songs discussed earlier, and to the music of the big bands. This was their popular music. During that same time period, many blacks listened to this music, too, but they also listened to more hard-line jazz, gospel music, blues, and R & B. All of these genres were their music, but R & B was created by black musicians and designed for black audiences. R & B was distinctly different from white popular music.

Black audiences favored diversified musical genres during the thirties and forties.

For example, the lyrics of R & B songs were earthier and more temporal in nature than the standard white ballad of the same time period. This is evident in a comparative study of the text of the popular song for white audiences written below and the R & B text that follows it. Both are love lyrics.

Compare the R & B lyrics to the lyrics of a contemporary song written for white audiences.

"White" Popular Song:

"You Are Too Beautiful" (lyrics by Oscar Hammerstein)
You are too beautiful my dear, to be true,
And I am a fool for beauty.
Fooled by a feeling that because I found you,
I could have bound you, too . . .
Love does not stand sharing,
Not if one cares.
Have you been comparing my every kiss with theirs?
If on the other hand, I'm faithful to you,
It's not through a sense of duty;
You are too beautiful and I am a fool for beauty.

© 1932 (Renewed) Rodart Music Corp. All Rights Reserved. Used By Permission.

R & B Song:

"Work with Me Annie"
Work with me Annie, work with me Annie,
Work with me Annie, work with me Annie,
Work with me Annie.
Let's get it while the gettin' is good
So good, so good, so good, so good.
Annie please don't cheat,
Give me all my meat,
Ah oo oo oo oo oo,
So good to me
Work with me Annie,
Let's get it while the gettin' is good.

The difference between the two is obvious. Now, not all R & B texts are as graphic as this, but generally speaking, R & B texts are simpler than white popular song texts, and less ladened with quasi-poetic imagery. The language is definitely down to earth.

Most R & B is in twelve-bar blues format.

As discussed in chapter 12, very few popular songs from the thirties and forties have the form and harmony of the twelve-bar blues. However, the majority of R & B vocal and instrumental numbers are cast in the twelve-bar blues format.

The basic beat of R & B was also very different from white popular songs. R & B developed a special accent pattern within the 4/4 meter that is characteristic of the style: the downbeat is accented, beats two and four are heavily accented, and beat three has no accent at all. Graphically illustrated the pattern looks like this:

Beat	1	2	3	4	1	2	3	4
4/4	x	X	o	X	x	X	o	X

The following recorded examples illustrate this pattern. Notice that the drummer consistently emphasizes beats two and four.

> "C. C. Rider" by Chuck Willis (*History of Rhythm and Blues,* vol. 3, side 2, band 5)
> "Jim Dandy" by LaVern Baker (ibid., vol. 3, side 1, band 7)
> "Shake, Rattle and Roll" by Joe Turner (ibid., vol. 2, side 1, band 6)
> "Honky Tonk (part II)" by Bill Doggett (*Great Hits of R & B,* side 1, band 1)

Having detected the beat pattern, listen to these same examples again. You will discover that they are all in the twelve-bar blues form.

The instrumentation of R & B was distinct from that of white popular music. It usually consisted of piano (or electric organ), drums, one or two guitars, and often a honking tenor sax. The sax and the lead guitar were the principal solo instruments.

Hard-core R & B singers often sang with rather raspy voices, and their delivery was often punctuated by a variety of whoops and yells. The backup vocal groups sang repetitive phrases and words, sometimes repeating nonsense syllables, or sometimes singing ooos or humms. This is evident in "Searchin' " by the Drifters (*History of Rhythm & Blues,* vol. 3, side 2, band 2).

In terms of lyrics, formal (and) harmonic structure, beat, instrumentation, and vocal style, R & B contrasted sharply with white popular music of the forties. But one of the major differences is less audible, and has to do with a basic attitude toward music; indeed toward life itself. Whereas white popular music was lush, polite, and dreamy, R & B was basic, sometimes brutally frank, and imbued with a carefree spirit. It was this spirit that took hold of the rock and roll audiences that emerged in the fifties.

The beat accent pattern characterizes R & B.

The R & B group featured a piano, drums, guitars, and tenor sax.

R & B lead singers were backed up by vocal groups.

Unique to R & B was its carefree spirit.

Country

Country music was also different from white popular music in terms of lyrics, instrumentation, and vocal style. The lyrics of country music songs were simple, down-to-earth, and free of poetic artificiality and dreams. The instrumentation of country music was very similar to that of R & B except that a raucous and wiry fiddle took the place of the honking tenor sax. The country singer sang very differently than the crooner or the big band singer. The country music singer produced a nasal quality that was punctuated by a variety of whoops (yodels) and groans. In addition, the beat of forties country music often resembled that of R & B. All of these qualities, including the beat, can be heard in the country hit of the late forties "I'm Walkin' the Floor Over You" by Ernest Tubb. (You should be able to find this recording in one of the several anthologies of country hits presently available.)

The attitude of the country singer bordered on arrogance; he or she was not ashamed of being different from mainstream popular singers. These people thoroughly enjoyed their music the way it was. Moreover, they didn't give a hang if not a single slick Yankee liked it or them.

Strange as it seems, white country music and black R & B had more in common with each other than either had with white popular music. They were both southern and both unimportant as far as the New York music industry was concerned.

Rock and roll, the first kind of rock music, is essentially an extension of R & B, though it also resembles country music. Considering the racial climate of the time and the disinterest of large audiences in country music, rock and roll definitely needed white performers in order to succeed commercially. It is therefore not surprising that the first giant of rock and roll was Elvis Presley, a white, southern singer and guitarist with a background in country music.

ROCK AND ROLL

Although rock and roll was essentially an extension of R & B, there were some differences between the two. For one thing, the language of R & B had to be cleaned up and purged of its too obvious sexual overtones. By law, radio stations could not broadcast such language as is found in "Work with Me Annie." So the language was scrubbed up in rock and roll and made legal for the general listening public. Many in the adult audience still didn't approve of the simple-minded language and the uncouth vocal style, but they could not argue that it was illegal. (Many still insisted that rock and roll was somehow immoral.)

Country music replaced the R & B sax with a fiddle.

Country music in the forties resembled R & B in some ways.

Country singers were proud of their music and their audience.

Elvis Presley brought his country music background to rock and roll.

Rock and roll grew out of R & B.

The texts of rock and roll songs were mainly about teenage puppy love, high school dances, cars, and similar topics. Songs dealing with love were free of the sentimentality and artificiality found in love songs from the thirties and forties. Elvis Presley's "I'm All Shook Up," Buddy Holly's "Peggy Sue," and the Drifters' "Why Do Fools Fall in Love" are typical. In much the same vein is a fine rock and roll song, "I'm Walkin'," by Fats Domino, a former R & B singer who had some success in the tamer and more broadly based world of rock and roll.

Some songs were part celebration of rock and roll and part anti-establishment. This is true of Chuck Berry's "School Days" (hail, hail rock and roll) and his famous "Roll Over Beethoven."

Apart from the thrill of the music itself, the self-ostracism of this music appealed greatly to a mass teenage audience looking for a means to express its own rebelliousness and anxious to assert its independence from the values of its elders. The music brought this motley, diverse audience together and became its rallying point. The music was theirs and theirs alone. No one else wanted it. With this music, northern and southern teenager, culturally different in so many ways, were united. Even more impressive, black and white youths found some common and mutually enjoyable ground in rock and roll, while race relations in the adult world were still in a deplorable state.

The older generation took a very dim view of rock and roll music and the effect it seemed to have on teenagers. They called it illiterate, mindless, filthy, the devil's own music, and void of any musical or poetic value. Rock concerts in the late fifties and early sixties were banned in some places, broken up in some places, and heavily policed in general. There were instances of riotous behavior by some teen rockers and alleged brutality by some officers of the law. This was partially caused by the enthusiasm and excitement of the music itself, and partially caused by a broadly based misunderstanding between parents and teenagers, something that came to be called the "generation gap."

The parents of these teenagers had recently suffered through a war and had a real sense of how grim and serious life can be. The sentimentality of the popular songs of their generation offered them solace. However, the grimness, seriousness, and sentimentality were lost on the younger generation. They rebelled against it. The more parents tried to forbid it, the more attractive rock and roll became to teenagers.

Rock and Roll Beat

Rock and roll took over the beat of R & B. Often in rock and roll this beat was underscored by a thumping, relentless pattern of quarter notes divided into eighth notes or into eighth note triplets. The two types are superimposed on the R & B beat illustrated in figure 13.1. In both cases the rhythm of rock and roll radiated vitality and the lure of dance.

Rock and roll lyrics were written to appeal to teenagers.

Some rock and roll was deliberately anti-establishment.

Teenagers found in rock a means of expressing their rebellion.

Rock and roll served as a common bond uniting all American teenagers.

Rock and roll music contributed in part to the generation gap.

Most adults found rock and roll to be less pleasing than their own sentimental music.

Rock and roll imposed a new rhythm on the R & B beat.

Fig. 13.1

The eighth note division is called "eight to the bar" and was borrowed from **boogie woogie,** a piano style that appeared in the thirties and forties, but is probably much older than that. A boogie takes the shape and harmony of the twelve-bar blues and, within that framework, the left hand plays a steady succession of eight eighth notes per 4/4 measure while the right hand plays figures and improvisations against it. (Pianist Meade Lux Lewis was an important boogie woogie player and can be heard in "Honky Tonk Train" [*Smithsonian Collection of Classical Jazz,* record 4, band 2].) Little Richard and several other rock and roll piano players adopted the "eight to the bar" pattern. You can hear it in two of Little Richard's biggest hits: "Lucille" and "Good Golly Miss Molly." The pattern is found also in several of Elvis Presley's early hits, including "Hound Dog."

Rock and Roll Instrumentation

The instrumentation of rock and roll is very similar to that of R & B. In the case of Little Richard and Jerry Lee Lewis, the piano is more prominent because they were piano players themselves. For others (Presley, for example) the guitar is the featured solo instrument.

By the late fifties it was clear to those in the New York music industry that there was a vast teenage rock and roll audience. The general affluence of the postwar years put money into the hands of this audience. Rock and roll record sales soared, and, little by little, radio stations across the country began to convert to a steady diet of rock and roll. This music was big business.

Soft Rock and Roll

In the late fifties and early sixties, a brand of **soft rock and roll** emerged. It was textually less abrasive, the rock beat was muffled (but not extinguished), and the background instrumentation sometimes included soft violins. The singer shied away from the harsh sounds of hardcore rock and roll, and took a position closer to old-style crooning.

Rock and roll's "eight to the bar" was borrowed from boogie woogie, a piano style form popularized in the 1930s and 1940s.

The instrumentation of rock and roll is similar to that of R & B.

The New York record industry's acceptance of rock and roll was motivated by economics.

Rock and roll was big business by the late fifties.

A softer rock and roll emerged in the late fifties and early sixties.

One of the most successful singers of soft rock and roll was Pat Boone. From his toothy grin to his white buckskin shoes, he seemed somehow clean and gentlemanly; even the teenager's parents could accept him. Among his biggest hits were "Ain't That a Shame," (actually a slow R & B song by Fats Domino), "I Almost Lost My Mind" (a country song disguised in soft rock and roll), and "Love Letters in the Sand" (a popular song from the thirties).

Pat Boone exemplified this soft rock and roll.

Other young solo singers, such as Frankie Avalon, Fabian, Paul Anka, and Ricky Nelson were also successful with soft rock and roll. Clyde McPhatter, who sometimes sang with the Drifters, was a black singer who was successful in both hardcore rock and roll ("Money Honey") and soft rock and roll ("The Treasure of Love," "Long Lonely Nights").

Other male singers contributed to the popularity of soft rock and roll.

FROM FIFTIES ROCK AND ROLL TO SIXTIES ROCK

Rock music began to change in the 1960s. American youth began to view the fun-loving, hard-driving rock and roll and the soft, syrupy kind of rock and roll as kid's stuff. The audience, who had recently reveled in rock and roll, began to look upon it as mindless and juvenile. Rock and roll was high school music, but the rock of the sixties was college music. Sixties audiences were ready for more sophisticated things: lyrics that did more than simply rhyme, instrumentalists who played more than three chords and who played with considerable skill, themes and harmonies that were thought provoking, and singers who had studied the great blues and jazz singers of the past, and were discontent with "doo-wat-da-doo-da-wah."

In the sixties a new rock for the college audience emerged.

The sixties rock audience sought more sophistication and complexity than rock and roll could offer.

Motown

But the changeover was neither complete nor universal. The echoes of rock and roll, somewhat altered, lingered in the sixties. Groups such as the Temptations and the Supremes (later Diana Ross and the Supremes) from Detroit produced music that was essentially an extension of rock and roll, though their lyrics were more high-toned and the Supremes were certainly sophisticated in manner and dress. The elegance of their singing and stage presence came to epitomize the Motown (Detroit) style. They sang such rock and roll songs as "You Can't Hurry Love" and "Run, Run, Run," but also songs by Rodgers and Hart. They recorded an album of Christmas songs and appeared at posh dinner clubs. Whereas their counterparts in R & B and rock and roll were raucous, even raunchy, the Supremes were beautiful and very ladylike. They personified Motown elegance.

The Supremes personified Motown in the sixties.

The Twist

The dance craze of the sixties was the twist.

The big dance craze of the early sixties was the twist, popularized by Chubby Checker (a play on the name Fats Domino) with the song "The Twist." Jet-setters and the rich were among those attracted to the fun of the twist. High society and teenyboppers who could afford the admission to the Peppermint Lounge, the national twist headquarters in Manhattan, danced to the "Mashed Potatoes," "The Slop," "The Pony," "Popeye," and of course "The Twist." Twist music was little more than rock and roll in the form of a game, providing a chance for the bored wealthy to go musically slumming. When the game was over, the twist died a quick death.

Rock became the dominant music form of the sixties.

Dolled up rock and roll and the twist were popular for a time, but peripheral to the major thrust of rock music in the 1960s. Many groups with serious musical and poetic intentions began to appear. The field of rock widened and deepened considerably in the sixties.

THE BEATLES

Rock has not been limited to the United States.

Though rock music was born and bred in the United States, it has not been limited to these shores. Since the sixties, rock has become an internationally cherished music, particularly among the young. Building upon the models of American blues, R & B, and rock and roll, a number of British groups created their own exciting brands of rock. One of these, the Beatles, from Liverpool, England, is regarded as the most successful, inventive, and influential group in the entire history of rock.

The Beatles dramatically influenced the direction of rock in the sixties.

The Beatles symbolized the revolution of an entire generation.

Not only their music, but also their hairstyle caused a revolution among young males: long hair for males became popular for the first time since the nineteenth century. The long hair, beards, and moustaches were visible symbols of commitment to the new rock generation. By the end of the sixties, beads, necklaces, army fatigues, and blue jeans with multiple patches fleshed out the symbolism. The looks, attitudes, values, and most importantly, the music of the Beatles stood at the center of an international revolution of youths angry about the war in Vietnam, the alarming depersonalization of society, and the questionable values of their elders.

The four Beatles were endowed with ordinary musical skills, but with work and with careful listening to their precursors such as Little Richard, Chuck Berry, Buddy Holly, and Elvis, the Beatles became a very accomplished and sophisticated musical group.

With time, the Beatles developed a sophisticated musical style.

Their early and late recordings are separated by a wide musical gulf. The Beatles, as musicians and as songwriters, were constantly growing and changing, setting the style for new trends in rock. The real

The Beatles in 1964

strength of the Beatles, however, lay in the melodic and poetic talents of John Lennon and Paul McCartney, who wrote many unforgettable songs. These songs ranged from the poignant "Eleanor Rigby" and "Yesterday," to the clever, as in "Polythene Pam" and "Taxman," to the philosophical, as in "A Day in the Life."

The poetic and musical talents of Paul McCartney and John Lennon gave the Beatles' music an unusual poignancy and cleverness.

Sgt. Pepper

The Beatles' masterpiece is the album *Sgt. Pepper's Lonely Hearts Club Band.* This album consists of twelve songs, and while each is interesting and enjoyable in its own right, they form a collective unity not unlike that of a nineteenth century song cycle. The songs are part of a larger whole and develop a central theme.

This theme is people in need: some are in desperate need; some don't even know they're in need. All of them need to be loved and some seek philosophical answers, such as the reason for their existence.

The songs in the *Sgt. Pepper's Lonely Hearts Club Band* album work together to develop a theme of human need.

The album begins with the title song, which is repeated as the second to last song in the set. In this song, the Beatles act as storytellers, recounting the lives of people in need. This glimpse of the contemporary human condition is presented as a variety show having numerous acts, evident in the lines from the opening song, "We hope you will enjoy the show" . . . "Sit back and let the evening go."

In the second song, "A Little Help from My Friends," a question is put to the individual: "Do you need anybody?" The reply is, "I need somebody to love." What will happen if you don't find such a somebody? "I'll get by with a little help from my friends," even "get high . . ."—a reference to the escapist comfort of some drug.

Song 3: "Lucy in the Sky with Diamonds." Composer Lennon maintained that this song has nothing to do with drugs. The fact remains, however, that the song speaks of someone's longing to escape an unwanted reality.

Song 4: "Getting Better." This song is about a person who is grudgingly optimistic about love and life. Things are improving because the individual's needs have been fulfilled by another.

Song 5: "Fixing a Hole." The song deals with a person who believes that he needs to be alone; he fears intervention by other people or ideas that might somehow pose a threat to his familiar lifestyle.

Song 6: "She's Leaving Home." The teenager runs away from home, hoping to fulfill "something inside that was always denied for so many years." The deserted parents are confused and hurt, with needs of their own.

Song 7: "Being for the Benefit of Mr. Kite!" The circus is being performed "for the benefit of Mr. Kite," suggesting the fulfillment of some need of his.

Song 8: "Within You, Without You." George Harrison's song, with its Eastern musical and philosophical overtones, is a desperate plea to see beyond one's self—to hurdle the illusions and snatch the truth. It is the only song in the cycle that directly points a finger at the listener. The songs asks, "Are you one of them?"

Song 9: "When I'm Sixty-Four." This is a nice replica of an old-fashioned British music hall song, but within the context of this song cycle the question, "Will you still need me?" is not as casual as it seems on its flippant surface.

Song 10: "Lovely Rita." Anyone, even the most casual acquaintance, might fill Rita's need for intimacy.

Song 11: "Good Morning." This is a song about a most ordinary bloke who is oblivious to the shallowness of his life: "I've got nothing to say, but it's O.K."

Song 12: "A Day in the Life." This song looks at a man who is frustrated by what he perceives around him—death and callousness.

The Beatles conclude the album on an optimistic note, suggesting that there are answers and ways to fill our needs, and offering to "turn you on" to them.

Sgt. Pepper's Lonely Hearts Club Band made generous use of brass and strings, something unheard of in earlier rock music. And in some of their recordings, the Beatles experimented with such electronic techniques as playing tapes backwards. The Beatles were clearly a long way from rock and roll musically, poetically, and conceptually.

The Beatles created a new dimension in rock music.

SOUL

The Beatles hit with such force that the collective attention was temporarily diverted from the activities of American rock performers. Though they were momentarily eclipsed, they were not inactive: the Americans—men, women, black, white, soloists, and groups—continued to create and change the makeup of rock. In the sixties rock received a major infusion of new blood with the emergence of soul music.

While the Beatles occupied the forefront of rock, other musicians were changing the makeup of the music.

The roots of this music can be traced to rural southern black religious music—a type called **gospel music.** The subject matter and texts of gospel music are religious in nature, but the singing style is almost indistinguishable from blues singing, a secular music. Drums, guitars, and piano are frequently used in gospel music as accompanying instruments. These are the same instruments used in blues, R & B, and early rock and roll.

White congregations were accustomed to and expected one kind of vocal style in church (nice, clean, and proper) and a different vocal style in popular music. They were also accustomed to the organ in church, not drums and guitars. The whites, then, made a definite distinction between sacred and secular music, and to allow any secular sound to enter the music of the church was to flirt with sacrilege. This is one of the reasons why some whites looked upon sacred and secular black music as "primitive," "childlike," or even "paganistic." They didn't understand that singing about Jesus with fire, passion, and pain in the voice was not sacrilegious, but was born of very deep religious convictions. Moreover, these were people whose singing style reflected the real, personal sufferings of black people at that time.

Most white Americans did not understand or appreciate black gospel music.

When this passionate singing style—part blues, part religious ecstasy—was applied to secular texts, it acquired the name **soul** music. In the mid-sixties Aretha Franklin emerged as the Queen of Soul. Many of her albums are readily available, but you should listen in particular to

When the passionate gospel style was brought to secular music, the result was soul.

Aretha Franklin's, James Brown's, and Otis Redding's sixties songs are vintage soul.

the songs "You Make Me Feel (Like a Natural Woman)" and "Satisfaction." James Brown and the late Otis Redding, both from Macon, Georgia, are vintage soul singers. Listen to Brown's "Please, Please, Please" and "Good, Good Lovin'," and to Otis Redding's "I've Been Loving You Too Long" and "Try a Little Tenderness."

WEST COAST ROCK

Rock music of the mid-to-late sixties reflected the turbulent cultural atmosphere.

Looking back, it seems certain that the mid-to-late 1960s was, among other things, a crazy time. The war in Vietnam, the explosion in drug use, and the relaxation of certain rules of social conduct contributed to the atmosphere. Rock music changed dramatically: like the "real" world, rock music (or some of it) became violent, revolutionary, and drug-oriented. The onstage gestures that some of the rock singers made and the lyrics they sang became far more explicit than had ever been true of R & B at its raunchiest.

Acid Rock

Acid rock was a product of the drug culture.

Increasingly the new sixties rock became a part of life, if not a way of life, for hippies, yippies, flower children, militant underground movements, and also for many "straights." A number of nonscientific surveys revealed that a surprisingly high percentage of American youths made some use or claimed to have made some use of pot (marijuana) or acid (LSD, a mind altering drug with unpredictable and sometimes tragic consequences for the user). A new branch of rock—**acid rock**—became an integral part of this scene.

Many acid rock bands were born in San Francisco, but their popularity was nationwide.

Several groups from San Francisco and other parts of the west coast created a music that blended into, and in fact reflected the mores of this psychedelic subculture. The music was heavily electronic and loud to the point of being ear-shattering. Jefferson Airplane was one of the most successful of the San Francisco bands, and their popularity quickly spread nationwide. Such songs as their "White Rabbit" left no doubt about the drug orientation, and eventually this message took root across the country.

Jim Morrison of the Doors epitomized the acid rock performer.

The Doors was a group with a similar and more violent orientation. "Break on Through" and "Light My Fire" were two of their songs that ranked high on the national charts. The leader of the group, the late Jim Morrison, was the epitome of the acid rock performer, who more than once found himself in trouble with drug and indecent exposure charges.

Jimi Hendrix's guitar-playing abilities bordered on virtuosity.

The sixties also produced some important solo performers. Jimi Hendrix, a young man from the northwest, was an amazing guitarist (left handed, at that!), whose playing bordered on true virtuosity when he chose to allow it. He used controlled feedback as the central part of many of his songs, such as "The Star Spangled Banner."

He had a wild, nihilistic stage act in which, drenched with sweat and full of contortions, he set his guitar on fire while the volume was turned up to full gain. It was as if the agonizing death screams of the electric instrument were being heard. Hendrix's "Purple Haze" is among the best known songs of the late sixties. Tragically, Hendrix died much too young.

Janis Joplin was another very talented singer whose career was also cut short by an early death. Joplin, from Texas, was a very gifted singer of the blues, and in her own way, was as much a virtuoso performer as was Jimi Hendrix. Part of her stage appeal was based on sex, though not in the explicit manner of Hendrix or Morrison. She was at her best singing the blues in a husky, full throttle voice, though she sang other songs with tenderness and poignancy. Her audiences were spellbound by her performances. Among her best known recordings are "Get It While You Can," "Piece of My Heart," and "Me and Bobby McGee."

Many acid rock performers and even more in their audiences were seething with anger and were vociferously antiestablishment. To be accurate, this anger was born not of madness, but was born out of a deep-rooted and bitter frustration with a culture that seemed to them to have lost its moral and ethical marbles.

Janis Joplin (1943–70)

Acid rock was a means of expressing frustration with the values of an older generation.

OTHER SIXTIES ROCK

Folk Rock

Folk rock music has been around since the late fifties. In 1959, the Kingston Trio introduced the sound to the American public with their song "Tom Dooley," which stayed at the top of the charts for several weeks. The popularity of the Kingston Trio helped set the stage for the success of **folk rock** of the sixties and early seventies.

Towering above all folk rock singers in the sixties was Bob Dylan. Dylan came from a true folk background, but beginning in the mid-sixties he edged closer to rock sound and subject matter. In the late sixties Dylan joined forces with a fine group that eventually took the name The Band. Together they recorded many great songs, including "Like a Rolling Stone." But Dylan's country-folk influence is evident in other solo songs by the Band, including some of the songs in their first album, *Music from Big Pink,* and their most famous song, "The Night They Drove Old Dixie Down," from the album entitled *The Band.*

The folk branch of rock music continued to flourish in the seventies with artists such as Arlo Guthrie, Joni Mitchell, and Judy Collins.

The Kingston Trio aroused interest in a music genre called folk rock.

Folk rock flourished in the music of Bob Dylan, Arlo Guthrie, Joni Mitchell, and Judy Collins.

Politics

Folk singers publicly
supported political causes
in the sixties.

In the volatile 1960s, folk lyrics with some depth and political lyrics with some punch became very popular in the United States, and composers and performers with a cause to support found an attentive audience. Peter, Paul, and Mary, Bob Dylan, Joan Baez, and a little later, Simon and Garfunkel were the principal players in that unfolding drama.

Surf

Surf rock resembled rock
and roll in its selection of
topics and lyrics.

The high school aura of old-fashioned rock and roll carried over to a new type of music from California called surf rock, popularized by the Beach Boys and their good-natured songs about surfing, sun, cars, and Californians. The Beach Boys found a large audience for such songs as "Surfin' U.S.A.," "Little Deuce Coupe," and "Fun, Fun, Fun." Surf rock enjoyed a mild comeback in the early 1980s.

Rolling Stones

One of the most famous and influential rock groups of the sixties was the Rolling Stones. The name of the group reflects their musical career for, like the Beatles, the Stones have never stood still stylistically for very long. In their evolution they have touched nearly all rock bases, from early R & B to hard core blues, hard rock, protest music, and a touch of jazz.

The Rolling Stones, still as
popular as they were
twenty years ago, have
performed nearly all rock
forms.

The Stones' success began in the mid-sixties with their most famous composition, "Satisfaction," and at that time their popularity rivaled that of the Beatles. Now, in their third decade together, they continue to play to packed houses around the world. Mick Jagger, the lead singer, is doubtless the most famous rock star alive.

MORE RECENT ROCK

No one branch of rock
characterizes the seventies
and eighties.

Throughout the 1970s and early 1980s, rock has been dominated by a profusion of diverse styles. In fact, so many different styles have emerged, and rock audiences have become so fragmented, that it is impossible to identify one branch of rock music as characteristic of the seventies and eighties. Some of the more influential branches of this period are examined here.

Blues Rock

Blues rock has emerged
from contemporary
musicians adapting
legendary blues music.

In the late sixties and early seventies some groups, both British and American, began to listen in earnest, perhaps for the first time, to some of the legendary blues performers, such as Big Bill Broonzy and Bessie Smith (both of whom are widely recorded, so you should seek out and listen to some of their records). The vocal and guitar styles of some of these legendary figures were important influences on the music of the **blues rock** musicians.

Years before Eric Clapton had a song on the top forty charts he was the guitar player in a British blues oriented group called Cream. Clapton is a fine rock guitarist on whom the influence of country blues is unmistakable; this is perceptible even in his less artistic, but more commercially successful, numbers such as *Lay Down Sally* (1978).

The same influence is apparent in several prominent American rock groups. Some of the best of these groups were from the South, like the Allman Brothers band of Macon, Georgia. An incredible number of singers from the American north and midwest, and singers from England, have developed southern accents, but the Allman Brothers were the real southern article, and the very sounds of their voices remind us anew of the southern ancestry of rock music.

Jazz Rock

The beat, the guitar, and the lyrics of mainstream rock, when fused with the swing, chord progressions, horns, and saxophones of jazz, create a branch called **jazz rock.** For a long time the typical rock group consisted of a basic quartet of players—keyboard, drums, bass guitar, and lead guitar, while one or more of the players handled the vocals. A New York-based group, Blood, Sweat and Tears, added to this basic rock quartet four nonrock instruments: alto sax, trombone, and two trumpets. The members of the rock quartet all had backgrounds in rock music; the four horn players had jazz backgrounds. Through much hard work and careful, painstaking attention to details, the musicians were able to accommodate themselves to each other's style. They were all very good players and sensitive musicians, which contributed to the group's success.

Other groups, like Chicago, and individuals such as trumpeter Miles Davis and pianist Chick Correa, have also met with some success in the attempt to blend jazz and rock.

Heavy Metal

Heavy metal rock emerged in the 1970s, and among its principal exponents were Led Zeppelin, Aerosmith, and Kiss. Its immediate ancestor is the acid rock of the sixties, though heavy metal bands tend to be more tightly controlled, and less venturesome and extravagant than their ancestors. Led Zeppelin's "Stairway to Heaven" is typical of the style. It is a long work that begins almost sweetly in the manner of a ballad, but near the end it becomes increasingly loud and violent.

Eric Clapton's work shows the blues influence on rock.

The music of the Allman Brothers reminds us of the southern roots of rock music.

Jazz rock resulted from the fusion of the beat, lyrics, and guitar of rock with the swing, chords, and instruments of jazz.

In the seventies, acid rock evolved into heavy metal rock.

Other Currents in Rock Music

Rock opera and broadway rock emerged in the late sixties and early seventies.

The late sixties and early seventies produced two rock operas: *Tommy,* by the Who, and *Jesus Christ, Superstar,* written by Andrew Lloyd Weber and Tim Rice. Rock even invaded the world of the Broadway musical with the very successful and long-playing *Hair.*

The seventies saw the rise of a new dance craze—disco. In some respects disco music, with its simplicity of language and style, was a throwback to the earlier twist music, although it was snappier. Like the twist, disco music appealed to a wide range of age and socio-economic groups, all of whom were anxious to strut their narcissistic stuff. The movie *Saturday Night Fever* was the catalyst for disco's appeal and success.

Disco's appeal was fueled by the movie *Saturday Night Fever.*

The 1970s also saw the emergence of **punk rock,** which began in England and traveled to America. Like the sixties' American rock music, punk rock was antiestablishment to the point of being offensive. This can be seen in the works of the Sex Pistols and the Dead Kennedys.

Punk rock was the anti-establishment music of the seventies.

From punk rock, new wave developed in the eighties.

The punk rock of the seventies spawned a more popular musical movement of the eighties, new wave, with such groups as the B-52s and the Talking Heads.

SUMMARY

Rock music, whatever the specific style, attempts to capture some element of the spirit of its time, and to give voice and focus to it. Our appreciation of each style can be enhanced by an understanding of the spirit of the times that produced rock music.

In the mid-to-late fifties musicians such as Elvis Presley, Bill Haley, and Little Richard notified the older generation of an approaching musical revolution that represented the widening "generation gap." The revolution came in the form of rock and roll.

The roots of rock and roll are found in rhythm and blues and in country music. R & B was black music created for black audiences in the thirties and forties. The twelve-bar blues form, a unique accent pattern, and explicit lyrics were characteristic of R & B. The R & B instrumentation consisted of a piano, drums, a guitar, and a tenor sax, playing with a free spirit that attracted the attention of the young.

Country music, on the other hand, offered simple lyrics and instrumentation similar to that of R & B, except that a fiddle replaced the sax. The accented second and fourth beat of the four beat pattern also resembled the R & B flavor.

Rock and roll in the fifties directed its appeal to teenagers with its songs of puppy love, dances, and cars. It offered a means of expressing rebellion against the older generation and acted as a force unifying teenagers of diverse geographic and socio-economic backgrounds. Rock and roll's "eight to the bar" pattern and guitar sound radiated an unmistakable new music. By the end of the decade, the music was also big business.

In the late fifties a softer rock and roll was popularized by Pat Boone, but this brand was quickly overshadowed by the sophisticated sixties rock of Motown musicians, exemplified by the Supremes and the Temptations.

The symbol of the new rock generation was the Beatles. These musicians created a musical revolution and set the style for the decade.

While the Beatles were in the spotlight, another genre of music was emerging in the background. Aretha Franklin, James Brown, and Otis Redding took black gospel music, added blues, and produced soul music.

Rock music continued to reflect the spirit of the times. The acid rock of the sixties was an integral element of the worldwide drug culture. Bands such as the Doors and soloists such as Jimi Hendrix were at the center of this scene.

The folk rock of Bob Dylan, Joan Baez, and others offered a rebellious generation music ripe with nontraditional political statement.

Rock in the seventies and eighties appeared in the diverse forms of blues rock, jazz rock, heavy metal rock, and punk rock.

The constant in rock has been the guitar. The rock of the 1990s will most likely continue to reflect the changing times through this instrument.

KEY TERMS

rocking and reeling (rocking and rolling)
rhythm and blues (R & B)
country music
boogie woogie

soft rock and roll
gospel music
soul
acid rock
folk rock

blues rock
jazz rock
heavy metal
punk rock

THINKING ABOUT IT

Examine the rock music of today—songs by recent performers and groups not mentioned in this chapter, plus the music of performers who have endured for years, such as Diana Ross, Grace Slick, the Stones or Crosby, Stills, and Nash. Analyze these songs in terms of musical and textual content and see to what extent each of these types of music owes something to early styles of rock.

14

Duke Ellington (1899–1974)

SOUNDS OF THE CHAPTER

Armstrong
"Hotter Than That" ♪
"West End Blues" ♪

Broonzy
"Baby Please Don't Go"
"I Got Up in the Mornin' Blues"

Brubeck
"Take Five" ♪

Coleman
"Happy House" ♪

Ellington
"Caravan"
"Mood Indigo"
"Solitude"
"Sophisticated Lady"

Gershwin
Rhapsody in Blue

Goodman
"Down South Camp Meeting" ♪

Henderson
"Down South Camp Meeting" ♪

Hooker
"Blues Before Sunrise"

Joplin
"Maple Leaf Rag" ♪

King Oliver
"Dippermouth Blues" ♪

Leadbelly
"The Bourgeois Blues"
"The Gallis Pole"

Morton
"Maple Leaf Rag" ♪

Parker
"Ornithology" ♪
"White Christmas" ♪

Spaan
"Worried Life Blues"

Trumbauer
"Riverboat Shuffle" ♪

Waller
"Numb Fumblin" ♪

"Groovin' High"
"Whispering"

THE NATURE OF JAZZ

Jazz did not develop as an isolated musical form. It is similar to other kinds of music, but in some important respects jazz is different from classical, popular, and folk music, so it is dealt with individually. In this chapter we will find out how and in what ways jazz differs from other kinds of music.

Jazz emerged in the American South in the early twentieth century.

Pure jazz emerged sometime in the early years of the twentieth century. Jazz was born in the South and its parents were black Americans. Its emergence was the result of the confluence of several different musical streams. Each of these streams—swing, improvisation, blues, rag, and the European tradition in instrumentation and harmony—has a history that is much older than jazz itself.

Several styles of jazz have evolved.

Like other music studied thus far, jazz continued to evolve, and it developed into several different styles: early New Orleans jazz, 1920s hot jazz, swing in the 1930s and 1940s, bop and cool jazz in the 1940s and 1950s, and new jazz since the 1960s.

Swing and improvisation are the core of jazz.

With the emergence of each of these styles jazz changed superficially, yet a permanent inner core has remained. At the heart of this core are swing and improvisation.

Swing

Though swing was briefly discussed in chapter 12, a more detailed investigation is now necessary. **Swing** is largely a temporal phenomenon. It is a manner of performing rhythm that is unique to jazz. Swing is the element most vital to jazz: without it, the music wouldn't sound like jazz. Swing musicians deliberately deviate from the true note values of a given melody. For example, a jazz musician confronted with this group of eighth notes:

Swing is the performance of a uniquely jazz rhythm.

True note values are deliberately avoided.

♪♪♪♪ ♪♪♪♪

will usually not play them thus. Instead, he or she might swing the even eighth notes like this:

♪.♪♪.♪♪.♪♪.♪

or this:

Some notes are held for longer or shorter periods than their notated values, some beats or fractions of beats are unexpectedly accented, and some pitches may be added to the notated melody, filling the gaps between the specified pitches of the melody. One of the striking things about swing is that it sounds so nonchalant, almost careless, but in fact it is very precisely controlled. One doesn't have to be born with the sense of swing—it can be learned—but many classical and rock musicians are unable to capture the rhythm, partly because swing cannot be precisely notated.

> **Swing cannot be precisely notated.**
>
> **Compare the swing and the more commonly heard version of "White Christmas." What's different?**

For instance, listen to the well-known song, "White Christmas," to hear what happens to its rhythm when Charlie Parker swings it on his alto sax. Listen as the melody is presented with relatively few alterations. Then compare Parker's swinging version with the way the song is usually sung by popular singers. Can you feel the difference?

The swing with which Parker plays is present in all true jazz. Swing is one of the core ingredients of jazz that transcends all stylistic boundaries.

Improvisation

Whereas swing has to do with *how* things are played in jazz, **improvisation** has to do with *what* is played in jazz. Simply stated, improvisation is a process in which musical ideas are created and played almost simultaneously. Improvisation is not something read off of a page or merely memorized; it is spontaneous rather than studied.

On the other hand, improvisation is by no means the product of accident. The improviser creates music within the bounds of a predetermined formal and harmonic structure. The improviser does not just play anything that comes to mind. To illustrate this let's return to Parker's recording of "White Christmas."

> **Improvisation is spontaneous, but structured.**

First, sing "White Christmas" to yourself. You should be able to detect that the song is in 4/4 meter and that it has four sections, each of which is eight bars long: A (eight bars), B (eight bars), A (eight bars), B' (eight bars). This thirty-two-bar pattern is called a **chorus.** Listen to the first chorus again. Notice that it is a full chorus of thirty-two bars. Now listen to the next chorus played by Parker. This second chorus is thirty-two bars long and it uses the same harmony as the first chorus, but there is a very noticeable difference between the two. The difference is improvisation in the second chorus. Parker plays an improvisation of great complexity and beauty, swinging the rhythm all the while. The melodic line of "White Christmas" all but disappears in this improvisation, but the song's formal structure and harmony are kept rigidly intact. The freedom of the improvisation is anchored to the preexistent harmony and form of the song. In a sense, freedom develops from control.

> **Each thirty-two bar pattern in "White Christmas" is called a chorus.**
>
> **In improvisation the melodic line almost disappears, while formal structure and harmony remain intact.**

Now listen to the next chorus played by Parker. In it is heard a new and different improvisation, but once more, the form and the harmony remain unchanged. Try singing the song softly to yourself as Parker plays these two choruses. If you maintain the tempo you will notice that in every case you and Parker come to the ends of phrases and sections simultaneously.

The recording continues with two thirty-two-bar choruses for trumpet. This is followed by a concluding chorus in which sax and trumpet repeat the melody of the opening chorus.

Though swing and improvisation were probably the most important precursors of jazz, now consider the other musical styles that led to its development.

EARLY JAZZ

The earliest jazz is associated with New Orleans.

New Orleans' divergent culture contributed to the makeup of jazz.

The earliest jazz is associated with the city of New Orleans. In the nineteenth century New Orleans experienced an influx of a variety of people, customs, and music. The Spanish, French, African, Cajun, and Creole heritage of New Orleans was, and is, clearly visible and audible even to the casual observer. These various cultures contributed to the musical style we now recognize as jazz.

Blues

African musical tradition is the basis for blues.

The blues scale is the major and minor third above tonic and the minor seventh above tonic.

Worried notes typify blues music.

In the late nineteeth and early twentieth centuries black country **blues** singers generally sang solo or accompanied themselves on the guitar. In either case, the vocal quality they produced was rooted in African rather than European musical traditions. The blues singer's delivery included various vocal scoops, groans, falsetto, and other ornaments. The melodic lines of blues often featured both the major and the minor third above tonic, and also the minor rather than the customary major seventh above tonic (this constitutes the blues scale). The blues singer's delivery also included **worried notes**—notes performed with a vocal shake or quiver, noticeably out of tune, sometimes, with European scales (some pitches smaller than the minor second).

These qualities can be heard in all of the following songs from the anthology *The Best of the Blues,* vol. 1: "The Bourgeois Blues" and "The Gallis Pole" by Leadbelly; "Blues Before Sunrise" by John Lee Hooker; "Baby Please Don't Go" and "I Got Up in the Mornin' Blues" by Big Bill Broonzy; and "Worried Life Blues" by Otis Spaan.

The twelve-bar blues was the most popular blues form.

Blues came in many sizes and shapes in the early twentieth century, but the twelve-bar blues, with which you are familiar, emerged as the most frequently used and the most influential pattern. The twelve-bar blues became the norm not only for singers, but also for jazz instrumentalists who adopted the form.

For the country blues singer the guitar was the required accompanying instrument since pianos were rare or nonexistent, especially for blacks, in the rural south. But urban blues singers, generally somewhat more sophisticated than rural musicians, began to use the piano for accompaniment. Eventually this led to the development of a whole school of blues/jazz piano players, among whom Ferdinand "Jelly Roll" Morton was a central figure.

Rag

In the St. Louis and Kansas City area, another brand of piano music developed in the 1890s: **ragtime,** or **rag.** Rag was a more cultivated style. It didn't swing, but syncopations dominated the right hand with space provided for improvisation.

An excellent demonstration of the stylistic difference between pure rag and early New Orleans jazz is Scott Joplin playing his composition, "Maple Leaf Rag." Next listen to Jelly Roll Morton playing the same piece but adding swing. The Joplin version, with its almost classical purity and stiffness, is clearly not jazz, but the Morton version definitely is, demonstrating a basic difference between New Orleans jazz and ragtime.

Rag music was an ingredient in the formation of jazz, though it was not as important as swing, improvisation, and blues.

Harmony and Instruments

With some exceptions, all rag pieces composed from 1890 to 1910 (when the craze for rags subsided) were written for the piano—a European, not an African, instrument. Thus, while ragtime and early jazz were essentially the products of black genius, European instruments and harmonies were important in the development of rag and jazz. In essence rag and jazz were the union of the two musical traditions—West African and European.

JAZZ: A EUROPEAN-AFRICAN COMBINATION

Marching bands were very popular in New Orleans before the turn of the century, and these bands utilized European harmony and instruments: trumpets, trombones, tubas, clarinets, drums, and others. However, the musicians were usually blacks who retained some of their West African musical traditions. The rhythm of tribal music is much more intricate and complex than that of Western art and folk music. **Polyrhythms**

Scott Joplin (1868–1917)

Improvisation is an ingredient of ragtime.

Compare the Joplin and Morton versions of "Maple Leaf Rag."

The majority of rags were composed for piano.

Ragtime and jazz combine elements of African and European musical traditions.

Blacks brought African music tradition to the American marching band.

African polyrhythms were considered by many to be chaotic.

(two or more different, simultaneously operating rhythms) are common yet so different from the European heritage that the Europeans of the early 1900s generally considered African rhythm to be chaotic.

The black musicians blended their musical heritage with the musical heritage of the Europeans, which resulted in a unique sound that helped to set the stage for the birth of jazz.

Jazz resulted from the blend of European technique and African delivery.

European musical traditions, then, provided the techniques (instruments) and theory (harmony), but African traditions influenced the delivery of the music—its soul.

In summary, the blending of swing, improvisation, blues, rag, and the fusion of West African and European musical traditions resulted in New Orleans jazz.

New Orleans Bands

New Orleans jazz bands consisted of: piano, bass fiddle, drums, clarinet, trumpet, trombone, and sometimes a guitar or banjo.

Early New Orleans jazz bands were small, normally consisting of piano, bass fiddle, drums, clarinet, trumpet, trombone, and sometimes guitar or banjo. Piano, bass, drums, and guitar or banjo formed the rhythm section, while clarinet, trumpet, and trombone were called "front line" instruments. Each of the front line instruments played solos, yet all three were also joined in ensemble, with the trumpet playing the main melody, the clarinet weaving improvisational embroidery above, and the trombone creating a line below.

These jazz bands played instrumental blues, rags, and short structures.

The repertoire of these bands consisted of instrumental blues (sometimes with vocals), rags, and other short structures such as stomps and breakdowns. Usually a performance consisted of the following:

One or two choruses for the ensemble
Solo chorus(es) for trumpet
Solo chorus(es) for clarinet
Solo chorus(es) for trombone
Closing chorus for the ensemble

Group improvisation is more important than the solo in New Orleans jazz.

King Oliver is a famous jazz artist.

Despite the importance of solos in New Orleans style jazz, group improvisation is valued above all else. The importance of group improvisation is obvious in many of the recordings of King Oliver's Creole Jazz Band. King Oliver was one of the early legendary jazz trumpet and cornet players. Listen to his recording of "Dippermouth Blues." (Oliver plays first cornet and the young Louis Armstrong plays second cornet in this recording.)

♩ **SOUND AND SENSE:** *New Orleans Style Jazz*

Title: "Dippermouth Blues"

Composer: King Oliver

A Closer Look:

"Dippermouth Blues" has the following structure:

Brief introduction by the ensemble
Chorus for ensemble—group improvisation
Chorus for ensemble—group improvisation
Chorus for clarinet
Chorus for clarinet
Chorus for ensemble—group improvisation
Chorus for cornet
Chorus for cornet
Two more choruses for ensemble
Brief coda

Notice that even during the solo choruses the other instruments remain active, particularly at the ends of phrases. Though each instrument improvises, there is a sense of group creation, unified by the common harmonies and the twelve-bar blues form they all share.

1920s HOT JAZZ

Jazz flourished in New Orleans, particularly in a section of the city known as Storeyville. Storeyville was a place of excitement and vice, with rough bars and brothels. In 1917 city officials closed Storeyville, and many jazz musicians found themselves out of work. As a result, New Orleans jazz went on the road.

> In 1917 New Orleans jazz was forced out of its element in Storeyville.

Prior to this, other centers of jazz had been developing in Chicago, Kansas City, New York, and other places. In the late twenties blues and jazz recordings became more popular in America. Some of the great New Orleans jazz musicians, such as Louis Armstrong, moved to Chicago in the early twenties. Armstrong had a tremendous impact upon jazz musicians there, but he began to deviate from the New Orleans jazz tradition, creating a kind of jazz that emphasized soloists. A sample of Armstrong's music at that time is found in his recording of "West End Blues."

> Jazz spread across America in the 1920s.

> Louis Armstrong put the focus on the jazz soloist.

Louis Armstrong (1900–71)

Hot jazz was Armstrong's style.

Economics played a role in the growth of jazz in Chicago.

A taste for jazz in Northern cities created a demand for jazz musicians.

Beginning in the 1920s white musicians began playing in jazz bands.

The white jazz musicians of the twenties became the leaders of swing bands in the thirties and forties.

Chicago style jazz featured the soloist.

SOUND AND SENSE: *Jazz Soloists*

Title: "West End Blues"

Composer: Louis Armstrong

A Closer Look:

A flashy, cadenzalike solo introduces "West End Blues."

Chorus for ensemble (note the twelve-bar blues structure)
Chorus for trombone
Chorus for clarinet with vocal interjections
Chorus for piano
Final chorus for ensemble

The hot side of Armstrong's jazz can be heard in "Hotter Than That." This is the kind of solo performance that set the Chicago and New York musicians on their ear. "Hotter Than That" is a thirty-two-bar structure that is prefaced by an eight-bar introduction. There is a chorus for ensemble, one for clarinet, and a half chorus for trombone, the other half for the ensemble. A spectacular chorus follows, with Armstrong singing instead of playing the trumpet. The piece ends abruptly with a clever duet with voice and guitar.

The expansion of jazz in Chicago was partly the result of economics. Jazz musicians from New Orleans and elsewhere in the south came searching for steady work in Chicago and other parts of the more affluent north during the Roaring Twenties. Many speakeasies (bars where liquor was sold illegally during Prohibition), restaurants, and clubs in Chicago catered to a white clientele that developed a taste for jazz, thus creating a demand for jazz musicians.

New Elements in Twenties Jazz

The jazz of the twenties changed in several ways as illustrated in "Riverboat Shuffle" played by Frankie Trumbauer and his orchestra. White musicians comprised the group, whereas jazz had formerly been played almost exclusively by blacks. Beginning in the twenties many white musicians became fascinated with and very adept at playing jazz. (This was the incubation period for white musicians who would become the leaders of many of the swing bands in the thirties and forties.)

"Riverboat Shuffle" has the drive of New Orleans style jazz and some of its group improvisation, but clearly the central feature of this Chicago style piece is the solo work of Bix Beiderbecke, the legendary white trumpet player who became a sort of jazz hero. While Chicago style is hot and bouncy, Beiderbecke's personal style is more lyric and not as raucous as Armstrong's forceful playing. Armstrong's solo improvisation, however, was assimilated by and became an important part of Chicago style jazz.

The saxophone became a prominent instrument for the first time with jazz. This piece features Trumbauer's instrument, the C-melody sax, which quickly gave way to alto, tenor, and baritone saxes in jazz. Whereas early jazz did not normally incorporate the sax, it became increasingly important in the twenties and in Chicago style jazz. Saxophones thus found a home in jazz, and before long a whole school of alto sax players and a school of tenor sax players blossomed.

Twenties jazz brought the sax to prominence.

"Riverboat Shuffle" also contains several short **breaks,** which are brief passages played by a soloist while the remainder of the group, including the entire rhythm section, remains silent. This type of break creates a cessation in the steady flow of the beat. The break is as old as jazz itself and was an integral part of blues and of New Orleans jazz. The break was not new in Chicago jazz, but the interesting harmony of the breaks in pieces like this one was innovative. The chord vocabulary of jazz was expanding to include new and more dissonant and complex harmonies.

During a jazz "break" the soloist plays while the rest of the band is quiet.

The first breaks in "Riverboat" occur near the beginning of the piece with five in the guitar. This is followed by a short piano break. Listen for the dissonance of these breaks. Later in the piece there is a clarinet break, two in the trumpet, three in the trombone, then one each in clarinet, trumpet, sax, and guitar, and sax.

Any of the jazz band instruments can play the break.

The standard size of a New Orleans band was five to seven players. Many groups in the twenties maintained that number, but groups of eight to ten or more became increasingly common and laid the groundwork for the big swing bands of the thirties. Trumbauer's group featured eight players and ten different instruments.

Toward the end of the 1920s jazz bands grew in size.

Thus "Riverboat Shuffle" exemplifies several new trends in twenties jazz: the inclusion of white performers, the focus on solo improvisation, the rise of the sax, the expansion of the harmonic language, and the move toward larger bands.

Name the characteristics of 1920s jazz.

Stride Piano

The twenties also saw the rise of new styles of piano playing: boogie woogie (discussed in chapter 13) and **stride piano.** Broadly speaking, stride style established three things: (1) left hand patterns that activated beats two and four in the 4/4 meter, resulting in a definite four-beat rather than a two-beat feeling; (2) right hand improvisations that often assumed the character of solo lines played by a trumpet or another single line instrument; and (3) an expansion of the harmonic language of jazz to include ninth and eleventh chords, and other complex chords and dissonances.

New styles of piano playing emerged in the 1920s.

Stride style established new left and right hand patterns.

In stride piano, the left hand plays four beats to the bar.

Can you distinguish the differences among jazz, rag, and stride piano?

All of the examples heard up to this point are in 4/4 meter, but they have the feeling of only two major beats to the bar (except in slow blues). Confirm this by listening to the examples again.

With stride piano, however, the left hand produces four distinct beats to the bar. A variety of patterns can be used to create this feeling: syncopation coupled with nonsyncopation, full chords on all four beats, melodic fillers on beats two and four, or extended countermelodies in the left hand.

By listening to the left-hand activity and by sensing the number of beats in the bar, the evolution from ragtime piano to New Orleans jazz piano to stride can be traced. With this in mind listen once more to the Joplin example, then to the Jelly Roll Morton example, and then to an example by the great stride pianist, Fats Waller: "Numb Fumblin'."

In Waller's stride style, notice the flexibility of the rhythm and beat, the intricacy of the improvisational lines, and the fullness of the harmonic language.

SWING IN THE THIRTIES AND FORTIES

Big swing bands combined ensemble playing and solo improvisation.

Whereas New Orleans jazz leaned heavily on group improvisation and twenties jazz emphasized solo improvisation, the big swing bands compromised, featuring both ensemble playing and solo improvisation. During this era popular songs were jazzed and thus became staples of the swing jazz repertoire.

The swing band of the 1930s was larger than the jazz band had been.

In a swing band each member was assigned a specific part to play.

The face of jazz changed with the emergence of the big bands. The size of the group was doubled as the solo clarinet, trumpet, and trombone swelled to three reeds, three trumpets, and two trombones. With a group of this size, it became necessary to indicate to the players specifically what they were to play and when to play it. Without this information, musical chaos would undoubtedly result. Either by notation or by rote each player had to learn and play his own part of the arrangement. The arranger thus became very much like a composer, writing out the ensemble sections and at least some of the underscore sections that supported the improvisational solos in the work.

Jazz Players

Paul Whiteman, called "the King of Jazz," was definitely not the reigning jazz musician. His inclination was to water down jazz, to popularize aspects of it, and to make it palatable to the general public. In his hands, personally, jazz was neither created nor very well served, but after the success of his famous Carnegie Hall concert of 1924 in which Gershwin's

Rhapsody in Blue was featured, Whiteman began, increasingly, to feature real jazz players as soloists with his orchestra. Among them were Bix Beiderbecke, Bunny Berigan, Red Nichols, Jimmy and Tommy Dorsey, and in the early thirties, Bing Crosby and the Rhythm Boys. When the jazz players left or sat out, Whiteman's orchestra deteriorated into pure corn. But when they played, these musicians offered most white Americans their first taste of jazz.

Black and White Jazz

Black and white swing bands played jazz differently as is noticeable in recorded performances. The black bands played swing first, played proportionately more of it than white swing musicians, and played for audiences who reveled in their performances. They played with an intensity, abandon, and drive unmatched by most of the white swing bands. The fire with which the best black bands played did not result, however, in ensemble sloppiness or imprecision, and the great sidemen (soloists) achieved a level of technical skill and creative inventiveness envied by all musicians.

The white bands, several of which were excellent performing groups, tended to play with more restraint. Not only was the volume more subdued, but all aspects of the rendition were presented without excess or extravagance.

These differences are best exemplified in a comparison of the black and the white swing band performances of the same composition. "Down South Camp Meeting" was composed by Fletcher Henderson and recorded by his black band in 1929. In 1934 Henderson became an arranger for Benny Goodman's band and in 1938 Goodman recorded "Down South Camp Meeting."

January 16, 1938, marked the first-known occasion of black and white jazz musicians publicly playing together. Teddy Wilson and Lionel Hampton joined forces with Benny Goodman (and others) in a legendary concert at Carnegie Hall. They broke the "color line" in jazz, just as nine years later Jackie Robinson and the Brooklyn Dodgers did in the world of professional baseball.

Certainly black and white musicians were aware of each other's work prior to this time, and it is a fact that some of the best of the black musicians had a profound influence on the development of many white jazz musicians; Goodman himself profited greatly from the exposure to certain black players.

As important as this Carnegie Hall concert was, it was in essence only the first step in a long journey. It did not tear down the walls between black and white performers on a wholesale scale and it had little immediate impact on the divisions between black and white popular music

Soloists in Paul Whiteman's orchestra became well-known jazz players.

Black swing bands were famous for intensity, drive, and creative inventiveness.

White swing bands were more subdued.

Compare the sounds of black and white swing.

In 1938 the "color line" in jazz was broken. Black and white musicians played together in a public concert.

The repertoires of black and white swing bands reveal the differences in their audiences' tastes.

and jazz audiences. From the beginning until the end of the swing era there remained differences between the tastes of the audiences, and these differences were reflected in the repertoires and performances of black and white swing bands.

The Genius of Ellington

Duke Ellington is respected as both a jazz musician and a jazz composer.

Jazz, like any other type of music, occasionally produces a musician of genius, one who clearly stands apart from his contemporaries and profoundly affects and influences others. Edward Kennedy "Duke" Ellington was such a figure. Ellington was an extremely prolific composer of diverse works, many of which have become standards: "Mood Indigo" (1931), "Sophisticated Lady" (1933), "Solitude" (1935), "Caravan" (1937), and others. He also composed hundreds of original jazz works, a number of more extended concert works, and some large-scale sacred works. His accomplishments are all the more impressive inasmuch as his schedule was jammed with performances almost throughout his entire career. It is astonishing that the man found the time to write as much as he did. Even under the constraint of this hectic schedule, Ellington's body of works contains little that is repetitious. Rather, it contains a seemingly endless flow of fresh and arresting musical ideas.

Ellington's abundant, original jazz compositions contain fresh and innovative musical ideas.

BOP AND COOL

Bop and cool emerged in the late 1940s.

Jazz was dominated by bop and cool in the 1950s and early 1960s.

Bop and cool groups were small in size.

After the swing era, the next significant devlopments in jazz came with the emergence of **bebop,** or **bop,** in the late forties, and **cool jazz** shortly thereafter. Bop and cool dominated jazz music through the fifties and into the sixties. Both styles have many similar characteristics. Each were reactions to the big swing bands and the style of jazz they played. The normal size of a bop group or cool group was five to seven players— three rhythm, and two, three, or four front line instruments. This was a drastic reduction from the size of a typical swing band.

Swing bands were actually dance bands, whereas bop and cool jazz were intended for listening.

Cool jazz was considered an art form when performed by the well-educated jazz musicians of the 1950s.

Bop was a hot, New York City-centered jazz style.

The swing bands played a kind of jazz that was designed for dance, so they were really dance bands. Bop and cool jazz, on the other hand, were more intellectual forms of jazz. Bop—with its complex rhythms and frantic tempos—was designed for listening rather than dancing. And many cool jazz musicians were well-educated, so cool jazz soon became infused with the harmonic language, counterpoint, and formal structure of classical music. It was at this time that some began to speak of jazz as an "art form."

Bop was a hot kind of jazz principally centered in the East (mainly in New York City). As its name implies, cool jazz was cooler and more detached. It flourished primarily in the Los Angeles area.

Charlie Parker (1920–55)

Characteristics of Bop

Bop is characterized by a frantic, almost angry quality noticeable in both the frenzied tempo and in the aggression with which the players performed. The complexity of the expanded chord vocabulary is another bop characteristic. The new chords and chord progressions struck some older musicians as wild to the point of being chaotic. But probably the most startling thing about bop is its rhythm: the bop drummer creates a fresh variety of polyrhythms, and the front line improvisers weave long and complicated lines filled with unexpected accents and sections of rapidly-played notes. The sound of the bop sax or trumpet is normally very tight and brittle in both fast and slow numbers. Lushness of tone is discarded in favor of a more aggressive sound.

Many musicians were responsible for the formation of bop, but two in particular—Charlie Parker and trumpeter Dizzy Gillespie—emerged as giant figures in the movement. Both are heard, together with Max Roach, one of the best bop drummers, in "Ornithology."

"Ornithology" is based on a thirty-two-bar theme that is first stated by the ensemble, followed by several thirty-two-bar improvisational choruses by Parker and Gillespie, and concludes with a restatement of the first chorus played by the ensemble. Notice that the theme sounds almost like an improvisation and is more complicated than that of a standard pop song. And though the solo choruses may sound complex, they have the same harmony and formal structure as that of the theme.

Bop is frantic and frenzied.

Aggressive rhythm is characteristic of bop.

Charlie Parker and Dizzy Gillespie were major figures in bop.

Notice the complex theme in "Ornithology."

New Orleans jazz exhibited two majors pulses: swing exhibited four, and bop exhibited eight.

The bass keeps the beat while the piano provides the harmony.

Max Roach keeps a relentless and furious pulse with brush on cymbal, while simultaneously creating an intricate web of polyrhythms and oddly distributed accents. The rhythm of bop takes the standard 4/4 meter and divides it into eight pulses, unlike New Orleans jazz (two major pulses) and swing (four pulses).

Each of the four quarter notes in bop is divided into a pair of eighth notes, and any one of these can be accented.

The bass player maintains the steady beat, playing either four or eight beats to the bar. The piano cooperates with the bass, supplying the harmonic underpinning, but also adding accents at various locations within the bar.

The format of Charlie Parker's "Groovin' High" is very similar. It is based on an old popular song, "Whispering." "Whispering" is a thirty-two-bar structure—*A* (sixteen bars) and *A* (sixteen bars). Once more, all of the solo choruses are based on the structure and chords of this song.

Characteristics of Cool Jazz

Cool jazz improvisation is gentle and smooth.

The cool jazz musician approaches the music with restraint and aloofness.

Since cool jazz uses many of the elements of bop, some musicians were active in both cool and bop at various stages in their careers. Cool, however, is characterized by a softer approach in general. The cool soloist's tone is softer and smoother than the brittle sound of bop. The improvisatory lines contain fewer notes and are gentle, rather than savage. The harmonic language is similar to that in bop, but where the bop musician can make a series of chords sound almost atonal, the cool musician makes the same chords sound much calmer. The cool drummer rides with brush on cymbal, but with a much gentler touch than the bop drummer, and the division of the 4/4 bar into eight pulses is less obvious in cool jazz. Where the bop musician plays aggressively, the cool musician plays with restraint and assumes a sort of aloofness.

Some of these qualities are evident in "Take Five," played by Dave Brubeck (piano) and Paul Desmond (alto sax), two legendary cool musicians.

This piece is in the rare 5/4 meter.

John Coltrane (1926–67)

NEW JAZZ

Since the 1960s jazz has become segmented, with each branch adopting names such as "the new thing," "funk," or "third stream." Many musicians have made significant contributions to the **new jazz,** but two particularly prominent figures are Ornette Coleman and John Coltrane.

Though Coleman's jazz may sound different at first, it is based in part on the old New Orleans group improvisation. Coleman attempted to free jazz from predetermined themes and chord progressions, allowing musicians greater freedom in improvisation. In Coleman's "Happy

Modern Jazz Quartet

House," each of the players is given a notated musical fragment on which to base his improvisation; chords and themes are freely invented by the performer on the spot. Complex counterpoint and pungent dissonances emerge from this musical tapestry, but notice that, through it all, the music swings just as any jazz does.

John Coltrane's "Alabama" commemorates the tragedy of local school children killed in a bombing. "Alabama" fluctuates between several different moods, reflective of Coltrane's multiple reactions to the event. The influence of blues, swing, and improvisation are evident in this composition.

Coltrane's "Alabama" exhibits the influence of blues, swing, and improvisation.

SUMMARY

As we began our study of jazz, we pictured it as having an ever-changing outer surface and a permanent inner core. This core contains the two elements basic to all jazz music—swing and improvisation. Swing describes how the unique rhythm of jazz is played. Improvisation describes the process through which spontaneous jazz music is created.

The history of jazz began with the influx of diverse elements in the city of New Orleans in the nineteenth century. This complex culture created musical forms that produced the earliest jazz.

Black country blues emerged from this culture in the late nineteenth century. The vocal quality of this music was rooted in African tradition. While country blues singers played the popular twelve-bar blues on the guitar, urban blues singers adapted the form to piano.

Piano playing took a different turn in the North where ragtime developed in the 1890s. Rag, unlike pure jazz, does not swing.

The marching band, popular in New Orleans during this period, blended the black musicians' West African musical traditions and polyrhythmic style with European harmony and instruments, to produce a unique sound that set the stage for jazz.

True jazz was first produced by small New Orleans bands. These jazz bands were made up of a piano, bass fiddle, drums, clarinet, trumpet, trombone, and sometimes a guitar and banjo. Group improvisation was the key element in the performance.

In the 1920s jazz moved north from New Orleans to become "hot" in the hands of famous composer/musician Louis Armstrong and others. Hot jazz was a central feature of the "Roaring Twenties."

1920s jazz showed these new elements: white performers, solo improvisation, a dominant sax, expansion of harmony, and larger band size. The twenties also witnessed the rise of two new piano styles—boogie and stride.

The swing bands that rose to prominence in the 1930s and 1940s were larger than the jazz bands of New Orleans and featured both ensemble playing and solo improvisation. Group improvisation lost some of its spontaneity when performed by these large bands. Black swing musicians reveled in intensity while white swing bands played jazz with more restraint.

Following on the heels of the swing era came the period of bop and cool. These forms dominated jazz in the fifties and early sixties. While the large swing bands played dance music, the small bop and cool bands produced music for intelligent listening.

Bop was a hot jazz style characterized by a frantic tempo, polyrhythms, and complex improvisation. The music of Charlie Parker and Dizzy Gillespie exemplifies this style. Cool jazz performs the characteristics of bop in a smoother, more gentle style.

The post 1960s jazz has exhibited a less formal structure and a diversity of melodic types.

Based upon our knowledge of jazz structure and our understanding of jazz history, we can predict that the jazz of the future will continue to swing and improvise while evolving in form.

KEY TERMS

swing	rag (ragtime)	piano stride
improvisation	polyrhythms	bop (bebop)
chorus	hot jazz	cool jazz
blues	break	new jazz
worried notes		

THINKING ABOUT IT

Now that you have some understanding of various styles of jazz, you should listen to several examples of each of the styles to reinforce the connection between what has been said about these styles and the actual performances of them. There are many fine recorded anthologies of jazz that should be available to you.

15

MUSIC IN THE NON-WESTERN WORLD

Feluccas on the Nile 1906

SOUNDS OF THE CHAPTER

''Gilak''
''Raghuvamsa''
''Song of Rejoicing After Returning from a
   Hunt''

Music is a priceless treasure around the world.

There are those who contend that something that has no price has no value. Music however, is an exception, for as stated in the first chapter, music is important in the most remote corners of civilization and in the deepest reaches of history, and though it is for all peoples a treasure that has great value, it has no price.

Music varies according to culture.

Music is universal, but there are differences between the music of one culture and that of another. Sometimes the differences are so pronounced that a person from one culture cannot automatically find enjoyment and satisfaction in the music of another culture. This happens because that person tries to interpret the foreign music in terms of his or her own understanding of music. Frustration and even annoyance sets in when the foreign music doesn't correspond to preconceived ideas about music. But the frustration and annoyance can be minimized as ideas about what music can be are broadened. Although great satisfaction in a given foreign music is not guaranteed, if it is understood it can be appreciated. It may still seem a little strange to us, but at least we can appreciate it as someone's music, and thus as a thing of value. The intelligent pursuit of this understanding is a worthy enterprise in and of itself, but given a world in which there is increased interdependence among cultures, this pursuit of understanding is even more important.

Characteristics of satisfying and enjoyable music also vary from culture to culture.

Understanding can lead to appreciation of foreign music.

As technology makes the world "smaller," an understanding of foreign culture is essential.

This chapter will deal with selected examples drawn from musical traditions of the non-Western world—cultures outside of Europe and North America. All musics of the world use time and sound, and all have form and meaning. In this chapter we will explore how the measurement of time, the quality of sound, the dimensions of form, and the meaning or function of music change from culture to culture.

Non-Western music is that music outside of the European and North American traditions.

We will look at non-Western time, sound, form and function in music.

AFRICA

The vast continent of Africa is home to nearly 500 million people living in more than fifty countries. There are hundreds of different languages spoken there, and almost as many practicing religions. Dozens of different forms of government, economies, customs, and ethnic groups enrich the continent.

Because of the diversity found on the African continent, we can consider only general musical characteristics.

In the space provided here it is impossible to examine even a handful of Africa's many musics, nor is it possible to cite a "typical" African music. There is simply too much diversity. However, some characteristics of African music, along with the music of a specific African people, will be covered.

General Characteristics

Some African cultures have art music and popular music, and some have sacred and secular music, but generally Africans do not make these distinctions. Music is not viewed as an art in the Western sense, nor as a phenomenon that is separate from the everyday functions of life. Rather, it is viewed as something that is inextricably tied to life itself.

Another important distinction is the absence of designated musicians in the African culture. In the Western world, the term "musician" applies to a select few whose musical talent and dedication set them apart from the average person. In Africa, however, all children learn at a young age how to make music. In a real sense, all Africans are musicians, for music is an integral part of African life.

For example, the tribe that depends upon catching wild animals for food would not dream of undertaking the hunt without performing the prescribed music before, during, and after the hunt. The music is just as important as the spear that kills the hunted animal. There can be no doubt that such music has meaning, not only in an aesthetic sense, but in a spiritual and even practical sense.

In most African music, rhythm is the central force. Melody and (in some cultures) harmony are important, but less so than rhythm. The music is driven by rhythm, an often very complex rhythm (to Western ears, not to African ears) that is consistently performed with precision. Rhythm suggests movement, and indeed a great deal of African music involves dance. Just as the dance is palpable, so the music has a tactile or percussive quality: drums, scrapers, rattles, xylophones, and other percussion instruments are prevalent.

In addition to percussion instruments, flutelike instruments, whistles, animal horns, and certain kinds of stringed instruments are employed in African music.

However, it is vocal music, with or without text, that dominates African music. This "instrument" is employed by all African societies.

Some African music uses many of the same intervals and some of the harmonies used in the Western world, but some make use of intervals that sound out of tune to Western ears. There is widespread use of pentatonic structures and some use of modes similar to those of the medieval (Western) church.

Very little of African music is notated. The music is learned through oral tradition, and improvisation is such a central part of the music that notation would be of limited value. There is little if any indigenous written musical theory.

African cultures consider music an integral element of daily life.

All members of an African society are "musicians."

Much African music has practical and aesthetic purposes.

Rhythm is often the central force in African music.

African music accommodates dance.

Although percussion instruments are prevalent, the voice is the dominant African instrument.

Pentatonic structures are heard in African music.

Notation is unimportant in African music.

Sub-Saharan musicians

Our focus will be on the music of sub-Saharan Africa.

Based on the geography, economics, and ethnicity of the continent, Africa can be divided into North Africa (the lands above the Sahara Desert) and sub-Saharan Africa. The music we will now examine is from sub-Saharan Africa.

The Ba-Benzélé Pygmies

African pygmies have become less nomadic.

The Ba-Benzélé is one of several different tribes of Pygmies who live in the jungle regions of central Africa. For centuries the Pygmies have been private, nomadic peoples, but in recent times, the Pygmies have settled in private camps for a more prolonged length of time.

Their communities are loosely organized and admirably democratic. The nomadic life dictates as a practical matter that there are few permanent possessions—possessions are too burdensome to carry. As a general rule, then, the Ba-Benzélé and other Pygmy groups do not carry

Pygmy music is primarily vocal.

musical instruments with them, except for whistles and small drums. As a result, their music is predominantly vocal. But the Pygmies traditionally have been very adept at using instruments fashioned by other tribes with whom they come into contact on their many journeys.

The pygmies' reputation as master musicians is legendary.

For centuries the Pygmies' reputation as master musicians was legendary. It is reported that even the Pharoahs of ancient Egypt included Pygmy musicians in their courts.

(A recording of the composition in the following Sound and Sense can be found on the Barenreiter Musicaphon-Unesco Collection, *An Anthology of African Music,* vol. 3, side 1, band 2.)

SOUND AND SENSE: *Non-Western Music*

Title: "Song of Rejoicing After Returning from a Hunt"

Composer: Ba-Benzélé Pygmies

A Closer Look:

Now listen to an example of the Ba-Benzélé's fascinating music: Ba-Benzélé Pygmies—"Song of rejoicing after returning from a hunt."

On the basis of one hearing this piece may seem chaotic, but with intent, repeated listenings, the chaos will evaporate and musical organization, sense, and pleasure will materialize. Given the foreign nature of this piece, you may have to listen more often and more intently to it in order to grasp it, but the terms, concepts and tools that we have used in listening to the various kinds of Western music can be applied to this kind of music also.

As you return to the piece, notice that there are two flutelike instruments. The lower flute enters first, playing a repetitive figure—a melodic ostinato that lasts eight beats—that is repeated again and again with only slight variations. The odd thing about the rhythm of this ostinato is that the eighth beat in the pattern is slightly shorter than the other beats, so we can't really fit this rhythmic pattern into any standard Western meters. However, it is still a meter, because the eighth beat is consistently shorter than the others. The pitches of this ostinato are drawn from a pentatonic scale and the melody stays within the range of an octave.

Before the completion of the first statement of this ostinato, a rattlelike instrument enters with its own rhythmic pattern, and shortly after, the second and higher flute enters. This higher flute plays two pitches from the same pentatonic scale. The flute plays a one-beat pattern, the downbeat always landing on the first or higher of the two notes in the pattern.

Try beating this pattern as you listen to the piece, but listen carefully to what the other flute and the rattle are doing. Notice that the downbeats of the three instruments do not coincide. They are three distinctly different rhythmic patterns.

A little further into the piece a chorus of low voices enters, singing yet another rhythmic pattern in long notes. The downbeat of this pattern does not coincide with the downbeat of any of the other patterns. The voices sing in chords made up of perfect fifths, creating a harmony reminiscent of Western medieval organum.

A little later, a lead solo voice slowly emerges and assumes a position of prominence. Higher voices then join the low chorus of voices, adding a new element and expanding the range of the texture, while also giving it a fresh new color. Near the end of the piece (of which this example is only an excerpt) a high yodeling solo voice dominates the texture.

In this celebratory song the Ba-Benzélé Pygmies create a musical fabric that crackles with rhythmic vitality, adorned with voices in harmony, solo voices, and instruments. Careful listening reveals that the piece is anything but chaotic or the product of chance; it is beautifully conceived and utterly consistent within itself. Particularly with rhythm, Western musicians have much to learn from the Ba-Benzélés.

The Ba-Benzélé Pygmies' music exhibits solo voice, harmony, and instrumentation.

Fig. 15.1

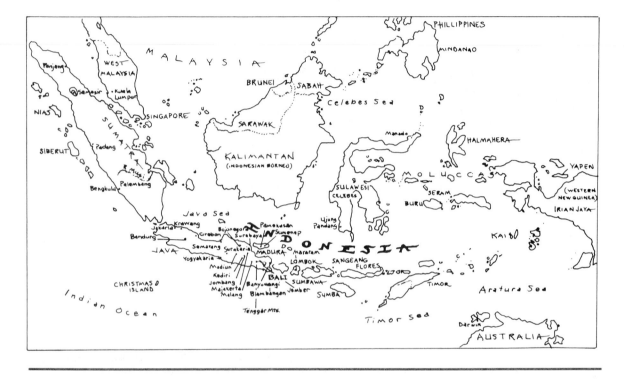

INDONESIA

Indonesian music reveals a diverse ethnic and religious tradition.

The Republic of Indonesia comprises the largest collection of islands in the world. There are about 6,000 individual islands, many of them quite small, and about half are populated (see fig. 15.1). There is considerable ethnic and linguistic diversity in Indonesia, though not to the extent that exists in Africa. The earliest cultural influences in Indonesia came from ancient China and India, but since about the thirteenth century the dominant religion has been a modified form of Near Eastern Islam. Coupled with this Islamic tradition in Indonesia is a mystical worship of nature and ancestors.

We will consider Balinese music.

Once more, it is not possible to investigate all of the musical traditions found in this part of the world, but one can be singled out—the Balinese—for consideration.

Gamelan musicians from Bali

Bali

The music of Bali contrasts sharply with the previously examined African music. For one thing, although solo and choral singing can be found in the culture, traditional Balinese music is primarily instrumental. Several kinds of instruments are combined to form an orchestra called a **gamelan.** In Bali and in neighboring Java, all cities, and even tiny rural villages, have at least one gamelan. Some of this orchestral music is intended for pleasure only, some of it is used to accompany native dances and pantomime dramas, but much of it is performed in conjunction with the religious ceremonies that are central to the Balinese culture.

A full-scale gamelan employs twenty-five to forty players and the following instruments:

Gongs of several sizes and pitches
Sarons—instruments with a series of bronze keys that are struck
    with a wooden mallet
Wooden xylophones
Hand-struck drums
Sulings—flutelike instruments
Rebab—a two-string fiddle

Balinese music is primarily instrumental.

The Balinese orchestra is termed a gamelan.

Much Balinese music is tied to religious ceremony.

The gamelan includes gongs, sarons, xylophones, drums, sulings, and rebab—each with a specific role.

Fig. 15.2

A nuclear melody is at the core of every gamelan composition.

The texture of gamelan music gives it a layered effect.

Drums provide the rhythm.

Gongs indicate the structure.

Gamelan music does not sound like the Western music with which we are familiar.

Each instrument has a specific role to play in the gamelan. At the core of a gamelan composition is the **nuclear melody.** This is a composed and frequently notated melody that is often quite old. It is thought that there are between three and four thousand nuclear melodies in the Balinese gamelan repertoire. In a performance some instruments play a nuclear melody, others play essentially the same melody but in longer note values, and still other instruments play an elaboration of the nuclear melody, but add many faster notes to it. This texture produces a layered effect that adds a shimmering quality to the music. In Western notation (which is different from Balinese notation) the music appears as in figure 15.2.

Drums provide rhythmic continuity and color. Gongs are used to indicate various parts of the formal structure: some mark the ends of phrases, some mark the ends of subsections, and others mark the formal divisions of the music. In many cases, pairs of gongs are used, one gong pitched slightly higher than the other, which adds to the shimmering effect of the music.

Much of this music at first seems out of tune to Western ears since many of the intervals and the whole tuning system are different than Western music. Once these differences are accepted as norms for this music, however, the beauty of gamelan music is better appreciated.

The short work *Gilak* provides an excellent introduction to Balinese gamelan music. It is a ritualistic piece used in the temple to accompany a particular dance. The piece is not hard to follow once you learn how to listen for its structure. (The piece can be found on Archiv: *Musical Traditions in Asia,* side 1, band 2.)

SOUND AND SENSE: *Balinese Gamelan Music*

Title: "Gilak"

A Closer Look:

The piece begins with a sixteen-beat pattern played by the drums. At the end of this pattern are two extra beats that are played rubato and lead directly to the exposition of the nuclear melody in the first section. Rubato is a common feature of gamelan music.

In the first section—A—the nuclear melody section is thirty-two beats long, followed by several other sections, most of which are thirty-two beats (sixteen plus sixteen) long, with the remaining sections sixteen beats long. A series of gongs articulate the formal structure: the large gong is sounded on beats one and seventeen of the thirty-two-beat pattern; the middle-sized gong is struck on beats one, nine, seventeen, and twenty-five; and the smaller gong sounds on beats one, five, nine, thirteen, seventeen, twenty-one, twenty-five, and twenty-nine (every fourth beat). The pattern is illustrated in figure 15.3.

The sectional structure of the whole work is as follows:

Drum introduction—Sixteen beats plus two beats to slow the tempo.
Section 1—Exposition of the nuclear melody, thirty-two beats long.
Section 2—Nuclear melody repeated, but with intricate improvisational elaboration in high-pitched instruments, thirty-two beats divided into two sixteen-beat subsections.
Section 3—Another sixteen plus sixteen beat pattern at a slightly faster tempo and with more animated drums.
Section 4—Same beat pattern, texture a little thicker, general sound somewhat brassier.
Section 5—Same beat pattern, softer sound.
Section 6—Same beat pattern, a shade faster tempo.
Section 7—Only sixteen beats long, somewhat softer sound.
Section 8—Sixteen plus sixteen beats, louder.
Section 9—Same beat pattern (sixteen plus sixteen), drums more prominent, rubato near the end.
Section 10—Same beat pattern, a shade faster.
Section 11—Same beat pattern, a little softer.
Section 12—Same beat pattern.
Section 13—Same beat pattern.
Section 14—Same beat pattern, a little faster and louder.
Section 15—Same beat pattern, more activity in upper part of texture.
Section 16—Same beat pattern.
Section 17—Same beat pattern, louder.
Section 18—Same beat pattern, drums more prominent.
Section 19—Same beat pattern.
Section 20—Sixteen beats, slower with rubato.

Fig. 15.3

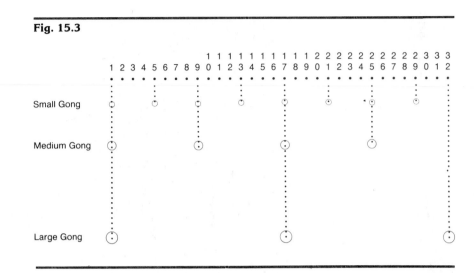

The beat pattern helps us to organize the gamelan music.

Once we perceive the beat pattern, the delicate sense of textural contrast, and shadings of dynamics, the music begins to make sense. Your ability to understand this piece will open the door to understanding a great many other gamelan works.

INDIA

India has two distinct music traditions.

We will examine the music of Southern India.

Two separate but closely related traditions dominate the art music of India: the north Indian or Hindustan tradition, and the south Indian or Karnatic tradition. Both are ancient traditions and both use essentially the same instruments, sounds, time measurement, formal structures, and performance practices, though the terminology may differ. The south Indian or Karnatic tradition is discussed here, but some of the techniques and principles are applicable to the Hindustan tradition as well.

India's classical music tradition is free from Western influence.

A tala is a set of beats organized into units.

Akshara is the Indian word for beat, while a unit of music is an anga.

Each tala has a name and an extra-musical connotation.

Although modern Indian music has been influenced by the West, India's classical music tradition is free of this influence. Some of the classical music—instrumental, vocal, and dance/dramatic—is designed for sacred purposes, some for entertainment, and some for both.

The secular side of Indian music is governed by repetitive time cycles called **talas.** A tala consists of a collection of beats grouped into various units within the cycle. A beat is called an **akshara,** a unit is called an **anga.** In modern practice there are dozens of different talas, and each of them has a specific name that has some extra-musical connotation. Illustrated in figure 15.4 is **adi tala.**

Fig. 15.4

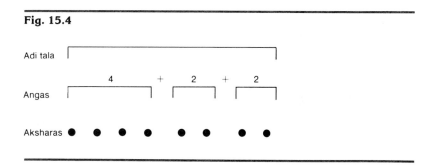

The Adi tala contains eight aksharas that are grouped into three angas. Notice that the angas are not all the same length: the first has four beats, the second has two beats, and the third two beats—4 + 2 + 2. The Western notion of downbeat and upbeat does not exist in this kind of rhythm.

For the performer, a tala is the rhythmic foundation from which further rhythmic improvisation springs. The performer's expertise is measured by this ability to improvise rhythmically within the structured bounds of the tala.

The sonorous aspect of Indian music is tied to the **raga.** A raga is somewhat like a scale in Western music, yet is more complex than a scale. A raga is like a scale in that it contains a set number of pitches arranged in some ascending and descending order. But whereas our chromatic scales have twelve pitches and our diatonic scales have seven, some Indian ragas have seven or fewer pitches, some have twelve or more, and many contain pitches not found in Western music. In other words, every raga has a set number of pitches, but they don't all have the same number of pitches. In addition, a raga and a Western scale differ in the order in which various pitches are introduced. For example, instead of playing:

    1 2 3 4 5 6 7
    c d e f g a b

a raga might introduce its pitches this way:

    1 4 2 7 3 5 6
    c f d b e g a

and the descending version of the raga may introduce the pitches in still another order.

Angas are of different lengths.

The bounds of improvisation are set by the tala.

The Indian raga has some characteristics of the Western scale.

Not all ragas have the same number of pitches.

Vina player

But a raga is more than a collection of pitches. A given raga is associated with certain melodic bits that belong only to that raga. And certain pitches of a given raga may require a specific kind of ornamentation. For example, the pitch "C" may be ornamented in one raga but not in another.

There are several dozen ragas in modern usage and all have extramusical names that may be associated with a certain mood or even a specific time of day. Thus, a raga has a kind of emotional, even a spiritual, quality.

The raga determines the emotional and spiritual quality of the piece.

Memorizing and mastering the many talas and ragas, and developing the enormous improvisational skill necessary to breathe musical life into them, is a full-time occupation requiring years of dedication and hard work. It is not surprising then that the Indian culture, unlike the Ba-Benzélé culture, has a specific class of musicians. The true masters of this class are called **gurus.**

Indian master musician/ teachers are called "gurus."

The principal musical instrument of southern India is the vina.

In south India the principal musical instrument of the guru is the vina, a relative of the harp family. The vina has four melody strings and three drone strings.

In classical music, the vina often plays solo.

Classical music for the vina is essentially soloistic music, though in concert a drum called a mridanga and a violin (held in front rather than under the chin) are sometimes used as accompaniment.

The basic formal structure of many Indian classical works has five parts as follows:

1. Alap—The alap section, played in free rhythm without tala, systematically reveals the notes and the special melodic characteristics of the raga. A drone played on one or more of the drone strings plays the central pitch (a kind of tonic), not continuously, but often enough that its location is always known.
2. Pallavi—The tala emerges and improvisation becomes more involved. The pallavi section plays mainly in the lower register of the instrument.
3. Anupallavi—The anupallavi is played in the higher registers; the improvisation reaches its climax.
4. Caranam—The caranam is a kind of denouement; a lowering of register and excitement.
5. Repetition of pallavi.

Many of these classical compositions are quite lengthy works. It is probably best to start with a shorter work, in which the various sections are fairly easy to grasp, before proceeding to a longer work. Listen to "Raghuvamsa" in raga Kadanakutuhalam, and tala adi (found in *Reflets de L'Inde,* Barclay 86 1205, side 1, band 5).

Short works provide the best introduction to southern Indian music.

SUMMARY

Our look at non-Western music focused on the music of the African Ba-Benzélé Pygmies, the Balinese, and the Karnatic Indians. In each of these cultures music plays a major role.

An appreciation of these non-Western music traditions can stem only from an understanding of how the musical components of time, sound, form, and function work together.

Although the continent of Africa is as diverse as it is large, we can generalize to a degree about its musical heritage. Music is an integral part of the African's daily life. For that reason, no class of musicians exists—all people are musicians. African music is primarily a vocal music with a dominant rhythm that sounds complex to us. Because improvisation is such a central part of the music, notation is of little use. Our musical example was from the Ba-Benzélé Pygmies of sub-Saharan Africa.

The music of Bali is primarily instrumental and designed to be performed by an orchestra—the gamelan. This gamelan music is composed around a nuclear melody, producing a layered effect. In Bali music, drums provide the rhythm and gongs indicate the structure. Our example of Balinese gamelan music was "Gilak."

Karnatic Indian music is organized by beats (aksharas), collections of beats (talas) and units (angas). The tala provides the rhythmic structure from which improvisation flows. The raga determines the emotional and spiritual quality of the music. Because of the skill necessary to work within the Karnatic musical boundaries, a class of musicians—gurus—developed within the culture.

We have had only a glimpse at non-Western music. The understanding and appreciation developed here, however, will serve you well as you explore other "foreign" musics.

KEY TERMS

gamelan   anga
nuclear melody   adi tala
talas   raga
akshara   guru

THINKING ABOUT IT

This chapter is intended to serve only as an introduction to specific examples of non-Western music. Nevertheless, the three examples we have considered serve as catalysts for examining the differences among many different kinds of music. As you reexamine these examples and as you listen to music from other cultures, compare and contrast them with one another.

APPENDIXES

APPENDIX A
Record Set Selections

Record 1, Side A   Chapters 1–2

1. Handel: "Halleluia" chorus from *Messiah*
   Philadelphia Orchestra, Eugene Ormandy, conductor; Mormon Tabernacle Choir, Richard Condie, director.
   (Example of note values in chapter 1, texture in chapter 2; can also be used in chapter 5 as an example of baroque music.)

2. Chopin: *Waltz,* op. 34, no. 2
   Dinu Lipatti, piano.
   (Example of note values and rubato in chapter 1.)

3. Haydn: Symphony no. 101, first movement
   New York Philharmonic, Leonard Bernstein, conductor.
   (Example of note values in chapter 1; sonata-allegro form in chapter 3. Can also be used to exemplify the classical symphony in chapter 7.)

4. Scott Joplin: "The Entertainer" (excerpt)
   David Frost, piano.
   (Example of note values and syncopation in chapter 1, rag form in chapter 3.)

5. Palestrina: "Agnus Dei"
   From *Masterpieces of Music Before 1750.*
   (Example of texture in chapter 2, Renaissance Mass motet in chapter 11.)

6. J. S. Bach: C Minor Fugue from *Well-Tempered Clavier,* vol. 1
   Glenn Gould, piano.
   (Example of imitative counterpoint in chapter 2; also useful in chapter 5 as an example of a baroque keyboard fugue.)

7. Griffes: *The White Peacock*
   Andre Kostelanetz, conductor.
   (Example of texture and harmony in chapter 2; also useful in chapter 9 as an example of impressionistic style.)

Record 1, Side B   Chapters 2–3

1. Barber: *Adagio for String Orchestra*
   Philadelphia Orchestra, Eugene Ormandy, conductor.
   (Example of string ensemble in chapter 2, "American" style in chapter 9.)

2. Beethoven: Symphony no. 6, third movement (excerpt)
   Philadelphia Orchestra, Eugene Ormandy, conductor.
   (Example of woodwinds in chapter 2.)

3.   Mussorgsky: "Promenade" from
      Pictures from an Exhibition
      New York Philharmonic, Leonard
      Bernstein, conductor.
      (Example of brass in chapter 2.)

4.   Varèse: *Ionization*
      Robert Craft conducts woodwinds,
      brass, and percussion.
      (Example of percussion in chapter 2.)

5.   Chopin: Mazurka, no. 44, op. 67, no. 3
      Alexander Brailowsky, piano.
      (Example of *ABA* form in chapter 3.)

6.   Chopin: Mazurka, no. 41, op. 63, no. 3
      Alexander Brailowsky, piano.
      (Example of *ABA* form in chapter 3.)

7.   J. S. Bach: "Allemande" from French
      Suite no. 1 in D Minor
      Glenn Gould, piano.
      (Example of *AABB* form in chapter 3.)

Record 2, Side A   Chapters 3–4

1.   Haydn: Piano Sonata in D Major,
      no. 50, last movement
      Arthur Balsam, piano.
      (Example of rondo in chapter 3.)

2.   Beethoven: Piano Sonata in C Minor,
      op. 13, *Pathétique,* second movement
      Glenn Gould, piano.
      (Example of rondo in chapter 3.)

3.   J. Baird: "I'm a Stranger Here"
      (excerpt)
      Brownie McGhee and Sonny Terry.
      (Example of twelve-bar blues in
      chapter 3.)

4.   Mozart: Symphony no. 40 in G Minor,
      first movement
      New York Philharmonic, Leonard
      Bernstein, conductor.
      (Example of sonata-allegro form in
      chapter 3, of classical symphony
      movement in chapter 7.)

5.   Beethoven: Piano Sonata in A♭ Major,
      op. 26, first movement
      Paul Badura-Skoda, piano.
      (Example of theme and variations in
      chapter 3.)

6.   Vivaldi: "Spring" from *The Seasons,*
      first movement
      St. Paul Chamber Orchestra, Pinchas
      Zuckerman, violinist/conductor.
      (Example of descriptive music in
      chapter 4.)

Record 2, Side B   Chapters 4–8

1.   C. M. von Weber: *Der Freischütz,* final
      portion of the Wolf's Glen Scene
      Grummer, Otto, Schock, Kohn, Berlin
      Municipal Opera Chorus.
      (Example of descriptive music in
      chapter 4.)

2.   Ives: *The Unanswered Question*
      New York Philharmonic, Leonard
      Bernstein, conductor.
      (Example of philosophical program
      music in chapter 4; also useful in
      chapter 9.)

3.   Handel: Trio Sonata in F Major, first
      and second movements (with no pause
      in between)
      (Example of a baroque trio sonata in
      chapter 5.)

4.   F. Couperin: "Le Croc-en-jambe" from
      Ordre no. 22
      Sylvia Marlowe, harpsichord.
      (Example of the rococo style in
      chapter 6.)

5.   J. C. Bach: Symphony in D Major,
      op. 18, no. 1, first movement
      Philadelphia Orchestra, Eugene
      Ormandy, conductor.
      (Example of style galant in chapter 6.)

6.   C. P. E. Bach: Symphony in B Minor
      (excerpt)
      Martin Galling, harpsichord; Mainz
      Chamber Orchestra, Gunter Kehr,
      conductor.
      (Example of *Sturm und Drang* in
      chapter 6.)

7.   Berlioz: *Roméo et Juliette* Symphony,
      op. 17, "Queen Mab" section (excerpt)
      New York Philharmonic, Leonard
      Bernstein, conductor.
      (Example of brilliant orchestration in
      chapter 8.)

Record 3, Side A   Chapter 8

1. Berlioz: *Roméo et Juliette* Symphony, op. 17, "Love Scene" (excerpt) New York Philharmonic, Leonard Bernstein, conductor. (Example of a dramatic scene from a choral/dramatic symphony.)

2. Brahms: Symphony no. 2, op. 73, first movement New York Philharmonic, Leonard Bernstein, conductor. (Example of classically oriented nineteenth century symphony.)

3. Chopin: Étude, op. 10, no. 5 Abbey Simon, piano. (Example of nineteenth century virtuoso keyboard work.)

4. Brahms: Intermezzo in A, op. 118, no. 2 Stephanie Brown, piano. (Example of a character piece for piano.)

Record 3, Side B   Chapter 8

1. Borodin: *In the Steppes of Central Asia* Philadelphia Orchestra, Eugene Ormandy, conductor. (Example of a tone poem.)

2. Chopin: Polonaise in A♭, op. 53, *Heroic* Philippe Entremont, piano. (Example of a dance fashioned into a character piece for piano.)

3. Schumann: Concerto in A Minor for Piano and Orchestra, op. 54, first movement Rudolf Serkin, piano; Philadelphia Orchestra, Eugene Ormandy, conductor. (Example of a romantic piano concerto.)

Record 4, Side A   Chapters 8–9

1. Rossini: *The Barber of Seville,* Act I, scene i Simone Alaimo, Paolo Barbacini, Leo Nucci, Orchestra and Chorus of Teatro alla Scala Milan; Riccardo Chailly, conductor; Romano Gandolfi, chorus master. (Example of nineteenth century Italian comic opera with set numbers.)

2. Debussy: *Danse bohémienne* Beveridge Webster, piano. (Example of Debussy's earliest style.)

3. Debussy: "Brouillards" from *Preludes,* Book II Walter Gieseking, piano. (Example of impressionism.)

4. Debussy: "La Flute de Pan" from *Chansons de Bilitis* Frederica von Stade, mezzo soprano; Martin Katz, piano. (Example of symbolist poetry set to music.)

5. Schönberg: *Pierrot Lunaire,* op. 27, "Mondestrunken" (first song) Bethany Beardslee, soprano; Isidore Cohen, violin/viola; Charles McCracken, cello; Robert Helps, piano; Ernest Bright, clarinet/bass clarinet; Murray Panitz, flute/piccolo; Robert Craft, conductor. (Example of expressionism with *Sprechtstimme.*)

6. Berg: *Wozzeck,* Act III, scene ii (excerpt) Walter Berry, Isabel Strauss; Orchestra of the Paris National Opera, Pierre Boulez, conductor. (Example of expressionism.)

Record 4, Side B   Chapters 9, 11

1. Berg: *Wozzeck,* Act III, scene v (excerpt) Childrens' Chorus of the Paris National Opera; Orchestra of the Paris National Opera, Pierre Boulez, conductor. (Example of expressionism.)

2. Satie: *Parade* (excerpt)
    Royal Philharmonic Orchestra,
    Philippe Entremont, conductor.
    (Example of dadaist music.)

3. Milhaud: *The Bull on the Roof*
    (excerpt)
    Minneapolis Symphony Orchestra,
    Dimitri Mitropoulos, conductor.
    (Example of polytonality.)

4. Josquin des Prez: Motet *Ave Maria*
    (Example of Renaissance motet with
    imitative counterpoint.)

5. William Byrd: *Christ Rising Again*
    (Example of English verse anthem.)

6. Marenzio: *S'io parto, moro*
    From *Masterpieces of Music Before
    1750*
    (Example of Italian madrigal.)

7. Morley: "Now Is the Month of
    Maying"
    (Example of Elizabethan madrigal.)

8. Gabrieli: *Gloria in Excelsis Deo*
    (excerpt)
    (Example of the mixture of vocal and
    instrumental elements in the late
    Renaissance.)

Record 5, Side A   Chapters 12, 14

1. Stephen Foster, "Jeanie with the Light
    Brown Hair"
    Jean Lemonds, soprano; Jay Fuller,
    pianist.
    (Example of a parlor song in the
    genteel tradition.)

2. S. Stept: "Please Don't Talk about Me
    when I'm Gone"
    The Side Street Ramblers.
    (Example of barbershop quartet with
    chromatic harmony.)

3. Fletcher Henderson: "Down South
    Camp Meeting"
    From *Original Big Band Hits,* vol. 1;
    Benny Goodman, clarinet.
    (Example of white swing.)

4. Fletcher Henderson: "Down South
    Camp Meeting"
    Fletcher Henderson, band leader.
    (Example of black swing.)

5. "Auld Lang Syne"
    Guy Lombardo.
    (Example of sweet band sound.)

6. M. Gordon, H. Revel: "Stay as Sweet
    as You Are"
    Sung by Lanny Ross.
    (Example of tenor or "clean" style.)

7. Jimmy Durante: "Can Broadway Do
    without Me?"
    Performed by Clayton, Jackson,
    Durante.
    (Example of talking style.)

8. Arthur Johnston, Sam Oslow: "Learn
    to Croon"
    Sung by Bing Crosby.
    (Example of crooning.)

9. Irving Berlin: "White Christmas"
    From *Archive of Folk Music,* jazz
    series; Charlie Parker, alto sax.
    (Example of swing and improvisation.)

Record 5, Side B   Chapter 14

1. Scott Joplin: "Maple Leaf Rag"
    Scott Joplin, piano.
    (Example of ragtime [non-swing] style.)

2. Scott Joplin: "Maple Leaf Rag"
    Jelly Roll Morton, piano.
    (Example of swinging style.)

3. Joe Oliver: "Dippermouth Blues"
    King Oliver, trumpet.
    (Example of New Orleans style jazz.)

4. Joe Oliver: "West End Blues"
    Louis Armstrong, trumpet.
    (Example of solo-oriented 1920s jazz.)

5. Lillian Hardin Armstrong: "Hotter
    Than That"
    Louis Armstrong, trumpet.
    (Example of solo-oriented 1920s jazz.)

6. Parish, Carmichael, Mills: "Riverboat
    Shuffle"
    Frank Trumbauer, C-melody sax; Bix
    Beiderbecke, cornet; Bill Rark,
    trombone; Don Murray, clarinet; Doc
    Ryker, alto sax; Itzy Riskin, piano;
    Eddie Lang, guitar; Chauncey
    Morehouse, drums.
    (Example of white jazz players.)

7. Fats Waller: "Numb Fumblin"
    (Example of stride piano.)

8. Charlie Parker: "Ornithology"
    (excerpt)
    Charlie Parker, alto sax.
    (Example of bop.)

9. Paul Desmond: "Take Five" (excerpt)
    The Dave Brubeck Quartet.
    (Example of cool jazz.)

10. Ornette Coleman: "Happy House"
    (excerpt)
    Ornette Coleman, alto sax; Dewey
    Redman, tenor sax; Don Cherry,
    pocket trumpet; Bobby Bradford,
    trumpet; Charlie Haden, acoustic bass;
    Ed Blackwell, drums; Billy Higgins,
    drums.
    (Example of new jazz.)

APPENDIX B

A Brief List of Composers and Their Works

Babbitt, Milton (b. 1916): American composer of serial and electronic music.

Bach, Carl Philipp Emanuel (1714–88): Son of J. S. Bach, a composer of chamber music, symphonies, and keyboard works, many of them in either *empfindsamer* or in *Sturm und Drang* style.

Bach, Johann Christian (1735–82): Youngest son of J. S. Bach, composer of symphonies, concertos, and other works in the style galant of the preclassic era.

Bach, Johann Sebastian (1685–1750): Great master of the late Baroque and of contrapuntal techniques. Best known works include the six *Brandenburg* Concertos, *St. Matthew Passion*, *Well-Tempered Clavier*, *Goldberg Variations*.

Barber, Samuel (1910–80): American composer of songs, opera, keyboard, and orchestral music. Best known works include *Adagio for String Orchestra*, *Knoxville, Summer 1915*.

Bartók, Béla (1881–1945): Hungarian composer much of whose music reveals his fascination with native folk music. Best known works are Music for strings, percussion and celesta, *Concerto for Orchestra*, the six *String Quartets*.

Beethoven, Ludwig van (1770–1827): Great master of the late classical and early romantic eras, and probably the consummate master of the developmental process. Best known works: Symphony no. 5, Symphony no. 9, Symphony no. 3, the *Moonlight* and the *Pathétique* piano sonatas, the *Missa Solemnis*.

Berg, Alban (1885–1935): Student of Schönberg and a leading expressionist composer. Best known work: *Wozzeck* (opera).

Berlioz, (Louis) Hector (1803–69): French romantic composer, especially prominent in the fields of dramatic and programmatic music. Best known work: *Symphonie Fantastique (Fantastic Symphony)*.

Bizet, Georges (1838–75): French composer, primarily of operas. Best known work is the opera *Carmen*.

Borodin, Alexander (1834–87): Russian composer with nationalist leanings. Best known works: *Prince Igor* (opera) and *In the Steppes of Central Asia* (tone poem).

Brahms, Johannes (1833–97): One of the central romantic composers, tempered by classicism; a master of counterpoint. Best known works: the Four Symphonies, *German Requiem*, numerous songs and shorter works for piano.

Byrd, William (ca. 1540–1623): Foremost British composer of the Elizabethan era. Best known for his Masses and verse anthems.

Caccini, Giulio (ca. 1550–1618): One of the central figures in the development of Camerata opera.

Cage, John (b. 1912): American composer known chiefly for his use of aleatoric procedures and other kinds of experimental music.

Chopin, Frederic (1810–49): Polish composer of the romantic era; generally regarded as the consummate master of romantic solo piano music. Best known works: Twenty Four Preludes, "Revolutionary" etude, *Heroic Polonaise*.

Copland, Aaron (b. 1900): American composer and a central figure in the "Americana" school. Some of his music is influenced by jazz. Best known work: *Appalachian Spring* (ballet).

Corelli, Arcangelo (1653–1713): Early baroque composer of trio sonatas.

Couperin, Francois (1668–1733): Composer of elegant and often fanciful keyboard works in the rococo era.

Debussy, Claude (1862–1918): Innovative French composer of the late nineteenth and early twentieth century; some of his works have been labeled "impressionistic." Best known works: *Prélude à l'Aprés-midi d'un Faune*, (*Prelude to the Afternoon of a Faun*), *Clair de lune*, "Nuages," *La Mer*.

Delius, Frederick (1862–1934): British impressionist composer. Best known works are tone poems such as *Brigg Fair: an English Rhapsody* and *On Hearing the First Cuckoo in Spring*.

Donizetti, Gaetano (1797–1848): Italian romantic opera composer. Best known work: *Lucia di Lammermoor.*

Dufay, Guillaume (ca. 1400–74): Flemish composer of the early Renaissance. Best known for his polyphonic Masses.

Dunstable, John (ca. 1370–1453): Important British composer of the early Renaissance.

Dvorak, Antonin (1841–1904): Prolific Czech romantic composer. Best known work: Symphony no. *9 (From the New World).*

Farnaby, Giles (1560–1600): Elizabethan composer best known for his works for the keyboard instrument known as the virginal.

Franck, César (1822–90): Composer-organist-teacher. Many of his works are rich in chromatics. Best known works: Symphony in D Minor, and the oratorio *Les Béatitudes (The Beatitudes).*

Gabrieli, Andrea (ca. 1510–86): Composer of colorful works for voices with instruments and for organ.

Grieg, Edvard (1843–1907): Norwegian composer. Best known works: Piano Concerto in A Minor, *Peer Gynt* suite.

Griffes, Charles (1884–1920): American composer who wrote in an impressionist style. Best known work is the tone poem "The White Peacock."

Handel, George Frederick (1685–1759): Great master of the late baroque and the central composer of opera seria, though today he is best known for works other than his operas. Best known works: *Messiah, Water Music.*

Haydn, Franz Joseph (1732–1809): A consummate master of the pure classical style; sometimes called "the father of the symphony." Best known works include several of his 104 symphonies, such as the *Surprise* (no. 94), String Quartet, op. 76, no. 3, and the oratorio *The Seasons.*

Honegger, Arthur (1892–1955): A member of the so-called "French Six," best known for works such as the oratorio *Le Roi David (King David)* and the tone poem *Pacific 231.*

Ives, Charles (1874–1954): American composer, boldly innovative in his day. Best known works: *The Unanswered Question,* Fourth Symphony.

Josquin des Prez (ca. 1450–1521): Known to some of his contemporaries as "the prince of music," he was a preeminent composer of the middle Renaissance; best known for his Masses and motets.

Liszt, Franz (1811–86): A prolific composer of many kinds of music and one of the greatest of the nineteenth century piano virtuosos. Best known works: the tone poem *Les Preludes,* many shorter works for piano.

Lully, Jean Baptiste (1632–87): The founder and leading practitioner of French opera in the middle baroque.

MacDowell, Edward (1861–1908): American composer. Best known work: *Woodland Sketches* (piano).

Machaut, Guillaume de (ca. 1305–77): Preeminent composer of the Ars Nova period, he was both a priest and trouvère and wrote both secular and sacred music.

Mahler, Gustav (1860–1911): Composer of several very large-scale works and a master orchestrator. Best known works: *Kindertotenlieder* (for voice and orchestra), Symphony no. 9.

Marenzio, Luca (ca. 1560–99): Important composer of Italian madrigals during the late Renaissance.

Mendelssohn, Felix (1809–47): A classically-oriented romantic who wrote in nearly all genres except opera. Best known works: Symphony no. 4 *(Italian), Hebrides* Overture, *Elijah* (oratorio).

Milhaud, Darius (1892–1974): A member of the "French Six," his music is eclectic, showing the influence of American jazz, Latin rhythms, and several folk melodies. Best known works: *Le Boeuf sur le Toit (The Bull on the Roof), La Création du Monde (The Creation of the World).*

Monteverdi, Claudio (1567–1643): The preeminent Italian composer of the early baroque. Best known work: *Orfeo* (opera).

Morley, Thomas (ca. 1557–1603): An important composer of English madrigals during the Elizabethan era. Best known madrigal: *Now is the Month of Maying.*

Mozart, Wolfgang (1756–91): A master composer in virtually all genres of music, instrumental and vocal. Among his best known works: *Don Giovanni,* Symphony no. 40, several piano concertos, and several piano sonatas.

Mussorgsky, Modest (1835–81): Russian nationalistic composer. Best known works: *Pictures at an Exhibition* (orchestrated by Maurice Ravel), *Boris Godunoff* (opera).

Okeghem, Joannes (ca. 1430–95): A master composer of the early Renaissance and the teacher of Josquin des Prez. Best known works are Masses and motets, especially the Mass *L'homme arme.*

Palestrina, Giovanni Pierluigi da (ca. 1526–94): The dominant composer in the field of sacred music during the late Renaissance. He is best known for his Masses such as the *Missa Papae Marcelli (Pope Marcellus Mass).*

Prokofiev, Sergei (1891–1953): Eminent and prolific Russian composer. Best known works include: *The Love for Three Oranges* (opera), *Peter and the Wolf,* Piano Concerto no. 3.

Puccini, Giacomo (1858–1924): Very popular Italian opera composer, some of whose works are imbued with *verismo.* Best known works: *La Bohème, Madame Butterfly.*

Purcell, Henry (1659–95): The leading British composer of the middle baroque era. Best known work: *Dido and Aeneas* (opera).

Rachmaninoff, Sergei (1873–1943): Russian composer and piano virtuoso best known for luxuriant melodies as found in his piano concertos.

Ravel, Maurice (1875–1937): French composer, often cited as an impressionist. Best known works: *Gaspard de la Nuit, Daphnis et Chloé.*

Rossini, Gioacchino (1792–1868): One of the giant composers of nineteenth century Italian opera. Best known works: *Il Barbiere di Siviglia (The Barber of Seville), William Tell* overture.

Satie, Erik (1866–1925): Associated with the dadaist movement for part of his career. Best known works: *Gymnopédie* no. 1 (for piano solo or for orchestra as orchestrated by Debussy), *Parade* (ballet).

Schönberg, Arnold (1874–1951): Inventor of the twelve-tone system. Best known work: *Pierrot Lunaire.*

Schubert, Franz (1797–1828): Prolific composer of Lieder, orchestral music, chamber music, and piano works. Best known works: *Die Erlkönig, Symphony no. 8 (Unfinished).*

Schumann, Robert (1810–56): Gifted, tragic romantic figure. Best known works: *Kinderscenen (Scenes from Childhood),* Piano Concerto in A Minor.

Sibelius, Jean (1865–1957): Finnish composer. Best known works: *Finlandia* (tone poem), *The Swan of Tuonela.*

Stamitz, Johann (1717–57): Important in the development of the early symphony in Mannheim.

Stockhausen, Karlheinz (b. 1928): Important composer in the development of electronic music. Best known work: *Gesang der Jünglinge (Song of the Youths).*

Strauss, Richard (1864–1949): Composer of tone poems, German operas, and other works. Best known works: *Till Eulenspiegels Lustige Streiche (Till Eulenspiegel's Merry Pranks), Der Rosenkavalier* (opera).

Stravinsky, Igor (1882–1971): Russian-American composer, one of the giants of the twentieth century. Best known works: *Le Sacre du Printemps (The Rite of Spring), Petrushka.*

Tchaikovsky, Peter (1840–93): Very popular Russian composer from the late romantic period. Several of his melodies have been made into popular songs. Best known works: *The Nutcracker, Symphonie Pathétique, Swan Lake.*

Torelli, Giuseppe (ca. 1650–1708): Important composer in the development of the concerto grosso in the middle baroque era.

Varese, Edgar (1883–1965): Important composer in the fields of experimental and electronic music. Best known works: *Ionisation, Poeme Electronique.*

Verdi, Giuseppe (1813–1901): The preeminent Italian opera composer of the nineteenth century. Best known operas: *Rigoletto, Aïda.*

Vivaldi, Antonio (ca. 1675–1741): Prolific composer of concerti grossi in the late baroque era. Best known work: the four concerti grossi comprising *The Seasons.*

Wagner, Richard (1813–83): Foremost composer of German opera in the nineteenth century. Developed the music drama with its system of leit motifs. Best known works: *Tristan und Isolde, Die Meistersinger von Nürnberg.*

Weber, Carl Maria von (1786–1826): Early romantic composer of German operas and other works. Best known work: *Der Freischütz.*

Webern, Anton (1883–1945): Early in Webern's career, he was an expressionist and student of Schönberg. Later, he developed serial techniques in works of emotional density, many of which are quite brief. Best known work: *Variations* (piano).

GLOSSARY

absolute music music that is not based on a program or story; the opposite of program music.

accelerando a speeding up of tempo.

accent stress or extra emphasis given to a beat.

accidental a ♯ placed in front of a note raises that note in pitch by a half step; a ♭ placed in front of a note lowers that note by a half step.

acid rock a heavily amplified and electronic form of rock that emerged in the mid-1960s, that reflected the mores of the then current psychedelic subculture.

adagio a slow tempo.

adi tala a particular tala in classical Indian music, consisting of a four-beat anga, followed by a two-beat anga, followed by another two-beat anga.

akshara a beat in classical Indian music.

aleatory *see* chance music.

allegro a fast tempo.

allemande a dance of moderate tempo, in duple meter, found in the dance suite of the baroque era, as in J. S. Bach's French Suites.

andante a moderately slow tempo that moves at a walking pace.

andantino a tempo that is somewhat faster than andante.

anga a smaller collection of beats within a tala in classical Indian music.

anthem a choral work with English text sung with or without accompaniment.

aria an elaborate solo song (with accompaniment) found in operas, cantatas, and oratorios.

Ars Nova the style period of the fourteenth century, at the end of the Middle Ages and just preceding the Renaissance, characterized by rhythmic complexity and secular attitudes.

atonal music not in a key, as in some of the works of Schönberg and Webern. Generally atonal music is more dissonant than music written in functional harmony.

ballade (1) a type of character piece for piano in the nineteenth century. (2) a fixed poetic-musical form of the trouvères.

bar a single unit of a metrical pattern; the same thing as a measure.

bar line in notating music, a bar line is drawn at the end of each repetition of a meter.

baroque the period from ca. 1600–1750.

basso continuo a bass line instrument such as a cello, and a chord-playing instrument such as harpsichord or organ; the basso continuo was used in most types of baroque music.

beat the basic rhythmic pulse of music, especially metrical music.

bebop *see* bop.

bel canto the "beautiful" style of singing associated principally with Italian opera.

binary a two-part form having the design *AB, AABB,* or *ABAB.*

bitonality music performed in two different keys simultaneously.

blues both a form and a manner of performance that grew out of southern black folk music, elements of which are used in pure blues singing, jazz, rhythm and blues, and other types of American popular music.

blues rock a type of rock from the early 1970s in which one senses the direct influence of pure blues singing and playing.

boogie-woogie an energetic style of piano playing that relentlessly plays on a pattern of 8 eighth notes to the 4/4 bar—the so-called "eight to the bar" style. The style developed in the 1920s and reached a pinnacle of popularity in the 1940s.

bop a wild, aggressive style of jazz from the 1940s and 1950s. Charlie Parker and Dizzy Gillespie were important performers of this style.

bowing pulling the bow across the strings of a stringed instrument.

break a short, solo improvisation found in many kinds of jazz; in a break, the beat of the rhythm section is temporarily suspended.

bridge a connective, often modulatory passage that leads from one theme to another, as in *A* theme . . . bridge . . . *B* theme.

cadenza a passage (often elaborate and showy) for the soloist at the end of recapitulation of the first movement of a concerto, as in the cadenza of a piano or violin concerto.

cantata a multisectional piece for voices and instruments, often with vocal solos (arias) and choruses. Many cantatas are based on sacred texts, some on secular texts. The history of the cantata began in the baroque.

chamber music small ensemble music, such as string quartets.

chance music music ordered by some kind of random directions; chance or aleatory music was developed by John Cage and others in the years following World War II.

chant a melody set to words (either scriptural or nonscriptural) designed for use in the early Christian church.

character piece a relatively short work for solo piano often with a descriptive or programmatic title; developed in the nineteenth century.

choral (dramatic) symphony a type of symphony developed in the nineteenth century that adds solo and/or choral voices to the symphony orchestra.

chorale text and melody of a Lutheran hymn, developed in the Renaissance and richly employed by J. S. Bach and others in the baroque.

chorale prelude a type of organ music based on a chorale melody.

chord two or more pitches sounding simultaneously.

chorus in jazz, an improvised solo, usually thirty-two bars in length.

chromatic non-diatonic pitches of a given key. Chromaticism may be used as a means of creating dissonance.

classical era the years roughly 1770–1810, best typified in the works of Haydn and Mozart, and the earlier works of Beethoven.

coda a section at the end of a movement. In many styles and works the coda serves as a kind of musical "stop sign"—it indicates that the movement is about to conclude.

comic opera a light-weight form of opera that developed in the mid-eighteenth century. Comic opera in England was called ballad opera; in France, opéra-comique; in Italy, opera buffa; in Germany, Singspiele.

concertino the solo group in the concerto grosso.

concerto a work (usually) for one soloist and orchestra.

concerto grosso the dominant form of orchestral music in the baroque, often in three movements (fast-slow-fast) as played by tutti (full orchestra) and concertino (small group of soloists) with basso continuo.

concerts spirituels public concerts in Paris in the preclassic era.

consonance the sense of tonal stability and restfulness; the opposite of dissonance.

contrapuntal a musical texture containing counterpoint.

cool jazz a sophisticated, mellow kind of jazz that developed in the 1940s and 1950s, almost simultaneously with the more aggressive bop style.

countermelody a subsidiary melody in a contrapuntal texture.

counterpoint a musical texture in which two or more different melodic lines are equally prominent and compelling.

country music a brand of white music formerly called hillbilly music. In some ways it resembled black rhythm and blues.

courante one of the basic movements of the baroque dance suite, with moderate tempo and triple meter.

crescendo a systematic, gradual increase in loudness; it appears as ⬁ .

crooning one of the dominant singing styles of American popular music in the 1930s and 1940s. The style is breathy and filled with vocal "scoops."

da capo aria aria in ternary form—*ABA*. Opera singers in the baroque usually ornamented or varied the repetition of the *A* section.

dadaism a radical, anti-establishment artistic movement that focused on and reflected the insanity of humankind. The movement emerged principally in Paris after World War I.

dance suite a collection of dances performed consecutively to form the larger whole. Nearly all of the dances in a suite have the binary form *AABB*.

decrescendo a gradual, measured decrease in volume; it appears as ⟩⟩⟩ in musical notation, and first became prominent in the preclassic era.

development the middle portion of a sonata-allegro form in which materials presented in the exposition section are elaborated.

diatonic tones that are "family members" of a key; the opposite of chromatic tones. Each key has seven diatonic members; for example, in the key of C only the pitches C, D, E, F, G, A, and B are diatonic—all others are chromatic.

dissonance harmonic tension or instability; the opposite of consonance.

dominant seventh one of the three basic chords in the system of functional harmony; it both resists and leads to the tonic chord.

double exposition a term used to describe the special nature of the exposition section in the classical concerto. The orchestra plays the exposition section first, then the soloist joins the orchestra for the repetition (a nonliteral repetition) of the material in the exposition.

downbeat a stressed or accented beat, such as the first beat in a metrical measure.

duplum the voice above the tenor in twelfth and thirteenth century polyphony.

dynamics levels of loudness and softness.

electronic music music in which some or all of the sounds are electronically generated.

empfindsamer stil the "sensitive style"; the melancholy, sentimental style of the preclassic era. A principal exponent of this style is C. P. E. Bach.

etude literally "a study," Chopin's etudes for solo piano present the performer with specific technical difficulties.

exposition the opening portion of a sonata-allegro form that introduces the dominant thematic materials.

expressionism an artistic movement that emerged in the early decades of the twentieth century. The deeply emotional and introspective style was fostered mainly by Schönberg, Berg, and Webern.

fermata the symbol ⌢ placed over a note indicating that the note is to be held for longer than its normal duration.

figured bass a kind of musical shorthand used by continuo players in the baroque era; it consisted of a notated bass line and a series of numbers and figures above it.

finalis the stable, ending pitch of a medieval church mode, somewhat analogous to the tonic pitch in tonal music.

flat notated as ♭, it lowers by a half step the pitch it accompanies.

folk rock a type of rock from the late 1960s and early 1970s that stressed less volume and electronics, and more politically oriented texts.

frequency the number of times per second a sound-producing body vibrates.

fugue a very important type of imitative counterpoint in which one or more "following" voices imitate the theme or subject of the "lead" voice.

functional harmony a system of organizing chords to produce the sense of being in a key. Tonic, dominant, and subdominant chords are the principal functional elements of the system.

gamelan an Indonesian orchestra (specifically Bali).

genteel tradition an era of American popular music from the mid-nineteenth century, consisting mainly of sentimental songs for voice and piano. Many of the songs of Stephen Foster belong to this tradition.

Gesamtkunstwerk Wagner's version of the synthesis of the arts—music, drama, poetry, dance, and architecture.

gigue one of the dances in the baroque dance suite, characterized by a lively tempo.

glissandos sliding from one note to another.

gospel music black religious music from the early twentieth century that had much in common with blues performance practice.

Gregorian chant the sanctioned (monophonic) music of the early Christian church; named after Pope Gregory I (Pope from 590–604).

ground bass a particular kind of ostinato much favored in the baroque era.

guru master performer/teacher of classical Indian music.

harmony in the broadest sense, harmony refers to the chords in music. One harmonic language differs from another because of differences in the types of chords employed.

heavy metal a more tightly controlled and less extravagant relative of acid rock; it emerged in the 1970s.

homophonic a musical texture in which one line— the melody—is clearly more prominent than any of the other accompanying or "harmonizing" voices or lines.

hot jazz a kind of jazz that emerged about 1917, featuring more solo improvisation than group improvisation.

humanism an ideal born in the Renaissance in which humanity took new and special pride in its own achievements.

idée fixe a recurring theme used in the course of an extended work, notably in Berlioz's *Symphonie Fantastique.*

imitative counterpoint texture in which a lead voice is echoed or imitated in one or more following voices, as, for example, in a fugue.

impressionism a late nineteenth century movement in French painting, dominated by Monet, Renoir and others. Some find the musical analogue to this movement in certain works by Debussy.

improvisation a musical creation in which the concept and the performance thereof occur almost simultaneously.

infinite melody Wagner's continuous flow of melody as used in his music dramas.

intermezzo a form of light musical entertainment that occurred between the acts of an opera seria in the late baroque. It was the earliest form of comic opera.

interval the distance between two pitches. Such intervals have names; for example, the distance or interval between the pitches c and d is called the interval of a major second or whole step.

inversion the upside down version of a melody or tone row.

isorhythm the repetition of the rhythm of one section of music in other sections of the same work; a practice of the fourteenth century.

jazz rock a type of rock from the mid-1960s in which the influence of jazz improvisation and swing are apparent.

key the proper ordering of tonic, dominant, and subdominant chords in functional harmony. A given key takes the name of its tonic chord; for example, the key of C major; the key of B minor, etc.

largo a very slow tempo.

legato playing a musical line in a smooth, connected fashion; the opposite of staccato.

leitmotif a musical motive (or even just a special chord) that is associated with a particular person, place, thing, or idea. Leitmotifs abound in the music dramas of Richard Wagner, but are also employed by others, Strauss among them, in orchestral works. (see, for example, Strauss' *Till Eulenspiegel lustige Streiche.*)

lento a slow tempo.

les six a group of then radical young composers active in Paris just after World War I. One of them, Milhaud, was noted for his use of polytonality.

libretto the story and complete text of an opera.

Lied German word for art song; plural of Lied is Lieder.

line synonym for a single voice or instrumental part of a musical texture.

liturgical item a melody, text, or bit of ceremony officially sanctioned for use in the Church.

liturgy the music, prayers, readings, and ceremony of a church, particularly the Roman Catholic church.

madrigal a piece usually for unaccompanied vocal ensemble set to pastoral texts or love lyrics in the sixteenth century.

Elizabethan madrigal the dominant form of secular vocal music in England in the late sixteenth century; Elizabethan madrigals tended to be lighthearted.

Italian madrigal the dominant form of secular vocal music in sixteenth century Italy; Italian madrigals tended to be more dramatic and emotional than Elizabethan madrigals.

major second (whole step, whole tone) comprises two minor seconds. On a piano keyboard, a whole step is produced by playing two keys that are separated from each other by one intervening black or white key.

Mass the Roman Catholic worship service consisting of Ordinary and Proper parts.

measure *see* bar.

melody a succession of pitches which form a continuity and create a sense of self-contained completeness.

meter a succession of beats organized into a pattern.

meter signature a meter signature has two factors: the upper factor tells the number of beats in the pattern; the lower factor tells what note value is to serve as the basic pulse of the meter.

metrical psalm (psalmody) music used in the early Calvinistic church that consisted of simple melodies and/or harmonizations set to metered translations of the texts from the 150 Psalms of the Bible.

mode 1) the special quality or sound of the minor mode as distinct from the sound of the major mode. A minor tonic triad establishes minor mode; a major tonic triad establishes major mode. 2) the several church modes of the Middle Ages and Renaissance, each mode having its distinctive or characteristic intervallic structure.

moderato a moderate tempo.

modified strophic a composition that incorporates both strophic and through-composed elements.

modulation changing from one key to another in the course of tonal composition.

monophonic a texture consisting of one voice line or a single line of music without accompaniment, as in a Gregorian chant.

motet a work for voices, usually with a sacred text. The motet was developed in the thirteenth century and reached a high artistic level in the Renaissance.

motive a brief musical figure, as in the opening measures of Beethoven's Symphony no. 5. A motive is shorter than a phrase and usually consists of just a few notes.

movement a unit of a larger work, as in the four movements of a classical symphony.

musical description music that imitates things beyond itself, such as babbling brooks, rain, thunder, bird calls, etc.

music drama Wagner's form of opera.

neoclassicism a movement (ca. 1920–50) that emerged after World War I and featured a return to forms and genres of eighteenth century music; seen in some of the works of Stravinsky, for example.

new jazz a broad label applied to several kinds of jazz that emerged in the 1960s after the fade of bop and cool.

ninth chord a triad with two additional thirds on top of the stack. From the bottom up the members are root, third, fifth, seventh, ninth.

nonimitative counterpoint a texture in which there are two or more different and equally compelling musical lines, as distinct from imitative counterpoint in which one dominant line is echoed or imitated in several voices.

note value sounds in music have durational values. These values are expressed in a set of symbols which are called note values.

novelty song a type of popular song that developed in the 1930s, featuring lyrics that were faddish.

nuclear melody the basic melody played by some instruments in a Balinese gamelan, elaborated in various ways by other groups of instruments.

octave the duplication of a pitch eight diatonic tones higher, as in the octave C-c.

opera seria a highly elevated and virtuosic brand of Italian opera from the early eighteenth century consisting of three acts, a small cast, da capo arias, recitatives, and small ensemble numbers.

opus literally, "a work." Composers often assign opus numbers to their works, such as Beethoven's opus (op.) 14, etc.

oratorio a large-scale work for soloists, chorus, and orchestra, the text of which is usually sacred. Unlike opera, the oratorio is not staged but is presented as a concert piece.

Ordinary Kyrie, Gloria, Allelulia, Credo, Sanctus, Agnus Die. Each of these has a prescribed text that is sung (or spoken) in a specific place in each celebration of the Mass.

ordres a French term for a collection or suite of short pieces for harpsichord, introduced by Francois Couperin in the rococo.

organum the earliest known form of polyphony, from about the ninth century, in which the two parts move parallel to one another.

ostinato a musical passage (sometimes just a rhythmic figure) that is repeated doggedly throughout a movement or a large portion of a movement.

parlor song a simple, often sentimental kind of song for voice and piano from the genteel tradition in nineteenth century North America.

philosophical program music a kind of music that expresses the essence and power of ideas and attitudes, such as nobility, integrity, love, etc.

phrase an internal division of a melody. A phrase is to a melody as a clause is to a sentence. Many phrases end with a temporary pause.

pitch determines the relative highness or lowness of a sound.

pizzicato plucking the strings of a stringed instrument with the finger tips, as opposed to bowing the strings.

polonaise a Polish dance arranged for solo piano, most notably by Chopin.

polyphonic a texture with more than one voice line. There are two major types of polyphony: homophony and contrapuntal.

polyrhythms two or more different rhythms operating simultaneously.

polytonality music written in three or more simultaneously sounding keys.

prelude (1) sometimes used as the first piece in a late baroque dance suite. (2) a short character piece for solo piano, introduced by Chopin in the mid-nineteenth century.

presto a very fast tempo.

program music instrumental music that is connected to or inspired by something beyond its acoustical self, such as a painting, a poem, a character, or a scene from nature.

Proper texts and chants of the Mass that are proper to and performed at specific times of the church year, as opposed to the Ordinary, whose texts never change.

psalm with antiphon chanted verses of a psalm bracketed by an antiphon, which is more active melodically than the psalm verses. Performed at Canonical Hours.

punk rock an aggressively anti-establishment, nihilistic form of rock that developed in the late 1970s and has carried over into the 1980s.

rag (ragtime) a syncopated kind of popular music that emerged in the late 1890s in the hands of Scott Joplin and others.

raga a collection of pitches used in a classical Indian composition; roughly similar to a scale in western music.

range the range of a melody is the distance between its lowest note and its highest note.

recapitulation the third portion of a sonata-allegro form, in which the turmoil of the development section is resolved.

recitative a kind of heightened speech utterance, usually quite static melodically; unlike the more active aria, both of which are found in operas, oratorios, and cantatas.

reciting tone in a church mode, the tone on which the bulk of a psalm or other text is sung. The reciting tone ultimately moves to the finalis of the mode.

Renaissance a cultural/artistic era comprising roughly the years 1450–1600.

Renaissance motet a large scale, one-movement work with Latin text, often featuring imitative counterpoint.

rest silence in music.

retrograde the backwards version of a melody, moving from the last note of the original melody to the first.

retrograde inversion the backwards and upside-down version of a melody.

rhythm having to do with all of the temporal aspects of music, such as beat, meter, tempo, and durational values.

rhythm and blues (R & B) a type of music that emerged in the 1940s which, with certain modifications, became the basis for rock and roll. It features the beat pattern and sometimes earthy lyrics.

ritardando a gradual slowing of tempo.

ritornello a patch of music that recurs several times in the course of a movement; often used in the baroque concerto grosso.

rocking and reeling (rocking and rolling) terms from certain types of black music from the early twentieth century, used to denote ecstasy.

rococo period between the baroque and classical styles (roughly 1730–50), generally characterized by lightness, polish, wit, and a lack of profundity.

rondo a musical form consisting of the alternation of an *A* section with two or more contrasting sections, such as *ABACABA*.

root the pitch upon which a chord is built; for example, the C major chord consists of C (root), E (third), G (fifth).

rubato a flexible tempo in which there is extensive use of accelerando and ritardando.

sarabande one of the dances in the baroque dance suite that employs slower tempo and triple-meter form.

scherzo a dance in triple meter at a fairly fast tempo; the scherzo and trio replaced the minuet and trio as the third movement of a symphony, beginning with Beethoven.

semitone *see* minor second.

sequence a liturgical chant proper to the Easter season.

serial music the roots of serialized music are found in Schönberg's twelve-tone system, in which the twelve chromatic pitches are presented as a series in a tone row. Later composers have also serialized such elements as rhythm, dynamics, and instrumentation.

set number a self-contained unit of a larger scene in nineteenth century Italian opera.

seventh chord a triad with an additional third on top of the stack. Reading from the bottom up, the members of the chord are root, third, fifth, seventh.

sharp notated as ♯, it raises by a half step the pitch it accompanies.

soft rock and roll a less abrasive and more insipid style of rock and roll that emerged in the late 1950s. It sometimes used violins as accompanimental background.

sonata a genre of music—usually for one instrument, as in a piano sonata, or for two instruments, as in a sonata for violin and piano. A sonata usually consists of three or four movements with contrasting tempos, moods, and content.

sonata-allegro a structure consisting of exposition-development-recapitulation-coda. In classical and many romantic symphonies, concertos, sonatas, and string quartets, the first movement is in this form; other movements may also be in the form.

song cycle a collection of poems set to music (voice and piano) that develop a central narrative theme.

soul a type of secularized gospel music.

Sprechstimme a type of utterance somewhere between speech and singing; used in Schönberg's *Pierrot Lunaire.*

staccato a manner of playing a musical line crisply; the opposite of legato.

stage (talking) style a singing style in American popular music that featured rough, raspy vocal quality and periodically lapsed into speech.

standard an American popular song such as "Night and Day" that retains a measure of mass appeal over a long period of time.

stride piano a piano style that established four-beat patterns in the left-hand, rather than the two-beat patterns of earlier jazz.

strophic a composition in which a number of stanzas or verses of a poem are sung to one strand of music, as is the case with most church hymns.

Sturm und Drang literally "Storm and Stress"; a somewhat violent movement in the late preclassic era, a reaction against the lighthearted rococo style.

style galant an elegant, often lighthearted style from the preclassic era of the mid-eighteenth century.

subdominant chord one of the three primary functional chords in functional harmony; its function is to lead to the dominant.

sweet dance bands bands of the 1930s and 1940s that did not play swing music.

swing a type of rhythmic performance in jazz.

swing era the years from the early 1930s to about 1945.

symbolism an essentially French literary movement of the late nineteenth century in which words were often used for their sonorous rather than their syntactical value. Some of Debussy's works can be seen as the musical counterpart of this movement.

symphony the dominant form of orchestral music in the classical and romantic eras.

syncopation a rhythmic disturbance in which accent is given to some beat other than the downbeat of a measure.

tala a rhythmic cycle in classical Indian music.

tempo the pace at which a piece of music progresses.

tenor (1) a high range male voice. (2) lower voice, usually in long note values, in twelfth and thirteenth century polyphony.

tenor (clean) style a singing style in American popular music in the 1930s and 1940s that stressed pure vocal quality and precise diction.

ternary three-part musical form—*ABA.*

texture having to do with the number and activity of voices in a musical fabric.

theme a dominating, memorable melody of a section or movement in instrumental music.

through-composed a composition in which new strands of music are created for each verse or stanza.

tie a tie connects one note to the next, thereby increasing the durational value of the note.

timbre the characteristic tone color of a given instrument, as the special color of a flute is distinct from the color of an oboe, trumpet, bassoon, etc.

Tin Pan Alley the hub of the popular music business in New York City in the late nineteenth century.

tonality functional harmony; the sense of being in a key.

tone (symphonic) poem an orchestral piece in one movement with some programmatic basis; a product of the nineteenth century.

tone row the basic set of twelve pitches in serial form found in music written in the twelve-tone system.

tonic the tonic chord is the center of harmonic gravity in tonal music, the chord to which all others must ultimately resolve if the piece is to sound as if it has ended decisively.

tragedie lyrique a form of French opera established by Lully in the late seventeenth century; it combined music, drama, and ballet.

triad a stack of major and/or minor thirds; the members of a triad, reading consecutively from the bottom of the stack upwards, are root, third, fifth.

trio sonata the dominant form of chamber music in the baroque era, typically consisting of two continuo instruments and two solo instruments.

triplum the voice above the duplum in twelfth and thirteenth century polyphony.

trouvères wandering poet-musicians of the later Middle Ages.

tutti the entire orchestra in a baroque concerto grosso.

twelve-bar blues has the structure of harmony:

A	A'	B	
1 2 3 4	5 6 7 8	9 10 11 12	
I	IV I	V₇ I	

twelve-bar blues has the structure and harmony: tonality. The twelve chromatic pitches are expressed in a tone row, no pitch being repeated until all the others have been presented.

upbeat the last beat in a measure, usually unaccented.

variations in a composition, the occurrence of an initially stated theme followed by a number of sections where, either the theme is embroidered upon, or the environment of the theme undergoes changes.

verse and refrain the standard American popular song format from the 1890s to the mid-twentieth century.

verse anthem similar to an anthem, but with one or more solo voices featured, along with the chorus.

volume (amplitude) the degree of loudness or softness of sounds.

worried notes in blues, notes played or sung with a quiver, while slightly and deliberately out of tune.

CREDITS

Text/Illustrations

Chapter 1

Pages 3–4: Shorey, Paul, LOEB CLASSICAL LIBRARY SERIES, Cambridge: Harvard University Press. Page 4: SOURCE READINGS IN MUSIC HISTORY, Compiled and edited by Oliver Strunk. W. W. Norton & Company, Inc., New York, N.Y. Copyright 1950 by W. W. Norton & Company, Inc. Copyright renewed 1978.

Chapter 4

Pages 73, 74, 75, 77–78: Extracts from "Programme Music In The Last Four Centuries" (Frederick Niecks). Reproduced by courtesy of Novello and Company Limited. Pages 74, 79: THREE CLASSICS IN THE AESTHETIC OF MUSIC, by Claude Debussy, Ferruccio Busoni, & Charles E. Ives, 1962, Dover Publications, Inc., N.Y.

Chapter 5

Page 97: Extract from "Programme Music In The Last Four Centuries" (Frederick Niecks). Reproduced by courtesy of Novello and Company Limited. Page 101: SOURCE READINGS IN MUSIC HISTORY, Compiled and edited by Oliver Strunk. W. W. Norton & Company, Inc., New York, N.Y. Copyright 1950 by W. W. Norton & Company, Inc. Copyright renewed 1978.

Chapter 8

Pages 195, 197–98: From Miller, Philip (editor). THE RINGS OF WORDS. Copyright © 1973 Doubleday & Company, Inc., New York, N.Y. All Rights Reserved. Reprinted by permission of Doubleday & Company, Inc., and Philip L. Miller. Pages 218–20: © 1962 RCA Corporation. Reprinted by permission.

Chapter 10

Page 277: Copyright 1946, 1949 by the President and fellows of Harvard College, © renewed 1974, 1977 by Alice D. Humez and Willi Apel. Reprinted by permission. Pages 282–83: From MASTERPIECES OF MUSIC BEFORE 1750, Compiled and Edited by Carl Parrish and John Ohl, by permission of W. W. Norton & Company, Inc. Copyright 1951 by W. W. Norton & Company, Inc. Copyright renewed 1979 by John F. Ohl and Catherine C. Parrish.

Chapter 12

Pages 311, 314: Margaret Bradford Boni, SONGS OF THE GUILDED AGE, Racine: Western Publishing Company, Inc., 1960, pages 131–32, 16–18.

Chapter 13

Page 336: "WORK WITH ME ANNIE" (Henry Ballard). © 1954 ARMO MUSIC PUBLISHING COMPANY. Copyright renewed and assigned to FORT KNOX MUSIC COMPANY. International Copyright Secured. All Rights Reserved.

Chapter 15

Fig. 15.1, p. 377: From Sadie, Stanley (editor). NEW GROVE DICTIONARY OF MUSIC AND MUSICIANS. Copyright © 1980 Grove's Dictionaries of Music, Inc. Used with permission.

Photos

Page 5: © George Holton/Photo Researchers. Page 6: AP Newsphoto. Page 8: © Ron Cooper/EKM-Nepenthe. Fig. 1.1 and 1.2, p. 14: St. Louis Regional Commerce and Growth Association. Page 31: © John Maher/EKM-Nepenthe. Page 37: Harry N. Abrams, Inc., The Times Mirror Company. Page 39, top row, left to right: © John Maher/EKM-Nepenthe; Bettmann Archive; Robert Eckert/EKM-Nepenthe; bottom row, left to right: Courtesy, Conn Corporation; © Jill Cannefax/EKM-Nepenthe; Courtesy, Ludwig Drum Company; Courtesy, G. Leblanc Corporation. Page 41, top row, left to right: © Jill Cannefax/EKM-Nepenthe; Courtesy, Scherl and Roth; © Jill Cannefax/EKM-Nepenthe; bottom row, left to right: Courtesy, Scherl and Roth; © Jill Cannefax/EKM-Nepenthe; Courtesy, Salvi Company. Page 43, top row, left to right: Courtesy, King Musical Instruments, Inc.; Courtesy, Selmer; © John Maher/EKM-Nepenthe; bottom row, left to right: © Jill Cannefax/EKM-Nepenthe; Courtesy, Selmer; Courtesy, G. Leblanc Corporation; © Robert Eckert/EKM-Nepenthe; Courtesy, Selmer. Page 45, top row, left to right: Courtesy, King Musical Instruments, Inc.; © Jean-Claude Lejeune/EKM-Nepenthe; Courtesy, Selmer; bottom row, left to right: Courtesy, Selmer. Page 46, left: Courtesy, Remo, Inc.; right (top): © Frank Siteman/EKM-Nepenthe; (bottom) Courtesy, Avedis Zildjian Company. Pages 50, 84, 270: Courtesy, The French Government Tourist Office. Page 68: © Tim Jewett/EKM-Nepenthe. Page 75: EKM-Nepenthe. From *Felix Mendelssohn Letters* "The Hebrides Overture from Fingal's Cave." Fig. 5.2, p. 88, pp. 180, 290: Art Resource. Pages 89, 97, 135, 141, 174 (seven photos), 245, 301: Free Library of Philadelphia. Pages 90, 116, 119, 121, 150, 187, 274, 285, 311, 317 (right), 357, 360, 365: The Bettmann Archive. Page 98: Courtesy, D. Jacques Way and Zuckermann Harpsichords, Inc. Pages 120, 132, 174 (Verdi and Wagner), 235, 240, 366, 374: Historical Pictures Service, Inc. Pages 139, 229, 239, 243: The New York Public Library. Page 228: Courtesy, The United Nations. Pages 232, 263, 332: Robert V. Eckert/EKM-Nepenthe. Pages 278, 313: Jane Kramer. Page 306: © Ron Cooper/EKM-Nepenthe. Pages 308, 325: EKM-Nepenthe. Page 317 (left): Courtesy, The Cole Porter Musical and Literary Property Trusts. Page 329: Springer/Bettmann Film Archive. Pages 323, 334, 335, 343, 347, 367: Wide World Photos. Page 352: Bob Coyle. Page 370: EKM-Nepenthe from the Burton Homes Collection. Page 377: © D. Chawda/Photo Researchers. Page 382: © Eugene Gordon/Photo Researchers.

INDEX